*In memory of my father, John Edwards
and in honor of my mother, Annie Kate Edwards*

Contents

The following appendices can be found at *www.ablongman.com/edwards1e*:

Figures and Tables

Tables

Foreword

Research shows that we must "think new" about parental involvement. No longer is *parent involvement* something that a few parents do on their own. Rather, improving *school, family, and community partnerships* is part of every school improvement plan. Educators are responsible for writing a plan for partnerships, just as they write plans for improving reading, writing, math, testing, and other essential components to create excellent schools and responsive classrooms. Like all aspects of school improvement, school, family, and community partners must work together to design, implement, evaluate, and continually improve programs of partnership—in effect, recognizing the shared responsibilities of educators, families, and others for promoting student success.

Presently, practicing educators are offered *inservice education* to learn how to conduct programs of school, family, and community partnerships linked to school improvement goals (Epstein, et al., 2001). However, inservice education provided on request to select sites is not enough to ensure that all teachers and administrators understand that school, family, and community partnership is part of every school organization and part of every educator's professional work. *Preservice education* also is needed to prepare prospective teachers to enter the profession with up-to-date knowledge, skills, tools, and approaches to school, family, and community partnerships (Epstein, 2001).

Patricia Edwards' book will help advance this agenda. Edwards knows that family involvement is not solely the family's responsibility. Using examples, observations, conversations, and moments to reflect, she guides elementary teachers to think about, discuss, and plan for the roles they will play to encourage families to become involved in their children's education. Three concepts and discussions are particularly important.

1. **Edwards reports that** *historic, humanistic, and cultural factors* affect the nature and extent of school, family, and community partnerships. She discusses how family structures have changed over time, how individuals' knowledge and attitudes about family involvement affect their behavior, and how the diverse cultures of children and families represent valuable resources for improving schools and enriching students' education.

Edwards provides a wealth of references that confirm what we have known for a long time: that family involvement is important for student success and that educators need to be better prepared to work with all students' families. It is surprising, therefore, that colleges and universities have not added the growing knowledge base on school, family, and community partnerships to courses for all prospective educators. This is not due to a lack of awareness. According to a national survey of colleges and universities that my colleagues and I conducted, deans of education and department chairs strongly agreed that school, family, and community partnerships are important for all teachers and administrators to understand and apply. They also strongly agreed that most graduates of their programs are *not* well prepared to implement practices of family and community involvement. Clearly, this discrepancy needs to be corrected so that all new teachers and administrators enter the profession able to effectively involve families and communities in students' education.

2. **Edwards calls for *interculturally competent teachers*** who can communicate and work with all students and their families. Today, cultural diversity is everywhere. Once homogeneous communities are now gloriously diverse. As they proceed in their professional careers, all teachers will work with students and families who differ in many ways. New teachers and administrators must leave the academy certified to teach diverse students and ready to collaborate with all families to help students reach their highest potential.

Many studies report that, regardless of racial and cultural backgrounds, family structures, languages spoken at home, or years of formal education, just about all parents care for their children and, with teachers, have high aspirations for their children's success in school. It is imperative, then, for teachers and parents to recognize their common goals for students, respect each other's efforts to educate and socialize children, and improve the work they do together to help students succeed at every grade level.

Thus, on one level, teachers need to know their students' families and be responsive to their *varied* cultures and goals for children. On another level, teachers need to understand the *common* goals that all families have for their children to achieve in school. Interculturally competent teachers will not only appreciate diversity but also create a sense of unity and community in their schools and classrooms. More than ever before, colleges and universities need to prepare teachers and administrators to understand their lives and cultures of families, and the hopes and dreams that all families have for their children.

It is always amazing to me that people judge whether children are "ready to learn" when they enter elementary school. We all know that the most eager and curious beings on the planet are children entering kindergarten and the first grade. A more appropriate question may be whether teachers and schools are ready to teach all children and communicate with all families. Edwards reminds us that many infants and toddlers learn things at home in ways that reflect culturally specific parent-child interactions.

Her discussions of family influence on young children's learning reinforce the need for colleges and universities to prepare interculturally competent teachers who can welcome and work with all children and families at all grade levels.

3. **Edwards illustrates how important it is for every school to develop a** *scope and sequence* of family and community involvement activities at each grade level to engage parents and community partners in ways that help students succeed at high levels. She worked with teachers at the Morton Professional Development School to create a scope and sequence for parent involvement on literacy-linked activities. Several studies that my colleagues and I conducted reveal that this is the most difficult and, yet, the most promising purpose of school, family, and community partnerships. Family involvement at home with children on reading, writing, and science activities measurably increases students' skills, report card grades, homework completion, or achievement test scores in the specific subjects in the elementary and the middle grades.

Our work, like Edwards', indicates that school, family, and community partnerships must be planned as a curriculum, just as reading, math, writing, science, and other subjects are planned, to outline and schedule the family and community involvement activities that will be conducted school wide at each grade-level throughout the year. As in any subject, a scope and sequence for school, family, and community partnerships is really about *equity*. Just as we would not approve a reading or math program that leaves it up to each student to figure out how to learn to read or compute, we cannot leave it up to each parent to figure out how to be productively involved in a child's education each year. Rather, schools benefit from writing detailed one-year action plans with well-planned activities that ensure that all families have many different opportunities to be involved at school and at home in ways that help their children progress through school each year.

Edwards' examples in Chapter 6 illustrate how teachers accomplish more by working together with grade-level colleagues than by working alone in designing and implementing literacy-linked approaches to school, family, and community partnerships. Similarly, my colleagues and I have found that an Action Team for Partnerships, linked to a school council, is the most important structure for producing excellent partnership programs. A team of teachers, administrators, parents, students, and community partners work together to plan and implement involvement activities that engage many others at the school. Team members may work as grade-level partners and school-level committees to increase the variety and quality of activities and the outreach and impact of a school's partnership program. To supplement Edwards' examples, see the TIPS interactive homework process on the Web site, *www.partnershipschools.org*, for another way that grade-level teams of teachers have worked with researchers to design homework assignments that enable students to involve family partners in math, science, and language arts activities. Edwards' and our experiences show that the work of a few teachers can help many other teachers improve curriculum-linked involvement of all families.

School-wide and Teachers-Specific Involvement Activities in a Comprehensive Partnership Program

Edwards' observations, experiences, and guidelines for elementary school teachers are fully "in sync" with other research-based approaches for developing comprehensive programs of school, family, and community partnerships at all school levels. By working with hundreds of schools and policy leaders across the country, colleagues and I have identified key structures and processes that help elementary, middle, and high schools, districts, and state departments of education to improve their leadership and programs of partnership. Based on a theory of overlapping spheres of influence, a research-generated framework of six types of involvement (*parenting, communicating, volunteering, learning at home, decision making,* and *collaborating with the community*), and the results of many studies, we have assembled a knowledge base for college courses on partnerships that complements Edwards' book with additional information and guidelines for elementary and secondary school teachers and for district and state leaders (Epstein, 2001).

Edwards' and our studies recognize that comprehensive programs of partnership include *school-wide* and *teacher-specific* involvement activities. *School-wide* activities involve all teachers, administrators, staff, families, students, and, often, the community. Examples include an open-house night, spring concert or drama production, football game, book fair, and other events that increase school spirit or that engage families and community partners to help students reach school-wide goals, such as improving attendance, behavior, or safety. Individual teachers may participate in school-wide involvement activities by leading, supporting, attending, or contributing to some events. For example, teachers may attend back-to-school night to welcome all parents and conduct an orientation session for their own students' families. Or teachers may work with their own students to contribute to school-wide goals to increase attendance, reduce lateness, or improve school discipline.

Teacher-specific and grade-level activities are conducted by teachers to involve families in helping students reach particular classroom learning goals. Examples in activities like those that Edwards developed with the teachers at the Morton School to help first graders' parents understand children's stages of reading development, to involve third graders' parents with students on writing assignments, or to enable fifth graders' parents to help students study and read for understanding.

One challenge in developing a comprehensive partnership is to coordinate school-wide and classroom-specific involvement activities in one scope and sequence for a school's curriculum on partnerships, linked to the overarching school improvement plan. Another challenge is to help each teacher in a school see that he or she is contributing to the climate of partnerships by participating in school-wide activities *and* by conducting his or her own classroom activities with students' families or the community. Edwards' discussions highlight the important roles that teachers play in supporting and extending a school's program of school, family, and community partnerships.

Conclusion

Edwards helps readers hear the real voices of elementary school teachers who are struggling to learn new ways to link family and community involvement to literacy goals for students. The teachers struggle, in part, because they did not have preservice education to help them understand how to think about family involvement as a professional tool for boosting students' literacy skills. Edwards quotes one teacher, Mrs. Novak, who both explains and complains:

> *"...In college we should have learned how to work with parents, but we didn't. Sometimes I feel like parents' involvement is not my job."*

In order to ensure that new teachers and administrators understand that family involvement is part of their professional work, colleges and departments of education must update courses for prospective teachers to include new research, policies, and approaches to school, family, and partnerships.

Today, there are many reasons to prepare educators to "think new" about school, family, and community partnerships. Federal legislation (e.g. the No Child Left Behind Act) requires every school to conduct a program of parental involvement and to communicate clearly with all families about student achievement and school progress in languages that parents can understand. Most states have policies on family and community involvement and have stipulated competencies in conducting partnerships among the requirements for state credentials. Many district policies require every school to implement effective programs of family and community involvement. School principals prefer to hire teachers who know how to involve families and the community to support student learning and success in school. Thus, new requirements and expectations have been set at all policy levels for educators to have knowledge and skills to conduct family and community involvement activities to help students succeed.

Edwards contributes important content and high spirit to the field of school, family, and community partnerships and provides a valuable resource for helping future teachers understand and work with students' families. This book helps show that conducting family and community involvement activities is part of all educators' professional work. It is professional for teachers and administrators to communicate clearly with all students' families. It is professional to mobilize family and community resources to enrich the curriculum, expand students' experiences, and help more students succeed at high levels.

With this book and the other references listed below, professors in schools, colleges, and departments of education can change the long-standing status quo of poor preparation on school, family, and community partnerships. It is time to improve course content and field experiences to ensure that all prospective teachers and administrators are prepared to be complete professionals.

References

Epstein, J. L. (2001). *School, family, and community partnerships: Preparing educators and improving schools*. Boulder, CO: Westview Press.

Epstein, J. L., Sanders, M. G., Simon, B. S., Salinas, K. C., Jansorn, N. R., & Van Voorhis, F. L. (2002). *School, Family, and Community Partnerships: Your Handbook for Action, Second Edition*. Thousand Oaks, CA: Corwin Press.

www.partnershipschools.org. (2002). Web site for the National Network of Partnership Schools at Johns Hopkins University that guides schools, districts, and states to develop research-based programs of school, family, and community partnerships.

Joyce L. Epstein, Ph.D.

Director, Center on School, Family and Community Partnerships and the National Network of Partnership Schools

Johns Hopkins University
Baltimore, Maryland

Preface

"Why did I write a book on family involvement when there are so many already available?" As a teacher-educator, I have found that there is a variety of books available for preservice and experienced teachers that focus on family involvement. The currently available texts, however, succumb to a variety of pitfalls. Some of the books offer "cookbook" approaches that help teachers neither reflect on their rationale for using a particular strategy nor discern whether any given strategy is the most appropriate for their particular community of families. Time and time again, textbook authors cite the old African proverb that "it takes a whole village to educate a child." Unfortunately, these texts on family involvement often fail to describe for teachers how to learn about the families and children in their village. For instance, most texts on family involvement include ideas that have been, for the most part, geared to middle-class families, which are both very familiar to and comfortable for teachers who are predominately white and middle-class themselves. These kinds of texts assume that all families are alike and what is effective for one group of families can be generalized to the larger population of families. Although this category of texts clarifies the philosophical underpinnings of why family involvement is important, these books generally do not go to the next step of providing guidance for applying family involvement theories and research in non–middle class school settings. Nor do they enable white middle-class teachers to effectively work with children from nonmainstream European American backgrounds who will increasingly dominate the student population of the twenty-first century.

There are other family involvement texts, which consist of (1) case studies of particular communities; (2) research reports, which build the rationale for why family involvement is important; (3) historical perspectives on the importance of the family to student achievement; and (4) texts, which offer both a diagnosis and prescription for America's failing education system. Although this kind of information can be interesting, anecdotal evidence and prescriptive advice do not guide preservice or experienced teachers in cultivating good relationships with their students' communities and families.

Within the last five years, a few family involvement texts have been written that provide a framework for thinking about, talking about, and actually building comprehensive programs for school and family partnerships at the elementary, middle, and high school level. Some texts show how teachers can create partnerships with families and students that facilitate participation in the schools while also validating home culture and family concerns and aspirations. Others explore several important debates, including the extent to which family involvement can mitigate the constraints of poverty for minorities and disadvantaged students, school of choice and equality of educational opportunity, and the effects that school-sponsored activities involving families have on children's educational performance.

Although these recent texts extend and expand our knowledge of family involvement, they, too, individually and collectively have several shortcomings. Information ignored in these texts includes: (1) comprehensive explanations of how theoretical arguments might translate into practice; (2) real-life case study examples to substantiate the validity of their theoretical arguments; and (3) suggestions to encourage teachers to integrate their knowledge of diverse family populations into creative involvement initiatives. Many of the recent texts only focus on family involvement without understanding that the level of involvement must be geared toward the actual learning objectives of the classroom and curricular practices of school. In contrast with the more typical portrayal of family involvement as getting parents to "be there" with little explanation of how their presence and involvement can and should support the academic opportunities of the student, I address the educational purposes underlying the development of family-school relationships.

Few available texts encourage elementary teachers, in particular, to come face-to-face with the underlying reasons of why they want families involved in their children's education. Although many elementary school teachers are willing to admit that they expect families to attend open houses and parent-teacher conferences, few are willing to openly admit that they also expect families to initiate learning activities at home to improve their children's performance in school (i.e., reading to them, helping with homework, playing educational games, discussing current events, and so on; see Edwards, 1991). Increasingly, family involvement at the elementary school level comes with the teacher expectation that families should support their children's literacy development (Edwards, 1991). Surprisingly, it appears that available texts ignore for the most part families' own literacy practices in urging parents' assistance in heightening children's literacy. Rarely addressed are questions like "What if the parents' literacy levels are too low to assist their children with homework assignments? What if families don't want to help their children or don't even want to walk into a school? What if they didn't like school when they were students? Or, how do parents' literacies and families' own experiences as students in school contribute to or detract from their involvement in their children's learning?" This book will address these questions.

Some educators might argue that education students should pursue interdisciplinary studies to develop family involvement strategies. Over the years, teacher educators have encouraged elementary preservice teachers to take courses related to families and children in the departments of sociology, social work, and human ecology, with an implicit understanding that "family involvement" or "parent involvement" is outside the realm of the formal teacher education curriculum. Although these courses provide some helpful information, they still do not fully serve the needs of preservice teachers. For example, sociology courses typically focus on sociological analysis of the family: its development as a social institution, its relationship to society, and changing roles of family members. Social work provides a lens for understanding child welfare movements, agencies, and family services. Human ecology may consider the interactive relationships of families with other social forces. These and similar issues about families raised in sources outside colleges of education are important, but they do little to help teachers think clearly and constructively about (1) how they will combine the distinctions between home and school; (2) their role and relationships with parents and families; (3) the increasingly wider range of socialization activities they will assume; (4) other activities that considerably go beyond the school's traditional tasks, and (5) families' involvement in children's schooling or in children's learning.

The aim of this book is to incorporate a more practical and comprehensive view of family involvement and its effect on children's literacy learning. Involved in a way that transforms the learning opportunities available to students, both in school and at home. From this perspective, family involvement in schools will lead to change, which is bi-directional. Family involvement is not only about bringing students "home culture" within the context of the classroom or just about getting parents to intentionally provide experiences at home which support the educational practices of the school. Home-school connections, I argue, involve rethinking the relationship between home and school such that students' opportunities to learn are expanded and better supported. It is important for teachers to be aware of diverse family dynamics and how they influence family-school relationships. My hope is that teachers will develop the skills necessary to encourage families to become more actively involved with schools after reading this book. I believe this book is unique because it includes practical applications, examples of quality family participation and in-depth commentary on the intricacies of families and how partnerships can be created between families and schools.

I have written this book to provide preservice and experienced teachers with a framework for thinking about, talking about, and actually building comprehensive programs for increasing family involvement in elementary schools. This book is also intended for professionals in the field, including school administrators, Title 1 staff, chief state school officers, state department of education personnel, Even Start and Head Start personnel, and community educators who are interested in learning more about working successfully with families.

The purpose of this book is to provide:

- Information on approaches to rethinking family involvement in school from a historical, humanistic, and cultural perspective

- Descriptions of multiple ways to view family involvement and illuminate the importance of each perspective
- Practical strategies for involving families in the literacy development of children, specifically developing a scope and sequence of family involvement around curricular issues
- "How-to" information on integrating knowledge about diverse family populations and the needs of specific school settings to develop creative family-school partnerships
- "How-to" information on connecting to communities via the Web, ways of recruiting families, organizing classroom and school-wide family demographic profiles, and conducting community scans
- Information on the complexities, struggles, and efforts of real teachers, administrators, families, and community leaders to increase family involvement
- Information on developing and refining definitions of family involvement
- Information on individual practices of working with diverse family populations and the barriers which prevent families from becoming involved
- Information on traditional "institutionalized" methods and "outside the box" techniques for opening lines of communication between home and school

How the Book Is Organized

Unlike most texts that are topically organized, this one is developmental in design. The introduction charts my own personal journey into family involvement. The first chapter of the book develops a general way to think about family-school partnerships and the reasons that underlie the continued interest in these partnerships. The next two chapters develop understandings related to the family-school partnerships. For example, Chapter 2 provides foundational information on why family-school partnerships are so problematic, and Chapter 3 highlights three different approaches—historical, humanistic, and cultural—that are critical when considering the possibilities for improving family-school partnerships.

The following three chapters focus on strategies for developing family-school partnerships. Chapter 4 focuses on teacher preparation for family involvement. I present information on specific strategies that can be incorporated in both preservice and inservice teacher development programs. Some of these strategies include reading autobiographies, incorporating parent involvement in field-based assignments and inservice workshops, developing family stories, and collecting parent stories of early literacy. Chapter 5 deals specifically with traditional "institutionalized" methods (e.g., parent-teacher conferences, newsletters, and parent-teacher organizations), as well as "outside-the-box" techniques of recruiting and communicating with families (e.g., bar owners, ministerial alliance, people sitting on the street corner, and so on). Chapter 6, the heart of the book, focuses on three sets of action steps for improving family-school partnership preparation. Finally, an epilogue provides additional context—and I hope inspiration—for the challenge of rethinking family involvement for the twenty-first century.

Special Features

I have included four special features to increase the effectiveness of the book and to address the most current resources in the field.

Chapter on Action Steps

Chapter 6 focuses on three sets of action steps for improving family-school partnership preparation. The action steps emphasize the methods and procedures for effectively gathering information on the families in schools, strategies for strengthening home-school partnerships, ways of developing definitions, deciding on types of family involvement, examining perceptions, and implementing practices. Readers will find a very practical aspect of this chapter is the provision of a scope and sequence of activities centered around the curriculum at each grade level designed to help families understand what kinds of things they can do to support their children's literacy development. The chapter also makes recommendations for how schools can develop an individualized scope and sequence of activities for families around their own literacy curriculum.

Chapter on Recruiting and Communicating with Families

Because of the extensive problems many educators experience in recruiting and communicating with families, Chapter 5 deals specifically with traditional "institutionalized" methods of communicating with families. I urge the reader to think "outside the box" and move toward more progressive ways to recruit and communicate with families. This chapter also addresses issues of communicating and working with bilingual families and families with special needs children and ways to make use of school resources that maximize the strengths and learning opportunities of both the home and community as well as the classroom.

Chapter on Teacher Preparation for Family Involvement

Chapter 4 focuses on teacher preparation for family involvement. I present information on specific strategies that can be incorporated in both preservice and inservice teacher development programs. Some of these strategies include reading autobiographies, incorporating parent involvement in field-based assignments and inservice workshops, developing family stories and personal life stories, and cultural self-analysis, as well as collecting parent stories of early literacy.

Chapter on Existing Possibilities

Chapter 3 highlights three different approaches—historical, humanistic, and cultural—that are critical when considering the possibilities for improving family-school partnership. Recognition of the historical, humanistic, and cultural dilemmas involved in constructive, productive, and mutually respectful partnerships is a prerequisite for the creation of better family-school partnerships.

Important Features for Students and Instructors

Students

When textbooks are organized so that you, as students, are actively involved in your own learning, it can motivate you to want to learn the information and implement what you learned when you begin teaching. This book is designed to do just that. There are (a) chapter goals at the beginning of each chapter to focus your learning; (b) introductory scenarios that tie the focus of each chapter to helping you understand more about the complex issues that surround involving families in the business of the school; and (c) pause and reflect activities in which problems, questions, or issues are posed for your reflection.

For you, the reader, I also provide a chapter overview, a chapter outline, chapter key concepts, and a summary at the end of each chapter. The appendices and the book's accompanying website *www.ablongman.com/edwards1e* list materials that you can use in thinking about and carrying out your own family-school partnerships. Key words dealing with family-school partnerships are defined in the glossary at the end of the book. These features are beneficial for the learning to take place through reading this book.

Instructor

College instructors have many demands on their time; this text has been designed to be as helpful to the instructor as possible. There are suggestions for thought questions and activities at the end of each chapter to make the class interactive, reflective, and stimulating.

This text employs the Internet as a teaching tool and provides Web addresses to help students get started. There are also lists of articles and books that can be used as class resources for assignments or as resources for students' pursuit of selected ideas on their own in greater depth.

Acknowledgments

Writing an acknowledgment is a challenge indeed, but crucial because no book is a solo effort. The fine quality of the many contributions made by so many people facilitated the shape and scope of this project. Like all books, this book reflects not only my own thoughts, work, and experience, but also that of countless other people—colleagues, teachers, research assistants, graduate, and undergraduate students. I acknowledge inspiring scholars who, although they might not always agree with me, were instrumental in stimulating my reflection.

Authors do not live or write in a vacuum. Writings are permeated with echoes, grace notes, images, and shadows from a lifetime of encounters with significant others. Over the years, I have had numerous conversations with teacher educators from around the country about preparing preservice teachers to work with parents. Some of these teacher educators included: Susan Florio-Ruane, P. David Pearson, Mary Lewis, Laura Roehler, Dorothy S. Strickland, Lauren S.

Young, Jeanne Paratore, Doris Walker-Dalhouse, Barbara Taylor, Patricia Schmidt, KaiLonnie Dunsmore, Jeanne Schumm, Mark Conley, Virginia Goatley, Clifford T. Bennett, Kathryn Au, Mary McVee, Lynne Paine, Cathy Zeek, Mary Rozendal, Margaret Compton-Hall, Gwendolyn T. McMillon, Patricia Bloem, Nancy Roser, Fenice Boyd, and Cynthia Brock. I wish I could name them all, but that would require a book in itself.

Crucial to this project are Fenice Boyd, KaiLonnie Dunsmore, and Gwendolyn T. McMillon—very special and talented people who played the most critical role of all. There is no way to adequately acknowledge the value and extent of their contribution.

Much of the research on which this book is based was funded by the Professional Development Schools Project at Michigan State University, the Center for the Improvement of Early Reading Achievement (CIERA), and by the Spencer Foundation. I gratefully acknowledge their assistance.

I acknowledge with pleasure the contributions of several doctoral students Leigh Hall, Youb Kim, Xiaohui Peng, Julia Reynolds, Stacie Tate, Jennifer D. Turner, and Linda Williams for helpful feedback and suggestions on one or more chapters in this book. I would like to thank the many students I have taught over the years, whose work and comments as they grappled with issues and assignments I tried out on them formed the ideas in Chapters 4 and 6. I am grateful to Clifford T. Bennett, Erica Buchanan, Laura Apol, Judy O'Brien, Brenda Childress, Barbara J. Diamond, Christopher Dunbar, Ernest Morrell, Kathryn Au, Gloria Smith, Doris Walker-Dalhouse, Geneva Rhodes, Vernicka Tyson, and Cathy Zeek for their encouragement in completing this book.

A special thank you to Allyn and Bacon who shared their expertise in finding appropriate pictures and artwork for the book. A special thank you also goes to Leigh Hall for assisting me with the Internet activities and Xiaohui Peng for her extensive research assistance. Thanks also to Heather Clemens, Elizabeth Horst, and Liane Matson for allowing me to include their parent stories of early literacy. Janet Chrispoels generously gave me permission to use some of the material from the *Home-School Partnership Planner* she developed. I gratefully acknowledge the teachers who provided helpful feedback and suggestions—Julie Bastow, Andrea McPherson, Coretta Perkins, Liane Matson, Elizabeth Horst, Mary Stevick, and Lynn Zurawski. I would also like to thank the following reviewers of this manuscript: Inge J. Carmola, Board of Cooperative Educational Services, Johnstown, NY; Roger Kroth, The University of New Mexico; Rosemary Polanco, Purdue University; Jeanne Schumm, University of Miami; Lee Schumow, Northern Illinois University; and Andrés J. Versage, Monte Vista Elementary School, Los Angeles, CA.

Finally, this book would not have been possible without the loving support and friendship of my family and friends: Callie R. Hall, Sandra Wright, Andrea Monique Lembrick, Demetrice L. Williams, Sam L. Russell, Delores Parker, Sharon Zarka, Vincent McMillon, Katie Robinson, and Linda Wright. I would like to thank Joyce Epstein for so graciously agreeing to write the foreword, and I am also very thankful for the patience and expertise of Aurora Martínez Ramos, Katie Freddoso, and Beth Slater of Allyn and Bacon.

Introduction

My Journey into Family Involvement

This book blazes a critical path toward assisting preservice and experienced teachers in developing the knowledge, skills, and attitudes to involve families as integral partners in the literacy support of their children's education. I believe that educators need to view partnerships with families as a necessary part of effective teaching and successful learning for *all* students who enter our classrooms. We most often think of students in regard to the teaching and learning that occurs inside of the classroom; we must also understand that outside of the classroom, parents are an important part of children's educational lives and have a great deal of affect on school experiences. Naturally, we want parents to be actively involved in their children's academic careers.

I believe, like David L. Williams (1992), that the responsibility for preparing teachers to work with families falls squarely on the shoulders of teacher educators. As a teacher educator, I spent a substantial amount of time examining the content of the courses in the Teacher Education Program at Michigan State University. Lengthy conversations with my MSU colleagues, as well as colleagues at other institutions, about how to prepare teachers and potential teachers to work effectively with families led to the development of a course focusing on family involvement. I concluded that if preservice and experienced teachers wanted to implement partnerships with families and communities to foster students' success, they needed resources or information to create a structure for involving families in the literacy development of their children, specifically around the grade level literacy curriculum. Unfortunately, many preservice and experienced teachers leave their teacher education programs without this vital information because we, as teacher educators, are still struggling to make sense of how to involve families in important curricular ways—particularly when these families have cultural, linguistic, and social experiences that might be very different from those lived by school administrators, faculty, and staff.

I agree with the suggestions offered by the California Assembly Bill 1264 Task Force Committee for implementing partnerships with families and communities

1

(see Ammon, Chrispeels, Safran, Sandy, Dear, & Reyes, 1998, p. 17). They concluded that educators must:

- Be aware of the importance of home-school connections and be committed to the concept of partnerships with the families of all children
- Be able to think systematically about their family involvement attitudes and practices and learn from their experiences
- Understand the goals and benefits of different types of family involvement, as well as the barriers to their implementation
- Be aware of the way cultural assumptions and life experiences influence interpretation of events and respect the beliefs, values, opinions, lifestyles, and childrearing practices of all families
- Be able to build on the family diversity in the classroom, at the school site, and in the home
- Be able to work collaboratively with each other, with other professionals, and with families and students to develop a common vision of partnership
- Be willing to assume responsibility for initiating, supporting, rewarding, and monitoring various types of partnership activities, ensuring access for all parents and respecting all types and levels of participation

Over the years, I have carefully selected skills, strategies, and illustrations of family involvement to empower educators to successfully implement family involvement initiatives. In creating this book, I draw from the knowledge I gleaned over the years from a host of teachers who have been students in my course at MSU called *Literacy for the Young Child at Home and School*. I also sifted through the array of practices and procedures proven effective for involving today's diverse family populations. I have deliberately and painstakingly chosen research-based, school-tested ideas as the focus of this book.

It is widely recognized that today's teachers need as many approaches and strategies in their repertoire as possible to work with parents and other family members. However, I have carefully culled out a critical path for educators to follow because it is important for educators to learn that "schools cannot and would not exist without parents [or families]. Parents [or families] supply the school with primary material about their children" (Harrington, 1971, p. 49). Understanding how to work with a wide range of families creates the confidence necessary to become partners with your students' first teachers—their families.

This book is the result of several of my personal and professional life experiences. As a child growing up in the South, I remember vividly that the family, the school, and the community contributed to the educational achievement of African-American children. I was born and raised in a midsize southwestern Georgia community. I entered school a few years after the 1954 U.S. Supreme Court landmark decision *Brown v. Topeka Board of Education*, which declared segregation in education unconstitutional. I grew up in a stable, close-knit neighborhood where I knew many eyes watched me and would tell my mama when I misbehaved. My elementary school principal and most of my teachers lived in my neighborhood. Consequently, there were many opportunities outside of school for my principal and teachers to talk with my parents about my progress and behavior in school. My principal, teachers, neighbors, and parents all shared and reinforced similar school and family values.

Before school desegregation, African-American parents had a place in the school. They felt comfortable coming and going to the school at their leisure. The faces of teachers and administrators were familiar to them because, in many instances, the teachers and administrators were their friends, neighbors, and fellow church members. Parents could voice their concerns, opinions, and fears about their children's educational achievement, and teachers and administrators listened and responded.

For many African-American parents whose children attended segregated schools, parent involvement connoted active participation, collaboration, and cogenerative discussions with teachers and administrators. It meant African-American parents had some control of the school and school systems that helped shape the character and minds of their children. For example, teaching personnel were accountable to the community and therefore had to teach effectively if they wanted to maintain their jobs. School performance was relevant to the life experiences and needs of African-American children and provided motivation to learn. African-American children developed self-worth and dignity through knowledge of their history and culture and through the images provided by community leaders and teachers. African-American parents had control through coalition. The schools maintained continuous communication with African-American parents and developed with these parents a structure that included them in the governing of the schools. African-American parents could exert influence to protect their most precious resources, their children. This involvement assisted schools in providing a more relevant education for students.

My mother was president of the Parent-Teacher Association (PTA) throughout my entire six years of elementary school, which meant that my sister and I had to attend all of the PTA meetings. In fact, we provided the entertainment at these monthly meetings, as we offered musical selections on the piano and xylophone. We also assisted Mama with fundraising activities. As I reflect back on these PTA meetings, I can remember hearing Mama telling parents: "Education is the key to a better life and brighter future for our children. We, as parents, must help the teachers help our children in school. We want our children to have a better life than we have right now." My mama's commitment to bridging the gap between home and school has shaped my understanding of what it means for families to be involved in their children's educational lives.

I want to make the point here that segregation was unequal, unfair, and wrong because the textbooks, equipment, and supplementary materials were often outdated and inferior to what was provided at all white schools. Despite this, African-American schools often implemented a curriculum that reflected high standards and compelled their students to exceed expectations to be successful in the "real world." Additionally, African-American parents had a sense of value and pride because the African-American principals and teachers in these segregated schools made them feel needed, wanted, and included in the business of the school.

Throughout high school and college, I became interested in family involvement. During the last two years of high school, I attended a desegregated school. Even though the quality of education for African-American children might have improved in desegregated schools, African-American parents seemed to be left out of their children's educational lives. What my parents and I noticed most strikingly in my desegregated high school setting was that we were not involved in PTA meetings as we had been in segregated school settings. My parents often reminisced about how the principals and teachers in segregated school contexts made parent involvement a top priority. What was missing but sorely needed in my desegregated high school setting was an invitation for African-American parents to be involved in the business of the school.

When I entered college, I knew automatically that I was destined to become a teacher, simply because I had been told all of my life that teaching was a good career for women, especially African-American women. I attended a small African-American teachers' college in the South (Albany State College, now Albany State University, located in Albany, Ga.) and was constantly reminded of how important my role would be as an African-American educator in the lives of boys and girls of color. My undergraduate professors often informed me that African-American students needed to see positive role models in the classroom. Specifically, they needed teachers who understood something about their cultural heritage, as well as their learning styles, to assimilate education with the family and community life.

My teaching career would begin within a new integrated system of education, and this caused concern from my undergraduate professors about the problems that I would encounter as an African-American teacher in a school with a majority white population. These professors agonized with me over the challenges for me as a minority teacher, given the fact that I might end up in contexts where I would be the only minority teacher in the school setting. The fact that this possibility existed prompted them to suggest I attempt to play an informal role in helping my white colleagues understand the African-American culture while using my white colleagues to assist me in understanding theirs. Despite, however, my professors' attention to the need for creating relationships that promoted understanding between the home cultures represented in the desegregated setting, provided no training or guidance as to how I could best interact with the families of the students in an integrated school setting. Furthermore, I had no formal guidance in understanding and appreciating the home literacy environments of my newly diverse population of students or knowledge of whether their culture did or did not resemble my own, and whether this would make a difference in my ability to work with the families of my students. My professors apparently were unaware that my lack of knowledge about home literacy environments could cause me to unknowingly alienate my students and their families, thus negatively affecting their quality of education.

Perhaps my undergraduate professors assumed that I would discover how to work with families based on "gut reaction" or "instinct," or that what I needed to know I would be able to infer easily from general descriptions of family life for a particular cultural group. However, these assumptions have serious limitations and in fact offer further problems for helping teachers understand the families of their students. Courtney Cazden (1999) in the foreword to Cynthia Ballenger's book *Teaching Other People's Children: Literacy and Learning in a Bilingual Classroom* provided the answer for me. She correctly noted that:

> Many people have remarked on the challenges confronting teachers who face children each morning from lives far from their own, especially now when that challenge can determine teachers' success across the country. For many years I thought the problem could be alleviated, even if not solved, by providing information about cultural differences as a part of pre-service and in-service education. Recently, Hugh Mehan and I have worried that such information, transmitted in readings and lectures about disembodied "others," may do more harm than good (Cazden & Mehan, 1989). With the best of intentions, it may reinforce, even create, stereotypes and lower expectations, and the information transmitted may make teachers less observant of their students rather than more.
>
> Instead, a more helpful process seems to be for teachers to learn *experientially* about students and families, and in the process to reflect on their own personal and cultural background instead of unthinkingly living it as an unexamined norm. But saying that only changes the terms of the problem; solving it is now up to each teacher (pp. vii-viii).

I believe like Cazden that, "it is up to each teacher." Also, I believe that learning about students' home literacy environments and learning how to interact with diverse families are the lifelines for creating better family-school partnerships in the new millennium. These lifelines will improve the academic achievement of all children regardless of race or economic status. Furthermore, today's teachers must make a concerted effort to reach out to diverse family groups even if they do not share the same heritage.

Several years after completing undergraduate and graduate school, my interest in family involvement was renewed once again when I received a W. K. Kellogg National Fellowship in 1983. As part of the Fellowship, I decided to focus on family involvement through employing multiple lenses, which draw from educational, psychological, sociological, cross-cultural, and policy perspectives. Over the three-year fellowship period, I visited more than fifty agencies, organizations, and institutions of higher education throughout the United States and abroad. This opportunity gave me the distinct opportunity to communicate with many noted experts who addressed family issues from multiple perspectives. Some of these experts included Joyce L. Epstein, Oliver Moles, Dorothy Rich, Shirley Brice Heath, Valora Washington, Dorothy S. Strickland, David L. Williams Jr., Barbara Rogoff, Eugene Garcia, Vincent Greaney, and Moncrieff Cochran.

After studying work on family involvement from various perspectives, I began thinking about how I could use the information I had gathered to both help my own community of Ruston, La., where I was living and working at the time, as well as fulfill the goals of the fellowship. It was at this point that I decided to volunteer to be a parent consultant at the local Head Start Center in this small rural northern Louisiana community. My goal was twofold: (1) to increase the families' awareness of the importance of supporting their children's educational development; and (2) to assess how low SES parents interpreted the request from teachers to read to their children (Edwards, 1989). What I found was that the ways parents interpreted the teacher request to "read to their child" was often quite divergent to the goals and practices intended by the teachers. Also, I discovered that while teachers thought that their requests for parent involvement was quite clear and specific, parents in fact where often confused or uncertain about what "read to child" entailed. Additionally, I found that there was little evidence that the teachers' requests acknowledged the enormous challenges faced by parents on a daily basis. Requests to "read to your child" or "come to school" did not account for the high illiteracy rate of parents or the difficulty poor parents face in arranging time away from a low-paying job or in finding child care for younger siblings.

After a successful year at the Head Start Center, I moved to Louisiana State University where I continued my research on parent-child book reading. I organized the *Parents as Partners in Reading Program* at Donaldsonville Elementary School located in Donaldsonville, La., a small, rural southern community. My goal was to train parents to participate in effective book-reading interactions with their children. It involved defining for parents the participatory skills and behaviors found in effective parent-child reading interactions. The most effective reading interaction techniques were also modeled for the parents.

Shortly after the program was implemented, the message of the *Parents as Partners in Reading Program* became clear to teachers and administrators. We must shift from only telling parents to read to their children to actually showing them the skills needed to create a quality interaction between child and parent. Parent efforts to learn these skills must be supported and reinforced. Thus began a unified effort on the part of parents, teachers, and community leaders to support the program, which produced benefits for all participants.

One of the critical factors in the success of the book-reading program was the fact that I was able to recruit parents and effectively communicate to them that the teachers truly valued their involvement in the program. I solicited the assistance of an unlikely group of community leaders (a bar owner, bus driver, grandmother, the ministerial alliance, and people sitting on street corners) who knew the parents in contexts outside of the school. These community members were liaisons between the parents and myself. They set the stage by encouraging or admonishing the reluctant parents to participate in the book-reading program.

After this experience, I wanted to share with teachers and administrators what I had learned about working with families and communities. Therefore, I authored two nationally and internationally recognized family literacy programs, which have also been published in Spanish: *Parents as Partners in Reading: A Fam-*

ily Literacy Training Program (1993, 1990) and *Talking Your Way to Literacy: A Program to Help Nonreading Parents Prepare Their Children for Reading* (1990). In 2004, the *Learning Together Company* in Greensboro, North Carolina, will publish updated versions of these two programs. As an integral part of both programs, I suggest ways that users can sensitively and successfully communicate with diverse family populations. As a result, teachers, administrators, librarians, researchers, and community groups around the country and abroad have implemented my book-reading strategies and methods of recruiting parents with similar success as that which emerged in my pilot work in Louisiana.

Because of my successful efforts in the Donaldsonville, Louisiana, community assisting low-income parents in how to share books with their children, I was invited during the 1988–89 school year to the Center for the Study of Reading at the University of Illinois at Urbana-Champaign. There, I continued my investigation of successful approaches for communicating with diverse family populations. However, this time I worked in an urban setting. My goal was to closely examine how to invite urban families to school. In other words, I wanted to explore creative strategies to reach out to these families in new and different ways, which would signal to them that they were welcomed. What I found was that these urban families, like the rural families, were excited about helping their children in school. Here again, I found it necessary to create a network for recruiting parents to participate in the book-reading program. A newsletter sent home, inviting parents to become involved, was nowhere near enough for people who have historically been disenfranchised from the system. I met with a demographer that shared background information on the neighborhoods in which the families resided. As a result, I was able to identify significant people who affected families' lives outside of school. These significant people were key to helping me solicit family participation. Like the Donaldsonville project, this project also was successful because it allowed me to transfer knowledge about book sharing that was acquired in a rural setting to an urban setting.

In the fall of 1989, following my year at the Center for the Study of Reading, I came to MSU, where I have continued to expand my research agenda on creating a structure for families to be involved in the literacy development of their children. This also includes the pursuit of a professional mission involving locating and testing ways to communicate with urban families. At Morton Professional Development School,* located in Lansing, Mich., I coordinated the Home Literacy Project. The goals of the project were (1) to respect the multiple literacy environments the families represented; (2) to become knowledgeable of the family's capability, responsibility, and willingness to be involved in the school; (3) to help educators recognize that not *all* families are the same; (4) to help schools reach out to diverse families in new and different ways; and (5) to develop a scope and sequence of family involvement activities coordinated around the grade level literacy curriculum. As part of this project, I created what I call a *scope and sequence*

---

* The school's real name has been changed and a pseudonym used.

of family involvement, which will be explained in greater detail in Chapter 6. At each grade level, I developed family involvement activities coordinated around the grade level literacy curriculum. In other words, family participation in these literacy activities was critical to their child's success. What I learned is that families were comprised of busy people and that I needed to consider their work schedules and other personal and professional commitments to develop approaches to and expectations for parent involvement. These are issues that will also be further explained in Chapter 6.

Currently, I am working at MSU as a teacher educator and was a senior researcher at the Center for the Improvement of Early Reading Achievement (CIERA). From 1997 to 2002, as I pursue my research interests in family involvement, I have noticed that the importance of family involvement has been emphasized in every national educational report over the past two decades, as well as by numerous political and education associations such as the National Governor's Association, National Association of School Boards of Education, and International Reading Association. Unfortunately, despite the widespread endorsement of family-school partnerships to support student learning, most educators in the United States have received little or no training on how to work effectively with families. Surveys of teacher educators, teachers, and administrators (Chavkin & Williams, 1988); evaluations of current professional education programs (Powell, 1991; Shartrand, Kreider, & Erickson-Warfield, 1994); and content analysis of certification tests in states that require them (Greenwood & Hankins, 1991) all support the conclusion that programs for prospective teachers neither provide student teachers with information and supervised experiences in working with families, nor expect them to demonstrate relevant competencies and skills for certification.

In the new millennium, we must create effective home-school partnerships with all of our families, and though we bring personal histories to the table, we can learn to communicate with each other in ways that support academic success for our students. Even though I am an African-American teacher educator and researcher, I feel that my experiences are ones that all ethnic groups can learn from. This book is not written for African-Americans only, but for any individual who is interested in learning how to involve a wide range of families in our nation's classrooms and schools irrespective of their ethnic identity or socioeconomic level. The time is now—we must prepare teachers to work with diverse families. This book will help you begin the journey toward bridging the gap between home and school. The experiences I share in this book are rich and insightful ones that will have meaning for all of my readers. It is my hope that this book will serve as a road map for expanding and broadening your knowledge of how to work with diverse families and children.

1

Why Family-School Partnerships?

Chapter Goals for the Reader

- To learn that the word *parent* refers to more than biological parents
- To become familiar with the definition of family involvement that acknowledges the expertise that both teachers and parents bring to such partnerships
- To become familiar with the benefits of family-school partnerships
- To become familiar with the key issues involved in the national discussion around the question: "Can parents teach their own children?"
- To become familiar with the goals and values implicit in the commitment that was made to parent education in the United States at the January 1979 Conference for the Commission of the States in Denver, Colorado, which continues to be reinforced by policymakers, academics, and professional educator organizations
- To understand why there is a continuing interest in family-school partnerships

Chapter Outline

Why Family-School Partnerships?

My Definition of Family Involvement

The Benefits of Family-School Partnerships: Multiple Perspectives, Multiple Interests

Can Parents Teach Their Own Children?

A Continued Interest in Family-School Partnerships

Chapter Overview

Many of the questions that Mr. Potts posed will be answered in this book, but this chapter addresses: (1) a definition of family involvement that reflects the changing nature of what constitutes the family and the realities of daily life that require new ways of envisioning family-school partnerships that are mutually transformative and effective; (2) the benefits of family-school partnerships for supporting students' academic needs and the educational goals that both parents' and teachers have for them; (3) the possibility of and extent to which parents can be successful teachers of their own children; and (4) reasons that underlie the continued interest in family-school partnerships. Throughout history, educational establishments have been interested in and infatuated with parent involvement. There is a continued interest in family-involvement in the new millennium as a vehicle for creating better schools for *all* students.

Introductory Scenario: Mr. Potts Speaks to Student Interns

As Mr. Potts, principal of Briarwood Elementary School, pondered what he would say to the new group of student interns, he quickly remembered the conversation that he had with last year's student interns, and their ongoing questions and concerns about parent involvement. When he had asked those interns if there was something that they really wanted to know more about, they had said almost in unison: "How do you deal with parents?" Other questions included "What are the school's policies? How have you involved parents in homework? Do most of the parents help their children at this school? What is the school's definition of parent involvement? Do you think that involving parents is beneficial?" He repeated these questions to the new group of interns and noticed as he was rattling off a list of "Top Ten" concerns about families that their heads were nodding in agreement. These were also their concerns.

Why Family-School Partnerships?

The concept of family-school partnerships is relatively simple. It is about a seemingly plausible idea: that teachers should encourage all families to become involved in their children's education and that we should reach out to families in new and different ways. This idea has heavily influenced educational reform over the past decade, and it lies at the center of most school restructuring initiatives. As with most complex reforms, it is difficult to decipher exactly what advocates of school restructuring want by way of family involvement. At some basic level, though, all advocates of restructuring seem to believe that acknowledging that they want families involved in the business of the schools will lead teachers and administrators to restructure how they think about family involvement, which will in turn increase the overall participation of families, and subsequently lead to improved performance of children. Unfortunately, this is not a reality in most schools. I believe like Epstein (1987) that although "parent involvement is on everyone's list of practices to make schools more effective, to help families create more positive learning environments, to reduce the risk of student failure, and to increase student success" (p. 4), this does not automatically occur. Epstein correctly noted that "parent involvement is everybody's job but nobody's job until a structure is put in place to support it" (p. 10). It comes as no surprise that there is little real parent involvement in schools, given the lack of support within the infrastructure to foster and support it. Schools seem to assume that merely stating a desire or preference for family involvement is the extent of their responsibility. I suggest that schools in the new millennium must make provisions to seriously respond to Epstein's observations about parent involvement. She revealed that:

> Parent involvement is not the parents' responsibility alone. Nor is it the school's or teachers' or community educators' responsibility alone. All groups need to work together for a *sustained period of time* to develop programs that will increase parents' understanding of the schools and their ability to assist their children, and that will promote student success and reduce failure at every grade level (p. 10).

One of my goals in this book is to seriously address the notion of parents and teachers working together and creating a structure for family involvement in grades kindergarten through five.

My Definition of Family Involvement

Four terms will be utilized quite frequently when referring to home-school relationships—family involvement, parent involvement, parent education, and family-school partnerships. I have selected to use in this book the term *family involvement* because it is broad enough to encompass the radical change undergone in what constitutes a family and the roles and responsibilities in the lives of the adults who nurture the children in today's schools. The family as a social institution has experienced many transformations that profoundly influence not only the ways in which we understand what constitutes *family* but also the function of the family unit as well (Tutwiler, 1998). Children are born into many different kinds of families, and parents create for children a wide variety of living arrangements. According to Morrison (1998), "A parent is anyone who provides children with basic care, direction, support, protection, and guidance…a parent can be single, married, heterosexual, homosexual, a cousin, aunt, uncle, grandparent, a court-appointed guardian, a brother, a sister, an institution employee, a surrogate, a foster parent, or a group such as a commune" (p. 472). Richard Clifford (1997), president of the National Association for the Education of Young Children (NAEYC) clarified how educators should view families when he stated:

> We agree that we must recognize the child in the context of the family; appreciate and support the close ties between the child and the family; respect the dignity, worth, and uniqueness of each family member; and help both children and adults reach their full potential (p. 2).

Springate and Stegelin (1999) correctly noted that:

This type of effort takes a partnership created by joining heads, hands, and hearts of loving adults—teachers, parents, grandparents, stepparents, administrators, caregivers, social workers, medical personnel, community members, and others. It also takes economic commitment and a willingness to advocate for resources for families. If partnerships are to be successful, all of those involved must be encouraged to make contributions of their gifts, talents, and resources to the lives of children and families (p. 52).

I believe the ultimate expression of education is the partnerships we develop with families because it prepares students to live in an increasingly diverse world. It is difficult to find a more authentic approach to learning than actual experience. As Dewey expressed in his famous *My Pedagogical Creed*: "…Education, therefore, is a process of living and not a preparation for future living" (see Archambault, 1964, p. 430). In other words, the efforts that schools make to develop collaborations between home and school engage families and students in lived experiences that are not a preparation for democratic involvement but are themselves transformative and educative. This process can best be achieved through involvement, partnerships, or collaborations. According to Lareau (2000): "What teachers want from parents [is] a partnership" (p. 15). Shockley, Michalove, and Allen (1995) pointed out that "a genuine partnership is constructed jointly by all the participants. Each participant has the responsibility to commit to both individual and shared goals" (p. 92). Based on her research, Swap (1993) feels that partnerships hold the most promise for transforming rather than transmitting knowledge. She calls for partnerships that encompass "long-term commitments, mutual respect, widespread involvement…, and sharing of planning and decision-making responsibilities" (p. 47).

I would like to add here that I believe that teachers want involvement or collaborations with families as well. Henderson (1993) has observed that: "…the enterprise of public education is inexorably coming to understand that careful, continuous collaboration between schools and the families they serve really pays off" (p. ix). Kagan (1991) defines *collaboration* as "organizational and interorganizational structures where resources, power, and authority are shared and where people are brought together to achieve common goals that could not be accomplished by a single individual or organization independently" (p. 3). Kagan suggests that several mediating variables can affect the nature and outcomes of collaborative efforts. These variables are (1) goals, (2) resources, (3) the power and authority structure, and (4) flexibility afforded to the participants of the collaborative effort. Kagan describes this phenomenon as a new *zeitgeist*, or way of viewing and conceptualizing the meaning of collaboration. Many families across this country are the leaders in these collaborative efforts at the school and classroom level. They see the need to become involved with the school to help children develop as successful learners. That's what my mother did. She started a grass roots movement to motivate parents to become involved in their children's education. However, many minority parents lack the skills and beliefs necessary to initiate collaborations with a system that they feel does not respect or value their involvement.

In the Introduction to this book, you learned that involving families in the education of their children was something I came to value at a very young age. My mother and the other parents my sister and I met at these monthly parent-teacher association (PTA) meetings believed in the notion that if parents are supported in developing knowledge, skills, and abilities relating to parenting, their children would have a better chance at succeeding in school. Morrison (1988) would view these supportive efforts "…as a sign [to the students] that their parents value education. When their parents are involved in their program, [children] recognize that their parents are not just 'leaving them off' and forgetting them" (p. 418). My mother and the other parents believed that if all families were involved in meaningful interactions with their children's school, then the consequences would be increased achievement of children in school settings, enhancement of their daily lives, and more self-fulfilled parents.

Perhaps by now you have a vague idea of what family involvement is, based on what I have shared with you about the experiences my sister and I observed at monthly PTA meetings. Well, there is more. After reviewing the current and past literature on parent involvement, I found numerous definitions of what it means to involve families in schools, but the definitions by Swick (1984) and Morrison (1998) are ones that I believe are still valid and relevant in the new millennium. Consequently, their definitions are the ones that I decided to draw on in developing my own definition of family involvement. Swick (1984) observed that:

> Parent involvement is a threefold process; it is "partnership between [families] and teachers and their helpers in the community,…a developmental process that is built over a period of time through intentional planning and effort of every team member, and a process by which [families] and teachers work, learn and participate in decision-making experiences in a shared manner"—a developmental process based on partnership and shared decision making (p. 115).

Morrison (1998) revealed that:

> …parent involvement is: *a process of helping parents use their abilities to benefit themselves, their children, and the [elementary school educators].* Parents, children, and [elementary school educators] are all part of the process; consequently, all three parties should benefit from a well-planned program of parent involvement. Nonetheless, the focus in parent/child/family interactions is the parent, and [elementary school educators] must work with and through parents if they want to be successful (p. 474).

I, also, believe that parent involvement or family involvement is a developmental process that is built over a period of time through intentional planning. Similarly, I agree with Springate and Stegelin (1999)—that there are traits of successful collaborative efforts that should be a part of this developmental process and intentional planning. These include the following:

- The context is fertile, especially the political and social climate
- The goals are clear
- Structure matches mission
- The mandate is facilitative, not restrictive

- People are really invested
- Resources are available
- Process and policies are clear (p. 318)

In short, Springate and Stegelin contend that:

> The school serves as a fertile ground for collaborative efforts among parents, teachers, administrators, community and agency representatives, policymakers, and other interested constituents. The school, because of its location and commitment to serve the public's young children, can become the hub of the community's successful collaborative efforts (p. 318).

They also suggest that [elementary] school teachers will be more successful in communicating and collaborating with parents if they keep the following guidelines in mind (Gargiulo & Graves, 1991, as cited in Springate & Stegelin, 1999):

- Explain terminology that is relevant.
- Acknowledge parents' needs and feelings.
- Listen to parents and validate their ideas.
- Adapt communication and planning to the specific situation.
- Keep parents informed and include them in planning.
- Be accountable on an ongoing basis.
- Recognize the part of cultural diversity in parent relations.
- Involve parents in all aspects of the process.
- Delegate parents to assume important roles.
- Keep a journal or record of collaboration efforts.
- Follow the general guidelines for interagency collaboration when working with parents and families.
- Document collaboration efforts and initiatives (p. 319)

It is important to keep in mind that collaboration in the school setting requires patience, planning, and a positive attitude. For four years I coordinated the Home Literacy Project at Morton Professional Development School, and I struggled to take my own advice to be patient, plan, and stay positive. A longitudinal perspective is required to develop productive collaborations with families. Parents did not become disenfranchised overnight; therefore schools need to have a long-term commitment to and plan for family involvement. The Home Literacy Project was designed to create a structure for parents to be involved in their children's development as readers and writers. The goals of the Home Literacy Project were to (1) respect the multiple literacy environments the families represent; (2) become knowledgeable of the families' capability, responsibility, and willingness to be involved in school; (3) help educators recognize the fact that not *all* parents are the same; (4) help schools reach out to families in new and different ways; and (5) develop a scope and sequence of family involvement activities coordinated around the grade level literacy curriculum.

My work at Morton Professional Development School led me to conclude that many elementary school teachers are willing to admit that they expect families to attend open houses and parent-teacher conferences, but few of these teachers initially were prepared to admit openly that they also expect families to initiate learning activities at home to improve their children's performance in school (e.g., reading to them, helping with homework, playing educational games, discussing current events, and so on [see Edwards, 1991]). As time passed and I helped teachers clarify both their goals and strategies for working with families, Morton teachers began to understand that family involvement at the elementary school level was associated for them with the expectation that families should support their children's literacy development (see Edwards, 1991). They were asking parents to be "involved" without being clear that involvement meant not merely presence at school functions but active participation in the learning activities of the students.

After teachers have become convinced of the wisdom of family involvement, they wonder how to go about the process. A primary requisite for involving families is the right attitude. Teachers have to *want* family involvement in the elementary school program; otherwise, family involvement won't be effective. A teacher must not feel threatened by families. The more confident the teacher, the less the teacher will feel threatened. Epstein (1987), for example, has shown that within schools, some teachers are *leaders* in recruiting parent involvement (Epstein & Becker, 1982; Becker & Epstein, 1982). These teachers are more successful in getting parents to become involved, regardless of social class, and are also less likely than other teachers to use social class as an explanation for why parents are not involved. Instead, they attribute parent involvement patterns to the strategies they did or did not use throughout that particular academic year. In other words, teachers who are effective in developing partnerships with parents recognize that parent involvement is a function of the knowledge and skills they possess as teachers and not just the interest level of parents.

Success also depends on how well teachers involve families in ways that are authentic and meaningful. Shockley and colleagues (1995) contend family-school partnerships contribute to student success, when "Parents knew that what they were doing was meaningful, saw direct benefits for their children, felt that schools were committed to them as parents, and knew that their involvement made a difference" (p. 94). In Chapter 6, I provide a detailed description of the scope and sequence of meaningful parent activities that I worked with teachers to develop at Morton Professional Development School (see Figure 1.1 for a brief outline of the family involvement activities). I strongly believe that just as most elementary schools have a scope and sequence of curriculum at each grade level, they also need a scope and sequence of family involvement, which is developmental, based on shared decision making and built around the elementary school literacy curriculum. In Chapter 6, you will also learn how other schools can develop a scope and sequence of activities; that is, tailor-made parent involvement initiatives based on families and children in particular school community settings.

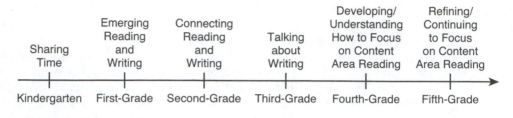

FIGURE 1.1 *Family Involvement Activities by Grade Level*

Planning is critical. Determine what families will do before they become involved but be willing to change plans after determining family strengths, weaknesses, and needs. Seek creative ways to involve *all* families. For schools and families to establish positive, effective partnerships, it is important for schools to ensure that the types of family involvement initiatives they want are appropriate for the types of family populations they serve. If they do not take this into consideration, schools, families, and communities will remain at odds with each other. Teachers must collaborate closely with parents and community members. In the long run, all involved will reap the benefits of an educational system that nurtures the learning of its students.

The Benefits of Family-School Partnerships: Multiple Perspectives, Multiple Interests

What I also learned early on was that an integral part of becoming a "good" parent resulted in parents' recognition of the importance of viewing themselves as their children's first and most influential teachers. Much of the conversation that my sister and I heard at the monthly PTA meetings had a recurring theme of: "Education is the key, and we as parents must first accept our responsibility for helping our children at home, as well as take responsibility for supporting our children's teachers any way that we can."

Over the years, researchers, policymakers, and national reports like *A Nation at Risk* (1983), and *Becoming a Nation of Readers* (Anderson, Hiebert, Scott, & Wilkinson, 1985) have acknowledged parents as their children's first teachers and have highlighted the benefits of family involvement. Below are some of the statements that have been used to describe the benefits of family involvement on student learning and academic achievement. Even though these statements reflect researcher views, I have heard statements such as these from parents and teachers with whom I have worked:

- Parents are the first teachers children meet. They are also children's teachers for the longest periods. Beginning at birth, children's experiences affect their success in becoming literate individuals. The success of the school literacy program frequently depends on the literacy environment of the home (Morrow, 1993, p. 40).

- Trying to educate children without the involvement of their family is like trying to play a basketball game without all the players on the court (Olson, 1990, p. 17).

- Parents act as role models for the literacy behaviors of their children, and the children of those parents who are poor models find that each year they slip farther behind in school. For them school is not the key to opportunity but to failure (Darling, 1988, p. 3).

- Literacy learning begins in the home, not the school, and that instruction should build on the foundation for literacy learning established in the home (Au, 1993, p. 35).

- Adults who live and interact regularly with children can profoundly influence the quality and quantity of their literacy experiences (Snow, Burns, & Griffin, 1998, p. 138).

- It may be that children can learn to become literate on their own without formal instruction, but when experiences with literacy take place in family environments, the emotional reactions of the parents can affect the child's progress significantly (Leichter, 1984, p. 46).

- Children will have many teachers in their lives, but only one family. It must be the family who help maintain the continuity of the child's education. The parents were the child's first teacher and will remain the most important throughout the child's life (Potter, 1989, p. 28).

- Although schools may have capable and dedicated teachers, schools are by their nature isolated from the larger world. Children learn from everything they see and do—at home, at school, and everywhere else (Schickedanz, 1986, p. 128).

- Every aspect of a family—the way it is organized, the way it works, the things it values, the relations that it has with the rest of society—all have some effect on what children learn…. All children are shaped by their families' teacher and the kind of environment their families create for learning (Weston, 1989, p. 1).

- Families form the nonconstructed, spontaneous institution which has principal responsibility for childrearing (Coleman, 1987, p. 35).

- Since parents are the closest, most intimate, and most persistent teachers that most children have, they teach their youngsters the basic attitudes, efforts, and conceptions of self, and for many, this occurs within the social environment of the household (Sutherland, 1991, p. 121).

- The family's main contribution to the child's success in school is made through the parents' dispositions and interpersonal relationships with the child in the household. Children receive essential "survival knowledge" for competent classroom role enactment from their exposure to positive home attitudes and communication encounters (Clark, 1983, p. 1).

- What parents do to help their children is more important to academic success than how well-off the family is (U.S. Department of Education, 1986, p. 7).

- You bear a responsibility to participate actively in your child's education. You should encourage more diligent study and discourage satisfaction with mediocrity and the attitude that says "let it slide"; monitor your child's study; encourage good study habits; encourage your child to take more demanding rather than less demanding courses; nurture your child's curiosity, creativity, and confidence; and be an active participant in the work of the schools (The National Commission on Excellence in Education celebrated report *A Nation at Risk,* 1983, p. 35).

As you can see, there have been strong mandates for the benefits of families in the educational lives of their children. Research has shown that the more comprehensive and long-lasting the parent involvement, the greater the influence is likely to be, not only on children's achievement but also on the quality of schools as institutions serving the community (Henderson, 1987). For example, Henderson (1987) conducted a study on a large number of young children divided into groups. One aspect of the study examines the home setting of very young children and the effects of certain behaviors or changes in behaviors when they later enter school; the other examines what occurs when their parents are enlisted to engage in supportive home activities in preschool or early elementary grades. Henderson noted that a positive learning environment at home, which included encouraging positive attitudes toward education and high expectations of children's success, has a powerful impact on student achievement across all social, economic, and ethnic backgrounds.

There is strong research support for partnerships that are developed by family-intervention programs at the preschool level. Research evidence shows consistently positive long-term effects on the quality of learning for children in part, because when families participate in these partnerships, they learn how to more effectively support their children's learning at home. For example, in their review of the effects of preschool education family-intervention programs, Goodson & Hess (1975) reported that the more a program focused on families, the more likely it was to produce significant and stable gains in children's learning. Similarly, Lazar (1981) found that students benefited more from educational programs when families directly participated in their children's education. Recent research on literacy also supports these findings. For example, Purcell-Gates (2000) reported that families with literacy-rich environments provide their children with the concept and skill development for learning about print. Richgels & Wold (1998) also reported significant increases in children's literacy knowledge when children

PAUSE AND REFLECT

Pause for a moment and think about the benefits I outlined above for involving families, then ask yourself, "Are there benefits that I as a teacher agree with, disagree with, or have serious questions about?"

were sent home with literacy-packed backpacks for their families to work on with them. The interactions between parents and children around the materials resulted in richer literacy conversations than might have occurred previously.

Most educators do not need research to know that parents strongly influence their children's behavior and learning in school (Kaplan, 1992). And, most educators do not need research to know that family-school partnerships help many families in their interaction and support of their children (Berger, 1991). Umansky (1983) as cited in Berger (1991) believes that:

> …teachers and parents need to establish a stronger bond with one another…Closer contact between parents and teachers will give each a more complete picture of the child's abilities and improve consistency in working toward desired goals. Most important, perhaps, the child will identify both the school and home as places to learn, and parents and teachers as sources of learning (p. 22).

Can Parents Teach Their Own Children?

I agree with Kaplan, Berger, and Umansky that family-school partnerships are important, and I think you might agree as well. However, a legitimate question that has been raised is: "Can parents teach their own children?" Also, questions have risen about the extent to which schools can and should expect parents to serve as instructional models and supports for children. Morrison (1978) believes that:

> The answer to this question is deceptively obvious; yes, they can teach their own children. This answer is obvious because all parents, whether they realize it or not, do teach their children…. However, many parents don't consider themselves to be teachers and conceive of learning as something which occurs only when the child enters school. For the most part, society in general and professional educators in particular have done a good job of reinforcing the idea that "real" education begins when school begins. In this sense, many parents feel that their role is that of caregiver and caretaker (p. 119).

However, Morrison was quick to point out that how effective a parent is as a teacher depends on many of the following factors:

- The psychological makeup of parents determines their particular temperaments. Parents may be high-strung, nervous, overanxious, etc., and this kind of behavior does not give them the patience necessary for teaching their children in any systematic way (p. 119).
- The feelings of the parent toward the child. For example, the parent may have a tendency to reject the child because [she or he] may be an unwanted or unexpected child, a child who does not meet the expectations of the parents, or a child who reminds one parent too much of the other parent. Or a parent may feel the child is an obstacle to some goal. For whatever reason, a parent

may reject a child and, therefore, not have a good parent-child relationship, which would promote the interaction necessary for teaching (p. 119).

- Time. Teaching children takes time. Time available to teach children is affected by many other interrelated factors, such as the number of other children in the home, housekeeping demands, demands from the other parent, health and nutritional problems, and so on (p. 119).
- Knowledge background of the parent. The knowledge a parent brings to the child-teaching process is also extremely important for the success of the endeavor. Many parents feel a great deal of frustration in knowing what or how to teach their children. When faced with not knowing what to do, the normal reaction is to do nothing. It is much easier to do nothing than to worry about doing something you don't know how to do. Besides if you don't know what to do and if you go ahead and do something, it may be wrong (p. 119).
- Availability of materials. Many parents are very well-intentioned and might want to read to their children, but because they don't have anything to read or because they don't know whether or not what they have is good enough to read to children, they end up not reading to them (p. 119). (I would add that many parents don't read to their children because they are illiterate [see Edwards, 1989, 1995].)
- Family problems. Problems facing the family, such as marital problems, employment problems, etc., determine how effective the parent is in dealing with the child. If parents are so immersed and consumed with problems, then certainly they are not going to have the time or desire to work with their children (p. 119).

I agree with many of the points Morrison highlighted, but these points do not lessen the importance of families becoming teachers of their children. Jenks (1972) and his colleagues argue that: "Children seem to be far more influenced by what happens at home than by what happens in school" (p. 255). Even Morrison (1988) agrees that the environment (including experiences, culture, objects, relationships with others, and so on), determines the extent to which the intellectual potential of the child will or will not be developed. The environment that most children are reared in is the home; every home should be as good and appropriate an environment as is possible to provide. More importantly, family-school partnerships should be developed so that schools can work with parents in providing an enriched home environment and experiences for the child. This rich home environment could ostensibly provide the child with the experiences necessary for optimum intellectual growth.

A Continued Interest in Family-School Partnerships

For the reasons above, there continues to be an interest in working with parents to provide them with the support, information, and expertise necessary for them to become the best educators of their children as it is possible for them to become.

However, I want to point out that for more than three decades in the United States, there have been federal programs and legislation for parent involvement (Head Start, 1965; Head Start Planned Variations, 1967–1971; Education of All Handicapped Children Act, 1975; Title I, 1981, and its successor, Chapter I, 1974–1975 [now Chapter I has reverted back to Title I]). A major focus in all of these federal initiatives was recognition of parents as those who have principal influence on their children's development and the importance of close cooperation between home and school. Edward Ziegler's remarks at a January 1979 Conference of the Education Commission of the States in Denver, provide the following excellent rationale for federal, state, and local support of parent involvement:

> Although there is controversy today over what the public schools should be trying to accomplish with the limited resources at their disposal, it is difficult to imagine any skill more basic than that of being a good parent, or any body of knowledge more crucial than that of knowledge of how to raise a sound family. In fact, as parents and families encounter new stresses and assimilate unfamiliar patterns of behavior at a rate we would have thought impossible several decades ago, more and more people are coming to feel that public schools have responsibility to provide help where it is needed, to offer programs that will assist in the education of Americans for parenthood.
>
> This conclusion—that schools should help people learn to be effective parents—is not a new one, but over the past few years it has been attracting increasing attention from educators, legislators, and the general public. It is part of a larger issue, which is the proper relationship between families and the major supportive institutions of U.S. society, such as schools, social agencies, and health care systems. That the relationship is changing is without doubt. The question facing policy makers is how to foster change in a direction that will strengthen the family and help to build strong communities.
>
> Parent education is not one of the subject areas traditionally included in school curricula. It has, nevertheless, been appearing with greater frequency in recent years, either as an element woven into other subject areas or as a discrete course on its own. The message appears to be that parent education is no passing fad. It is here to stay, and it is challenging public schools to reassess the scope of their educational mission. In view of the growing interest and the profound social values at stake, the time has come for serious consideration of the feasibility of implementing parent education in the public schools (p. ix).

The 1979 Conference of the Education Commission of the States in Denver, where Ziegler made these remarks, set in motion the direction and course of action schools needed to assume as it relates to parent involvement. Even though many schools have been slow to develop parent involvement initiatives, the research is clear that school practices and policies need to be related to family involvement (Henderson, 1987; Henderson & Berla, 1995). Also, the need for parent involvement is now clearly highlighted and supported in federal policies such as the 1988 Elementary Secondary Education Amendment (ESEA) and the Goals 2000 Educate America Act. Moles (1993) revealed that in the 1988 ESEA different kinds of parent participation were supported by then–Secretary of Education

Lauro Cavazos, who recommended a number of steps that should be taken by the federal government, schools, and parents to help children learn and parents select a quality education for them. More specifically, Moles stated that:

> Three tangible results of this renewed interest at the federal level are incorporated in the 1988 ESEA amendments: new parent involvement requirements for all Chapter I projects, a special grant program on family-school partnerships, and Even Start. Chapter I aid to low-income-area schools now requires a parent-involvement program in each participating school district, although no additional federal funds were added for this purpose. Parents are to provide "meaningful consultation" on the planning and implementation in this program. Annual meetings for all parents, more often if requested, are to be supplemented with reports on children's progress. Parent-teacher conferences are encouraged to discuss the child's progress and placement, and methods by which parents can support the child's instruction. A number of activities may be included in local programs to train parents and educators to work effectively together and to support the efforts of parents to work with their children at home, including opportunities for parents who lack literacy skills and whose native language is not English (Public Law 100-297).
>
> The family-school partnership program supports projects in Chapter I school districts designed to help school staff and parents work effectively together. Even Start is designed to integrate early-childhood education (1–7 year olds) and adult education in programs that promote adult literacy, train parents to support the educational development of their children, and coordinate with existing services. Child care and transportation must be provided (Public Law 100-297).
>
> Thus the confrontations of earlier years between parents and schools seem to be giving way to a new spirit of cooperation centered on helping disadvantaged parents prepare their children more effectively for school learning. It is significant that the training for this is directed at helping parents and school staff to work together. Without reestablishing parent advisory councils, the 1988 federal legislation calls for significant consultation with parents on parent-involvement-program design and operation (pp. 25–26).

More than ten years later, the federal government proposed Goal Eight of the Goals 2000 Educate America Act to encourage school staffs to work with families. Specifically, Goal Eight states, "By the year 2000, every school will promote partnerships that will increase parental involvement and participation in promoting the social, emotional, and academic growth of children" (National Education Goals Panel, 1998, p. 6). In the National PTA's publication *Building Successful Partnerships: A Guide for Developing Parent and Family Involvement Programs (2000)*, it was revealed why the U.S. Congress added Goal Eight of the Goals 2000. They stated that:

> Congress added this voluntary goal to encourage and increase parent participation in schools across America. It calls upon schools to adopt policies and practices that actively engage parents and families in partnerships that support the academic work of children at home and share decision making at school. Therefore, it prompts schools to examine how their policies, practices, and program designs affect parent involvement. (p. 16)

Family involvement as stated earlier "is no passing fad," and "it is here to stay." That's why there is a continuing interest in family-school partnerships and schools must begin to examine their policies and practices. The federal government has and continues to provide funding to encourage states and communities to voluntarily form partnerships at the local level with parents, educators, and business and community groups to meet the challenges of educating children for the twenty-first century.

Summary

Parent involvement is an integral part of a successful schooling experience for students. By participating in various activities and supporting the school's literacy curriculum, parents show their children that they value their education. Similarly, by encouraging family involvement, teachers show that they value the vital input that parents can contribute to their children's education.

Although several factors can reduce their teaching effectiveness, parents are their children's first and most influential teachers. The identity of the person(s) fulfilling parental responsibilities has changed over the years, mirroring the transformation of the family and a wide variety of living arrangements. However, these changes have not decreased the importance of family-school partnerships. Schools continue to request that parents become actively involved, and many schools offer workshops to assist parents with various concerns.

Chapter 1 Key Concepts _____

- Teachers should encourage all families to become involved in their children's education and should reach out to families in new and different ways.
- There is little real parent involvement in schools, given the lack of support within the infrastructure to foster and support it.
- The term *family involvement* in used to reflect the radical change undergone in what constitutes a family and the roles and responsibilities in the lives of the adults who nurture the children in today's schools.
- *Parent* is defined as anyone who provides children with basic care, direction, support, protection, and guidance.
- Successful parent involvement is a process of helping parents use their abilities to simultaneously benefit themselves as well as their children.
- Parents are their child's first and often the most influential teacher, however, some factors may affect their effectiveness as teachers. These factors include: the psychological makeup of the parent, the parent's feeling toward the child, the amount of time available to work with the child, the knowledge background of the parent, availability of materials at home, and family problems that might prevent successful learning to occur.

Suggestions for Thought Questions and Activities _____

1. In Chapter 1 the word *parent* is described in a variety of ways. On a sheet of paper, write your personal description of an "ideal" parent.

2. Survey an elementary school class to identify the number of ways that *parent* can be described in that particular classroom. Write a list of the types of parents included in the survey.

3. After studying the list compiled from the survey and considering your personal definition of the "ideal" parent, assess any personal biases that might prevent you from developing an effective family-school partnership with parents who do not fit into your linear model of an "ideal" parent.

4. Share your list with a fellow classmate and brainstorm barriers that may prevent different parent types from becoming actively involved in school.

5. Now develop ways to address the barriers and your biases. In other words, devise a plan of action that will encourage *all* parents to become involved. If possible, try to implement at least one idea on your list every month. Preservice teachers may be able to share their ideas with the teacher in their field experience.

Internet Activities _____

• Using a major search engine, look up the term *family-involvement*. How does this definition compare with or enhance your own?

• Using a major search engine, look up the home pages for school districts on the Internet. In what ways do these districts attempt to establish family-school partnerships?

For Further Reading _____

Building successful partnerships: A guide for developing parent and family involvement programs (2000). National PTA. Bloomington, IN: National Education Service.

> Based on research, *Building Successful Partnerships* provides a blueprint for developing quality parent involvement programs that work. This practical resource focuses on ways to implement the six National Standards for Parent/Family Involvement Programs: communicating, parenting, student learning, volunteering, school decision making and advocacy, and collaborating with the community.

Chavkin, N. F. (1993) (Editor). *Families and schools in a pluralistic society.* Albany, NY: State University of New York.

> Part 1 provides a historical look at the general topic of parent involvement in education. In Part 11, the voices are clearly research-focused. The authors present specific research studies on current parent involvement issues. In Part 111, teachers, parents, college professors, social workers—each from a different conceptual framework—present their ideas on effective practice. In Part IV, the recommendations for the future are derived from experience in research, practice, and the political world.

Edwards, P. A. (1993). Before and after school desegregation: African-American parents' involvement in schools. *Educational Policy*, 7(3), 340–369.

Edwards focuses on the nature of parental involvement in historically African-American community schools compared with that experienced by African Americans in desegregated schools. Returning to her childhood community, Edwards recounts her own experiences in a historically African-American community school and shares recollections from her mother, elementary school principal, and first-grade teacher. She presents with first-person accounts of how the people who studied, worked, and sent their children to one African-American school in Georgia viewed the changed nature of parental involvement in desegregated schools controlled by the local European-American elites.

Fuller, M. L., & Olsen, G. (1998). *Home-school relations: Working successfully with parents and families*. Boston: Allyn and Bacon.

Home-School Relations is a thoughtful guide to more productive relationships between parents and teachers, homes, and schools. It begins with the premise that parents are their children's first and most important teachers, and further, that the dispositions, language, values, and cultural understandings that help guide children and young people are learned most fully within families (and, importantly, this book makes the conception of families inclusive of the many child-nurturing arrangements that exist).

Shockley, B., Michaelove, B., & Allen, J. (1995). *Engaging families: Connecting home and school literacy communities*. Portsmouth, NH: Heinemann.

During four years spent studying what "the students [they] worried about most," Shockley, Michaelove, & Allen became increasingly aware of the importance of children's literacy experiences outside of the school. Although their students talked regularly about home literacy events, there was no real link between home and school: no way to learn what families valued and practiced, no way to communicate to families how their children were becoming literate at school. *Engaging Families* details how these teachers and families of the students created a connection between home and school, developing respected partnerships in the teaching/learning process.

Swap, S. M. (1993). *Developing home-school partnerships: From concepts to practice*. New York: Teachers College Press.

Swap discusses how schools and families share responsibility for increasing every student's motivation and success in school and how collectively, schools, families, and communities share responsibilities for the success with which this nation's students will be able to compete with students from nations in the future.

Tamis-LeMonda, C.S., & Cabrera, N. (2002) (Editors). *Handbook of father involvement: Multidisciplinary perspectives*. Mahwah, NJ: Lawrence Erlbaum Associates, Publishers.

Four salient themes/questions, regarding the nature, determinants, and outcomes of father involvement inspire thought and recur throughout the book: (a) What is father involvement, what dimensions comprise the construct, and how are those dimensions changing over time? (b) What factors contribute to and/or play a role in explaining father involvement within and across time? (c) Which outcomes in children are affected by which dimensions of father involvement at which stages in development? and (d) How and why might father involvement vary across culture and ethnicity?

2

Family-School Partnerships

Why Are They So Difficult to Create?

Chapter Goals for the Reader

- To learn why family-school partnerships are so difficult to create
- To become familiar with the questions that were raised about parent education at the January 1979 Conference more than twenty years ago and learn why many of these questions still remain unanswered
- To become familiar with the multiple personal meanings, understandings, and interpretations of parent involvement
- To become familiar with the many terms and phrases used to describe family-school partnerships
- To become familiar with various types of family-school partnerships

Chapter Outline

Family-School Partnerships:
Why Are They So Difficult to Create?
    Too Many Unanswered Questions Regarding
       the Commitment to Parent Education
    Where Are We Now?
    Overburdened Schools Not Seeing Parent
       Involvement as a Top Priority
    Limited Participation of Families in Life
       Inside Schools: Some Possible Reasons
    Lacking a Common Understanding of
       Parent Involvement

Shifting Definitions of Parent Involvement
    Task Approach
    Process Approach
    Developmental Approach
    Comprehensive Approach
Changing Terminology
    Local Definitions of Parent Involvement
    Literacy-Centered Parent Involvement
    Classroom/School-Based Definitions of
       Parent Involvement

Chapter Overview

This chapter is organized into four main sections that highlight the reasons that I believe have led to the difficulty in creating family-school partnerships. In particular, this chapter provides insight into the complexity surrounding the developing of family-school partnerships.

In the first section, I put forth the argument that we, as educators, have not successfully answered all of the questions that were raised at the January 1979 Conference for the Commission of the States in Denver. Consequently, this might be, in part, one of the reasons we still find ourselves struggling to develop family-school partnerships.

In the second section, I propose that with schools struggling to meet all of their responsibilities, providing effective parent involvement opportunities is not always a top priority. Thus, the promotions of family-school partnerships have been put on the back burner. Also, Berger (1991) quickly reminds us that, "…not everyone in the school will be comfortable with increased parent-school collaboration" (p. 116). Why would some educators not want families to be involved in school? Although most educators believe that home and schools should work together because they share the same goals for the students, other teachers might think that schools can achieve their goals to educate most efficiently when school and home remain separate, because the "professional status is in jeopardy if parents are involved in activities that are typically the teacher's responsibilities" (Epstein, 1986, p. 227). As educators, we must realize that there is room for families' involvement in our classrooms and schools and that their presence enhances our professionalism rather than decreases it.

In the third section, I candidly address five reasons I think family-school partnerships have been difficult to create—(1) too many unanswered questions regarding the commitment to parent education, (2) overburdened schools not seeing parent involvement as a top priority, (3) the limited participation of some families in life inside schools, (4) lacking a common understanding of what is *parent involvement*, and (5) changing terminology used to describe *family-school partnerships*. I argue that the kinds of relationships desired depend on how particular individuals (e.g., teachers, administrators, researchers, policymakers, parents, community leaders, etc.) define parent involvement. The wide variability in which all of these individuals have defined parent involvement is another reason that has led to the confusion around creating family-school partnerships.

In the fourth section, I suggest that confusion in terminology and about the meaning of what counts as "involved" is yet another reason why family-school partnerships have been difficult to create. When I first read the literature on family-school partnerships, I noticed that several different terms or phrases have been used to describe parent involvement initiatives: *family involvement, parent involvement, business partnerships, home-school partnerships, family literacy, community as family,* and *home-school-community partnerships.* This confusing variability in terminology reflects differing perspectives of the goals for and nature of school-home interactions and makes it difficult for educators to decide what kind of family involvement practices are needed for the families they serve. In this section, I provide some examples of partnerships that some schools have developed with families to illustrate my definition of parents as educationally productive entities.

Introductory Scenario:
Dr. Zurawski and Her Reading Methods Class _____

While leading a discussion on emergent literacy in her reading methods class, Dr. Zurawski realized that her students wanted more information about the role families should or could play in helping their children as they develop as readers and writers. She quickly pointed out to her students that parent involvement in children's emergent literacy skills has been considered important for some time. She continued by citing some research to support her point. Parents support emergent literacy in their young children by creating literacy-rich environments and interactions. In these environments children are often read to, see others reading, are provided with accessible reading and writing materials, and are encouraged to ask and answer questions (Teale & Sulzby, 1986, 1987). Physical environments, such as homes where books are accessible to children, promote their perception of competence with print (Snow et al., 1991). The accessibility of books in the home, as well as the quantity and quality of parent-child interactions, may be strengthened when parents have levels of literacy that allow them to feel competent with print, speech, and other literate behaviors (Edwards, 1989, Leitcher, 1984). Effective parent-children interactions are created when parents and children solve problems using a high degree of verbal interaction (Rogoff, 1990). In this way, parents can influence the children's motivation to acquire, develop, and use literacy. According to Wigfield & Asher (1984), parents' attitudes and expectations for their children's performances are good predictors of children's attitudes toward learning, effort in school, and classroom performance.

The students were nodding their heads in agreement with Dr. Zurawski's comments about the importance of parent involvement in children's emergent literacy skills. However, many students expressed that their field observation of kindergarten and first-grade children had led them to conclude that all too often, many children arrive at school unprepared for literacy instruction because they have not received adequate support and literate experiences at home. Other students concluded that when parents help their children at home they have a better chance of successfully emerging as readers and writers—a point discussed by Dr. Zurawski. The students provided personal vignettes about the ways in which their own parents had been involved in their schooling in such ways as reading to them, volunteering in their classroom, and going on field trips.

Because there was so much interest in learning more about families and the role they should assume in the educational lives of their children, Dr. Zurawski decided to ask her students to define what they meant by parent involvement. Chances are when Dr. Zurawski asked her students this question, she was unaware of the multiple ways in which parent involvement has been defined and all of the questions that have been raised about the nature and role of schools in providing parent education. She would likely have been caught off guard if her students had decided to pursue the issue further and challenged her to explain why, with all the known benefits of family involvement, effective family-school partnerships continue to prove difficult to create and sustain. This chapter will help you, the preservice or experienced teacher, learn more about (1) the complexities surrounding developing family-school partnerships, (2) the many questions about parent education that still remain unanswered, (3) the reasons why overburdened schools have not made parent involvement a top priority, (4) the reasons for the limited participation of some families in life inside schools, (5) the multiple ways parent involvement has been defined, (6) the terms and phrases that have been used to describe family-school partnerships, and (7) various types of family-school partnerships that have been developed over the years.

Family-School Partnerships: Why Are They So Difficult to Create?

Strong evidence exists that validates the importance of families in the educational lives of their children. Swap (1993), Henderson (1981, 1987), and Henderson & Berla (1994) shows that family involvement improves (1) student achievement, (2) attitudes toward learning, and (3) self-esteem. Schools that undertake and support strong, comprehensive family involvement efforts and have strong linkages with the communities they serve are more likely to produce students who perform better than schools with identical student populations but do not explicitly involve families. Children from low-income and culturally and racially diverse families experience greater success when schools involve families, enlist them as allies, and build on their strengths. Family involvement in a child's education is a more important factor in student success than family income or education.

Despite this strong evidence, we are still faced with a nagging question about why family-school partnerships are so difficult to create. In the following pages, I discuss several possible explanations to account for this persistent problem.

Too Many Unanswered Questions Regarding the Commitment to Parent Education

Since the invocation of parent education in the United States in the late 1970s, many questions still remain unanswered. Once the parent education movement was in motion in the United States, educators and researchers began asking: Where was it going? Whom would it serve? How would it serve them? At the 1979 conference of the Education Commission of the States, Ira Gordon emphasized "the need to clarify the goals of parent education before plunging into program development, because different goals will pose different problems in implementation" (Gordon, 1979b, p. xi). In a 1977 article, Gordon (p. 73) questioned our motives: "Are we climbing aboard a new educational bandwagon? Do we see parent education and parent involvement as a new kind of panacea?" He went on to explain his concern "about the American tendency to seek the short-term, easy, package-solution to problems and, within that context, to view the school as the remedial agent for society's ills. This single shot approach often ignores the social context, assumes a power for formal education it most likely does not possess, and overlooks the fact that schools are but one subsystem within the society" (p. 73). From that concern, he raised these critical questions:

1. What are the philosophical assumptions underlying programs? Do they still perpetuate the separate mainstreaming and middle-class movements?
2. What is the place of parent education outside of parent involvement in the school?
3. What is the role of the school in parent education vis-à-vis the role of the family in parent involvement in the school? If there are parent-directed emergent group efforts, as we have seen in the middle-class tradition, and government-required parent involvement in the decision process in the mainstreaming movement, how do these roles of parents relate to those parents as receivers of child development or educational information?
4. What are the evidences that various programs have been successful and what is meant by success? (p. 73)

Assuming that answers could be found to those questions, Gordon saw newcomers to the parent movement as having to face another set of questions:

1. What are the comparative advantages of home visitor, center, or mixed type of programs?
2. How do you select and train and supervise home visitors, if that is the model you plan to use?
3. What should be the level of training of personnel who work with parents?
4. How do you design multi-discipline approaches; build flexibility into a program?
5. How do you get parents to participate, and then sustain their level of involvement?
6. How do you convince legislators and educational bureaucrats that educational dollars should be spent outside the classroom? (p. 73)

If the school system is to be viewed as the major social agency, then Gordon suggested yet another set of questions:

1. Where do schools acquire the wisdom to know what parents need? Where do school personnel get the training and develop the attitudes and skills necessary for working with parents from diverse backgrounds?
2. Do programs run the risk of seeing parents as clients and lowering parent self-esteem and sense of potency in relationship to the system?
3. Are there universal parent-child behaviors we wish to foster? What is the evidence? And how do we reconcile conflicting views about what is good for children?
4. How do we solve the possible struggle for power over the programs? How do we resolve the maximum feasible misunderstanding in which school systems may want (or permit) parent involvement in decision-making if it enhances the school as is, and parents may want to make major modifications in that very system? (pp. 75–76)

From the questions Gordon posed in his 1977 article he warned that: "We should ask ourselves strategic questions [about parent education in public schools]. Why are we doing this? How does it fit into the larger social scheme? What do we hope to accomplish within the narrow confines of a specific program? What else ought to be done? What are our basic assumptions about people—what they need and want, and how they learn and grow, what we desire for them?" (p. 78). While acknowledging that a commitment to parent education was important, Gordon (1979b) felt that it was equally important that the federal government, as well as state and local agencies, address these questions in a serious manner.

Another important participant in the 1979 Conference of the States Education Commission was a state senator from Minnesota, Jerome M. Hughes. Senator Hughes strongly agreed with the notion that "…no matter how well conceived, well financed, and well intended, an education program for children alone that cannot counteract the profound cultural effects of the home will not achieve its goals" (Hughes, 1979, p. 6). But Hughes recognized that the parent education movement was creating yet another function for families in addition to a whole list of other traditional family functions and felt that public schools needed to help parents in meeting and talking with teachers, principals, and other experts, namely, doctors, social workers, and psychologists. He further states that "our goals must be to help parents maintain a sense of power, dignity, and authority in the rearing of their children…if parents have the power to do so, most of them will accept the long-term responsibility of caring for and supporting their children" (p. 9). To effectively accomplish this goal, Hughes argued that a series of questions needed to be answered. "How can the parent coordinate the professionals with whom they share the task of raising their children? How does the parent deal with the early childhood expert who is armed with special credentials and sometimes a jargon that most parents cannot understand? How do parents retain responsibility for their children's lives when they rarely have the voice, the authority, or the power to make others listen to them?" (p. 8).

PAUSE AND REFLECT

Take a few minutes to initiate a conversation with a partner in your class/group of colleagues, university professor, or with a cooperating mentor teacher about the questions posed by the speakers at the 1979 Conference of the States Education Commission. In particular, discuss how you think these questions should be addressed in the new millennium.

As a result of concern over the many questions raised about parent education at the 1979 Conference of the States Education Commission, the federal government and state and local agencies have made important steps toward disrupting the cycle of poverty experienced by a larger sector of the American public. These agencies have made these important strides based on our social belief that public education was designed, in theory, to provide an equal opportunity for all children to learn and develop—it was designed to create a chance for upward mobility and achievement, regardless of the advantages or disadvantages associated with family circumstances.

However, since the United States has faced a serious crisis of poverty and ethnic conflict that has produced social isolation and economic disadvantage for many members of certain ethnic minorities, members of some of these cultures have felt ignored, unknown, unappreciated, and sometimes even oppressed by the dominant groups who controlled important extrafamilial institutions. Salient among these institutions is public education, which to many has appeared unable or unwilling to adapt itself to the special needs of poor and ethnic minority children (Laosa, 1985).

Over the years, the federal government and state and local agencies have recognized the distrust and alienation of some families, particularly those of color and who are poor, have about public education. Consequently, attempts to reverse this situation have involved, among other things, the provision of providing monies for improving the literacy skills of poor and minority families, heightening the awareness of school officials of the need for family involvement in the schooling process, creating mandates within federal- and state-subsidized programs that parents be included in decision making, and attempting to remove obstacles that have prevented families from becoming involved, such as transportation, child care, and so on.

Since the 1960s, researchers in reading, linguistics, both educational and developmental psychology, and sociology have attempted to understand the factors in the home that might contribute to children's success and failure in school. This research was mostly an outgrowth of President Johnson's *War on Poverty*, concentrating on the poverty-stricken community in general and the African-American community in particular (Gadsden, 1994). Durkin (1974–75) explored the factors found in the homes of low-income parents from Chicago in African-American children's reading development, performance, and behaviors. Labov (1965) explored the linguistic components related to African-American children's code structures within urban homes and communities and the influence of these structures on their literacy. Coleman and his colleagues (1966) delineated the situation of African-American families in America and the challenge their children encountered to secure admittance in the educational system. Moynihan (1965) described the obstacles African-American families confronted in connection to national agendas. Bilingsley (1968) studied the sociology of black families, whereas Blassingame (1972) wrote a historical perspective on African-American families.

With the large sums of monies the federal government provided to researchers to understand how to connect with African-American families and find ways to invite them to participate in the education of their children, one could conclude that there is little doubt that a commitment to parent education did exist. But the difficulty of getting results is hardly to be minimized. Francis Roberts

(1979) argued, "the process of moving a community to accept serious parent education in the schools can be like the war of the worlds" (p. 10). Roberts then raised a critical question about parent education: "What makes us think the public schools are capable of taking on parent education?" More recently, Powell (1991) noted that "for schools, appreciation of the social context of family life leads to a central question: to how many elements of the ecology of family functioning can schools effectively respond?" (p. 311). Although Powell did not offer any answers to his question, Roberts (1979) did offer an answer to the question he raised about parent education. He broached his question with the observation that "lumping of social problems into the box labeled *need for parent education programs in schools* seems too inclusive. Especially since the schools are in a period when educational goals are being narrowed rather than enlarged, there is reason to be clear about what can be done" (p. 11). Roberts also summarized the comments of Arthur Wise, presented in an article in the *New York University Quarterly*, "The Hyper-rationalization of American Education." He stated: "...Given a broad array of applications of a proposed policy (in our case parent education) and knowing how hard it is to get any practical application, we will choose things we think are measurable not because they are most central to the policy but because they do appear measurable" (Roberts, 1979, p. 11). This is a very real threat to schools as they begin incorporating family involvement into their schools, namely, the selection of approaches that look good on paper but involve little transformation of either educational experiences for students or in the relationship between the home and school.

Perhaps one of the problems facing those supporting parent education has been the notion that policy and decisions should be made on a more centralized basis. A compulsive tendency has been noted in both large and small school systems to operate on the apparently logical but quite simplistic assumption that there is more wisdom at the center than on the periphery and that decision making, evaluation, and program creation is best done by those most removed from the lived experiences of students (e.g., that the superintendent knows better than the principal, teachers, or parents what a school needs). This has hampered the overall commitment to parent education. The ease with which everybody talks about parent education and the importance of a commitment to it, raises the question: What have school systems across the country done (beyond formal commitment) to make parent education a reality for all parents and especially poor and minority parents?

Few would argue that much has been done to raise teachers' and administrators' levels of awareness about the need for parental involvement and that many have proposed plans designed to foster parent involvement. Unfortunately, we have yet to capture the "human element" that is so central to understanding and developing parent involvement initiatives. Douglas R. Powell, of the Merrill-Palmer Institute in Detroit, has pointed out that (1979) "parent education brings new clients to schools" (p. 14) and that "parent education offers public schools an opportunity to develop a new orientation to children and families, a new sense of what it means to serve a community's educational needs" (p. 17). However,

Roberts (1979) appropriately noted that this presents a major challenge for some public schools. More specifically:

> In talking about [parent] education in the schools, we are apt to easily slide into proposals that deal at surface levels with the deep-seated ways of people. How they work with their own children and how they are prepared for this are matters differing from one subculture to another and, even in these times, from locale to locale. We are dealing with personal meanings, with patterns of culture and ways of people, not with some technical need for information. (pp. 11–12)

Where Are We Now?

Even though the discussion regarding the commitment to parent education in the United States occurred more than twenty years ago, it appears that many educators continue to say, as Henderson, Marburger, & Ooms (1986) put it, "killer phrases…[that] are also expressions, used often without thinking, that can stop [parent involvement initiatives]" (p. 66). Some of the phases that have been used are as follows (p. 67):

- A good idea, but…
- The Superintendent won't go for it.
- Against policy.
- Too hard to administer.
- All right, in theory.
- We have been doing it this way for a long time, and it works.
- Be practical.
- Why hasn't someone suggested it before, if it's a good idea?
- Costs too much.
- Ahead of the times.
- Don't start anything yet.
- Let's discuss it.
- It needs more study.
- Let's form a committee.
- Let's make a survey first.
- We've never done it that way.
- Let's sit on it for awhile.
- That's not our problem.

PAUSE AND REFLECT

I invite you to keep track of the number of times you hear these phrases.

In addition to saying these "killer phrases," it appears that many of the questions that were raised at the January 1979 Conference of the Education Commission of the States in Denver are ones on which today's educators are still trying to reach consensus. Some of these recurring questions are as follows:

- Are we climbing aboard a new educational bandwagon?
- Do we see parent education and parent involvement as a new kind of panacea?
- What are the evidences that various programs have been successful, and what is meant by success?
- What should be the level of training of personnel who work with parents?
- How do you get parents to participate and then sustain their level of involvement?
- Where do schools acquire the wisdom to know what parents need? Where do school personnel get the training and develop the attitudes and skills necessary for working with parents from diverse backgrounds? (Gordon, 1977, pp. 73–75).

Even though many of today's educators have not arrived at plausible answers to the above questions, some believe that for educators to make the commitment to "parent education" or "parent involvement" they must come to understand that they can no longer continue to think of equality in terms of "things" such as buildings, books, and curriculum. According to Hawkins (1970), "In all that is done in the name of equalization of opportunities, it is necessary that educators keep in mind that *what* is done is important, but *how* it is done is more important" (p. 43). The relationship between the home and the school must be one of depth where assumptions are challenged and new practices are formed and not merely another term on a list to be done.

The pleas from many researchers call for educators to develop a closer working relationship with the home. Fletcher (1966) was quick to build the case that: "Education is simply not something which is provided either by teachers in schools or by parents and family members in the home. It must be a continuing cultivation of the child's experiences in which both schools and families jointly take part" (p. 66). Potter (1989) continued this line of thought by candidly stating "teachers have the important responsibility of working with and relating to families, not just children" (p. 21). Seeley (1985) argues that: "The crucial issue in successful learning is not home or school—teacher or student—but the relationship between them. Learning takes place where there is a productive learning relationship" (p. 11). In Gordon's (1979a) plea to educators to develop a closer working relationship with the home, he stated that:

> Parent involvement holds the greatest promise for meeting the needs of the child—
> it can be a reality rather than a professional dream. Of course, the bottom line is not
> only that involving parents holds the most realistic hope for individual children

but also it serves as a hope for renewing the public's faith in education. This faith is needed if public schools are to continue as a strong institution in our democratic form of government, which, ironically, can only survive with a strong educational program (pp. 2–3).

Berger (1991) made a very realistic and logical plea to educators on the need to make a commitment to parent education or parent involvement. She stated that: "Schools have more contact with families than any other public agency. Almost every child from the age of 5 spends 9 months a year, 5 days a week, 5 or 6 hours in school. If child care centers and preschools are included, the school-home-community relationship begins at an even earlier age" (p. 118). Berger also correctly notes that: "The school and home...have a natural opportunity to work together" (p. 118).

I agree with all of the pleas for parent involvement and developing family-school partnerships, but I argue that educators must address the recurring questions regarding parent involvement. I realize that many schools have felt overburdened and have failed to address these questions, which is another reason why family-school partnerships have been difficult to create. In Chapter 6, I will show you how to begin addressing these critical questions. However, I want to provide some additional explanations as to why when it comes to parent involvement "...Parents favor it. Principals expect it. Teachers want it" (Chavkin & Williams, 1988, p. 88), yet parent involvement continues not to be a top priority in most schools.

Overburdened Schools Not Seeing Parent Involvement as a Top Priority

As I stated in Chapter 1 and earlier in this chapter, parent involvement research has resulted in an increase in legislative mandates requiring school programs to include parent involvement components. These include creating parent advocacy committees and traditional parent-teacher association (PTA) groups. Some even provide monetary incentives to encourage parents to participate in the schooling of their children. The burden, however, has once again been placed on the schools to manage this outreach. Schools are public institutions that on a daily basis are being pulled in all directions. Dye (1992) provides a poignant example of the numerous demands that our society places on schools:

Today's schools are expected to do many things: resolve racial conflict and build an integrated society; inspire patriotism and good citizenship; provide values, aspirations, and a sense of identity to disadvantaged children...reduce conflict in society by teaching children to get along with others and to adjust to group living...fight disease and poor health through physical education, health training, and even medical treatment...end malnutrition and hunger through school lunch and milk programs; fight drug abuse and educate children about sex.... In other words, nearly all the nation's problems are reflected in demands placed on the nation's schools (p. 162).

The public scrutiny, pressure to perform, and the responsibility of a child's future are tremendous burdens for schools to effectively handle, burdens that are very likely hindering progress in building family-school partnerships. With schools struggling to meet all of their responsibilities, providing effective parent involvement opportunities is not always a priority. Bob Witherspoon, executive director of the National Coalition of Title 1/Chapter 1 Parents, has evidence to support that Title I schools are doing none or only part of what is required even though the 1994 amendment of Title l mandated the development of school-parent compacts. In particular, he notes that "The problem is implementation, monitoring, and making it a priority—schools still look at partnerships as way down on the list" (p. 1).

Witherspoon's comments echo a finding in a 1999 Education Department report, *Promising Results, Continuing Challenges: The Final Report of the National Assessment of Title 1*, or the NAT1 report. It was the culmination of five years of studies and asserts that "research supports the direction taken by the 1994 legislation," but many schools have not made the commitment to supporting meaningful parent partnerships. The analysis says that school officials find compacts helpful in promoting desired behaviors, but they are used in only 75 percent of Title I schools and parents are still not as involved with their schools as is desirable.

The research is clear as to what schools and teachers should be doing to increase family-school partnerships. Schools may play the role in the national effort to improve the education of children but they cannot accomplish it alone. More recently, Lareau (2000) revealed that: "Teachers do not want parents to turn over to them the whole responsibility for educating the child. Instead they want parents to play an active role in the schooling process" (p. 15). However, this is not a new request; it was brought to our attention by Croft (1979) more than twenty years ago. She stated that: "Today's teachers are so overworked writing reports, attending meetings, keeping records, and planning curriculum materials that they feel they hardly have time to devote to the children they are supposed to be teaching (p. 4). Epstein (1982) expressed a similar view: "School cannot always provide individual attention to children who need extra help on skills, nor can schools always offer a range of activities to enrich the basic education program" (p. 1). It is not surprising that LeGrand (1981) found that the children who need the most help tend to be children from minority groups: "Some children achieve and progress, and others don't; and of the others who don't, more than is conscionable are member of minority groups" (p. 680), and most are especially from lower socioeconomic status backgrounds within these minority groups. Shuck, Ulsh, & Platt (1983) point out that, unfortunately, "lower [socioeconomic status] parents appear more reticent about communicating with the school because they often lack confidence, communication skills, and knowledge about learning processes" (p. 524). However Grimmett & McCoy (1980) and other researchers (Bronfenbrenner, 1974; Evans, 1971; Shelton, 1973) have argued that when lower socioeconomic status parents (and minority parents) receive assistance from the school system, they become more involved with children's academic programs. One limitation is that too many school systems have been unsuccessful at attempting to establish family-school partnerships with diverse parent groups.

As a society, we have focused our energy on what schools can do and have ignored the home experience. It is possible that in placing so much of the responsibility of developing successful adults into the hands of the schools, we have not been clear about what we want from parents. We have not been able to clearly express to parents what we would like for them to do for their children beyond suggesting general activities such as "help with homework," "read, talk, and listen to your child," "tell them stories, play games, share hobbies," and so on. Although schools cannot assume sole responsibility for developing family-school partnerships, they should be the ones to make the first step in initiating the partnership process. In many cases, parents do not know the discourse of school well enough or have the confidence in their own educational abilities to take the lead in fostering academically supportive relationships with their children and their children's teachers.

The social, emotional, physical, and academic development of a child is a shared and overlapping responsibility of the school, the family, and other community agencies and institutions. Epstein (1987) correctly points out that:

> Parent involvement is not the parents' responsibility alone. Nor is it the schools' or teachers' or community educators' responsibility alone. All groups need to work together for a sustained period of time to develop programs that will increase parents' understanding of the schools and their ability to assist their children, and that will promote student success and reduce failure at every grade level (p. 4).

Parents are the acknowledged first teacher of their children and need to maintain their role in their children's academic life. Unfortunately, most parents do not know where to start. Must they wait for schools to provide opportunities for involvement or are there ways to become involved independent of the public school system? There are ways for parents to become involved independent of the public school system, but some parents are at a loss as to what to do. Some parents are at a loss because they don't always know how to help their children in school. On the other hand, some parents might not have the time and are not comfortable asking their child's teacher for assistance.

Are parents at the mercy of the overburdened schools? My answer is "yes." If schools feel overburdened and simply don't develop family-school partnerships, many parents feel disconnected and frustrated as to how they could or should help their children. And what is it exactly parents should be doing to help their child become academically successful? Many parents have begged for teachers to instruct them in what to do, but they have not been, for the most part, given clear directions at each grade level as to what to do, especially as it related to the literacy curriculum. The failure of schools to successfully address these questions is yet another reason why family-school partnerships have been difficult to create.

Although schools might feel overburdened by all the roles they are already expected to assume, I would like to suggest that by taking seriously the role of parents in the educational process and becoming specific about the actual help from families needed, burdens actually become lifted as responsibilities are shared. This requires that teachers and parents establish collaborative relationships around specific goals. General ideas such as "helping the child succeed this year" or "providing a good education" can be frustrating and confusing to parents because expectations and goals are not explicit enough to provide direction to parents who themselves may have a history of school failure. When vague pronouncements dominate, important differences between teachers and parents remain unexplored. Little negotiation about meaning and action occurs, and the collaborative effort suffers (Corbett, Wilson, & Webb, 1996).

Before collaborating with parents, Edwards & Danridge (2001) suggest: "Teachers think about the specific goals and expectations. It would be helpful for teachers to connect these goals and expectations to curricular and instructional practices" (p. 254). Moll and colleagues (1992) assert that when cultural information (e.g., traditions, values, expectations) from the home informs classroom pedagogy, *strategic connections* (p. 132) between teachers and parents are formed. These strategic connections are integral to collaborative relationships because they foster reciprocity and establish mutual goals. Consequently, when teachers tap into parents' funds of knowledge, they can craft school-based literacy instruction that resonates with home-based literacies and cultural practices.

Limited Participation of Some Families in Life Inside Schools: Possible Reasons

It is easy for school administrators, teachers, and families to give reasons why the school-family connections are tenuous and parent involvement in schools is low or even nonexistent. There are a number of reasons for the limited participation of families in life inside schools and the overall lack of commitment to parent education or parent involvement:

1. **A history of distrust and miscommunication in family-school interactions.** Many schools have not kept a close watch on the population make-up of parents that they serve (i.e., single, teenagers, employed, new literates, functionally illiterate, illiterate, minority parents, and so on). Additionally, schools often make assumptions about parents, which cause them to be distrustful of their involvement. When left unexplored, this lack of understanding of and acceptance for the families and communities of the students, act to further substantiate parents' own mistrust of the educational system. In many instances, neither the school nor the family are sure what steps to take in order to rebuild the trust or create better lines of communication. Edwards, & Danridge (2001) recognize that many educators would like "to increase collaborative relationships between parents, schools, and communities, [but] there are very few practical examples of how to do so" (p. 251). Furthermore, Edwards & Danridge (2001) believe that:

> One important reason for teachers' inability to create these collaborative relationships with parents from diverse backgrounds is their strong reliance on traditional

methods of parent-teacher interactions. Open houses, parent-teacher conferences, and special school events such as plays and talent shows should not be the only ways that teachers communicate with parents from diverse backgrounds because these interactions are infrequent and superficial (p. 252).

Lightfoot (1978) explains:

> There are very few opportunities for parents and teachers to come together for meaningful, substantive discussion. In fact, schools organize public, ritualistic occasions that do not allow for real contact, negotiation, or criticism between parents and teachers. Rather, they are institutionalized ways of establishing boundaries between insiders (teachers) and interlopers (parents) under the guise of polite conversation and mature cooperation (pp. 27–29).

Lightfoot's explanation illuminates the exclusionary nature of traditional forms of interaction between teachers and parents from diverse communities. Because these forms of communication are deeply rooted in academic, middle-class discursive practices, parents from poor, minority, or immigrant communities might feel alienated and inferior (Edwards & Danridge, 2001; Edwards with Pleasants & Franklin, 1999; Purcell-Gates, 1995). As a result, the ensuing frustrations, tensions, and conflicts can prevent the formation of collaborative relationships between teachers and parents from diverse backgrounds.

Moreover, conventional teacher-parent interactions might not provide access to school literacy. Many parents from diverse communities need sustained exposure to mainstream social and cultural practices to feel comfortable collaborating with teachers and competent working with their children (Purcell-Gates, 1995). When their contacts with teachers are limited, parents from diverse communities can become discouraged and frustrated. Consequently, these parents might be wary of helping their children read and write for fear of "doing it wrong." Goldenberg (1987) provides an excellent example of a Hispanic mother who wanted to help her first-grade daughter, Violeta, learn to read. Although the directives in the teacher's note had been "teach your child the consonants in the alphabet," Violeta's mother was unfamiliar with the school-based methods for doing so. Although Violeta's mother attempted to teach her daughter, she eventually stopped because she was afraid that would confuse her child. Edwards & Danridge (2001) suggest that "teachers who want to build collaborative relationships with parents from diverse backgrounds move beyond the boundaries of traditional teacher-parent encounters" (p. 253).

2. Issues of power between teachers and parents. When parents are not sure how to support their children's literacy learning or how to integrate themselves into the business of the school many feel paralyzed, inadequate, and powerless. Clark (1988) offers some insight into the problem by stating that:

> Very often, parents don't know to which standards, methods, and content their school-age child should be exposed. Their sense of uncertainty, anxiety, and fear increases because they begin to perceive themselves as inadequate. They feel they should know how to respond to their child's out-of-school linguistic and social capital needs, and they feel increasingly frustrated at hav-

ing failed due to their incomplete knowledge about how best to help their children learn increasingly complex school lessons. When schools fail to provide these parents with factual, empowering information and strategies for supporting their child's learning, the parents are even more likely to feel ambivalence as educators (p. 95).

If the situation persists, both the school and the parents begin to blame each other. However, we need to keep in mind that inadequacy and powerlessness may stem from the school failing to make clear what they want parents to do and offering support to those parents who request assistance. Or, when parents do not request assistance extending an invitation to them so that they might feel comfortable approaching the school for assistance.

Edwards, Danridge, McMillon, & Pleasants (2001) presented four stories as a way to illuminate that teachers can use their power in ways that empower students and families from diverse backgrounds. One story that provides an example is Donaldsonville Elementary School, which demonstrates how teachers can reach poor, low-achieving students by building partnerships with parents and communities. Donaldsonville teachers were successful once they recognized that parents' concern about their children's education was greatly mitigated by low literacy. By using powerful community alliances, these teachers supported the literacy development of students and their parents. In doing so, teachers affirmed their commitment to listening to parents from diverse backgrounds. In a second illustration also taken from my own research, "parent stories" have been used as a practical way for teachers to glean pertinent information about children's rich home literacy experiences during their conversations with parents (for further discussion of this, see Edwards with Pleasants & Franklin, 1999). Parent stories will also be discussed later in this book as a strategy for developing knowledge about parents' beliefs and practices and the literate experiences of the child.

As a third example, Edwards et al. assert that teachers become more appreciative of cultural diversity when they identify and understand their own cultural heritages. They highlight Mr. Andrews, an effective urban teacher, because he understood his European American cultural heritage, and he openly shared his cultural experiences with his students. In doing so, he created a classroom environment that invited students to also share their cultural knowledge. Moreover, Mr. Andrews elicited information about parents' home literacy experiences and cultural practices during home visits, which provided him with further opportunities to publicly acknowledge and draw from the cultural practices of students' own community.

In the fourth case story, Edwards and her colleagues demonstrate how two students, Marcus and B.J., were accustomed to building close, trusting relationships with Sunday School teachers and other adults in the African-American church environment. When they were unable to make similar connections with their teachers at school, Marcus and B.J. felt frustrated and confused. Although some teachers may feel uncomfortable with the idea of establishing close bonds with their students, it is their responsibility to find creative ways to reach beyond the idiosyncrasies in different cultural communities or personal preferences for privacy and detachment to ensure success for their culturally diverse students. As Cazden (1988) asserts, teachers must make "personal adjustments" to reach students in their classrooms each year. The four story examples highlighted by Edwards and her colleagues provide opportunities for teachers to encounter "real life" situations that help them understand the lives and experiences of culturally diverse students and their families.

   3. **The changing nature of parents' roles in children's lives.** Increasingly, some parents feel that if they simply send their children to school that they have fulfilled all of their responsibility. After sending them to school they don't want to become involved in their children's school lives (see Lareau, 2000). They feel that it is the school's responsibility to educate their children. Many parents work long hours to put food on the table and feel they are doing all that they can for their children at home, so teachers can ensure that their children learn at school.

   To help you see up close why some parents might feel this way, I share with you the case study by Lareau (2000). Case studies can simulate for preservice and experienced teachers what they might face within schools when they must deal with students whose backgrounds are different from their own. Analysis of cases may also help to break down myths associated with social class. In addition, the cases may offer some options for ameliorating within the schools some of the grave injustices that have been inflicted by society.

   In her case studies, Lareau (2000, 1989) investigated family-school relationships in white working-class and middle-class communities. She discovered that the teachers and principals had a certain expectation regarding the appropriate role of parents in the schooling process. Through interviews with parents, Lareau found that working-class parents wanted their children to do well but tended to leave the education up to the teacher. Middle-class parents on the other hand saw themselves as partners with teachers in their child's education. In the first case, the working-class parents tended to be ill at ease in the school. Many of them had not received a high-school diploma. In the second case, the middle-class parents were generally at ease with the teachers. Most were professionals in their own right and had known successes throughout their education. The different backgrounds between working-class and middle-class parents made for different behavior in parents' compliance to school requests.

   Lareau interpreted her study using the cultural capital model (Bourdieu, 1984). Bourdieu (1977; Bourdieu & Passeron, 1977) argues that schools draw unevenly on the social and cultural resources in the society. For example, schools use particular linguistic structures, authority patterns, and types of curricula; children of higher socio-economic standing enter school already familiar with these social arrangements. Bourdieu maintains that the cultural experiences in the home differentially facilitate children's adjustment to school and academic achievement. This transforms elements of family life, or cultural resources, into what he calls cultural capital. Lareau (2000) believes that even though "Bourdieu does not examine the question of parent involvement in schooling…his analysis points to the importance of class and class cultures in facilitating or impeding parents' negotiation of the process of schooling" (p. 8).

Lareau suggested that the school take into account the difference in class backgrounds before assuming that the working-class parents do not want their children to succeed. More studies in the ethnographic tradition are needed to begin to understand some of the misconceptions parents have of schools and schools have of parents, particularly when the category of social class is considered.

4. An unintentional exclusion of poor, minority and/or immigrant parents from school activities. With all of the many families that schools have to serve, they may not have the expertise to address the needs of all these families. Many poor, minority, and/or immigrant parents often feel that the school's activities are not culturally sensitive and do not address their concerns. Perhaps the activities do not address these parents' concerns because the school has not taken the necessary time to listen to these parents.

Recognizing that schools and families do not communicate effectively prompts the need to regroup and work together to meet the needs of America's children. How can schools begin to instigate better systems of gathering and sharing information from/with parents? Edwards with Pleasants & Franklin (1999) argue that to construct the two-way communication necessary to build the groundwork for "parent stories" to evolve, schools and teachers must enter a partnership not unlike an arranged marriage. Trust must be developed to gain maximum information. Through the use of stories, Edwards and her colleagues believe that trust will begin to develop between teachers and parents. Edwards and her colleagues (1999) define *parent stories* as the narratives gained from open-ended conversations and/or interviews. In these interviews, parents respond to questions designed to provide information about the traditional and nontraditional early literacy activities and experiences that have happened in the home. They also define parent stories through their ability to construct home literacy environments for teachers and by their ability to connect home and school. By using stories as a way to express the nature of the home environment, parents can select anecdotes and personal observations from their own individual consciousness to give teachers access to complicated social, emotional, and educational issues that can help to unravel for teachers the mystery around their students' early literacy beginnings. In Chapter 4, I will discuss in more detail how to construct "parent stories."

Lacking a Common Understanding of Parent Involvement

Despite the resounding calls for extending the family's role in children's learning, the reality in most schools remains "high rhetoric and low practice." Could it be, like the term *restructuring*, the meaning and definition of family-school partnerships, family involvement, and parent involvement varies widely (Moles, 1987)? It is educationally sound to want more family/parent involvement, but the kinds of relationships desired depend on how particular individuals (i.e., teachers, administrators, researchers, policymakers, parents, community leaders, and so on) define the concept, which leads to the confusion around the definitions of family/parent involvement. It is also, in my opinion, another critical reason schools have struggled to develop successful family-school partnerships.

In their review of parent involvement research, Baker & Soden (1998) pointed out the problems of research in this field as being difficult to untangle:

> While most practitioners and researchers support the policy direction of increased parent involvement, few agree about what constitutes effective involvement. Confusion persists regarding the activities, goals, and desired outcomes of various parent involvement programs and policies. A major source of this confusion is the lack of scientific rigor in the research informing practice and policy. Because of this, less is known about parent involvement than commonly is assumed. Nonetheless, early studies suggesting the importance of parent involvement are treated as definitive, regardless of the equivocal nature of the data, and they are used to support the position that all types of parent involvement are important. Moreover, many programs and policies promoting parent involvement are not explicitly based on the evidence that does exist. Reliance on such compromised data may lead to unrealistic expectations of what parent involvement programs and practices actually are able to accomplish (p. 3).

As you can see, several factors work together to create the problem regarding parent involvement for practitioners and researchers. One of the most prevalent problems is the shifting definition of parent involvement. Morrison (1978) pointed out "…that there has been a tendency to have too narrow of a definition of parent involvement" (p. 21). Ascher (1988) said, "Parent involvement may easily mean quite different things to different people" (p. 10). She continues by saying that,

> It can mean advocacy: parents sitting on councils and committees, participating in the decisions and operation of schools. It can mean parents serving as classroom aides, accompanying a class outing or assisting teachers in a variety of other ways, either as volunteers or for wages. It can also conjure up images of teachers sending home notes to parents, or of parents working on bake sales and other projects that bring schools much needed support. Increasingly, parent involvement means parents initiating learning activities at home to improve their children's performance in school: reading to them, helping with homework, playing educational games, discussing current events, and so on. Sometimes, too, parent involvement is used more broadly to include all the ways in which home life socializes children for school (p. 10).

Meanings of parent involvement are conveyed conceptually in Figure 2.1, which marks the way in which involvement is embedded in the interpretations, understandings, and personal meanings of the participants. This figure is intended to represent some of the phrases, comments, reflections, and statements that teachers, administrators, researchers, policy makers, parents, and community leaders have used when asked to define or describe parent involvement.

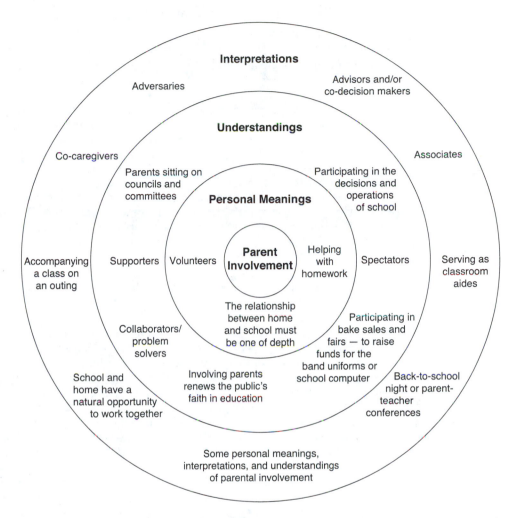

FIGURE 2.1 *Personal Meanings, Interpretations, and Understandings Associated with Parent Involvement*

Shifting Definitions of Parent Involvement

In the following section you will see just how broadly parent involvement has been defined. What I want you to notice is that these definitions, in most cases, are definitions that are most commonly used irrespective of whether employed by teachers, administrators, researchers, policy makers, parents, or community leaders. When I have had the opportunity to sit in on group or individual meetings with teachers, administrators, researchers, policy makers, parents, and community leaders, I have observed that the interpretations, understandings, and personal meanings found in Figure 2.1 surfaced in all of the conversations I have had with these different groups of individuals.

Henderson, Marburger, & Ooms (1986) share Ascher's (1988) contention that educators are not always clear about what they mean by parent involvement. They point out that:

> Most [educators] are probably referring to parents' participation in home-school activities such as bake sales and fairs to raise funds for band uniforms or school computers. Or they may be referring to parents helping in the classroom or on school trips. Some may be referring to special programs designed to encourage parents of young children to become more involved with their children in learning activities at home. Other educators feel less positive about parent involvement, thinking instead about incidents where parents have insisted that certain books are banned from the school library, particular courses are not taught, or a teacher is fired. Yet others are ambivalent about parent involvement, thinking about "Back-to-School" nights or parent-teacher conferences, which on some occasions turn out to be useful and constructive, but on others are boring rituals or even quite hostile encounters (p. 2).

Chrispeels (1992) provides an insightful definition of what teachers and schools mean by parent involvement. She argues that:

> From the school's perspective, teachers want parent involvement to mean parents send the child to school ready to learn. Teachers also perceive that the school has good parent involvement if there is a ready pool of volunteers who help to raise funds, provide other resources, and attend all meetings called by the school. Early primary teachers frequently work to involve parents in the classroom, but upper grade elementary and secondary teachers rarely encourage this kind of involvement. Less direct involvement of parents in the classroom is appropriate as children mature and develop; however, this distancing has also meant that important opportunities for home-school collaboration and support are lost (pp. 1–2).

Morrison (1998) defines parent involvement and family involvement in terms of four approaches: task approach, process approach, developmental approach, and comprehensive approach. These four approaches are described in the next sections.

Task Approach

The most common and traditional way to approach parent involvement is through a task orientation. This method seeks to involve parents in order to get assistance completing specific tasks that support the school or classroom program. In this orientation, faculty, staff, and administration work to involve parents as tutors, aides, attendance monitors, fundraisers, trip monitors, and clerical helpers. This is the type of parent and family involvement many professionals are comfortable with and the sort that usually comes to mind when planning for some kind of parent or family involvement. However, while this type of parent involvement has many benefits, by itself it does not represent a sufficient program of family involvement (p. 475).

Process Approach

In this approach, families are encouraged to participate in certain activities that are important to the educational process, such as curriculum planning, textbook review and selection, membership on task forces and committees, teacher review and selection, and helping to set behavior standards. This approach is becoming popular because professionals realize the importance of sharing these processes and decisions with parents, family members, and members of the community. Parents and others need preparation and support for this kind of involvement. Some professionals may think parents lack the necessary skills to help in certain areas, but with some assistance and an opportunity to participate, many family members are extremely effective (p. 476).

Developmental Approach

This orientation seeks to help parents and families develop skills that benefit themselves, children, schools, professionals, and families and, at the same time, enhance family growth and development. This humanistic orientation is exemplified in cooperative preschools, community schools, and Head Start programs (p. 476).

Comprehensive Approach

A comprehensive approach to parent and family involvement includes elements of all of the preceding approaches, especially the developmental approach. It goes beyond the other three approaches, however, in that it makes the family the *center* or *focus* of activities. This method does not seek involvement from parent or family members for the sake of involvement or the benefit of a particular agency. Rather it works with, in, and through the family system to empower, assist, and strengthen the family. As a result, all family members are helped, including children.

The comprehensive approach seeks to involve parents, families, and community persons in school processes and activities, including decisions about the school. It is also provides parents choices about which school or program their children will attend.

A comprehensive program also provides involvement through family development and support programs. Many programs are not only encouraging involvement in family-centered programs, they are providing them. These family support programs include parenting programs, home visitations, substance abuse education and treatment programs, discussion and support groups, job training and referral programs, basic skills training programs, and linking parents to existing community resources programs (p. 476).

PAUSE AND REFLECT

Explore the different definitions and/or views of parent involvement and relate them to your personal experiences. How do you think these definitions/views influence a school setting?

Changing Terminology

The last reason I believe that family-school partnerships have been so difficult to create has to do with the confusion in terminology. Some schools have tried to implement what they have read about or seen other schools doing to involve parents, not realizing that individual schools must examine the types of parent involvement initiatives they create based on the needs of parents in their school. Consequently, when schools use the "same terminology" as that of another school, and it does not work the way the other school's family-school partnership worked, there is usually confusion as to why it did not work. What schools have to recognize is that parent involvement is different even if their school uses the same terminology that another school used. Parent involvement can be different from school to school and community to community.

Local Definitions of Parent Involvement

A number of broad terms have been used to describe parent involvement including *business partnerships, home-school partnerships,* and *home-school-community partnerships.* These types of partnerships can be categorized as *local* because they consider how local community members can join with parents, teachers, and administrators to become more actively involved in family or parent involvement initiatives. This "team model" of schooling, which is the foundation for "Accelerated Schools" in California and those developed by Comer (1980), positions parent involvement as a powerful element, and strives to empower all parents rather than just a few parent volunteers (Seeley, 1989). In these partnerships, parent involvement is not a separate project, rather it is an integral part of the school's comprehensive plan to mobilize all available resources (e.g., parents, neighbors, community leaders) in an effort to help children achieve.

One of the most popular and well-known types of these partnerships is the business partnership. And, perhaps the momentum for the business partnerships came from a challenge by Geiger (1992). He stated that:

> We cannot expect the parental involvement that is essential to improved education unless and until employers demonstrate real and meaningful respect for parenting—and for parents. If corporate America expects today's children to take their places as tomorrow's productive workers, that respect must be translated into policies that reflect appreciation for the unprecedented challenges confronting today's families (p. 309).

Wissbrun & Eckart (1992) extended this challenge further by noting that:

> Communities have become concerned with the business of education. Among the complaints are that students who graduate from high school and apply for entry-level positions cannot properly complete employment application forms. In response to this concern, businesses can: (1) outline skills that high school graduates need to enter the job market and share them with schools; (2) bring local students, teachers, and parents to the company site and explain the skills their employees need; (3) hire students in work-study programs; and (4) supply equipment, such as computer labs, to schools (pp. 128–129).

Wissbrun and Eckart also believe that employees can become involved in the educational system. They can:

1. Become a mentor for at-risk students
2. Promote time off to team teach in schools
3. Trade roles, so teachers could work in business and industry while they teach in schools
4. Find out how their company is involved in remedial training for job applicants
5. Put pressure on statements for school reform
6. Sponsor college days for high school students
7. Provide money for achievement incentives, special projects, and college funds (p. 129)

Local definitions of parent involvement are powerful because they make it possible to consider unusual or unique circumstances that require empathy and sensitivity. For example, the notion of *community organizations as family* is included in local definitions of parent involvement. Heath & McLaughlin (1991) explain the concept:

> Policy makers and practitioners concerned with American youth acknowledge the special and critical contribution of community organizations as resources that extend beyond family and schools. Their view recognizes the limitations of today's schools and families. Schools as social institutions are inadequate because they are built on outmoded assumptions about family and community. Too many families simply lack the emotional, financial, experiential, or cognitive supports that a developing youngster requires. Policy makers and practitioners no longer need to be convinced of the importance of positive local alternatives to a family- and school-based system of support (p. 624).

As educators, we must be cognizant of the fact that "parents" can come in different forms. For many students, other people—grandmothers, aunts and uncles, siblings, Big Brother/Big Sister organizations, and court-appointed guardians (e.g., foster parents)—act as parents, and they should be welcomed and involved within the classroom as much as possible. The term *community organizations as family* broadens the definition of "parent" to include community leaders and youth workers (e.g., Boys and Girls Clubs of America, Future Farmers of America) who are invested in the lives, dreams, and development of the children in their care.

Literacy-Centered Parent Involvement.
Literacy learning begins at birth. In the years before school, parents play a vital role as their children's first literacy teachers (Morrow, 1993), and especially with respect to reading (Taylor & Strickland, 1986). Book reading is the parent-involvement activity most commonly requested by teachers (Vukelich, 1984), and parents need to understand that storybook reading is the cornerstone of reading instruction in the early grades (Edwards & Garcia, 1991; Taylor & Strickland, 1986).

Parents' reading aloud to their children is assumed to be a prerequisite for success in school. As early as 1908, Huey revealed "the secret of it all lies in the parents reading aloud to and with their child" (p. 32). In *Becoming a Nation of Readers*, the authors state that: "Parents play roles of inestimable importance in laying the foundations for learning to read" (Anderson, Hiebert, Scott, & Wilkinson, 1985, p. 57). Mahoney & Wilcox (1985) concluded, "If a child comes from a reading family where books are a shared source of pleasure, he or she will have an understanding of the language of the literacy world and respond to the use of books in a classroom as a natural expansion of pleasant home experiences" (p. ix). Among families who routinely read stories to their children, Adams (1990) estimates that the children spend from 1,000 to 1,700 hours in one-to-one literacy activities before entering school. Adams suggests that these children experience another 2,000 hours of print "guidance" by watching *Sesame Street* and perhaps another 1,000 or 2,000 hours by playing with magnetic alphabet letters, participating in reading and writing activities in playgroup or preschool, exploring with paper and pencils, and playing alphabet games on a computer (p. 85).

But for children in many families, there are no storybook routines, no magnetic letters on the refrigerator, no easy access to paper or pencils for creating messages, and no literacy games to play on a computer. Perhaps there is not even *Sesame Street.* Such children will begin first grade without the "thousands of hours of school-like reading experience" (Adams, 1990, p. 90) that other families have the resources to provide. Adams' findings point to the fact that many preschool children who enter school each year have not been marinated or soaked in print. But, they still come!

However, it should be noted that when children enter school, the suggestions most commonly made for parent involvement, according to Carol Vukelich (1984), are as follows:

1. Read to your child.
2. Be a good literate role model.
3. Provide books, magazines, and so on for your child to read.
4. Build a reading atmosphere at home (place, time, library area).
5. Talk and listen to your child.
6. Exemplify a positive attitude toward reading.
7. Provide experiences for children that are reading related (e.g., library trips) or that can be used to stimulate interest in reading.
8. Read environmental signs; capture reading opportunities in the environment.
9. Provide contact with paper and pencils.
10. Be aware of your child's interest.
11. Point out similarities and differences in objects in the environment (p. 473).

All of these are excellent suggestions and/or activities for bridging the gap between home and school. However, what I found in my classic 1989 study entitled, "Supporting Lower [Socioeconomic Status] Mothers Attempts to Provide

Scaffolding for Book Reading," is that book reading is a very simple teacher directive, but a very complex and difficult task for some parents (see Edwards, 1989). I put forth the argument that to simply inform parents of the importance of reading to their children is not sufficient. Instead we must go beyond *telling* to *showing* lower socioeconomic status parents how to participate in parent-child book reading interactions with their children and support their attempts to do so.

I contend like Gadsden (1994) that "many parents want assistance in using school-like models for literacy" (p. 14) and book reading is one of those school-like models. For more than three decades, studies have shown that when parents read to and with children, their children's literacy is developed (Anderson, Hiebert, Schoot & Wilkinson, 1985; Chomsky, 1972; Laosa, 1982; Teale & Sulzby, 1986). This school-like model is another form of a local parent involvement initiative characterized as *family literacy*.

Family Literacy. Numerous studies have attempted to define family literacy (e.g., Harris & Hodges, 1995; Morrow, Tracey, & Maxwell, 1995; Tracey, 1995) without being able to agree on a definition. Most attempts have failed to define the concept of home literacy in a way that can be of use to both researchers and practitioners in fostering children's literacy development within a family context. As a result, there has been ambiguity about the concept of family literacy and an absence of theoretical frameworks.

This vacuum has forced literacy specialists to create their own definitions and to conceptualize their own theoretical framework. Multiple domains (e.g., adult literacy education, parent education and support, children's literacy education) were integrated to encourage parents to provide quality time with their children. They developed the concept of family literacy reflecting several domains, including emergent literacy, early reading intervention, parent involvement, and parent education. Researchers have used these domains to define the term, identify their theoretical framework, conduct studies, and develop programs accordingly. Currently, studies on family literacy have concentrated on cross-cultural and social situations or on understanding family ecology, family within school contexts, and mother-child interactions (Bronfenbrenner, 1986; Scott-Jones, 1987; Willett & Bloome, 1992). Various researchers (e.g., Delgado-Gaitan, 1987; Diaz, Moll, & Mehan, 1986; Taylor & Dorsey-Gaines, 1988) augmented the family literacy definition to include literacy of practical use found in the home, such as notes, bills, and grocery lists.

Aiding Parents in Sharing Books with Their Children. Family storybook reading is one of the strongly supported family literacy activities. The notion that parents could profit from receiving assistance in book reading has been suggested by a number of researchers. Spewock (1988) proposed that parents who have poor attitudes toward school because of their own negative experiences as students could profit from training in the use of children's literature to teach their children. Pflaum (1986) suggested, "Children with little experience in one-to-one verbal interaction with their parents may profit from instruction that provides such interactive focus. Parents may be able to supplement their interactions through training" (p. 89).

Several researchers have developed successful book-reading models. For example, Arrastia (1989) developed the Mothers' Reading Program, which taught adults to read through group creation of literature. Participants in this program would "read" the world, through dialogue about issues in the community—such as literacy, education, parenting, and the myriad of issues that affect mothers in present-day New York City. The dialogue was then transformed into written texts. This community literature became the core reading material used to build language skills.

Another effective program is the MOTHERREAD program, designed by Gaj (1989), for mothers separated from their children by imprisonment. The program focused on creating connections between parents and children around books, capitalizing on the shared history, intimacy, and motivation that make the parent unique as a teacher.

One program in particular was based on emergent literacy principles. I developed *Parents as Partners in Reading*, a book-reading program for low-literate parents (see Edwards, 1990, 1993). The program operated from October 1987 to May 1988 in a rural Louisiana community and consisted of twenty-three two-hour sessions divided into three phases: coaching, peer modeling, and parent-child interactions. Each phase lasted for approximately six to seven weeks.

During the first phase called *coaching*, I met with the mothers as a group. I modeled effective book-reading behaviors and introduced a variety of teacher videotapes, which highlighted specific book-reading techniques. The tapes often began with the teacher providing a rationale for why a book was appropriate for accomplishing a particular objective. The objective could include such activities as pointing to pictures, labeling and describing pictures, and making connections between the events in the book to one's own life experiences and vice versa. The teacher, working with a child, would then model book reading, highlighting the particular objective they had selected. After parents viewed the teacher tape, I involved them in a guided discussion of the applications of the strategy modeled by the teacher. The parents could stay after the sessions to review tapes and interact with me on an individual basis.

During the peer-modeling phase, I helped the parents manage the book-reading sessions and strategies. This phase was based on Vygotsky (1978); see also Edwards & Garcia, 1995, which states, "the zone of proximal development defines those functions that have not yet matured but are in the process of maturation" (p. 86). I assisted the parents by (1) guiding their participation in book-reading interactions with one another, (2) finding connections between what they already knew and what they needed to know, (3) modeling effective book-reading behaviors when such assistance was needed, and (4) providing praise and support for their attempts.

During the last phase, parent-child interactions, I ceded total control to the parents and functioned primarily as a supportive and sympathetic audience. In this final phase, the mothers shared books with their own children and implemented book-reading strategies they had learned in the previous two phases (coaching and peer modeling). From these interactions, the mothers learned the importance of involving their children in a book-reading interaction. This program appears to model kinds of interaction with parents that are similar to the ones used to engage children in reading.

Classroom-Based Definitions of Parent Involvement

As educators, our definitions of parent involvement are particularly influential because we interact directly with our students and their families. Many teachers use a *delegation* model of parent involvement, where the types and forms of parent involvement are teacher-directed. For example, many teachers request that parents chaperone their children and other students on field trips. Although the parent is technically "involved," the teachers have directed the involvement (i.e., telling parents to "keep your group together at all times") so that the parent has little or no input into the nature of the task.

I suggest that teachers begin to use a *collaborative* model for parent involvement. Collaborative involvement will enable parents to support teachers and their instruction because teachers and parents talk about activities and set goals for the involvement together. Thus the nature of the parent involvement is more in-depth than when the parent merely supervises field trips or bakes cookies for isolated occasions. The nature of the involvement is much more achievement-oriented. In collaborative parent involvement, parents have the opportunity to interact with students and teachers so that they can begin to learn the inner workings of the classroom. Collaborative parent involvement easily interfaces with more specific types of parent involvement that closely connect it to academic achievement.

Parents are willing to become involved in schools, but they want their involvement to have a significant impact on their children's achievement and educational experiences. Delpit (1995) argued that parents have little interest in having the school reinforce what children already know and instead "want to insure that the school provides their children with discourse patterns, interactional styles, and spoken and written language codes that will allow them success in the larger society" (p. 29). Delgado-Gaitan (1993) also addressed the school's responsibility to teach parents what they need to know to support their children in school. She suggested a critical proposition as a basis for working with parents:

> The knowledge required to participate in school is socioculturally bound and transmitted in socially constructed settings. Thus, organized efforts are necessary in order to provide parents with explicit knowledge about schools and how the educational system operates…if this information is not made available to all parents; parent participation is limited to those who have the means to gain access (p. 140).

Parents need to be aware of the school's goals and objectives and how classroom instruction meets these objectives. Teachers can discuss their curriculum in these terms with parents. Many of the *delegation* and *collaborative* model programs are specifically designed for target groups of parents to encourage them to become involved in their child's educational achievement. According to Rich (1985), "If teachers had to choose only one policy to stress…the most payoff, [would] come from teachers involving parents in helping their children in learning activities at home" (p. 19). Hamby (1992) points out that:

> The "parents as teacher" model is probably the most appropriate for widespread and sustained involvement of families. It is the approach that research links most directly with improvements in academic achievement and is well suited as a way to involve not only single parents, but also families in which both parents work (p. 63).

The following *delegation* and *collaborative* program models demonstrate the range of parent-child interactions recommended to further a child's development as a reader. In particular, these program models are illustrative of some of the ways parents have been encouraged to participate in their children's learning. The goal of most of the programs is to teach parents to engage their children through specific types of activities. Another goal of some of these program models was to help minority parents support their children's language development. The expectation is that this involvement will give parents additional ways of influence, assessment, and encouragement to take responsibility for fostering their children's learning.

Delegation Program Models

Helping Parents Develop Instructional Games.   Cassidy & Vukelich (1978) developed a program that focused specifically on parents' construction of games to reinforce what were considered to be survival-reading skills. An unusual feature was an informal pretest, sent to parents before each workshop, in which the parents assessed their children's knowledge of the skill to be stressed so that they would know how difficult to make the game. Vukelich (1978) designed the Preschool Readiness Outreach Program (PROP) to help parents enhance their children's beginning reading skills. For twenty-six weeks, parents constructed games and activities to use with their children to develop oral language, visual discrimination, auditory discrimination, and listening. Although organized around more traditional "skills," the program design encouraged the parent to plan the game and activities with their child's level of functioning in mind.

Clegg (1973) provided low-income, African-American parents with individually planned learning games to help them increase the reading achievement of their second-grade children. Raim (1980) developed a reading club for low-income Hispanic parents. The purpose of the reading club was to show parents how to construct instructional devices appropriate for their children and to rehearse how to use these devices before using them with the children. Burgess (1982) provided eight two-hour workshops for parents in which the educator presented some information about reading and the parents prepared a game to take home to use with their preschoolers. In the following session, the parents first shared their experiences with the previous week's game and then were presented with more information, with which they designed a new game. The programs all suggested close communication with parents, concerning their children's reading progress.

Developing Reading Activities for Parents to Help at Home. Sittig (1982) provided parents with packets of ideas for sharing reading activities at home. Families were asked to complete a minimum of eight activities over a two-week period. The project was designed as a parent involvement program that would be noncompetitive, open to all grade levels, and would focus on children's experience of success in reading as an enjoyable pastime. Lengel & Bagbhan (1980) developed a family reading program and a Sustained Silent Reading (SSR) program. The major objective of the program was to encourage parents to read to their children for 15 minutes a day, seven days a week, for a period of nine weeks. Siders & Sledjeski (1978) provided parents with activities in the form of a calendar with a home activity given for each day for seven months.

Involving Parents as Tutors of Their Children. Criscuolo (1974) suggested that parents could learn a great deal about reading by observing in the classroom. Crosset (1972) involved low-income black parents in a Parent Participation in Reading (PPR) program. Parents observed their child at school in a reading group and then received personal instruction and materials for home study with the child from a teacher at a family learning center.

McWilliams & Cunningham (1976) designed Project Parents Encourage Pupils (PEP) to teach parents in the community how to help their school-age children benefit from reading instructions in the schools and how to provide a home environment that would help their preschoolers develop those readiness skills expected of a beginning reader. Shuck, Ulsh, & Platt (1983) encouraged low socioeconomic status parents in a large inner-city school district to tutor their children using PEP calendar books and individualized homework activities tallied by means of a progress chart. The results indicated that the parent-tutoring program had a significant impact on the improvement of children's reading scores.

Collaborative Program Models
Participating in Parent Programs in Bilingual Education. Shanahan, Mulhern, & Rodriguez-Brown (1995) explained that Project Family Literacy: Apprendiendo, Mejorando, Educando (Learning, Improving, Educating) (FLAME) was based on some key assumptions: that a supportive environment is essential to literacy development, that parents can have a positive effect on their children's learning, and that parents who are confident and successful learners will be effective teachers for their children. Studies of outcomes of Project FLAME (Shanahan, et al., 1995; Rodriguez-Brown, Li, & Albom, 1999) indicate that it led to improved English proficiency for parents, improvements in children's knowledge of letter names and print awareness, more frequent visits by parents to school, more literacy materials in the home, and more confidence in helping with their children's homework.

Paratore (2001) organized the Intergenerational Literacy Project in 1989 to achieve three goals: (1) to improve the English literacy of parents, (2) to support the literacy development and academic success of their children, and (3) to conduct research on the effectiveness of an intergenerational approach to literacy. To accomplish these goals, the Intergenerational Literacy Project offers literacy instruction to parents of preschool and school age children. No direct instruction is provided to children; rather, the project is based on the premise that as parents improve their own literacy skills and knowledge, they will promote literacy learning among their children. In other words, as parents share reading and writing with their children, they will support their own literacy learning through practice and application.

In the following section, I describe a variety of *collaborative* program models that schools have employed to work with parents.

Conversing with Parents Through Dialogue Journals.   Baskwill (1996) had been looking for a way to establish a more effective means of communication with parents and decided to try using dialogue journals with parents of her primary students. These journals provide a means for teachers and parents to carry on a conversation over time about a variety of topics, especially when so many parents are unable to make school meetings for very legitimate reasons. As Baskwill continued to use dialogue journals with parents of the children she taught, she found another benefit, one that she had not considered at the onset. She found that through dialogue journals, she came to know the families better than she had ever known before. In addition, the families of the children in Baskwill's class came to know her better. She notes "…[the families were able to know her] not simply as a name on a door; or a face across a meeting table, but as a person who shares an interest in the development of their children" (p. 61).

Using Home Literacy Bags to Promote Family Involvement.   Barbour (1998–1999) describes home literacy bags as a strategy to encourage family participation and engage parents in children's early literacy development. Home literacy bags contain collections of books, and sometimes activities, that children take home from school. The materials within the bags encourage parents and children to read books and do related activities together in a relaxed, informal fashion.

Home literacy bags appear to "reach" all families, even those that typically do not participate in school-based events. Families that lack transportation and/or child care, or whose members do not speak English or do not understand the school system, still can profit from home literacy bags. The bags put appropriate, high-quality literature directly into the hands of parents, and other informal, interactive activities for extending children's language and literacy acquisition. In other words, home literacy bags can empower all parents to be teachers of their own children.

As you can see, there are many terms and phrases that have been used to describe family-school partnerships. Even though schools have worked hard to develop partnerships, these partnerships, in many instances, have not necessarily met the needs of all of the families they serve. Consequently, many schools continue to struggle to create family-school partnerships, especially when they serve many different family groups with a variety of needs and wants.

Summary

Educators agree that student achievement increases when parents are involved, however, parent education must be provided to help parents learn effective ways to support the school's literacy curriculum. In an attempt to develop successful approaches to parent involvement, in 1979 a Conference of the Education Commission of the States was held. Several educators and politicians raised critical questions that have never been fully answered. Instead of pausing to reflect on the Commission's concerns and trying to answer their questions, many educators forged ahead developing family-school programs that have been, for the most part, unsuccessful.

Even though the discussion regarding the commitment to parent education in the United States occurred more than twenty years ago, many educators continue to use *killer phrases* when responding to issues related to parent involvement. They often leave the task of developing effective family-school programs to individual schools. These schools may be overburdened with many other issues that prevent them from having parent involvement as a top priority. Additionally, various actors within the school culture may view parent involvement differently. Parents, teachers, and administrators may have varying definitions, understandings, and interpretations of parent involvement, thus making family-school partnerships difficult to create.

There are numerous challenges that one must face in developing effective family-school partnerships, but several have been established, including business partnerships, home-school partnerships, and home-school-community partnerships. These partnerships have broadened the definition of "parent" to include community leaders and others who are invested in the lives of children.

Chapter 2 Key Concepts

- Family involvement in a child's education is probably the most important factor in student success. It improves student achievement, attitudes toward learning, and self-esteem.
- Educators and politicians attending the 1970 conference of the Education Commission of the States posed a series of critical questions that are still unanswered in the new millennium.
- Currently, educators often use *killer phrases* in responses to suggestions related to parent involvement initiatives. *Killer phrases* are the excuses used to prevent parent involvement initiatives from being implemented.
- As a society, we have focused our energy on what schools can do, often ignoring the importance of the home, thereby unintentionally not clearly communicating what parents should be doing to help their children at home.
- There are several possible reasons for the limited participation of some families inside of schools, including a history of distrust and miscommunication in family-school interactions; issues of power between teachers and parents; the

changing nature of parents' roles in children's lives; and an unintentional exclusion of poor, minority, and/or immigrant parents from school activities.

- Multiple definitions, understandings, and interpretations of parent involvement are probable sources of confusion around the development of successful family-school partnerships.

- Parent involvement can be defined in terms of three views: (1) *Task orientation:* most common way to approach parent involvement by assigning a specific task to assist the school or specifically in a classroom; (2) *process orientation:* parents are involved in activities related to the educational process, such as curriculum planning, textbook review and selection assisting with behavior standards, and so on; (3) *developmental orientation:* parents develop skills that will benefit themselves, children, schools, teachers, and families while simultaneously enhancing the process of parent involvement.

- Local definitions of parent involvement include (1) *business partnerships*: corporations assisting with educating students to ensure that they have productive workers in the future; (2) *home-school partnerships:* parents and teachers work together as a team to help students achieve; and (3) *home-school-community partnerships:* establishing a team including parents, teachers, and businesses and/or community organizations (e.g., churches, YMCA, and so on) to assist students.

Suggestions for Thought Questions and Activities ⎯⎯⎯⎯⎯⎯⎯⎯⎯⎯⎯⎯⎯⎯

1. Parent involvement has multiple meanings, understandings, and interpretations. Based on your experiences as a child and teacher (preservice and/or inservice), define parent involvement.

2. Compare and contrast your definition of parent involvement with those discussed in Chapter 2. What are the similarities? What are the differences?

3. Chapter 2 may have presented some areas of parent involvement that you had not previously considered. Revise your definition of parent involvement by adding ideas that you found appealing while answering Question 2.

4. Based on your revised definition of parent involvement, what type(s) of family-school partnership(s) do you prefer?

5. Depending on your family-school partnership preference(s), parents may need some training. List three possible ways to provide the training that they will need to successfully participate in your preferred family-school partnership(s). Finally, list three ways that you can motivate parents to become involved in your family-school partnerships.

Internet Activities ⎯⎯⎯⎯⎯⎯⎯⎯⎯⎯⎯⎯⎯⎯⎯⎯⎯⎯⎯⎯⎯⎯⎯⎯⎯⎯⎯⎯⎯

- Using a search engine such as Yahoo! or MSN, locate a community-based program designed to help connect families and children.

- Using the Web site *http://www.proteacher.net*, search for activities that could help create family-school partnerships.

- Enter the term *parent involvement* into a major search engine. How do different groups and organizations define this term? How do these definitions help you think about the different ways people interpret this term?

For Further Reading

Henderson, A. T., Marburger, C. L., & Ooms, T. (1986). *Beyond the bake sale: An educator's guide to working with parents*. Columbia, MD: National Committee for Citizens in Education.
> *Beyond the Bake Sale* is an educator's guide to working with parents. The text provides clear and concise descriptions of ways educators can involve parents in what happens to their children in school. This book is a great starting place for thinking about various forms of parent involvement, and the contributions such involvement makes to children's learning. Suggestions about effective ways to build partnerships between schools and families are included throughout the book.

Kaplan, L. (Ed.) (1992). *Education and the family*. Boston: Allyn and Bacon.
> This volume is written by members of the Association of Teacher Educators' (ATE) Family Ties Commission. This final report is a comprehensive response to the Commission's charge: to study what constitutes appropriate relationships between home and school and to make recommendations to ATE regarding teacher educators' roles in preparing beginning teachers to initiate and carry out strategies for strengthening home-school relationships.

Moles, O. C. (1996). *Reaching all families: Creating family-friendly schools*. Washington, DC: U.S. Department of Education Office of Educational Research and Improvement.
> This publication is designed for the school administrators and teachers, to help them involve parents and families as more active participants in their children's education. The strategies suggested here are appropriate for all students, including students with special needs.

Phi Delta Kappan, January 1991, 72(5).
> The January 1991 issue of *Phi Delta Kappan* includes a special section on parent involvement, with Joyce Epstein as guest editor. This is an excellent resource for gaining a broad sense of the major themes, contributors, dilemmas, and references on parent involvement.

Sarason, S. B. (1994). *Parent involvement and the political principle: Why the existing governance structure of schools should be abolished*. San Francisco: Jossey-Bass Publishers.
> Sarason's searching analysis of American school governance raises what may be the most fundamental questions confronting school reform: Who participates? Who decides? On what basis? His answers strike to the heart of democratic life and create new possibilities for democratic education. Sarason pushes us to look beyond the bureaucracy—to invent inclusive forms of schooling that engage the minds, hearts, and voices of parents, students, and teachers together. It is impossible to leave this book without a commitment to work toward an answer that will work for children.

Weiss, Heather B. (1995). *Raising our future: Families, schools, and communities joining together*. Cambridge, MA: Harvard Family Research Project, Harvard Graduate School of Education.
> *Raising Our Future* presents a national resource guide that characterizes the genre of programs being implemented in schools today to serve families with young children, from preschool to the early elementary grades. Nine chapters roughly plot a continuum of programs, from those that are relatively self-contained to those that are more comprehensive and interconnected to the school and broader community.

Improving Family-School Partnerships

Existing Possibilities

Chapter Goals for the Reader

- To become familiar with three different approaches for thinking about family-school partnerships: (1) historical, (2) humanistic, and (3) cultural
- To become familiar with how the American family has changed over the last several decades
- To understand how poverty has affected the American family
- To become familiar with some of the myths about poverty
- To become familiar with concepts like *textbook children, differentiated parenting,* and *parentally appropriate*
- To understand the importance of teachers learning about family cultures

Chapter Outline

The Morton Story: A Case Example of
Historical, Humanistic, and Cultural Issues
    School History

Dealing with Reality: Schools as a
Microcosm of Society

Chapter Overview

This chapter highlights three different approaches—historical, humanistic, and cultural—that are critical when considering the possibilities for improving family-school partnerships. Many, if not most, preservice and experienced teachers have an incomplete understanding of ways, or approaches, for thinking about family involvement in schools. Many of us would like to believe that we comprehend the whys, wherefores, and details of family involvement until we realize two things: (1) how often educators are puzzled by all of the complexities they are expected to consider when structuring family initiatives and (2) how often what educators think should be done to initiate successful family involvement diverges from how things are "really" done and why. This divergence between what educators want to do with families in school and what they actually do is an important topic that we must address if we want families to get involved with their children's academic lives. It is all too easy for us to reach oversimplified conclusions or to make generalizations about families and ways to involve them or fail to understand the factors that have changed the American family and ultimately impact the kinds of roles they play in school.

In the first section of the chapter, you will learn about the historical approach. In particular, you will learn about the changes in the American family and the nature of family involvement in schools. Also, discussed here are the effects of poverty on American families, which are highlighted in the historical approach.

In the second section of the chapter, I will focus on the humanistic approach that views "parents as people." Stories from real teachers and schools are used to describe how families and children have changed over the years and to explain why it is important to understand the needs of families.

In the third section of the chapter, I will focus on the cultural approach. The cultural approach focuses specifically on the needs of diverse families and emphasizes the fact that parents' cultural differences should not be viewed as deficits. Such differences can actually enhance the educational process.

In the last section of the chapter, I discuss the need for educators to increase their knowledge about families in general and to acknowledge that there has been a struggle to connect home and school literacies. Acknowledging this, I believe, provides hope for creating better family-school partnerships.

Introductory Scenario:
Dr. Edwards Speaks to Undergraduate and Graduate Students

November 2001, two members of the Michigan State University College of Education community, the first a doctoral student and the second an assistant professor, invited me to speak to their students. I was invited by Mrs. Youb Kim to speak to the undergraduate students in her TE 250 "School and Society" class. The following day, I spoke to

Dr. Christopher Dunbar's graduate students in an education administration course entitled, "Schools, Families, and Communities." Both instructors invited me to speak to their students about the importance of families in the educational lives of their children. They knew that I was in the process of writing this book on parent involvement in schools and wished for me to share my thoughts with their students.

As I pondered what I would share with the two groups of students, several thoughts came to mind. First, I wanted to talk about what I had uncovered in the research literature about the lack of training preservice teachers have received in working with parents before their entry into the teaching profession. Second, I decided to share some of my personal experiences that motivated me to advocate the need for preparing preservice and experienced teachers to work with families. This would build a case, I decided, for my third point that teachers should begin to think about family-school partnerships from three different points of view: (1) historical, (2) humanistic, and (3) cultural. The substance of those two lectures, given in late November 2001, provides a framework for this chapter. I have reframed them a bit later on to introduce you to this issue. My lecture began as follows:

Broad consensus exists on the importance of the family's role in education. Nearly twenty-five years ago, Ira Gordon (1969) suggested that parental involvement in education could be traced back to Biblical times. However, David L. Williams, Jr. (1992), after closely examining the research literature on parent involvement, argued that "...the beginnings of programs to prepare teachers for integrally involving parents as partners in their children's education cannot be traced to such a historic origin" (p. 245). What he found glaringly missing from this literature were documented examples of teacher educators preparing teachers to work with parents. Almost twenty years earlier, Safran (1974) surveyed the research literature for examples of teacher educators preparing teachers to work with parents. He, too, was surprised to find that there were few documented examples. Safran lamented that "...despite the growing interest in and demand for parent and community participation in schools, despite the continuing controversy over school governance issues and the extent to which parents should or should not be involved, teachers are no more being prepared to work with parents and facilitate community participation now than they were ten years ago" (p. 7).

Although teacher educators may agree that parents are important participants in the educational process, teacher educators have not moved beyond simply acknowledging the importance of parents. The lack of documented examples of teacher educators preparing teachers to work with parents is particularly alarming when over and over again the research literature has highlighted the fact that parents are their child's first teacher and teachers are children's second teacher.

Williams Jr. (1992) and Safran's (1974) arguments that teacher educators have failed to prepare teachers continues to hold true precisely because teacher educators have been unable to produce documentation that invalidates their argument. In other words, teacher educators continue to fail to provide training to their students, who are future teachers, in how to work with and involve parents. Garibaldi (1992) noted, "...preservice teacher education programs [have failed to] devote...attention to the important roles that the home, parents, and community play in the effective education of children, especially those who come from inner-city and rural communities" (p. 35). She concluded that "...young teachers must be trained how to communicate better and work more closely with the parents of their students" (p. 35). Evans & Nelson (1992) also advocate for a teacher education curriculum that provides educators with the skills they need to empower and involve real families (in whatever form that family may be defined) of children and youth. Evans & Nelson warned, "In the absence of solid pedagogy that permits teachers to employ a variety of appropriate strategies for teaching children and youth, teaching will be a frustrating and generally unsuccessful activity. New goals for teacher preparation and professional development must be advanced" (p. 236).

In an earlier study (Edwards & Young, 1992), we concurred with this point that teacher educators are to be commended for preparing teachers who are knowledgeable about their subject matter. However, we were quick to point out that, in this day and time, knowledge and skill development in subject matter instruction is simply not enough to effectively teach in the multicultural world of today's schools. Krevotics & Nussel (1994) further emphasized this point by noting that:

> Many teachers find themselves ill-prepared to comprehend the multiple cultures that students bring to the classroom, let alone bring dignity and respect for those cultures. They are taught subject matter, but not what to do when the subject matter does not pertain to the life experiences of the students. Teacher education programs rarely prepare teachers to make education meaningful to diverse groups of students [and their parents]...(p. xi).

When I read this quote, the students nodded their heads in agreement, perhaps as you are when reading this book. My point is best reflected in a statement by Foster & Loven (1992) who noted that, "Most teacher education programs have [preservice teachers] involved with children throughout their preparation, but few, if any consider having students involved with parents prior to their entry into the profession" (p. 17).

At that juncture in my discussion, I decided to share with the students some personal experiences that made me committed to preparing teachers to work with families. I highlighted how my thinking about the importance of preparing teachers to work with families was affected when I taught at a historically black university in the late 1970s and a predominately white university in the early 1980s.

Experiences at a Historically African-American University

After completing my doctorate at the University of Wisconsin-Madison, I accepted a position at a small, southern black university located in a rural, northern Louisiana community (Grambling State University). This experience allowed me to share some of the frustrations African-American teacher educators at primarily African-American colleges/universities are facing (e.g., declining enrollments in teacher preparation programs, large numbers of students failing teacher competency tests, and academically weak students choosing to become teachers). As a teacher educator at Grambling State University, I addressed in my seminar class the issue of families and children because my students continually told me that their parents had struggled with the "system" to get them through it, and after getting through it, they still felt that they had been "dealt a bad deal," so to speak. For example, one student named Cassandra told a chilling story of how her parents had to fight with the principal, teacher, and supervisor when she was in fourth grade to prevent them from putting her in a special education class. Angela, another student in the seminar class, commented that she and her parents experienced teachers quickly giving up on her and wanting to track her into lower sections or special education classes. Other students indicated that their parents had fought similar battles. These students wanted to be teachers who reconstructed the public school system to improve educational opportunities for African-American students. Intrigued by these revelations, I began to explore with my students the possibilities of what it would mean to improve the "system" that they said had not served them and their families adequately. What I discovered was that there was overwhelming agreement among the students that the "system" needed to devise ways to meaningfully involve *all* the families they serve. In particular, the students felt that the school system needed to refrain from making generalizations about minority families.

Reflecting on my Grambling students' comments led me to conclude that teacher educators must help preservice teachers to understand that mere knowledge of generalized family statistics is not sufficient for a teacher to be effective in dealing with students in a classroom. Houston & Houston (1992) reiterate my point that: "Statistics synthesize the generalized conditions in our nation about families and family life, but the classroom teacher must be concerned with particular families and specific instances with real students" (p. 256). As a teacher educator, I began to really see that our methods for the preparation of preservice teachers to work with parents needed immediate attention. Even though I agree with Chavkin & Williams (1988) that "It is clear that teacher training about parental involvement is exceedingly complex" (p. 89), I still felt strongly that teacher educators had to give explicit attention to the preparation of preservice teachers in ways to work with families even if it was "exceedingly complex." In a 1992 paper, Williams, Jr., demonstrated just how complex teacher training about parental involvement really is by outlining three tough challenges that teacher educators face—*self-development challenges, challenges within the profession and with colleagues, and challenges for teaching candidates successfully.* According to Williams, Jr., "In terms of their own dispositions and their preparation for providing parental involvement training, teacher educators themselves will face the greatest challenges" (p. 250). Among these *self-development challenges* are:

- How to develop, accept, articulate, and demonstrate the belief that parents are legitimate partners in education.
- How to become more familiar and well versed with the parental involvement philosophical, theoretical, research, development, implementation, practice, and evaluation literature.
- How to become more knowledgeable about various national, state, and local parental involvement program efforts or activities.
- How to identify, locate, obtain, compile, and use an array of parental involvement materials, documents, resources, and so on for teacher training.
- How to observe and participate in a variety of parental involvement activities at different levels of elementary schooling and in different socioeconomic, cultural, racial/ethnic, linguistic, and geographic settings.
- How to internalize the tenet that teachers must work in partnership with parents to ensure the success of students at home, at school, and in life.
- How to take part in parental involvement training activities as part of faculty professional growth and development (e.g., conferences, workshops, meetings, etc.).

- How to volunteer, advise, consult, and/or otherwise work with one or more local, state, district, regional, or national parental involvement program(s) for a sustained period.
- How to conceptualize and make parental involvement an integral part of the elementary teacher preparation subject areas (e.g., reading, writing, computing, social studies, and so on).
- How to become proficient at instilling in prospective teachers the importance of teaching and working with parents, as well as students (pp. 250–252).

Williams, Jr., believes that: "Another serious set of challenges to teacher educators are the environments (colleges/schools/departments of education) where they work and the various faculty with whom they work and interact" (p. 252). This involves *challenges within the profession and with colleagues* such as:

- How to develop a logical place(s) for incorporating parental involvement preparation into teacher education that enhances rather than intrudes upon the process.
- How to inform and convince colleagues within the department/school/university and across other related higher education fields about the value, need, and importance of parental involvement training.
- How to facilitate the inclusion of parental involvement throughout the curriculum/coursework of elementary teacher instruction/training.
- How to minimize or eliminate the attitudes, beliefs, and practices among many teacher educators that relegate parent involvement to being at best merely an attachment to mainstream teacher preparation experiences.
- How to develop a cadre of parents and parent involvement experts to take part in the preparation of prospective elementary teachers.
- How to make parental involvement training experiences part of the competencies that states and districts require for teacher certification and renewal.
- How to establish a comprehensive materials resources base or collection of parental involvement documents and resources to supplement or complement teacher education curriculum and instruction in this area (pp. 252–253).

Williams, Jr., warns, "The ultimate challenge for teacher educators is to ensure that their elementary teachers are prepared to involve parents more fully in children's education at home and at school" (p. 253). The *challenges for teaching candidates successfully* might be considered good indications of this challenge being met:

- Increased opportunities and experiences for candidates that enable them to make parental involvement instruction applicable to their elementary teaching/learning efforts.
- Increased methods for and development of skills in the implementation and assessment and refinement of home/classroom/school parental involvement efforts among elementary education teacher candidates.
- Better candidates' skills in working with parents as partners in education and as adult learners.

- Wider use of innovative ways to assess the parental involvement knowledge, understanding, and skill levels of elementary teacher candidates other than the traditional classroom or standardized tests.
- Increased learning experiences for candidates that clearly connect college/university-based parental involvement theory with school/community-based reality.
- Increased beliefs and actions by candidates demonstrating that parents and their full involvement are essential to school improvement and children's academic success.
- Increased candidates' knowledge/skills in facilitating parental involvement in schools where there is teacher and/or principal resistance, where they are unaware of how to develop effective parental involvement programs or activities, and where they do not see parental involvement's relationship to study (p. 253).

In addition to the complexity of training teachers is the fact that many teacher educators, like public school teachers, are not adequately prepared themselves to help preservice teachers work with families. Preservice teachers, I explained to the surprised students, are unprepared in large part because their professors are ill equipped themselves in how to go about addressing this topic.

Experiences at a Predominately White University

While teaching at a predominately white southern university located in a rural, northern Louisiana community (Louisiana Tech University), I was faced with another challenging situation. My white students often complained that their "teacher preparation program had not done a very good job in showing them how to work with families, especially families of social and ethnic groups different from their own." They would cry out to me, "We desperately need to know how to do this." Consequently, I reframed my courses to better address these issues. The illustration below helps explain why I saw the need to really explore, in a structured way, how to prepare preservice teachers to work with parents.

Susan, a twenty-two-year-old white female began her first year of teaching in Shreveport, Louisiana. Susan was assigned to teach a group of twenty-nine first-grade African-American "repeaters" (i.e., twenty-nine students who had already failed first-grade at least once). She struggled to build a learning community, but nothing seemed to be working in her favor. She also struggled to involve parents, but they did not respond to her requests. The other teachers were telling her that she was in a helpless situation while offering little or no assistance. The principal and supervisor were constantly giving her negative feedback. She became frustrated and called me, her former professor. I encouraged her to set up a meeting with the principal, supervisor, and myself so that all of us could come up with a reasonable solution to this situation. I shared with the principal and supervisor that when they completed college 20 and 25 years ago, respectively, they were not faced with teaching in an all-black setting and most certainly not teaching a class of all-black repeaters. They both agreed. I then asked, "How can you expect Susan to deal with this situation without any assistance or support?" The situation for Susan was resolved because I was willing and able to work with her in making contact with parents and successfully involving them in the literacy support of their children.

Susan's encounter and the past school encounter and those of other teachers, both black and white, with whom I worked forced me to pursue more seriously the issue of helping preservice teachers think about parental involvement. Due to the declining number of minority students selecting teaching as a profession, it occurred to me that we are going to have more Susans around the country struggling to communicate with parents and children different from themselves. Similarly, Colleges of Education will always have a few minority students who might be angry and frustrated by their past school experiences and will need help in identifying these attitudes and feelings, working through them so that they can improve the school learning environments for those students of color who might have had similar experiences. Finally, regardless of their own race, students will need help in working with white students and other ethnic minorities who are different from them.

In my lecture, I emphasized to both the undergraduate and graduate students that understanding how comprehension of multiple cultures impacts classroom instruction and relationships with families is a *must* for today's teachers. Also, I shared with the students a set of questions to which we must attend that were posed by Marilyn Cochran-Smith as cited by James Fraser (1997). She stated:

> What assumptions do teachers and students of all ages bring to school with them about "the self" and "the other"? What understandings do they have about meanings, cultures, and families that are not like their own?…Is it possible and/or desirable to strike a balance between pedagogy and curriculum that is supportive of the racial, cultural, and language identities students bring to school with them and that, at the same time, prepare students to negotiate but also critique the current power structures of schooling and society? (p. vii)

I then asked the students: "What do you think I learned from my students at Grambling State University and Louisiana Tech University?" None of the students responded, but I could tell in their body language that they were interested in what I had to say.

I responded by saying, my Grambling State University and Louisiana Tech University preservice teachers recognized that they needed more information about how to interact with diverse families and children. They needed this information to help them understand "something" about the home literacy environments of their students. Similar results have been reported by Hadaway, Florez, Larke, & Wiseman (1993) and Holm & Johnson (1994). Hadaway, Florez, Larke, & Wiseman (1993) reported that: "…[preservice] teachers were aware of the shortcomings of their backgrounds, and they realized they would be working in multicultural environments for which they were inadequately prepared. Thus, they were eager to obtain more training and skills" (p. 62). They further noted that "[preservice students] reported few personal experiences in culturally diverse settings" (p. 62). Holm & Johnson (1994) revealed:

> …that the preservice teachers each had a keen desire to become multiculturalists;…that the preservice teachers were seriously underprepared to shape cultural partnerships;…that the preservice teachers identified two kinds of experience that they valued as critical components in the multicultural preparation but found deficient in their program of study: carefully guided participation with model teachers who have particular facility in their work with diverse student populations, and multicultural course work that is tied to participation experiences (p. 86).

Researchers like Florio-Ruane (1994), McDiarmid & Price (1993), Cazden & Mehan (1989), and Paine (1988) have raised similarly serious concerns about preservice teachers' lack of preparation to teach diverse learners and their ability to appreciate the impact of the relationship between families and schools.

One of the first documented studies of undergraduate students' perspectives on parental involvement was conducted by Foster & Loven (1992). They examined the views of early childhood and elementary education students who were working in two different professional preparations contexts: the larger, comprehensive state university and a small, private liberal arts college. The students were asked to complete a questionnaire designed to address five research questions:

(1) Do undergraduate education students believe that parental involvement in children's education is necessary? (2) What do undergraduate education students believe contributes to successful relationships between families and schools? (3) What specific ways do undergraduate education students believe they can involve parents in the education process? (4) What specific difficulties do undergraduate education students anticipate in working with parents? And, (5) In what ways do undergraduate education students' personal views and values affect their thinking about involving parents in the educational process? (p. 14)

PAUSE AND REFLECT

Take a few moments to ask yourself these same questions, which were raised above. Then compare your answers with the findings of Foster & Loven below. Do you see your answers as reflecting a realistic picture of home-school connections? Why? Why not? As you were reflecting on your answers, were you thinking about specific memories and examples of your own school experiences? How did your own memories and examples compare with Foster & Loven's findings?

After examining the questionnaire findings, Foster & Loven admitted that the undergraduate education students' responses to these five questions were naive and decidedly answered from a middle-class perspective. For example, they noted that "...most of the [students] had adequate knowledge of traditional techniques for involving parents, but, unfortunately, many of the traditional ways [the students] mentioned did not take into consideration the changing lifestyles and needs of families in the 90's." (p. 17) They also noted that "although students overwhelmingly reported that they did not anticipate difficulty working with parents who are socioeconomically, ethnically, or language different from themselves,...[the] students responses did not seem to consider that an interaction might exist between socioeconomic and cultural backgrounds and the parent role" (p. 17). The last finding highlighted by Foster & Loven is one that was also highlighted by Lareau (1989) and was discussed in more depth in Chapter 2. Lareau connected variance in parent participation in schools to social-class membership, noting a strong influence of social class on the density of connections between parents and schools, regardless of parents' aspirations for their children. Inequalities in parents' resources and dispositions (e.g., education, occupational status, and income) critically affected levels of parent involvement (Lareau, 1989).

The Foster & Loven (1992) and Lareau (1989) findings call for the need for all teachers, preservice and inservice, to learn how to work with culturally different children and families. Once again, the students nodded their heads in agreement. Perhaps one of the overriding reasons for this training is that the culture of poor, minority, and immigrant children is in direct conflict to the middle-class educational vision that a primarily white, middle-class, K–12 teaching staff may bring to the classroom and school environment (McDiarmid & Price, 1993; Paine, 1988). It is not surprising that researchers have reported that such teachers, in most instances, often cannot envision people who think and act differently from themselves or have different cultures and/or experiences (Florio-Ruane, 1994; McDiarmid & Price, 1993; Cazden & Mehan, 1989; Paine, 1988). These researchers further revealed that primarily white, middle-class, K–12 teaching staffs rarely come to the classroom equipped with the skills and abilities to teach diverse learners. According to Florio-Ruane (1994), "This lack of shared background is particularly troublesome as teacher candidates prepare to teach the school-based literacy skills of reading comprehension, written composition, and interpretation of literacy and subject-matter texts" (pp. 52–53).

All too often this lack of shared background has made it difficult for teaching staffs to connect subject matter to the lives of their students. The inability to do this is problematic for these students' parents, and it may prevent them from becoming involved in school affairs, simply because parents may become discouraged and dissatisfied with teachers' inability to successfully teach their children. As a result, the attitude that some parents may exhibit is: "Why should I bother coming to school when everything my child's teacher has to say about my child is negative?" Unfortunately, this often leads to the unraveling of the relationship between home and school. Because of this miscommunication, children are caught in the crossfire and ultimately suffer academically.

The inability of teaching staffs to understand the lives, histories, or cultures of communities different from theirs is yet another factor that has made it difficult to connect home and school literacies. It has also hampered family-school partnerships. In addition to the complexity of parent involvement training itself is the fact that many teacher educators, like public school educators, are not adequately prepared to help preservice teachers work with families. The main reason I decided to write this book was to help teacher educators better prepare preservice and inservice teachers to work with families. The authors of the Holmes Group Report *Tomorrow's Schools* admitted that "student [and parent] diversity has received inadequate or inappropriate attention by school and university faculty, most of whom enter education with little personal experience of people different from themselves" (Young, Sykes, Featherstone, Elmore, & Devaney, 1990, pp. 36–37). The problem is compounded, as Kochan & Mullins (1992) note, by the perception of schools as the sole source of knowledge. Many parents, teachers, administrators, and teacher educators fail to consider the integration of the home, school, and other environmental factors as the basis of a fusion of knowledge. Kochan & Mullins (1992) observe that "Teachers are not prepared to detect, nor deal with, differences that might exist between the family and the school. Teacher educators expressed concern that they were not adequately informed about families to address these concerns in their classes" (p. 272). They continued by asserting:

While the awareness of the need to build relationships with families is growing, both administrators and teacher educators argue that the curricula are already overloaded and it is impossible to add additional requirements. Many believe that the knowledge, skills, and attitudes for working with parents flow naturally from the teaching experience. Yet, teachers in classrooms are frequently just as uncomfortable dealing with families as are the teacher educators who trained them (p. 272).

As we see in the statement above, many classroom teachers are uncomfortable dealing with families; teacher educators have similarly voiced their discomfort with preparing pre-service teachers to work with families. When educators continually place these difficulties in the foreground, what evolves is a *passing of the buck* syndrome. However, as Williams, Jr., (1992) pointed out, the preparation of preservice teachers to work with families rests squarely on the shoulders of teacher educators. This last point is strongly supported by Epstein (1988) in her statement that "...connections between schools and families must be an integral part of educational programs [and that teacher educators]...need to begin new directions in research, practice, teacher training, and policy development" (p. 59). As educators, we must strive to remove the obstacles that we ourselves have erected as rationales for avoiding or giving a superficial treatment of parent involvement issues. Only when these obstacles have been removed will we be able to forge the connections of which Epstein speaks. Epstein (1985) correctly noted that:

Schools are at the crossroads of yesterday's traditions, today's demographics, and tomorrow's technologies. This three-way intersection is, at this time, a hazardous crossing. We are getting a variety of messages about whether and how to proceed to improve schools. We are seeing red signals to stop and head back toward traditional curricular designs with all students taking the same courses, as if all students were headed in the same direction. We are seeing yellow signals of caution about innovative curricula, school and business partnerships, changing teachers' roles, and changing the structures for teachers' salaries. We are getting green signals to go quickly in many directions with technological advances, to invigorate the students' role away from passive toward active learning, and to prepare students' role away form passive toward active learning, and to prepare students for the demands of society in the future. Although it may be easier and safer not to cross the street at all, it is more interesting to step, with due caution, in new directions to improve education. One new direction involves parents...Schools of the future will improve, it is believed, if schools and families, teachers and parents, understand each other's potential for improving the education of the children they share (p. 18).

I could see that the students really agreed with the last statement. I hope that as you read what I shared with the undergraduate and graduate students that you are in agreement with what I had to say. I hope that I was able to successfully convey to you that improving family-school partnerships in today's school is a *must*. Lastly, I hope that I was able to successfully prepare you to read with great interest why I wholeheartedly believe that to improve family-school partnerships you need to seriously think about these partnerships from a historical, humanistic, and cultural perspective, which is the focus of Chapter 3.

Learning about Historical Issues
Involving Families and Communities

The American Family: A Changing Institution

According to Morrison (1988), "A parent is anyone who provides children with basic care, direction, support, protection, and guidance…a parent can be single, married, heterosexual, homosexual, a cousin, aunt, uncle, grandparent, a court-appointed guardian, a brother, a sister, an institution employee, a surrogate, a foster parent, or a group such as a commune" (p. 414). These changing patterns of who is a parent are having important implications for today's teachers.

What constitutes a family and or parent has undergone a radical change over the years. The family as a social institution has experienced many transformations that profoundly influence not only the ways in which we understand what constitutes "family" but also the function of the family unit as well (Tutwiler, 1998). Children are born into many different kinds of families, and parents create for children a wide variety of living arrangements. These family structures affect, in obvious and subtle ways, children's development and how teachers relate to them.

For statistical and reporting purposes, the U.S. Census Bureau classifies family households into four types: (1) married-couple families, (2) families with female householders (no husband present), (3) families with male householders (no wife present), and (4) nonfamily households. A *household* is a person or group of people who occupy a housing unit. The *householder* is a person in whose name the housing unit is owned, being bought, or rented. The term *householder* has replaced *head of family*. A *family household* consists of a householder and one or more people living together in the same household who are related to the householder by birth, marriage, or adoption—it may also include people unrelated to the householder. If the householder is married and living with his or her spouse, then the household is designated a *married-couple household*. The remaining types of family households not maintained by a married couple are designated by the gender of the householder. A *nonfamily household* consists of a person living alone or a householder who shares the home with nonrelatives only (e.g., with roommates or an unmarried partner).

In 1990, the categories of *unmarried partner, adopted child, stepchild, foster child,* and *grandchild* were added to the relationship item to measure the growing complexity of American households. Two additional categories were added to the question in Census 2000 to further measure household composition—*parent-in-law,* and *son/daughter-in-law*. Finally, people who wrote in responses *brother/sister-in-law, nephew/niece, grandparent, uncle/aunt, or cousin* were also coded into separate categories instead of remaining in the *other relative* category as in previous censuses.

Overall, the number of households in the United States increased 15 percent from 91.9 million in 1990 to 105.5 million in 2000. Family households increased

TABLE 3.1 *Households by Type: 2000*

Household type	Number	Percent
Total households	105,480,101	100.0
Family households	71,787,347	68.1
Married-couple households	54,494,232	51.7
Female householder, no husband present	12,900,103	12.2
Male householder, no wife present	4,394,012	4.2
Nonfamily households	33,692,754	31.9
One person	27,230,075	25.8
Two or more people	6,462,679	6.1

Source: U. S. Census Bureau, Census 2000 Summary File 1.

11 percent, from 64.5 million in 1990 to 71.8 million in 2000, whereas nonfamily households increased faster, 23 percent, from 27.4 million in 1990 to 33.7 in 2000.

Table 3.1 shows that the vast majority of family households in 2000—households containing at least one person related to the householder by birth, marriage, or adoption—were married-couple households (54.5 million). Family households maintained by women with no husband present numbered 12.9 million, almost three times the number maintained by men with no wife present (4.4 million). Nonfamily households predominated (27.2 million) and were more than four times as common as nonfamily households with two or more people (6.5 million).

Despite increases in both the number of households and people in the United States since 1990, both the average household size and average family size decreased over the decades—from 2.63 to 2.59 people, and from 3.16 to 3.14 people respectively. These declines continue the downward trends in these indicators since the end of the Baby Boom in the 1960s.

The number of households within each category type increased in the last 10 years, including married-couple households, from 50.7 million people in 1990 to 54.5 million people in 2000. Despite this increase, Figure 3.1 shows that in 2000, 52 percent of all households were comprised of married couples. However, 10 years earlier (1990), the number was slightly higher—55 percent of the households included married couples. For each of the other types of households, both the numbers and percentages share an increase slightly from 1990 to 2000.

Today's families have changed and do not resemble the families of the 1950s and 1960s. However, in the 1950s and 1960s, many American families identified with the television program *Leave It to Beaver.* In the following excerpt, Johnson (1990) provides a vivid description of this *Leave It to Beaver* type family:

"Ward, I'm worried about the Beaver." With those words, spoken to her husband, June Cleaver led us, enthralled, into one of the *Leave It to Beaver* episodes that were

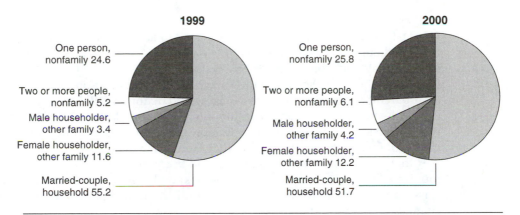

1999

One person, nonfamily 24.6

Two or more people, nonfamily 5.2

Male householder, other family 3.4

Female householder, other family 11.6

Married-couple, household 55.2

2000

One person, nonfamily 25.8

Two or more people, nonfamily 6.1

Male householder, other family 4.2

Female householder, other family 12.2

Married-couple, household 51.7

FIGURE 3.1 *Households by Type: 1990 and 2000*

Source: U. S. Census Bureau, Census 2000 Summary File 1; 1990 Census of Population, *Summary Population and Housing Characteristics, United States* (1990 CPH-1-1).

to become the archetype for American family life in the middle of the Twentieth Century. It was a time when the big problems, like World War II, the Nazi Holocaust, Corregidor, Hiroshima and Nagasaki were behind us. And it was a time when the awesome legacy of those events, racism, pollution, nuclear proliferation, and global poverty, were not yet in the American vernacular. We were lucky to be alive and living in the good old USA, and we celebrated our good fortune with the gusto of an adolescent nation still somewhat astonished by its own might...what could go wrong? Listening to June, Ward, Wally and the Beaver, we would conclude, "not much"...Those episodes, combined with other elements of the popular culture of the day, inexorably shaped our view of families. And even if the one on the screen wasn't like ours, it seemed that it showed the way families were *supposed* to be...Most of us do not have to look very far into our own personal histories, though, to find out that the Cleavers lived only on the screen and in our collective imaginations about what we *wished* all families to be...It was not until the 1960s that "family" problems, such as chemical abuse, poverty and domestic violence became social policy issues, and the hidden problems of unhappy marriages, teenage pregnancy and a host of others came out of the nation's closet and into our mainstream institutions: the courts, the press, and, most important for us, the *schools* (pp. 1–2).

However, reluctantly, Americans are coming to grips with the changing American family. These changes are not just projections of what is to be in the future, they are ones that have already taken place. Since families have changed dramatically, so too should schools. Yet schools have been more resistant to change than any of our institutions.

Teachers must understand that cultural and ethnic diversity can be a key to identifying and respecting changes in American family life. Tutwiler (1998) believes that "School and home connections are likely to be enhanced when teachers and other school personnel are respectful of a family's living circumstances, as well as the unique ways a family might support the education of their children" (p. 41). Houston & Houston (1992) see a need to acknowledge the changing structures and culture of the family—the "new reality," which is what those teachers find in today's schools. Evans & Nelson (1992) aptly describe these changes as the "...urbanization of 'Dick and Jane'" (p. 236). Communication with students and their parents is essential to acknowledging and dealing with these changes. If family involvement is to become a reality in schools and classrooms rather than simply a professional dream, close attention must be paid to how the family has changed. Johnson's (1990) warning that "somebody had better wake up and realize" that American society is changing and becoming more complex should communicate to educators that we must also acknowledge that the cultural makeup of classrooms is changing in conjunction with the ethnic, cultural, and economic changes occurring in families.

These changes are encroaching on the school and lives of the families we serve. The recurring message is that "families today are just not like we used to know them...time and people have changed..." (Leitch & Tangri, 1988, p. 73). Unfortunately, many schools are still trying to serve the two-parent, two-child family. However, this family configuration, according to Hodgkinson (1991, p. 10) "...constitutes only 6% of U.S. households today." Jones & Blendinger (1994) raise another important point by noting that when schools think of "the phrase 'the American family' [it] generally brings to mind a white, middle-class family with a father who works and mother who stays at home with the children, living in a nicely furnished one-family house, with a dog in the yard. Unfortunately, this description of the mythical American family does not widely exist in the 1990s if it ever did" (p. 80). (See Figure 3.2 for a pictorial description of the families with whom schools will have to open lines of communication.)

J. K. Footlick (1990) supported this figure with a description of the diversity of family situations in America:

> The American family does not exist. Rather, we are creating many American families, of diverse styles and shapes. In unprecedented numbers, our families are unalike: we have mothers working while fathers keep house; fathers and mothers both working away from home; single parents; second marriages bringing children together from unrelated backgrounds; childless couples; unmarried couples, with and without children; gay and lesbian parents. We are living through a period of historic change in American life (p. 15).

PAUSE AND REFLECT

Changing demographics, deterioration of inner-city communities, and the diverse combinations of individuals that represent the modern family require not only restructuring within schools but also a radical change and restructuring of the ways schools and families work together. Based on this statement, write down as many different types of family structures of which you can think. With a partner, brainstorm creative ways that you can work with the families that you listed.

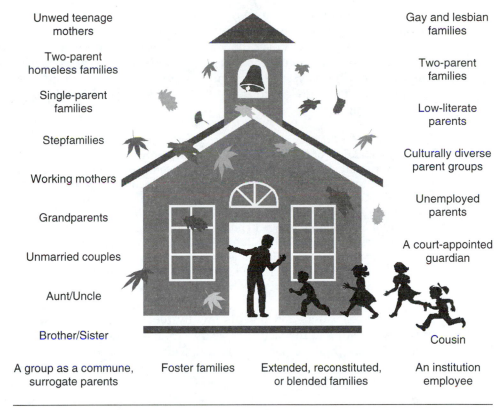

Unwed teenage mothers

Two-parent homeless families

Single-parent families

Stepfamilies

Working mothers

Grandparents

Unmarried couples

Aunt/Uncle

Brother/Sister

Gay and lesbian families

Two-parent families

Low-literate parents

Culturally diverse parent groups

Unemployed parents

A court-appointed guardian

Cousin

A group as a commune, surrogate parents

Foster families

Extended, reconstituted, or blended families

An institution employee

FIGURE 3.2   *Schools Are Communicating with a Variety of Parent Groups*

To this profile of American family life, one can add the observation of Edwards with Pleasants & Franklin (1999) of how: "Schools and teachers must realize that children do not live in a utopia free of the problems that plague adults. Children are a part of society, and what happens in their family, community, and school affects them and all aspects of their development" (p. xix).

It is an unfortunate fact that children today are living and dealing with social problems. Many teachers would agree that what happens in a child's community, and especially in their family, has a direct effect on their development. Overwhelmingly, these problems and circumstances also influence classroom learning, which makes home-school connections especially critical. Even though many teachers agree that family involvement is necessary and important, there are some teachers who might wish that they could just forget about their students' families and the needs of those families. But teachers can't easily do that. Why not? The answer to this question has historical significance.

Thirty years ago, Harrington (1971) predicted that "Schools cannot and would not exist without parents. Parents supply the school with primary material—their children—around which the formal educational and organizational program for that school is constructed" (p. 49). It is important to remember that schools and teachers are here to serve students and families, and oftentimes schools focus their efforts on parents. The recognition of this fact has occurred in various stages and ways over the years, depending on changes in society. Berger (1991) noted that in recent years "…schools and government agencies stressed the importance of teachers working with parents as if a new strategy were emerging…Actually, a traditional concept was being re-emphasized" (p. 30). She continued by saying that:

> The history of parent education and involvement can be pictured as the constant ebb and flow of the ocean's tide. Some eras portray a calm; others are characterized by tumult. As rapid changes, social problems, poverty, and political unrest produce turbulence for families, their need for stabilizing forces increases. So in the 1960s with the call of a "War on Poverty" and the achievement of a "Great Society," there emerged a focus on the family as one institution that could affect the lives of millions of disadvantaged children. The call was strong and resulted in renewed interest in programs in child care centers, home-based education, and combined home-school intervention projects. The emphasis on individualism and families in the 1980s and 1990s has called for increased parent involvement. Concentrating on the fabric of recent programs, we tend to overlook the threads of the past (p. 30).

Many educators and parents vividly remember these threads. They reminisce by pointing to the fact that "years ago, when the parents hired the teacher, lived with her [in the same community], went to church with her, and even monitored her free time, teachers and parents were in close communication. Parents not only knew what their children did in school, they often dictated every move the teacher made." Think back to your own memories of how your parents and teachers interacted and communicated. This knowledge probably gave you some explicit and implicit notions of the types of parent-teacher roles and relationships that are possible.

Most would agree that Gordon and Breivogel's (1976) statement describes a time in our history that, for the most part, characterizes the close working relationship that existed among the home, school, and community. Some of you may have your own thoughts of why such a close working relationship among the home, school, and community no longer exists. Your thoughts may include changes in the family, parents' mistrust and dissatisfaction with schools, parents not feeling invited to come to school, etc. Additionally, you may have specific memories and examples that you are drawing on to support these thoughts. However, I encourage you to consider some important observations made by Tutwiler (1998). She stated that:

> The relationship between parents and schools may be affected by faulty perceptions schools hold of given groups. Typically, school expectations of families reflect behaviors, value orientations, and capabilities of middle-class nuclear families. In this way, uniform standards for measuring familial competency exist that often ignore or negate the diversity among families as well as the contributions families bring to the educational settings…While traditional bonds between white middle-

class families and schools must be maintained, a need exists for recognition of the variety of ways in which families not fitting this form conceive of their roles in the educational lives of their children (pp. 41–42).

Poverty and the Changing American Family

The authors of the Holmes Group Report, *Tomorrow's Schools,* stated that "More [children] will be raised by single parents. More will come from families different from the mainstream culture. More will speak languages other than English. The biggest shadow falling over tomorrow's children will be the scourge of deep poverty" (Young, Sykes, Featherstone, & Elmore, 1990, p. 29).

Perhaps, it comes as no surprise to you that a large concentration of people in poverty areas is most pronounced in the nation's large cities. This growing concentration of poverty reflects changes in the inner-city class structure and has been accompanied by increasing rates of joblessness, families headed by females, and welfare dependency. The typical inner-city neighborhood today tends to include almost exclusively the most disadvantaged segments of the urban minority population, such families plagued by persistent poverty and welfare dependency, workers who experience long spells of joblessness, and individuals who are pushed into street crime and other forms of aberrant behavior because of a limited opportunities structure (Neckerman & Wilson, 1986; Leibowitz, 1977; Stafford & Hill, 1974).

Added to this bleak outlook for urban families, is a problem that researchers and educators face: many school professionals do not fully understand the interaction of these different factors and how they make the necessary adjustments in school to sufficiently address the needs of urban families. Kozol (1994) describes a chilling reality for many urban black children and their families. He states that:

> On an average morning in Chicago, about 5,700 children in 190 classrooms come to school only to find they have no teacher. Victimized by endemic funding shortages, the system can't afford sufficient substitutes to take the place of missing teachers. "We've been in this typing class a whole semester," says a 15-year-old at Du Sable High, "and they still can't find us a teacher"…In a class of 39 children at Chicago's Goudy Elementary School, an adult is screaming at a child: "Keisha, look at me…Look me in the eye!" Keisha is fighting with a classmate. Over what? It turns out: over a crayon, said *The Chicago Tribune* in 1988. Last January the underfunded school began rationing supplies…The odds these black kids in Chicago face are only slightly worse than those faced by low-income children all over America. Children like these will be the parents of the year 2000. Many of them will be unable to earn a living and fulfill the obligations of adults; they will see their families disintegrate, their children lost to drugs and destitution. When we later condemn them for "parental failings," as we inevitably will do, we may be forced to stop and remember how we also failed them in the first years of their lives (p. 75).

Poverty, homelessness, drugs, and teen pregnancy are among the many social and economic problems that have been highlighted in the media to underscore the decline of urban America. However, these problems that urban families face are similar to those faced by families all across the country. For example, poverty is not just an "urban issue." Fuller & Tutwiler (1998) revealed, "Approximately 22 percent of all American children live in poverty. To make matters worse, more than 25 percent of all children under the age of six (the most important years developmentally) live in poverty" (p. 260). They provided two reasons for the rise in child poverty in recent years: "(1) the failure of hourly wages to keep pace with inflation, particularly for young workers and those with less than a college education, and (2) the increase in the number of families headed by a single parent—usually the mother. Mother-only families are at high risk for poverty due to the absence of a second adult earner and the historically lower earning power of women" (p. 260). Poverty has always been a part of American life. Kozol (1994) describes the grim situation as he portrays the children of the poor as social outcasts. He warns us of the gulf that is being perpetuated between the *haves* and *have nots* and wonders what kinds of adults the latter will become. He cites differences in school expenditure, infant mortality rates, homelessness, and school standards, all of which compound the problems of the poor.

Poverty affects children in devastating ways. Kozol (1994) poignantly describes the lives of homeless children and explains what it tells us about the disregard our society has shown for vulnerable people. He points out that:

> Many of these kids grow up surrounded by infectious illnesses no longer seen in most developed nations. Whooping cough and tuberculosis, once regarded as archaic illness, are now familiar in the shelters. Shocking numbers of these children have not been inoculated and for this reason cannot go to school. Those who do are likely to be two years behind grade level…many get to class so tired and hungry that they cannot concentrate. Others are ashamed to go to school because of shunning by their peers. Classmates label them "the hotel children" and don't want to sit beside them. Even their teachers sometimes keep their distance. The children look diseased and dirty. Many times they are. Often unable to bathe, they bring the smell of destitution with them into school. There *is* a smell of destitution, I may add. It is the smell of sweat and filth and urine. Like many journalists, I often find myself ashamed to be resisting the affection of a tiny child whose entire being seems to emanate pathology…Their parents—themselves—too frequently the products of dysfunctional and underfunded urban schools—have nonetheless been lectured on their "lack of values" (p. 77).

Kozol's words might be shocking, but there are teachers who work with these children each day. Fuller & Tutwiler (1998) provided some "reality" about the myths that teachers and most people have about poverty. Educators should play close attention to these myths, and the actual realities, so that they will better understand how to respond to children who are living in deplorable conditions. Paying attention to these myths does not mean, "rushing to judgment" by making the assumption that these myths are representative of all children from impoverished backgrounds. Further, teachers should be aware of the fact that their preconceived notions about poor children could cause them to neglect or to provide less-effective instruction to them (Rosenthal and Jackson, 1968; Rist, 1970). These myths can be found in Table 3.2.

Many of you may be asking yourselves, "Why do teachers have these myths?" I believe that it is more comfortable for teachers to create myths about children and families that they do not know than to pursue the kind of deep relationships necessary to develop accurate portrayals of the family lives of their students. I believe, as well, that most of the prejudices that people have about poor people are connected to the American myth that anyone can be successful if willing to work hard. Consequently, economic failure is perceived to be a personal rather than social problem (i.e., "you're lazy, stupid, or immoral). The impoverishment of inner-city neighborhoods and the flight to the suburbs by middle- and working-class residents have significantly altered the family in which children grow up (Neckerman & Wilson, 1986). Therefore, many teachers believe that among the possible consequences for education are a deterioration of the ability of families and neighborhoods to supervise children and support the schools. In addition, class or ethnic tension between middle-class teachers and lower-income

---

TABLE 3.2 *Myths about Poverty*

Myth: We have all heard the stereotypes concerning poor people. They are people of color who are too lazy to work. This stereotype is not only inaccurate and unfair, but it makes understanding the dynamics of poverty more difficult and, consequently, harder to consider appropriate interventions.

Reality: The reality is that the percentage of people of color in poverty may not be greater than that of white children. In fact, there are more poor white children than children of color.

Myth: Poor people live in the inner city.

Reality: More children in rural settings (twenty-seven percent) are poorer than children in the inner city (eleven percent) (Sherman, 1994).

Myth: Families are poor because they are lazy and don't work.

Reality: The reality is that most of the children of poor families have at least one parent who is working; these children receive twice as much support from the paid work their parents do than from welfare programs (Children's Defense Fund, 1996).

Myth: If they just worked harder, they wouldn't be poor.

Reality: The reality is that a person can work forty hours a week at minimum wage and the salary earned won't raise a family above the poverty line. And, finally, contrary to popular opinion, welfare is not a way of life for most poor people. The majority of families who received welfare benefits receive them for less than two years (Sherman, 1994).

Source: M. L. Fuller and S. W. Tutwiler, "Poverty: The Enemy of Children and Families," *Home-School Relations: Working Successfully with Parents and Families,* M. L. Fuller and G. Olsen, eds. (Boston: Allyn and Bacon, Inc., 1998).

parents discourages parental involvement in school (Ogbu, 1974; Mitchell, 1982; Fitchen, 1981).

Fuller & Tutwiler (1998) were quick to point out that "parents in poverty, like parents of all other socioeconomic groups, love their children, but may feel uncomfortable in their children's school. They often feel helpless in their relationships with schools and teachers" (p. 260). Haberman (1995), in his book, *Star Teachers of Children in Poverty*, discusses the difference between "star" teachers' perceptions of parents of poverty and those of other teachers. Haberman says, "Star teachers do not blame parents. As much as they may find out about the child and/or the family, they use the information as a basis for helping children learn more or want to learn more" (pp. 11–12).

Learning about Humanistic Issues Involving Families and Communities

The humanistic approach views "parents as people." In the historical approach section, you heard repeatedly that teachers recognized that families have changed but did not fully understand how to respond to these changes. The humanistic approach highlights for educators the need to move beyond simply recognizing the changes in families to responding and rethinking how they interact with families. In particular, educators need to refrain from using a double standard in dealing with families.

Double Standard in Dealing with Families

In 1988, the commission members of *One-Third of a Nation: A Report of the Commission on Minority Participation in Education and American Life* recommended a call for action. They stated that:

> Minority Americans are burdened not by a sudden, universal, yet temporary economic calamity, but by a long history of oppression and discrimination. They remain largely segregated in minority neighborhoods and minority schools. For many, full participation in the dominant culture imposes a painful choice: to dilute or abandon a rich and distinctive heritage. Above all, they are marked by the color or their skin as different, and therefore more vulnerable…yet, minority citizens are not separate. They are, in a real sense, the new America. In a few years they will comprise one-third of the nation's children; soon afterward they will be one-third of the nation's adults…they are not other; they are us. How well and under what conditions minority groups are integrated into American life—and the extent to which they participate in and contribute to our educational system and the economy—will determine the continuing strength and vitality of the nation as a whole (p. 6).

Recognizing the fact that schools are dealing with people rather than technical information, the National Education Association organized four subcommittees to address the special needs and concerns of ethnic minorities—African American, Hispanics, Asian/Pacific Islanders, and Native Americans/Alaska Natives. One of the major findings was that educators tend to use a double-standard approach in dealing with parents. In such cases the behavior of some parents is singled out while others are overlooked. For example, teachers and school districts can hold different views of various minority groups. However, it is of critical importance that schools recognize that all parents can make significant contributions. It is of equal importance that teachers and administrators not prejudge parents and children from certain groups. Among the biggest barriers to successful parent involvement are (1) the false labeling of some minority groups as not interested and/or unwilling to support their children's education is an unfair generalization most frequently made about minority groups (e.g., African Americans, Hispanics, Native Americans/Alaska Natives) and (2) communicating to other minority parent groups that it is acceptable if they choose not to become involved in the school because their children have no "real problems" with school (e.g., Asians/Pacific Islanders).

Asians and Pacific Islanders are sometimes described as "a minority of convenience," as noted by one of the individuals testifying before the National Education Association (NEA) Study Committee (Joe, 1987). In fact, according to the Asians and Pacific Islanders Subcommittee (Chase, 1987), "Asians and Pacific Islanders are often not perceived as minorities" (p. 12), and in many instances, their treatment "borders on neglect" (Tso, 1987). The "good mouthing" of citizens, as well as immigrants, and refugees of Asian and Pacific Islander extraction "has been so effective and so successful today, that after 25 years of falsely portraying Asians [and Pacific Islanders] as successful members of a so-called *model minority*, too many people—both white and black—believe that [they] have no real problems" (Inocencio, 1987). That perspective was emphasized again and again as the committee heard more than 50 witnesses and visited 14 schools.

Public school administrators and teachers have not so positively viewed African Americans, Hispanics, and Native Americans/Alaska Natives. In most instances, a number of problems have been pinpointed by administrators and teachers that they tend to have with these three groups of minority parents—poor literacy skills, language deficits, inability to implement suggestions, cultural distance between school and community, unwillingness or inability to attend meetings, and the inability to recognize their importance in their children's achievement. Unfortunately, teachers and administrators often become angry in these circumstances and complain that the very parents who most need to come to school fail to become involved, making their job even tougher. Some school personnel, in disgust, even come to the conclusion that nothing can be done with these children, since their parents do not support and reinforce their children's school achievement. More than twenty-five years ago, White (1975) expressed a similar opinion about the impact that families have on their children's educational lives. He stated that "The informal education that families provide for their children makes more of an impact on a child's educational development than the formal educational system. If the family does its job well, the professional can provide effective training. If not, there may be little the professional can do to save the child from mediocrity" (p. 4).

Ron Edmonds, a strong advocate in the school effectiveness movement vehemently disagrees with White's position. Ulric Neisser (1986) summarized the remarks Edmonds made at a Cornell conference before his death on July 15, 1983. Edmonds argued that:

> Minority children's failure to learn can just as easily be seen as the school's failure to teach them. The fact that many poor and minority children fail to master the school curriculum does not reflect deficiencies in the children, but rather inadequacies in the schools themselves. Variability in the distribution of achievement among school-age children in the United States derives from variability in the nature of the schools to which they go. Achievement is therefore relatively independent of family background, at least if achievement is defined as pupil acquisition of basic school skills (p. 6).

While many teachers and administrators agree that children from different family backgrounds can acquire basic school skills, the general consensus among them is that to master these skills, children must receive some minimal assistance from their families. Families who cannot help their children with their homework, for example, can at least encourage them to do their best in school and support their efforts to do so. Epstein (1986) suggested that teachers could increase the amount of involvement of parents (including minority parents) who have little education. Epstein compared teachers who were active in seeking parental support with those who were not. Differences in these parents' reports of their involvement in learning activities at home from those of more educated parents were significant only in classrooms of teachers who failed to show leadership in parental involvement. Epstein concluded that teachers who got parents involved "…mitigated the disadvantages typically associated with race, social class, and level of education" (p. 279). This is encouraging.

Now, more than ever before, some teachers and administrators believe wholeheartedly that certain minority parent groups (African Americans, Hispanics, Native Americans/Alaska Natives) simply do not care and strongly resist being involved in the school's parent-involvement efforts. More recently, the label of "not caring" or "unwilling to support" their children's education has also been associated with poor, uneducated white parents. The schools' apparent neglect of these parents is similar to that of Asian/Pacific Islander parents. The message is that these parents and children have "no real problems." Of course, we know that this is not at all the case. Poor, uneducated white parents want, like anyone else, to have a sense of belonging. Purcell-Gates (1995) provides a poignant example of one such family. She highlights the point that if asked to identify those children who rank lowest in relation to national educational norms, who have higher school dropout and absence rates, and who more commonly experience learning problems, few of us would know the correct answer: white (not African American), urban Appalachian children.

These children and grandchildren of Appalachian families migrated to northern cities in the 1950s to look for work. They make up this largely "invisible" urban group, a minority that represents a significant portion of the urban poor. The school loses a great deal when it fails to include the voices and perspectives of poor and uneducated white parents. McLaughlin & Shields (1987) would argue that "What's lacking, in most schools and school districts are appropriate strategies or structures for involving minority parents" (p. 157). Strategies and structures must be developed, for, as Rodriguez (1981) warned, "The failure to involve minority groups (as well as poor and uneducated white families) in educational policy-making activities of a school represents a tremendous loss in human resources for the parent, the child, the minority group to which he or she belongs, and the school as a whole" (p. 40).

Parents Are Not All the Same

We, as educators, must understand that parents are not all the same. Parents are people, too. They have their own strengths and weaknesses, complexities, problems, and questions, and we must work with them and see them as more than "just parents." In my work with parents, I coined two terms, *differentiated parenting* and *parentally appropriate* to help teachers find new ways to think about who parents are. *Differentiated parenting* means recognizing that parents are different from one another in their perspectives, beliefs, and abilities to negotiate school. Although parents might have the same goals for their children (i.e., to read, write, and spell well), they might have different ideas about how they can help their children accomplish these goals. *Parentally appropriate* means that, because parents are different, tasks and activities must be compatible with their capabilities. For example, parents who don't read well might be very intimidated and frustrated by teachers who expect them to read to their children every night, and teachers might need to select other activities to support them in developing reading fluency. Parents who work multiple jobs or who are raising their children by themselves might not be able to attend parent conferences after school or in the early evenings, and teachers might need to make other arrangements to accommodate them. When we as teachers plan these activities and tasks, we must remember that parents want to successfully accomplish them, and we need to provide them as much support as possible. When we as teachers ask parents, for example, to "read to their child," more times than not, we assume that parents know what we mean. Unfortunately, many do not. I found this to be true in my study of the book-reading practices of poor and minority parents at Donaldsonville Elementary School (Donaldsonville, Louisiana). The following anecdote illustrates my point:

> Donaldsonville Elementary School had been recognized for its "good curriculum," even though teachers were disappointed with the progress of their students. Eighty percent of the student population was African-American children, and 20% was white children; most were members of low-income families. Teachers felt that they were doing all they could to help these children at school. Without parental

assistance at home, the children at Donaldsonville were going to fail. The teachers' solution was to expect and demand that parents be involved in their children's education by reading to them at home.

The teachers felt that this was not an unreasonable request. There is good evidence of positive gains made by "disadvantaged" elementary students when parents and children work together at home on homework and learning packets. What the teachers did not take into account was that 40% of the school's parents were illiterate or semi-literate. When the parents didn't seem willing to do as the teachers asked, teachers mistook parents' unfamiliarity with the task being asked of them, coupled with low literacy skills, for lack of interest in their children's education. The continued demand that parents read to their children at home, which had a particular meaning in teachers' minds, sparked hostility and racial tensions between teachers and parents. Each group blamed the other for the children's failures; each felt victimized by the interactions. Children were caught between their two most important teachers—their classroom teacher and their parent (Edwards & Young, 1992, p. 76).

To further illustrate this point, I share with you the thoughts of one mother and the response of a first-grade teacher. Angela, a thirty-two-year-old African-American mother with five children ranging in ages from twenty-two months to sixteen years old, becomes fearful and sometimes defensive when her child's teacher requests that she read to her child. The mother quietly admitted to me something that mirrors the reality of some parents:

I'm embarrassed, scared, angry, and feel completely helpless because I can't read. I do care 'bout my children and I want them to do well in school. Why don't them teachers believe me when I say I want the best for my children? I know that my children ain't done well in kindergarten and first grade and had to repeat them grades. My older children are in the lowest sections, in Chapter 1, and are struggling in their subjects. My children are frustrated, and I am frustrated, too. I don't know how to help them especially when the teacher wants me to read to them. These teachers think that reading to children is so easy and simple, but it is very difficult if you don't know how to read (Edwards, 1995, p. 54).

Mrs. Colvin, a first-grade teacher at Donaldsonville Elementary School, expressed her frustration with parents or other caregivers like Angela:

Year in and year out these parents who are mostly low-income African American and white send their children to school with serious literacy problems. It seems as if the children have no chance of passing. They don't recognize letters of the alphabet, numbers, and they can't even recognize the letters in their own name. Consequently, it is not surprising that most of them have had to repeat kindergarten and first grade. All of the kindergarten and first grade teachers have seen similar behaviors in these children. These behaviors include limited language skills and the inability to interact with adults. We feel that these children have not been read to and have rarely engaged in adult-child conversations. Each year when we see parents at the beginning of the school year we tell them the same old thing,

"Please read to your child at least two to three times per week. It will make a world of difference in how well your child does in school." We know the parents hear what we are saying, but we don't think they have read or plan to read one single book to their children. We, as kindergarten and first grade teachers, cannot solve all of these children's literacy problems by ourselves. The parents must help us (Edwards, 1995, p. 55).

Gardner Jenkins (1969) challenged schools by posing this question: "...[schools] are accustomed to making the concept of individual differences in the children central to much of [their] planning and thinking, but do [schools] also apply [the concept] to [their] contacts with parents of the children?" (p. 35). Making her case even stronger, Gardner Jenkins categorized five differences in parents, which pointed to the complexity and significance of schools and teachers knowing the parents they serve or being "parentally appropriate." These five categories are as follows:

- *Parental dynamics.*   Teachers have been trained to understand child differences. We try to be patient with a child who cannot learn as quickly as some others and offer extra help to the youngster whose background is inadequate. We may recognize that a child has an emotional problem and try to work with him in as supportive a fashion as possible. But we do not consider parental differences. We are more likely to think of parents and even plan for them as a group labeled *parents*. So when [our efforts to involve parents follow in an] orderly fashion, [and fail to] recognize that parents are different, we may find ourselves frequently distressed or disappointed at the failure of these parent involvement efforts (p. 35).

- *Parent feelings regarding school.*   Parents respond to schools based on their past experiences, or frozen memories, in addition to the current situation. Most parents form ideas about what goes on in school from their own school experiences. If these experiences were unpleasant, parents might not feel comfortable returning when their children are in school. Thus, "...debilitating experiences with school, feelings of inadequacy, poor achievement by children, and pressures of the present can cause some parents to stay away from the school" (Berger, 1991, p. 118). However, parents can also be very involved in their children's schooling, based upon their positive school experiences or even the wish that their parents had been more involved in their school experiences. This complex issue of parents' frozen memories in school will be discussed later in Chapter 6.

- *Parent relationships with their children.*   Today's parents have different relationships with their children. Some parents relate to their children as friends. Other parent figures, such as grandparents who are raising their grandchildren, might have a totally different way of relating. Even though they may love them, some parents are better able to relate to their children than others. Some are warm and supporting, others may be rejecting or even negligent. Some we find highly intelligent, competent people; others may be mentally inadequate, unable to grasp the meaning of situations involving their children.

• *Parent values and goals.*   Values differ among parents. The goals and standards for their individual families will differ one from another and, indeed, may be quite different from our own (p. 35). Also, parents value education differently. Gardner Jenkins (1969) notes, "…some have a high regard for education, but there will be others who view schooling as something to be lived through because it is required by law" (p.35).

• *Variety of parents' attitudes toward participation in parent involvement efforts and the school's responsibility to acknowledge and accept that these parent differences do exist.*   Parents bring their individuality to parent involvement and efforts. Until the school knows parents as individuals and is sensitive to and willing to accept their individuality, it will be difficult to establish any clear communication between them (p. 35).

Gardner Jenkins' description of the categories of parent/families' differences provides insights into the importance of gaining a deeper knowledge of understanding the "human side" of families. If educators begin to think seriously about Gardner Jenkins' categorized five differences of parent/families when planning family involvement initiatives, it will move them closer to implementing my notion of *differentiated parenting* and *parentally appropriate*. Also, it will enable educators to develop more inclusive and sensitive practices of family involvement. In Chapter 6, I will show you how to develop a demographic profile of families in a school. This data will help you capture critical characteristics of the families you serve.

PAUSE AND REFLECT

Take a few minutes to closely examine the categories of parent differences described by Gardner Jenkins. You can respond independently, work with a partner in your class/group of colleagues, or work cooperatively with a cooperating/mentor teacher to discuss the issue of parent differences and the terms I coined: *differentiated parenting* and *parentally appropriate*. As you think about the meaning of parent differences, *differentiated parenting,* and *parentally appropriate,* try to relate these issues to your own school situation or classroom. If you are not presently teaching, try to think about these issues in terms of conversations you might have with your cooperating teacher or university professor.

In the next section, I provide some additional information that educators should consider when looking at the "human side" of the families they serve. Gardner Jenkins' categories of parent differences are closely connected to how parents interact with their children at home and to their general perceptions and attitudes toward school. However, Berger (1991) expands on Gardner Jenkins' category of parent feelings regarding school. She points out that parents respond to schools based on their past experiences, as well as the current situation. Berger characterizes parent responses to school as follows:

> Debilitating experiences with schools, feelings of inadequacy, poor achievement by children, and pressures of the present can cause some parents to stay away from the school. On the other hand, some parents tend to dominate and to be compulsively involved with the schools. Between these two extremes are parents who need encouragement to come to school, parents who readily respond when invited, and parents who are comfortable about coming to school and enjoy[ing] some involvement in the educational process [see Figure 3.3]. Each group requires a different response from the professional staff (p. 118).

Potter (1989) also focuses on parent responses to school in terms of their desire to participate, their past memories about schools, and the feeling that they have nothing to contribute. He argues that:

> There will be degrees of participation by parents and this must be accepted; teachers must be aware of the parents' desire to participate in the education program. The participation may vary from passive to very active and will vary in quality depending on the attributes of the child, parent, and teacher as well as on the social stresses placed on the family and school alike. Parents sometimes feel uneasy in the school environment and this may be simply a hangover from unhappy days at school for them; they may feel threatened by the teacher, unsure of the "new approaches" being taken in schools or they may have experienced failure at school. It may well be that it is this feeling of failure, which keeps the parents home from school meetings or from class activities, even though a warm invitation has been sent home. It may explain why the parents are never home when the teacher makes the scheduled home visit.

Parents who avoid schools like the plague	Parents who need encouragement to come to school	Parents who readily respond when invited to school	Parents who are comfortable and enjoy involvement in school	Parents who enjoy power and are overly active

FIGURE 3.3 *Parents Respond to Schools Based on Their Past Experiences and Their Current Situations*

Sometimes the parents do not see themselves as educators and do not recognize the important role they have in supplying experiences to the child, which enrich his life and contribute to his ever-growing body of knowledge. Perhaps the parents feel that teaching and learning go hand in hand and it all happens at school; they do not appreciate their role at home. Perhaps the parents feel that they have nothing to contribute to the classroom's activities, a reflection, maybe, of lack of self-esteem. Perhaps the parent has too many personal problems and simply is unable to cope with something else in their lives. In fact, the parents may be crying out for support, to have some of their own needs met, and the role of family helper is one, which is becoming increasingly part of a teacher's professional life. This necessitates a good knowledge of the support systems in the community, available to families in need; it does not mean that the teacher must add "counselor" to his or her role description (p. 22).

Berger and Potter's descriptions of parent responses depict the realistic ways in which families react to being invited to come in school. Parental differences are real, and this is an issue that teachers in the new millennium must seriously consider and appropriately address. Failure to acknowledge and respect parental differences will more than likely result in strained relationships between the home and school. Educators can no longer expect successful family involvement without strongly considering and responding to the "human side" of families.

PAUSE AND REFLECT

If parents in your building or individual classroom have negative memories of school, what can you, the principal, and other teachers do to counter these parents' negative memories about school? Discuss your ideas with a partner in your class/group of colleagues, or with a cooperating/mentor teacher.

Learning about Cultural Issues Involving Families and Communities

Viewing families from a historical and humanistic stance is important, but there is one other approach that educators must consider—the cultural approach. The cultural approach focuses specifically on the needs of diverse families and emphasizes the fact that families' cultural differences should not be viewed as deficits. Berger (1995) revealed that:

Two challenges face the schools as they work with culturally diverse students. One is to understand each child's abilities and actions. The other is to eliminate ethnic discrimination. The more the school and home become involved with each other in a positive relationship, the greater are the opportunities for understanding the family and reducing discrimination (p. 105).

In addition, today's educators cannot afford to make damaging and inaccurate judgments that families who comprise these new family structures are uncaring, incompetent, or apathetic [parents] (McLaughlin & Shields, 1989, p. 157). Because certain families may not respond to the school's invitation to participate, it does not imply that successful partnerships cannot be developed. Even though today's teachers may not fully understand the possible differences that exist between themselves and observed families, they cannot simply conclude that these "differences" translate into a defect in families. As a preservice or experienced teacher, you can work to not only adeptly interpret these changes but to find successful ways of helping your students deal with these changes. The differences can actually enhance the educational process.

We must keep in mind that children do not learn in a vacuum; they bring their culture, family experiences, and community experiences with them to school. It is apparent that when people talk about diversity, it always tends to come back to where children come from. At an early age, children become literate as they interact with family to meet personal needs, gain self-identity, and establish behavior patterns that reflect cultural values and beliefs (Heath, 1989; Schiefflin & Cochran-Smith; 1984, Wertsch, 1991). Berliner (1986) correctly noted that "Teachers have no choice but to inquire into each student's unique culture and learning history, to determine what instructional materials might best be used, and to determine when a student's cultural and life experiences are compatible, or potentially incompatible, with instruction. To do less is to build emotional blocks to communication in an already complicated instructional situation" (p. 29).

The involvement of families in schools moves closer to becoming a reality when teachers understand more about the cultures of families. Many teachers may be well intentioned and sensitive to different cultures. But they may lack the experiences and knowledge to understand and meaningfully teach diverse students and to successfully interact with families. Connecting home and school literacies can be difficult for teachers because it requires a deeper understanding of the lives, histories, or cultures of families and communities different from their own.

In teaching in the twenty-first century, there is an overwhelming need for teachers to understand the culture of students and families. Irvine correctly points out that teachers must understand the cultures of their students, because culture is "the sum total ways of living that are shared by members of a population," consisting of "rites, rituals, legends, myths, artifacts, symbols, language, ceremonies, history, and sense-making that guide and shape behavior" (Irvine, 1992, p. 83). Culture is what children bring to school; John Ogbu (1995) referred to this process as students bringing into the classroom, "their communities' cultural models or understandings of social realities and the educational strategies that they, their families, and their communities use or do not use in seeking education" (p. 583). According to Diamond and Moore (1995), "the child's culture, home, family, and community form the sociocultural backdrop for school learning. The classroom must be sensitive to these multiple histories, which are the ways of knowing and learning that students bring" (p. 18).

In the new millennium, it is critical for educators to reexamine their classrooms to determine if they are knowledgeable of the multiple histories and ways of knowing that students bring to the learning environment.

In this section, you will learn the importance of teachers learning about family cultures, and what research has to say about the value of home literacy environments. The title of this section reflects my reading of an important article written by Lisa Delpit (1988), in which she critiques aspects of progressive pedagogy. Delpit claims that those children who do not learn these particular conventions at home have difficulty acquiring them at school. In many ways this section on culture is an exploration, and I hope a further formulation, of the tension Delpit so importantly identifies—the tension between honoring the child's home discourse or way of communicating as a rich source of knowledge and learning itself, and yet wishing to put that discourse into meaningful contact with school-based and discipline-based ways of talking, acting, and knowing. When teachers do not respect what children bring to school; it has direct implications on family involvement. When families feel that teachers are not successfully working with their children, it oftentimes hampers their involvement in the school.

Funds of Knowledge: Drawing on Children's Resources Outside the Classroom

In her book on *Culture in School Learning*, Etta Hollins (1996) describes several successful interventions that improve the academic achievement of groups traditionally underserved in the nation's public schools. Some of these interventions include:

1. Legitimizing the knowledge the children bring to school.
2. Making meaningful connections between school learning and cultural knowledge or knowledge acquired outside of school.
3. Creating a hybrid culture in school that is congruent with many of the practices and values children bring from the home and peer culture.
4. Creating a community of learners where collaboration is the norm rather than competition.
5. Balancing the rights of students and teachers.
6. Providing curriculum content and pedagogical practices that support a consistent and coherent core of identity and intergenerational continuity with the past (p. 14).

In critically examining what Hollins has suggested, you need to look at your schools, structures, or teaching practices to determine which of the six successful interventions have been addressed, which have not, and what additional information might be helpful. In particular, you might start by asking how teachers can begin to celebrate and respect students' diversity. Traditionally, some teachers think of addressing cultural diversity as what Derman-Sparks (1989) refers to as a *tourist curriculum*, which focuses on artifacts of other countries, such as food, traditional clothing, folk tales, and household items. Derman-Sparks criticizes the *tourist-curriculum* as follows:

> Tourist curriculum is both patronizing, emphasizing the "exotic" differences between cultures, and trivializing, dealing not with the real-life problems and experiences of different peoples, but with surface aspects of their celebrations and modes of entertainment. Children "visit" non-white cultures and then "go home" to the daily classroom, which reflects only the dominant culture. The focus on holidays, although it provides drama and delight for both children and adults, gives the impression that that is all "other" people—usually people of color—do. What it fails to communicate is real understanding (p. 7).

So, how do teachers move from seeing culture as "tourism" to seeing it as an important part of our experiences and lives? One way is for teachers to understand how various cultures may foster specific interactive styles that differ from the teacher's expectations. Christine Bennett (1999) believes that culturally relevant teachers seek "intercultural competence"—the knowledge and understanding of their students' cultural styles. Bennett further explains that these teachers:

> ...feel comfortable and at ease with their students. Intercultural competent teachers are aware of the diversity within racial, cultural, and socioeconomic groups, they know that culture is ever changing, and they are aware of the dangers of stereotyping. At the same time, they know that if they ignore their students' cultural attributes they are likely to be guided by their own cultural lenses, unaware of how their culturally conditioned expectations and assumptions might cause learning difficulties for some children and youth (p. 38).

Hollins (1996) points out that "as a classroom teacher, you bring your own cultural norms into your professional practice. The extent to which your teaching behavior will become an extension of your own culture exclusively or will incorporate the cultures of the students you teach may be influenced by your perceptions of the relationship between culture and school practices, political beliefs, and conceptualization of school learning." As teachers, then, you must seriously examine the relationship between your own cultural beliefs and practices and those of your students. Your role as teacher ought not and should not provide legitimacy to your values and discourse practices at the expense of those of your students. Specifically, you should consider the ways in which accomplished teachers are able to weave together their own cultural patterns with those of their students.

PAUSE AND REFLECT

Take a few moments to closely examine the six successful interventions Hollins outlined that improve the academic achievement of groups traditionally underserved in
our nation's public schools. If you are a preservice teacher, as part of your field observation, see if you observe any of these successful interventions. If you are an inservice
teacher, critically examine your classroom to determine if any of these successful
interventions exist.

Looking to Research for Home Literacy Information

In the Introduction, I pointed out that if preservice and inservice teachers wanted
to implement partnerships with families and communities to foster students' success, they needed resources or information to create a structure for involving families in the literacy development of their children, specifically around curricular
issues. To successfully do this, teachers need to understand the connections
among literacy, culture, and family involvement. Learning about children's literacy environments is a way to learn about the families' goals, motives, strategies,
accomplishments, difficulties, and engagement with literacy.

Good teachers have always seen the importance of the parent role in their
child's learning (Hollins, 1996). Similarly, I believe that good teachers have always
seen the importance of closely examining the research on families and children
with the primary mission of achieving what Etta Hollins (1996) calls *cultural
accommodation*. According to Hollins, "The primary goal of cultural accommodation is to facilitate teaching and learning in situations where teachers and students
do not share the same culture and there is a standard curriculum. Teachers practicing cultural accommodation need to be knowledgeable about the students' cultural background…" (p. 145).

Teachers have the tremendous responsibility of teaching children in school.
But we know that students have prior knowledge and experiences that they have
learned at home. Since culture is a component of family life, different families
enact different cultural practices, and these practices can shape the experiences
and the learning of children before they enter the classroom. How can teachers
learn more about the familial experiences of their students, particularly if parents
are not very involved with school? One way is to explore the research literature to
see how families teach their children, and more specifically, how they engage their
children in literacy activities.

Literacy is a broad term, and the school is a particularly crucial institution for
mediating the process by which the individual becomes literate for the reflecting
societal and cultural views of what constitutes literacy. Roth (1984) put it this way:

Social/cultural control is tied directly to the structure of knowledge and to the
manner in which knowledge is presented in the schooling context. Schools, acting

as agents for the culture, control the extent to which personal knowledge may enter into the public knowledge of school curriculum; they thus have a direct influence upon cultural continuity and change. In selecting what to teach and how it is to be taught and evaluated, schools reaffirm what the culture values as knowledge.... (p. 303)

Roth acknowledged the "potential cultural conflicts" in the structure and presentation of knowledge. She highlighted controls placed on cultural variables that might enter school curriculum through the "personal knowledge" students from different cultures bring to the classroom. Although multicultural curriculum in teacher preparation programs has helped "the cultures" of school accommodate the customs of other cultures; multicultural education has not permeated pedagogy. Too often teachers focus on historical or group cultural traditions in their classrooms and fail to consider the "personal knowledge" of students that accompanies those traditions. In the section below, you can gain some "personal knowledge" about the literacy environments of a variety of home cultures.

Hidden Literacies

Anderson and Stokes

Anderson & Stokes (1984) conducted ethnographic observations in the homes of twenty-four low socioeconomic status Hispanic, African-American, and white families. One of the goals of the research was to uncover "hidden" literacy in the everyday lives of families and their children. Hidden literacy events may or may not match school expectations. Anderson and Stokes contended that many of the literacy experiences that occur in the homes of poor families were easy to underestimate because mainstream educators tend to look for activities such as reading storybooks to children and helping children with homework. Consequently, mainstream educators may inadvertently overlook a range of reading and writing experiences that these young children engaged in or observed.

Anderson and Stokes uncovered multiple examples of reading and writing experiences that young children engaged in from poor families. Sources of experiences in literacy, in addition to typical school or "literacy-for-literacy's sake" activities, included literacy events for daily living needs (e.g., paying bills, obtaining welfare assistance), entertainment (e.g., solving a crossword puzzle, reading a television guide), and religion (e.g., Bible-reading sessions with children). Similarly, Denny Taylor and Catherine Dorsey-Gaines' (1988) in-depth account of the families and lives of African-American, urban six-year-olds who were successful in learning to read and write revealed that these parents engaged in daily literacy activities that provided their children with authentic interactions with print.

Schiefflin & Cochran-Smith

Schiefflin & Cochran-Smith (1984) revealed still another path to literacy through sharing the experiences of a Sino-Vietnamese family, where the son had entered school in Philadelphia in second grade and was successful in learning to read and write at nine years of age. A prominent feature of this home was a lack of reading materials or an abundance of print. Parents neither read to their children nor provided children materials to read on their own. However, literacy was functional, meaningful, and relevant in the lives of this family and other Asian refugees studied. In addition to being part of the long Chinese tradition of literacy, this family and others placed a high value on becoming literate in English. Furthermore, although book reading was not a prominent feature of the home, literacy played an important role in maintaining relationships with others. Exchanging letters with relatives occurred often. Also, children often helped parents complete forms and correspond with others in the community because the children had stronger skills in written English.

These two important studies strongly support the notion of multiple literacies and the necessity for teachers to realize that these ways of knowing should be sought out and explicitly recognized. For more information on "hidden literacies" in children's home lives and learning, uncovering multiple literacies that need to be valued in their own right and that can become additional tools to develop print literacy, see the recent text written by Voss, which I briefly summarize next.

Multiple Literacies

Voss

Voss (1996) tells the stories of three fourth-grade children: Kelly, talkative but lacking confidence in her ability to read and write; Eric, struggling with print but handy with tools and mechanical things; and Janette, literate in print and successful—though quiet—in school. With insight and sensitivity, Voss describes how the children interact and learn in their homes and portrays their classroom teacher's efforts to tap their varied literacies in school. Influenced by Howard Gardner's theory of multiple intelligences and Denny Taylor's research on family literacy, Voss demonstrates how familial influences on children lead them to develop particular strengths, and she describes the features of home learning that teachers should understand and consider. She suggests we broaden our concept of literacy to include more than print—media literacy, consumer literacy, and especially interactive and mechanical literacy—so that we might see and value the multiple literacies children already have.

Moll

Moll and his colleagues (1992) at the University of Arizona-Tucson worked to develop innovations in teaching that drew on the knowledge and skills found in local Latino households. They predicted that, by capitalizing on household and community resources, they could organize classroom instruction that far exceeded in quality the rotelike instruction currently being used. They established strategic connections that took the form of joint household research between classroom teachers and university-based researchers, which subsequently led to the development of ethnographically, informed classroom practices. The approach they employed involved studying how household members use their "funds of knowledge" in dealing with and changing difficult social and economic circumstances. They were particularly interested in how families developed social networks that connected them with their social environments (most importantly with other households) and how these social relationships facilitated the development and exchange of resources, including knowledge, skills, and labor, that enhance the households' ability to survive or thrive.

Moll and his colleagues noted that in contrast with classrooms where a student's relationship with a teacher is often one-dimensional (that is, they typically interact on a limited number of levels in a limited setting), the family social network is "flexible, adaptive, and active, and may involve multiple persons from outside the homes" (p. 133). Moll et al. term this kind of network *thick* and *multi-stranded*, and note that "The person from whom the child learns carpentry, for example, may also be the uncle with whom the child's family regularly celebrates birthdays or organizes barbecues, as well as the person with whom the child's father goes fishing on weekends" (p. 133). Teachers need to be able to recognize, learn about, and draw on these networks as they teach children. Recognizing and acknowledging these home networks will provide impetus for and foster communication with parents or adults involved at home with the students. This recognition can open up the classroom, make it accessible and relevant for families, and build parents' and communities' trust of teachers and schools. Then, the human social interdependence or "reciprocity" that Moll et al. speaks of can develop. They noted, "Reciprocal practices establish serious obligations based on the assumption of "confianza" (mutual trust), which is reestablished or confirmed with each exchange and leads to the development of long-term relationships." The research on multiple literacies should encourage you, as a teacher, to "dig out" the hidden literacies that culturally diverse families and children have and expand your definitions of literacy in multiple ways.

The continued lack of connection between home and school literacies is because few researchers have designed ways to connect these two important institutions. However, researchers have identified some "cultural variables" that contribute to this disconnect. These cultural variables may be compatible or incompatible with the expectations and structures of schools (see Table 3.3) for a listing of the cultural variables.

As listed in Table 3.3, Tharp (1989) has suggested at least four variables that may be compatible or incompatible with school expectations and structures: social organization, sociolinguistics, cognition, and motivation. Similarly, Phelan, Davidson, and Cao have identified four patterns, which may offer an explanation for why the degree of cultural continuity between home and school can vary. These four patterns as cited in Sleeter & Grant (1988) include (1) congruent worlds among home, school, and peer group, with smooth transitions from one setting to the next; (2) different worlds with boundary crossings from one to the next that are manageable; (3) different worlds with unabridged boundary crossings that are hazardous for the student; and (4) different worlds with insurmountable barriers (p. 57). If the four patterns are ignored, conflict might erupt. Gilbert & Gay (1985) have identified four areas of potential cultural conflict: learning style, interactional

TABLE 3.3 *Cultural Variables/Patterns Compatible or Incompatible with the School Expectations and Structures*

Researcher	Cultural Variables/Patterns
Tharp (1989)	1. Social organization 2. Sociolinguistics 3. Cognition 4. Motivation
Phelan, Davidson, and Cao (1991)	1. Congruent worlds among home, school, and peer group, with smooth transitions from one setting to the next; 2. Different worlds with boundary crossings from one to the next that are manageable; 3. Different worlds with unabridged boundary crossings that are hazardous for the student; and 4. Different worlds with insurmountable barriers (p. 57).

or relational style, communication, and differing perceptions of involvement. If teachers try to dismantle, rearrange, or ignore the ways in which students interact outside of school, students may rebel and resist. What teachers need to do now is consider these "cultural variables" in conjunction with the potential areas of conflict—that is, they need to think more about how particular ways of living, communicating, and thinking affect learning, interactions, and perceptions.

Following are three examples from important research studies, which highlight how students may rebel and resist at school. Phelan, Davidson, & Cao (1991) reported that students did reasonably well academically with teachers who tried to adapt their teaching to the students' ways of learning and interacting outside of school. They found that when forced to choose between the peer group and the school, or between home and school, many students did not choose school and consequently failed. For example, Trueba (1989) described immigrant children who were unable to comprehend classroom instruction or who responded to the teacher in a way different from that which the teacher expected. Over time, the children's academic performance dropped, as did their effort. Although teachers viewed the students as exhibiting learning disabilities, Trueba argued that the students' learning abilities were normal, but that the culture of the classroom was substantially different from the home culture as to make it impossible for them to function well. Because of the stress of repeated failure, the students stopped trying.

In another example, Jordan (1985) and her colleagues identified a few key practices that were interfering with native Hawaiian children's learning. Hawaiian children spend considerable time working with peers outside of school; if they are punished for interacting with peers in the classroom, especially if punishment involves isolating them, then they will put their energy into establishing illicit contact with peers. If a moderate level of peer interaction is allowed, they tend to stay on task. These examples point to the importance of understanding the cultures of families and children.

Further conflicts between teachers and students can occur when home and school cultures are not compatible. Au & Mason (1983), for example, investigated this issue with students of Polynesian-Hawaiian ancestry. Teachers who insisted that Hawaiian children speak one at a time in answering their questions had great difficulty in conducting effective reading lessons. On the other hand, teachers who allowed the children to cooperate or speak together in answering questions could conduct highly effective lessons.

Teachers who used this second style of interaction were teaching in a manner consistent with the rules for talk story, an important nonschool speech event for Hawaiian children. In talk story, speakers cooperate with one another in telling stories. Rather than one person telling the whole story, two or more speakers take turns, each narrating just a small part. Use of a cooperative talk-story style was important to the students, perhaps because it seems to reflect the value many Hawaiians attach to the performance and well-being of the group or family, as opposed to the individual. This example illustrates how the effectiveness of reading depends on how teachers use students' cultural backgrounds to broaden or deepen their view of the context of literacy—the process of learning to read.

Preservice and experienced teachers need to be aware of deeper and broader views of literacy. It is important because culturally diverse children might not be familiar with school-based forms of literate activities. For example, Michaels (1981, 1986) discovered that culturally different children might not be familiar with "sharing time" (or "circle time," "show and tell," etc.) even though it is a common speech event in early elementary school classrooms. She reported that when the children's discourse style matched the teacher's own literate style and expectations, collaboration was rhythmically synchronized and allowed for informal practice and instruction in the development of a literate discourse style. For these children, sharing time could be seen as a kind of oral preparation for literacy. In contrast, Michaels noted that when the child's narrative style was in variance with the teacher's expectations, collaboration was often unsuccessful. For example, the teacher would often interrupt students while they were talking rather than guiding or supporting them in making the most out of the event. She concluded that "sharing time could either provide or deny access to key literacy-related experiences, depending, ironically, on the degree to which teacher and child start out 'sharing' a set of discourse conventions and interpretive strategies" (p. 423). Michaels observed that:

> The discourse of the white children tended to be tightly organized, centering on a single, clearly identifiable topic, a discourse style…"topic-centered." This style closely matched the teacher's own discourse style as well as her notions about what constituted good sharing. In contrast to a topic-centered style, the

> [African-American] children and particularly the [African-American] girls, were far more likely to use a "topic-associating" style that is discourse consisting of a series of implicitly associated personal anecdotes (p. 423).

Heath (1983) discovered that culturally different children might not be familiar with classroom question-answering routines. She compared the use of questions in three settings: Trackton, a working class African-American community; the classrooms of the children from this community; and the homes of their teachers. In the classrooms and teachers' homes, Heath found that teachers often asked questions for the purpose of "training" children. The children were expected to give answers already known by the adult. When the child was looking at a book, such questions would include: "What's that?" and "Where's the puppy?"

In Trackton, on the other hand, children were not generally asked questions for which the adult already knew the answer. Instead, they were asked open-ended questions with answers unknown to the adult. For example, in the passage below, the grandmother's first question has to do with what her grandson is planning to do next with the crayons. Another type of question often asked of Trackton children called for them to make comparisons, stating how one thing was like another. As shown in the passage, the grandmother's second question called the boy's attention to the fact that one of the crayons was the same color as his pants. Heath writes:

> At early ages, Trackton children recognized situations, scenes, personalities, and items, which were similar. However, they never volunteered, nor did adults ask them, to name the attributes, which were similar and added up to one thing's being like another. A grandmother playing with her grandson age 2 years and 4 months, asked him as he fingered crayons in a box: "Whatcha gonna do with those, huh?" and "Ain't dat [color] like your pants?" She then volunteered to me, "We don't talk to our chil'un like you folks do; we don't ask 'em' bout colors, names, 'n things" (p. 117).

When they first entered school, then, Trackton children were unprepared to answer teachers' questions, which often had to do with such information as telling the colors or names of objects. As Heath's work suggests, when teachers and children are unable to collaborate or "hook up" in a way that allows teaching to take place, students' learning to read is bound to suffer.

Preservice and experienced teachers need to know about families and cultures even though they might feel a little uncomfortable about addressing cultural differences. Lewis (2001) revealed that schoolteachers are often in a dilemma between the idea of respecting student diversity and unexamined personal beliefs about color-blindness. If this might be your case, I encourage you to learn about families and cultures because it can help you move closer to fostering family-school relationships. More importantly, it can help you gain a greater understanding and sensitivity toward culturally different families. Sonia Nieto (1992) highlighted this issue when she stated that:

Many teachers and schools, in an attempt to be color-blind, do not want to acknowledge cultural or racial differences. "I don't see black or white," a teacher will say. "I see only students." This statement assumes that to be color-blind is to be fair, impartial, and objective. It sounds fair and honest and ethical, but the opposite may actually be true. That is, to see differences, in this line of reasoning, is to see defects and inferiority. Thus, to be color-blind may result in refusing to accept differences and therefore accepting the dominant culture as the norm. It may result in denying the very identity of our students, thereby making them invisible. What seems on the surface to be impeccably fair may in reality be fundamentally unfair. Being color-blind can be positive if it means being nondiscriminatory in attitude and behavior. However, it is sometimes used as a way to deny differences that help make us who we are (p. 109).

Garcia (1994) echoed this problem when he wrote, "diversity is a wonderful gift to our society, but often it's an unrecognized gift—at times easily discarded or even scorned" (p. xiii).

To be effective, preservice and experienced teachers need to understand that a range of home-based reading and writing experiences occur that can be easily silenced by schools. Anderson and Stokes pointed to literacy events for daily needs, and Schiefflin and Cochran-Smith provided the example of the importance of letter writing in a Sino-Vietnamese household.

How, then, do teachers connect home and school literacies to reduce the potential for "at-risk" behaviors in various circumstances? Perhaps they can do so by acknowledging and valuing different literacies equally. Children come from different literacy environments and these environments should be understood and appreciated. But then the question that Nieto asked arises: "What are the educational implications of 'Equal is not the same'"? In other words, although we value as "equally" legitimate differences in family cultural patterns, we must also acknowledge that such differences do not provide the same kinds of preparation for school-based literacy tasks. Nieto (1992) responded to this question with three important answers.

First, it means *acknowledging the differences that children bring to school,* including their gender, race, ethnicity, language, and social class. Not acknowledging these differences often results in schools and teachers labeling children's behavior as deficient (p. 110). Second, it means *admitting the possibility that such differences may influence how students learn*. This should in no way devalue children's backgrounds or lower our expectations of them, yet this is precisely why so many educators have a hard time accepting "equal is not the same"—that is, they are reluctant to accept this philosophy because they may feel that in doing so, they must lower their expectations or water down the curriculum so that all children can learn. Yet neither of these practices should be seen as necessary (p. 110). Third, *accepting differences also means making provisions for them*. These students' cultural and linguistic backgrounds should be viewed as a strength on which educators can draw. However, the best of educational practice, which asserts that differences must be taken into account in teaching consideration of student differences, often overlooks cultural and linguistic variability (p. 110).

In Nieto's responses are echoes of Berger's (1995) comments on the importance of teachers focusing on children's' differences. Berger stated that:

Children are like snowflakes.
At first they appear to be alike,
But on close examination they are all different.
Focus on their similarities,
But understand their differences. (p. 104)

This is good advice. Yet few teachers are comfortable following it. In many instances, they aren't even sure how to follow this advice. Sometimes it is more comfortable to focus on student similarities rather than their differences. Some teachers fear that if they select to focus on student differences, they will be unable to integrate those characteristics into their personal approach to teaching and into their classroom curriculum as a whole. In fact, some teachers may feel that by recognizing differences they will be opening "Pandora's box" and creating more work for themselves and the schools in which they teach. However, if teachers fail to recognize and appreciate differences of children and their families, these children and their families will continue to be alienated and disconnected from the school. If you become what Christine Bennett (1999) calls an "interculturally competent teacher" or a teacher who uses the six strategies that Hollins mentions, I firmly believe that you will be able to more easily and confidently recognize and appreciate differences of children and families. More importantly, you will be able to motivate alienated families to become involved in school in meaningful ways.

The Morton Story: A Case Example of Historical, Humanistic, and Cultural Issues

For four years I coordinated the Home Literacy Project at Morton Professional Development School (not it's real name; a pseudonym is used for the school and all teachers and parents described). The Home Literacy Project was designed to create a structure for parents to be involved in their children's development as readers and writers. The goals of the Home Literacy Project were to: (1) respect the multiple literacy environments the families represent; (2) become knowledgeable of the families' capability, responsibility, and willingness to be involved in school; (3) help educators recognize the fact that not *all* parents are the same; (4) realize that schools must reach out to families in new and different ways; and (5) develop a scope and sequence of family involvement activities coordinated around the grade-level literacy curriculum.

The Morton Project began in the fall of 1990. However, I met with the principal, K–2 teachers, and the reading specialist during the spring of 1990 to introduce myself and invite consideration of the following questions: (1) How do teachers think about parent involvement?, (2) How do teachers communicate to parents the importance of supporting their children's literacy development?, (3) How do teachers foster and/or encourage parental involvement?, (4) How do teachers address parental differences?, (5) How do teachers view parents who choose not to become involved in and/or support their children's literacy development?, (6) How do teachers use demographic data about parents and children to develop parental involvement programs?, (7) How do teachers incorporate parents' perceptions of their role in their children's literacy development? and (8) How do teachers build on the multiple home literacies represented in their classrooms?

PAUSE AND REFLECT

In a group or by yourself, discuss how teachers at a school where you are currently teaching or have worked in the past would answer these eight questions.

It should be noted that at the spring 1990 meeting, I did not solicit specific responses to these eight questions. Instead, these questions were simply introduced to provide the principal, teachers, and the reading specialist with a general idea of some of the parental involvement issues that we could possibly address for the upcoming year.

In addition to asking them to think about the above eight questions, I also conducted two structured, individual interviews with each of the eight K–2 teachers and the reading specialist. The *first interview* was designed to assess their general thoughts about parental involvement (see Table 6.2 in Chapter 6). The *second interview* was designed to assess their thoughts regarding working with diverse parent populations, their beliefs about parental involvement/support of the school, and their reactions to parents' perceptions about schools (see Table 6.7 in Chapter 6). These results are discussed in Chapter 6.

School History

I had to gather historical information about Morton because, as noted earlier, when using a historical approach, the history of the school is very critical to understanding current patterns of parent involvement. In 1952, when Morton Elementary School was built, it served primarily middle-class white families. These families were young, first-time homeowners. The school served many purposes for them. Many of the community's social events were held at school. The school was also a place where the young families discussed national, state, and local politics, goals and aspirations for their children, and ways they could help the school better serve the needs of their children. An interview with the first Morton parent-teacher association (PTA) president was quite revealing. She said that:

In 1952 because there were few obvious differences between parents and children and teachers and administrators, Morton was a place where parents and teachers worked closely together. We were able to work closely together because we were friends, neighbors, church members, and we even saw each other at the local grocery store. We shared so much in common. We had a shared sense of goals and aspirations for our children.

The PTA president's description did not resemble Morton in *1990*. In a second meeting on October 5, 1990, I shared with the principal, K–2 teachers, and the reading specialist the demographic parent profile data that I had collected. These data forced them to recognize that the parents and children at Morton in *1990* were very much unlike the parents and children some of them may have interacted with or remembered interacting with in *1952*. They were slowly beginning to understand two very important points that were highlighted by Stevenson & Baker (1987) and Nieto (1992). Stevenson and Baker stated that although it is true that parental involvement through activities such as attendance at parent-teacher conferences, participation in PTA, and influence over their child's selection of courses predict student achievement, such parental involvement is becoming more and more scarce. Nieto warned that:

> In a society increasingly characterized by either one-parent families or two-parent families in which both work outside the home, traditional kinds of parent involvement become more problematic. PTA meetings help during the day, parent-teacher conferences during school hours, and the ubiquitous cake sales are becoming remnants of the past. Most parents nowadays, regardless of cultural or economic background, find it difficult to attend meetings or otherwise to be involved in the governance of the school (p. 82).

From Stevenson and Baker's and Nieto's comments, it appears that these forms of parent involvement are not only remnants of the past at Morton, they are also remnants of the past in other school settings. Teachers across the nation can no longer consider only "textbook children" and "textbook parents" in their classrooms. I define *textbook parents* as those parents who baked cookies and who were available to come to school anytime teachers wanted them to come. Haberman (1993) defined *textbook children* as those that "teachers trained in traditional programs of teachers education are taught 'normal' children are like" (p. 2). He noted that in those traditional programs "how all children behave, think, and perceive the world is laid out in terms of a 'normal' universal development, year by year" (p. 2).

In preservice preparation programs in the new millennium, students must look beyond the idea of a single, model child. They must break through "textbook expectations" and understand that "what middle-class youngsters of a given age do is formed by the experts who write the texts and make the films into 'normal,' meaning desirable, behavior. The word *normal*, which began with the meaning of 'frequently observed', is thus changed into 'behavior considered healthy'" (Haberman, 1993, p. 2). Haberman warned of the danger in supposing that child development proceeds "...in the same way and at the same year-by-year rate in all groups and cultures and under all life conditions," calling such an assumption "dangerously naïve" (p. 2). Specifically in regard to urban communities like Morton, Haberman (1993) wrote that:

> Children develop by interacting with specific people in particular environments. What is "normal" in one set of circumstances will not be "normal" in another. In fact, given the facts of life in growing up in urban poverty today, it is clearly unreasonable to expect children to resemble the textbook models future teachers are trained to regard as normal. The important point is that the urban poor are quite normal. *They are making perfectly reasonable responses to those who raise them and to the life conditions under which they live and grow (p. 2).*

After a lengthy discussion about "textbook children and parents," the principal, K-2 teachers, and the reading specialist admitted that the parental involvement climate at Morton needed to be restructured. As we continued to talk, the principal and several of the K-2 teachers began to make comments that reflected that they were aware of differences in family structure and opportunity of the current students versus those those that had been in the school when it first opened.

- Many families at Morton lived in poverty, and some of the families lived in fear.
- Many families at Morton lacked the ability to "parent," meaning that they struggled with illiteracy issues, allowed their children to be raised by other family members, and did not speak English.
- Several types of abuse occurred in the homes of the families who had children attending Morton (drug, physical, child, and sexual abuse, and so on).

The comments by the principal and teachers raised questions about the blurring lines between home and school. As we talked, their comments highlighted the effects of the ecological environment on schools' and teachers' expectations. Although they understood in part, at least, some of the differences and difficulties that the families of their students faced, many expressed their need for guidance in how to use this knowledge to purposefully alter their teaching in ways to accommodate and meet the needs and values of today's families. The principal's and teachers' comments also reflected their concern for family configuration and stability, as well as their concerns about family violence, young and uneducated parents, nonnative English speakers, and the large number of children who enter school from unstructured home environments. Listen to their specific comments:

> *Mrs. Jones:* My concerns are that parents are beginning to give me their parental responsibility. I have notes in my room on homework that parents have written...Please talk to Susie about completing her homework and not talking back to me and not doing those things; so then I become the parent for the parent so to speak. Which tells me again that the parents don't have a lot of parenting skills. I'm feeling somewhat perplexed though by the limited skills that some of the parents have in parenting.

Mrs. Benton: The problem [is] now at Morton, we are dealing with a lot of problems where the children have had years of issues from home that they are dealing with. When the child comes to us, it is totally different, and teaching is much more difficult. You are dealing with so many other issues that when you say, "All right I want the...[grade] level in reading" that seems ridiculous when they cannot even deal with life at home. So you are dealing with all of those issues too, which is a different child from twenty years ago. And I'm sure in ten years more, the child's living conditions are even going to be more difficult.

Mrs. Bates: It's not like you want to pry, but I think it is very important to know what kind of home situation the child is coming from. If there is, let's say, a low economical area, which several children are in [in] our building or if there are drugs in the home, I've had parents come right out and tell me that there are drugs in the home and at the time that they were pregnant they were on a certain drug.

Mrs. Miller: One parent told me that she and her family were living in two rooms and four children were sleeping in one bed...Things like that are what we need to be paying attention to...

Mrs. Bell: I'm now dealing with children who have emotional problems, drug problems, physical abuse, sexual abuse, the children are so far behind in grade level that I didn't know what to go for first. Do I try to get them up to grade level?...Do I try to get their home more stable?... sometimes I feel at a loss...

Mrs. Terry: ...some of the neighborhoods that the students live in are frightening to go into for me. Sometimes parents are embarrassed [by] their surroundings and how they live. I have one parent I knew was in the house and didn't open the door.

Mrs. Tate (Principal):   Because we have so many children that aren't being raised by their mother and father, they are not even being raised by their mother, they are being raised by an aunt, uncle, or a grandmother because the father is in jail and the mother is on drugs...I really feel sorry for some of the children we have at Morton now.

Mrs. Terry: I have a lot of young five year olds, and a lot of them have not had previous academic exposure prior to coming to school. They tend to be more timid [or] shy. I have several children that are violent. I really do have violent children.

Mrs. Benton: I have seen a sharp decline in the literacy levels of the parents of the children I teach. I have a parent who said to me that her husband is a "nonreader." This mother said that her husband is getting concerned now because their son is starting to read and he doesn't know how he is going to be able to hide from his son his inability to read.

Mrs. Jones: I've noticed that a lot of the parents are younger. I had one parent who told me that a lot of the work was hard for her to do, and she is a very young woman. She looks young. Her child would bring her work that she's unable to do; she has to get her sister to help. I guess a lot of the parents now, I wonder if they even get through high school. It seems like they don't know a lot about second grade.

Mrs. Gregory:　I have one kid in my class whose dad came to the conference and he said that the mother was ashamed to come to school because she doesn't speak English very well.

Mrs. Andrews:　...a lot of kids come to school now that don't even know what a rule is, and they are not under any adult rules at home. That's a problem.

From these voices of concerned school professionals, we get a glimpse of what it is like to be a teacher in a classroom with children who are very different from them. In these situations, teachers have legitimate questions and issues: How do they reach these children? How can they take on the role of being parents in light of the many responsibilities that they have?

It is important for teachers and administrators to talk "in specifics" when they are dealing with children and parents so that they don't begin to generalize based on cultural, class, or linguistic differences. At Morton, the principal, K-2 teachers, and reading specialist shared with me four specific cases that further highlighted their concerns about the social and physical well-being of the their students.

Case #1: The drug bust. A first-grade student was absent for 16 consecutive days. The student's concerned teacher did what most teachers would do: she attempted to contact the child's parent. She sent several letters home and telephoned the parent. The teacher even called one of the parent's neighbors to inquire if the neighbor would inform the parent of the need to arrange a conference. None of these efforts to reach the parent proved successful.

Sharing her concerns with the principal, the teacher learned that the mother had previously been arrested for drug use. The principal's fear that the mother might have resumed her involvement with drugs was borne out when the mother was arrested a few days later. The children were placed in foster homes; the mother faces a 20-year prison sentence.

Case #2: My sister's children. A teacher's attempt to contact a third grader's parent led to the discovery that the parent was missing. The child's seventeen year-old aunt stated that she had not heard from her twenty-two-year-old sister and did not know where she was.

Case #3: Caught in the middle. A mother who has custody of her five-year-old son suspected that her former husband had been sexually abusing the boy. Consequently, the mother did not want the school to contact her former husband about their son's performance in school. The father, however, demanded that he be kept informed by receiving the same communications from the school that were sent to his former wife. He further charged that the mother was an alcoholic and that he was in a better situation to respond to the child's needs.

Case #4: Bewildered in kindergarten. A kindergarten teacher with more than twenty years of experience was at a loss as to how to develop a workable instructional program for a child who was acting, according to the teacher, "strange." The child's learning style did not fit any pattern that the teacher had observed in all her years of teaching. She arranged a conference with the parent to better understand how best to work with this child. During the course of that conversation, the parent revealed that her daughter had tested positive for the virus that causes AIDS. The mother added, "I want the best for my child, but I just don't know what is going to happen to her school wise." Although the teacher did not verbalize her feelings at the time, she later confided to a colleague that she did not know the best way to develop the child's learning potential (see Edwards and Young, 1992, p. 76).

Dealing with Reality:
Schools as a Microcosm of Society

The comments from the faculty at Morton Elementary School and the four case examples I have provided illustrate the complex ways in which schools reflect the social reality of the larger society. School is a microcosm of society, and no matter what exists in the larger community (e.g., drug abuse, child abuse, teen pregnancy, alcoholism, poverty, illiteracy, and so on), these societal problems are slowly beginning to surface as real concerns in the school and the classroom environment. (See Figure 3.4 for a pictorial description of the school as a microcosm of society.)

FIGURE 3.4 *Pictorial Description of the Schools as a Microcosm of Society*

Teachers in public schools may have no control over whom they will teach, because everyone has the right to attend public schools. In that way, Morton is no different from any other school. Violence, drugs, teen pregnancy can happen in a suburban affluent school, as well as in schools located in the inner city. However, there is a double standard. When violent acts occur in the inner-city schools, it is no surprise, and it is expected. Many will say, "Those people are *prone* to act violently." On the other hand, when violent acts occur in suburban affluent schools, people are shocked, surprised, and tend to make up excuses or justifications for these violent acts. In the past, people have suggested that these violent acts in suburban schools are not the violent acts of students who attend these schools. Instead, students from inner-city schools are often assumed to be the perpetrators of these violent acts on the families who live in these suburban affluent communities. Yet, as tragic recent events have revealed, white children in both affluent suburban and isolated rural schools also bring hatred and violence into their schools. In this day and time, many schools, whether located in inner city or suburban affluent communities, are all struggling with the problems like Morton's.

Bronfenbrenner's (1986) macrostructure model provides a further illustration of the connection between society and school (see Table 3.4). Bronfenbrenner describes the ecological environment of the child as a macrostructure with four levels, with an underlying belief system.

The Morton teachers had described characteristics about their students' families that fit in each of the four levels in Bronfenbrenner's macrostructure. For example, at level 1, teachers reported that they recognized that some parents needed assistance in how to "parent," some parents were illiterate, and families live in poverty. At level 2, they noted that parents were unable to volunteer even if they wanted to. Moreover, the "textbook children and parents" who were involved in Morton in 1952 do not resemble the children and parents at Morton in 1990. At level 3, they talked about the parents who need to work and that some parents did not have money beyond buying the basic necessities. At level 4, they alluded to the fact that several Morton families lived in poverty and that some lived in fear. Even though not always clearly stated, I could sense that the teachers worried about the children who come to Morton each day from these families.

TABLE 3.4   *Bronfenbrenner's Description of the Child's Ecological Environment*

Level 1 is the child's immediate, primary setting (home, school, and so on).

Level 2 is the interaction between immediate settings.

Level 3 involves settings beyond the child (e.g., parents' jobs).

Level 4 includes a wide range of developmental influences such as a war or national economic crisis, which produce subcultures.

Source: Urie Bronfenbrenner, *The Ecology of Human Development* (Cambridge, MA: Harvard University Press, 1979).

In particular, teachers worried about the children's academic performance. As Mrs. Benton stated:

> The problem [is] now at Morton, we are dealing with a lot of problems where the children have had years of issues from home that they are dealing with. When the child comes to us, it is totally different, and teaching is much more difficult. You are dealing with so many other issues that when you say, "All right I want the...[grade] level in reading" that seems ridiculous when they cannot even deal with life at home. So you are dealing with all of those issues too, which is a different child from twenty years ago. And I'm sure in ten years more, the child's living conditions are even going to be more difficult.

The conversations, which I had with the Morton administrators and teachers about the current relationship between the school and its community and the vision that we collectively would use to re-imagine this relationship, were sometimes painful. It is not easy to rethink existing structures and practices. Although the Morton staff had in the past made structural adjustments in an effort to address the needs of the *1990* versus *1950* parents, these had been in traditional modes of home-school relations (e.g., scheduling parent-teacher conferences to accommodate parents' work schedules, providing transportation for parents, and so on). The Morton staff was frustrated with the families of the children they served. In our initial conversations, they expressed the belief that families did not care and were unconcerned about their children's academic achievement. This thinking negatively affected their ability to successfully reach out to families. It was through the discussions about who the new family of *1990* really was (including educational level, family structure, cultural modes, and goals) that they began to see their need for rethinking their parent involvement structures, purposes, and practices. In Chapter 6, you will learn how the Morton staff was able to move to more effective family involvement. In particular, you will learn more about the scope and sequence of activities I helped the Morton staff develop.

PAUSE AND REFLECT

> After reading the Morton story, list at least three things you learned. With a peer or one of your colleagues, discuss how what you learned from the Morton story will affect how you think about parents in your school.

The Morton story illustrates how the three approaches to understanding family involvement described earlier (i.e., historical, humanistic, and cultural) provides a first step to rethinking existing practices. The historical approach showed how the teaching context within which many of these teachers began their teaching had radically shifted over the twenty to thirty years of their professional career. The humanistic approach provides a caution for us to examine the judgments and assumptions we make about why parents behave in particular ways toward schools. Specifically in the Morton case, we see how lack of involvement was attributed to apathy and unconcern. Finally, the cultural approach provides the necessary framework for beginning to explore how predominately white, middle-age teachers who live themselves in the suburbs can effectively build relationships with poor, urban, and predominately minority families.

The Morton story also highlights poverty and its effects on teachers and parent involvement initiatives. The teachers at Morton were not the *Star Teachers of Children in Poverty* that Haberman spoke of; they initially held very stereotypical views of the families and children they served, and much of the previous discussion in

TABLE 3.5 *Some Key Points to Remember*

1. Poverty is relative. If everyone around you has similar circumstances, the notion of poverty and wealth is vague. Poverty or wealth only exists in relationship to known quantities or expectations.

2. Poverty occurs in all races and in all countries. The notion of middle class as a large segment of society is a phenomenon of this century. The percentage of the population that is poor is subject to definition and circumstance.

3. Economic class is a continuous line, not a clear-cut distinction. In 1994, the poverty line was considered $14,340 for a family of four. In 1994, seven percent of the population made more than $100,000 per year. Individuals are stationed all along the continuum of income; they sometimes move on that continuum as well.

4. Generational poverty and situational poverty are different. Generational poverty is defined as being in poverty for two generations or longer. Situational poverty is a shorter time and is caused by circumstances (i.e., death, illness, divorce, etc.).

5. This work is based on patterns. All patterns have exceptions.

6. An individual brings with him/her the hidden rules of the class in which he/she was raised. Even though the income of the individual may rise significantly, many of the patterns of thought, social interaction, cognitive strategies, and so on remain with the individual.

7. Schools and businesses operate from middle-class norms and use the hidden rules of middle class. These norms and hidden rules are not directly taught in schools or businesses.

8. For our students to be successful, we must understand their hidden rules and teach them the rules that will make them successful at school and at work.

9. We can neither excuse students nor scold them for not knowing; as educators we must teach them and provide support, insistence, and expectations.

10. To move from poverty to middle class or middle class to wealth, an individual must give up relationships for achievement (at least for some period of time).

Source: R. K. Payne, *A Framework for Understanding Poverty* (Baytown, Texas: RFT Publishing Company).

the section on poverty represented the thinking of the Morton staff. However, the school staff at Morton Professional School wanted to learn more about the families and children they served because they recognized that they were serving more children who lived in poverty, and they became star teachers because they were willing to make changes in the ways they thought about, taught, and interacted with their students and their families.

Ruby K. Payne, a professional educator from Baytown, Texas, decided to address the issue of urban poverty by gathering information about poverty, middle class, and wealth that would be of interest to other educators. Earlier in her career when she served as a principal of an affluent elementary school in Illinois, she began to rethink so much of what she had thought about poverty and wealth. Payne (1998) recalls, "The Illinois students had no more native intelligences than the poor students I had worked with earlier in my career. And I noticed that among affluent black, Hispanic, and Asian children, their achievement levels were no different from the white children who were affluent" (p. 9). Payne then highlighted ten key points educators should remember when working with children living in poverty (see Table 3.5).

Educators around the country are slowly noticing Payne's ideas about poverty, but it is clear that in the last two decades of the twentieth century, the urban family in the United States has undergone profound changes and Morton is no different.

Summary

Teachers need to begin thinking about family-school partnerships from three different points of view: historical, humanistic, and cultural. Students suffer when their teachers have limited understandings of ways to promote family involvement in schools. From a historical perspective, the definitions of parent, family, and household have changed drastically over the years. Poverty, teenage pregnancy, drug addiction, and other social ills have been the sources of many of these changes. Teachers must assess their biases about the "ideal family" and be willing to solicit support from the "real families" of their students. Regardless of their plight in life, parents are people too, and teachers are responsible for encouraging parents to become involved in their child's education. A humanistic view of parent involvement requires teachers to rethink how they interact with families. It is critical that teachers and administrators refrain from prejudging parents and children from certain groups. Statistics and stereotypes can be the greatest sources of miscommunication between parents and teachers. They must not fall into the pitfall of basing decisions on prejudiced and biased ideologies. Finally, teachers should view cultural differences as differences, not deficits. The cultural perspective of family-school partnerships challenges teachers to draw from their student's out-of-school experiences to help them make connections and improve in-class learning. It is not enough for teachers to *accept* diversity in a classroom. They must *embrace* it, and *celebrate* it. By utilizing the historical, humanistic, and cultural views of family-school partnerships, teachers can develop effective relationships with *all* types of parents and students.

Chapter 3 Key Concepts

- School cannot and would not exist without parents.
- The history of parent education and involvement can be pictured as the constant ebb and flow of the ocean's tide. Some eras portray a calm; others are characterized by tumult.
- Today's families have changed and do not resemble the families of the 1950s and 1960s. Culturally relevant teachers understand that the needs of parents can be a key to identifying and respecting changes in American family life.
- The American family does not exist. Rather, we are creating many American families of diverse styles and shapes.
- Poverty is something that most schools recognize but have failed to make the necessary adjustments to sufficiently address.
- Poverty, homelessness, drugs, and teen pregnancy are among the many social and economic problems that have been highlighted in the media to underscore the decline of urban America.
- The two reasons for the rise in the child poverty in recent years are (1) the failure of hourly wages to keep pace with inflation, particularly for young workers and those with less than a college education, and (2) the increase in the number of families headed by a single parent, usually the mother. Mother-only families are at high risk for poverty due to the absence of a second adult earner and the historically lower earning power of women.
- Four myths about poverty include (1) People of color are too lazy to work; (2) poor people live in the inner city; (3) families are poor because they are lazy and do not work; and (4) if they just worked harder, they would not be poor.
- Parents in poverty, like parents of all other socioeconomic groups, love their children but may feel uncomfortable in their children's school.
- School staff must seek to learn more about the families and children they serve, especially if they live in poverty.
- Teachers across the nation can no longer consider only "textbook children" and "textbook parents" in their classroom. They must understand the myth of "textbook" individual and seek to broaden their views of the school's clientele.
- School is a microcosm of society and no matter what exists in the larger community (i.e., drug abuse, teen pregnancy, alcoholism, poverty, illiteracy, and so on) all of these "things" come to school.
- Educators must understand that parents are not all the same. *Differentiated parenting* means recognizing that parents are different from one another in their perspectives, beliefs, and abilities to negotiate school. *Parentally appropriate* means that, because parents are different, tasks and activities must be compatible with their capabilities.
- There are five differences in parents, which point to the complexity and significance of schools and teachers knowing the parents they serve: (1) parental dynamics, (2) parent feelings regarding school, (3) parent relationships with their children, (4) parent values and goals, and (5) variety of parents' attitudes toward participation in parent involvement efforts.

- Parents respond to schools based on their past experiences and some parents feel that they have nothing to contribute to the school.
- Today's educators may not fully understand the possible differences that exist between themselves and the families they serve, but educators cannot simply conclude that "differences" translate into deficits within families.
- The backdrop for school learning is a combination of the child's culture, home, family, and community.
- A "tourist curriculum" focuses on artifacts of other countries, such as food, traditional clothing, folk tales, and household items.
- Successful interventions that improve the academic achievement of groups traditionally underserved in the nation's public schools focus on the following: (1) legitimizing the knowledge the children bring to school, (2) making meaningful connections between learning and cultural knowledge or knowledge acquired outside of school, (3) creating a hybrid culture in school that is congruent with many of the practices and values children bring from the home and peer culture, (4) creating a community of learners where collaboration is the norm rather than competition, (5) balancing the rights of students and teachers, and (6) providing curriculum content and pedagogical practices that support a consistent and coherent core of identity and intergenerational continuity with the past.
- Teachers should seek "intercultural competence"—the knowledge and understanding of their students' cultural styles.
- There are hidden literacies in the everyday lives of families and their children, and the literacy events may or may not match school expectations.
- Families have their own "funds of knowledge," and teachers can learn to draw on the resources of these funds of knowledge of the child's world outside the context of the classroom.
- There are at least four cultural variables that may be compatible or incompatible with the expectations and structures of schools: (1) social organization, (2) sociolinguistics, (3) cognition, and (4) motivation. If these cultural variables are ignored, conflict might erupt. Four areas of potential cultural conflict have been identified: (1) learning style, (2) interactional or relational style, (3) communication, and (4) differing perceptions of involvement.
- The educational implications of "equal is not the same" are as follows: (1) acknowledging the differences that children bring to school, (2) admitting the possibility that such differences may influence how students learn, and (3) accepting differences also means making provisions for them.

Suggestions for Thought Questions and Activities _____

1. Organize a small group of three or four members. Each member must develop a composite student and parent that least fits within their perception of "ideal." The student must be from a different culture, have a different type of family life, and the parent should fit within the broad definition of parent—not the traditional definition of an American family.

2. Each group member must pass his or her composite student and parent to another group member. What is your first reaction to the description? Total honesty is required. Identify and discuss your biases concerning the student and parent.

3. All group members must pass their composite students and parent to the next group member. Brainstorm and write three ways that you could develop a family-school partnership from a historical perspective. For example, how could you learn more about the student's family situation? If the student were in a foster home, what would you need to know in order to assist the student and motivate the foster parents to become involved?

4. Pass the composite students and parent to the next group member. Brainstorm and write three ways that you could develop a family-school partnership from a humanistic perspective. For example, what biases do you have that might prevent you from developing a good relationship with the student and parent?

5. Pass the composite student and parent to the next group member. Brainstorm and write three ways that you could develop a family-school partnership from a cultural perspective. For example, would you and your students benefit from inviting parents as guest speakers to talk about some aspect of their culture?

6. Make copies of the information gathered within your group and use the ideas in your classroom in the future.

Internet Activities

- Using a major search engine, look for pictures that portray the American family over the last fifty years. In what ways have these pictures changed? How do these pictures compare with what you know about the makeup of the American family?

- Using a major search engine, look for schools that use a variety of ways to get parents involved. What methods do they use? How do they attempt to connect families with schools?

- Using a major search engine or *www.proteacher.net*, search for parentally appropriate activities that involve literacy. I also suggest that you use the National Network of Partner School Web site (*http://www.partnershipschools.org*) for some ideas for developing partnerships with families.

- Keeping in mind the term *Intercultural Competence*, use a major search engine to locate and learn more about a specific culture that is represented in your classroom.

For Further Study

Allen, J., & Mason, J. M. (1989). *Risk makers, risk takers, risk breakers: Reducing the risks for young literacy learners.* Portsmouth, NH: Heinemann.
> *Risk Makers, Risk Takers, Risk Breakers* contains chapters by teachers, researchers, and policy analysts who are concerned with how school systems, curricula, and timetables for "success" can put young children at risk. The book provides portraits of children who are beating the odds, teachers who are learning from children in order to teach them, and parents who are supporting their children as they become readers and writers.

Au, K. H. (1993). *Literacy instruction in multicultural settings.* Fort Worth, TX: Harcourt Brace Jovanovich College Publishers.

Literacy Instruction in Multicultural Settings was written to acquaint preservice teachers with issues they will face in teaching reading and writing to students of diverse cultural and linguistic backgrounds.

Berger, E. H. (1995). *Parents as partners in education: Families and schools working together.* Fourth Edition. Englewood Cliffs, NJ: Merrill.

In this book, Berger builds the case that the school and home are intertwined. She wrote this book with the hope that it might help bring about collaboration between home and school. She provides suggestions for effective home-school-community relationships, communication and parent programs, leadership training in parent education, school-based programs, home-based programs, working with parents of the exceptional child, and the abused child.

Clark, R. M. (1983). *Family life and school achievement: Why poor black children succeed or fail.* Chicago: The University of Chicago Press.

Clark offers ten intimate portraits of African-American families in Chicago. Visiting the homes of poor one- and two-parent families of high and low achievers, Clark made detailed observations on the quality of home life, noting how family habits and interactions affect school success and what characteristics of family life provide children with *school survival skills*, a complex of behaviors, attitudes, and knowledge that are the essential elements in academic success.

Delgado-Gaitan, C. (1990). *Literacy for empowerment: The role of parents in children's education.* New York: The Falmer Press.

Literacy for Empowerment is an innovative study that describes the ways in which twenty Mexican Spanish-speaking parents participate in their children's home literacy acquisition and in the school in general. This important book reveals how some families, schools, and one community defy the stereotypic constraints and become empowered by their collective work toward building educational opportunities for Mexican children in the home and in the school.

Delgado-Gaitan, C., & Trueba, H. (1991). *Crossing cultural borders: Education for immigrant families in America.* New York: The Falmer Press.

Children of Mexican and Central American immigrant families in the Secoya Community crossed a national border, and today continue to cross linguistics and social and cultural borders that separate the home, school, and community. *Crossing Cultural Borders* describes the day-to-day interaction of children with adults, siblings, and peers in the home, school, and community at large. These families demonstrate their skills in using their culture to survive in a new society.

Delpit, L. (1995). *Other people's children: Cultural conflict in the classroom.* New York: The New Press.

Drawing on her extensive teaching experience, Delpit uses analyses of cultural clashes in classrooms from Alaska to Papua New Guinea to get at the highly charged issue of race in our schools, discussing what must happen if we are to educate teachers to accommodate ethnic and cultural diversity. Delpit introduces the idea of teachers as "cultural translators" for students struggling to understand the sometimes "foreign" ways of American public schools. She also acknowledges the voices of African Americans and other non-mainstream students and teachers, many of whom have been alienated by schools inhospitable to non-Anglo cultures.

Dickinson, D. K. (1994). *Bridges to literacy: Children, families, and schools.* Cambridge, MA: Blackwell Publishers.

In increasingly technological economies around the world, workers need to be able to read and write complex material. Yet demographic changes—resulting in minority languages and cultures, some without family traditions of literacy, and poverty persisting from generation to generation—present serious impediments to full literacy. *Bridges to Literacy* reviews the progress that has been made in developing school and community-based programs to help beginning students surmount these difficulties. The authors, leading researchers and practitioners, describe and analyze the effectiveness of programs that have been in operation for a number of years. They offer sufficient detail to enable a broad audience to understand how each project has been implemented and how it has solved the problems of program delivery, communication, and collaboration with parents and teachers.

Dickinson, D. K., and Tabors, P. O. (2001). *Young children learning at home and school: Beginning literacy with language*. Baltimore, MD: Paul H. Brookes.

In this exciting book, early childhood professionals, educators, and parents will travel into the homes and schools of more than seventy young children from diverse backgrounds and observe parent-child and teacher-child interactions. Based on research gathered in the Home-School Study of Language and Literacy Development, *Beginning Literacy with Language* reveals for readers the relationship the authors found between these critical, early interactions and children's kindergarten language and literacy skills.

Edelman, M. W. (1987). *Families in peril: An agenda for social change*. Cambridge, MA: Harvard University Press.

This book constitutes a thorough and powerful presentation on behalf of poor children. It has the substance and rationale to awaken the national consciousness and should become a powerful influence on the thinking of Americans and their political leaders.

Ferreiro, E., & Teberosky, A. (1982). *Literacy before schooling*. Portsmouth, NH: Heinemann.

Emilia Ferreiro and Ana Teberosky are enriching a growing, although small, body of research, which is exploring literacy development in young children before school instruction in reading and writing. As psychologists and researchers based in Piagetian traditions, the authors have ingeniously devised reading and writing tasks within the framework of Piagetian theory to explore how children come to know literacy.

Garcia, E. (1994). *Understanding and meeting the challenge of student cultural diversity*. Boston: Houghton Mifflin Company.

This book provides the basis for responsive teaching by exploring the roots of diversity. This basis consists of the social, cognitive, and communicative roots of diversity; how children of diverse backgrounds learn to think and communicate with their home, community, and school environments is the pivotal framework of this book.

Goelman, H., Oberg, A. A., & Smith, F. (1984). *Awakening to literacy*. Exeter, NH: Heinemann.

How do children become literate without formal schooling? This issue is the main subject of this volume in which eighteen distinguished researchers with extensive and overlapping backgrounds in anthropology, linguistics, psychology, sociology, and education discuss the most recent research findings on pre-school literacy.

Haberman, M. (1995). *Star teachers of children of poverty*. West Lafayette, IN: Kappa Delta Pi, an International Honor Society in Education.

Dr. Haberman shares composites from more than 1,000 interviews in *Star Teachers* to illustrate how star teachers think and behave differently from those who fail with students or quit the profession, providing a guide to effective action for those committed to students' successful learning through teaching excellence.

Hart, B., & Risley, T. R. (1995). *Meaningful differences in the everyday experience of young American children*. Baltimore, MD: Paul H. Brookes Publishing Company.

Meaningful Differences charts the course of the authors' search for the roots of intellectual disparity. Examining the daily lives of one- and two-year-old children in typical American families, Hart and Risley found staggering contrasts at the extremes of advantage—and within the middle-class—in the amount of interaction between parents and children. These differences in early family experience translate into striking disparities in the children's later vocabulary growth rate, vocabulary use, and IQ test scores—critical measures of an individual's ability to succeed at school and in the workplace.

Heath, S. B. (1983). *Ways with words: Language, life, and work in communities and classrooms.* Cambridge, MA: Cambridge University Press.

> *Ways with Words* is a stimulating and challenging study of children learning to use language at home and school in two communities only a few miles apart in the southern United States. "Roadville" is a white, working-class community of families steeped for four generations in the life of the textile mills; "Trackton" is a black working-class community whose older generations grew up farming the land but whose current members work in the mills. In tracing the children's language development, the author shows the deep cultural differences between the two communities, whose ways with words differ as strikingly from each other as they do from the pattern of the townspeople, the "mainstream" blacks and whites who hold power in the schools and workplaces of the region. Against the social historical background of textile mills in the Southeast, the book portrays how differences in language use are linked to the systemic relations between education and production for members of the three groups—Roadville, Trackton, and the townspeople.

Henry, M. (1996). *Parent-school collaboration: Feminist organizational structure and school leadership.* Albany, NY: State University of New York Press.

> Mary E. Henry examines in close detail public schools' relationship with parents and communities. Using an anthropological approach and feminist theory, she argues that for educators, knowledge of family and social contexts, and work with communities is essential. Henry argues convincingly that the school structure has to change, that more demands can't be made of parents while schools remain the same.

Hoffman, E. (1989). *Lost in translation: A life in new language.* New York: Penguin Books.

> A classically American chronicle of upward mobility and assimilation, *Lost in Translation* is an incisive meditation on coming to terms with one's own uniqueness, on learning how deeply culture affects the mind and body, and finally, on what it means to accomplish a translation of one's self.

Hollins, E. R., & Oliver, E. I. (Editors, 1999). *Pathways to success in school.* Mahwah, N. J.: Lawrence Erlbaum Associates, Inc.

> This text is designed to help preservice and inservice teachers identify pathways to productive teaching and learning for students from culturally and experientially diverse backgrounds.

Hull, G., & Schultz, S. (2002) (Editors). *School's out!: Bridging out-of-school literacies with classroom practice.* New York: Teachers College Press.

> This timely book uses research on literacy outside of school to challenge how we think about literacy inside of school. Bringing together highly respected literacy researchers, this volume bridges the divide in the literature between formal education and the many informal settings—such as homes, community organizations, and after-school programs—in which literacy learning flourishes. To help link research findings with teaching practices, each chapter includes a response from classroom teachers (K-12) and literacy educators. This book's unique blending of perspectives will have a profound effect on how literacy will be taught in school.

King, J. E., Hollins, E. R., & Hayman, W. C. (1997). *Preparing teachers for cultural diversity.* New York: Teachers College Press.

> In *Preparing Teachers for Cultural Diversity*, editors Joyce E. King, Etta R. Hollins, and Warren C. Hayman have gathered together some of the top researchers in teacher education to explore both the theoretical parameters and practical dimensions of transforming teacher education programs to educate teachers for diversity. The contributors identify the competence, skills, knowledge, and attitude needed to teach diverse populations effectively and equitably, including methods and experiences to expand understanding of diversity, racism, social justice, and culturally responsive instruction.

Koerner, M. E., Hulsebosch, P. (1996). Preparing teachers to work with children of gay and lesbian parents. *Journal of Teacher Education, 47*(5), 347–354.

The authors describe a curriculum and a structure to engage teachers in discussions on family diversity and summarize several themes consistently emerging through these discussions. These authors suggest that the entire curriculum, or parts of it, can be used in preservice classes, school-based inservices, and professional workshops.

Kotlowitz, A. (1991). *There are no children here*. New York: Anchor Books-Doubleday.
This book follows Lafeyette and Pharoah over a two-year period as they struggle with school, attempt to resist the lure of the gangs, and mourn the death of friends, all the while searching for some inner peace.

Kozol, J. (1991). *Savage inequalities: Children in America's schools*. New York: Crown Publishers.
Savage Inequalities is a plea for fairness and decency in the way we pay for education of all children in this country, an argument for saving at least some of them from destruction and despair.

Lareau, A. (2000). *Home advantage: Social class and parental intervention in elementary education*. Second Edition. Lanham, MD: Rowman, & Littlefield Publishers, Inc.
This book illuminates the relationship between family background and parent involvement in schooling in very telling and powerful ways. Focusing on a working-class and upper middle-class community, this work helps us understand the dramatic differences in family-school relationships in these two communities and highlights the influence of social class on opportunities that are afforded children in schools and other social institutions.

Polakow, V. (1994). *Lives on the edge: Single mothers and their children in the other America*. Chicago: The University of Chicago Press.
Lives on the Edge draws on social, historical, feminist, and public policy perspectives to develop an informed, wide-ranging critique of American educational and social policy. Stark, penetrating, and unflinching in its firsthand portraits of single mothers in America today, this work challenges basic myths about justice and democracy.

Purcell-Gates, V. (1995). *Others people's words: The cycle of low literacy*. Cambridge, MA: Harvard University Press.
If asked to identify those children who rank lowest in relation to national educational norms, who have higher school dropout and absence rates, and who more commonly experience learning problems, few of us would know the answer: white, urban Appalachian children. These are the children and grandchildren of Appalachian families who migrated to northern cities in the 1950s to look for work. They make up this largely "invisible" urban group, a minority that represents a significant portion of the urban poor. Literacy researchers have rarely studied urban Appalachians; yet, as Victoria Purcell-Gates demonstrates in *Other People's Words*, their often severe literacy problems provide a unique perspective on literacy and the relationship between print and culture. A compelling case study details the author's work with one such family.

Rodriguez, R. (1983). *Hunger of Memory: The education of Richard Rodriguez*. New York: Bantam Books.
Hunger of Memory is the poignant journey of a "minority student" who pays the cost of his social assimilation and academic success with a painful alienation—from his past, his parents, his culture—and so describes the high price of "making it" in middle-class America.

Schmidt, P. R. (1998). *Cultural conflict and struggle: Literacy learning in a kindergarten program*. New York: Peter Lang.
This story began in an educational setting where two children who were physically and culturally different experienced conflict on a daily basis. Peley's family immigrated from Cambodia and Vietnam and Raji's from Bombay. Both children struggled throughout their first year of formal education in a predominately white suburban school district. Social and academic problems developed during work and play, formal literacy learning, holidays and celebrations, and home/school communications. Their teacher, Ms. Starr, also

struggled as she tried to understand the two children and their families, watching help-lessly as Peley and Raji became isolated in the kindergarten program. At the end of this compelling account, specific classroom recommendations are offered to present and future educators.

Schorr, L. (1988). *Within our reach: Breaking the cycle of disadvantage.* New York: Doubleday.
There is growing consensus about the need for comprehensive, integrated services for children who are vulnerable to a number of social and health conditions. Schorr describes several intensive health, family support, and education programs that have shown success in breaking the cycle of disadvantage. One chapter in particular, "Schools, Balance Wheel of the Social Machinery," highlights what schools can do as one of several social institu-tions in the broader community context.

Swap, S. M. (1987). *Enhancing parent involvement in schools: A manual for parents and teachers.* New York: Teachers College Press.
Swap examines the benefits of and barriers to parent involvement. She then outlines three models of home-school interactions (the protective model): the school-to-home transmis-sion model, the curriculum enrichment model, and the partnership model. She concludes by discussing three proven paths to partnership. Swap places special emphasis on reach-ing out to parents and guardians of diverse ethnic, racial, language, and class back-grounds to create alliances for children's school success.

Taylor, D. (1983). *Family literacy: Young children learning to read and write.* Exeter, NH: Heinemann.
In her attempt to find out more about literacy activities within the family context, the author spent three years doing fieldwork with six families. At the time of the study, each of the families contained a child who was considered by his or her parents to be success-fully learning to read and write. This study represents an attempt to develop systematic ways of looking at reading and writing as activities which have consequences in, and are affected by, family life.

Taylor, D., & Dorsey-Gaines, C. (1988). *Growing up literate: Learning from inner-city families.* Portsmouth, NH: Heinemann.
In early 1982, Denny Taylor and Cathey Dorsey-Gaines made the first of what were to be many visits to families living in the inner city of a major metropolitan area in the Northeast. Their aim: to study the familial contexts in which young African-American children living in urban poverty are growing up literate. Through their focus on children who were successfully learning to read and write despite the extraordinary economic hardships of their lives, this multiracial team presents new images of the strengths of the family as educator and the ways in which the personal biographies and educational styles of families shape the literate experience of children.

Taylor, D. (1997). *Many families, many literacies: An international declaration of principles.* Portsmouth, NH: Heinemann Trade.
At a time when family literacy policies and practices are confusingly fragmented and often deficit driven, *Many Families, Many Literacies* provides much-needed guidance on developing policies and practices that build on the strengths families bring to any learn-ing situation: their diverse languages and literacies and their complex problem-solving capabilities. This collection features the opinions of leading international education experts and family literacy practitioners, together with those of families participating in literacy programs. It is essential reading for any educator, researcher, or community-based practitioner concerned about the political implications of the family literacy movement.

Weiner, L. (1993). *Preparing teachers for urban schools: Lessons from thirty years of school reform.* New York: Teachers College Press.
In *Preparing Teachers for Urban School,* Lois Weiner poses the question, "Do urban teachers of at-risk students require special preparation, and if so, who can best provide it? Unique from other works in that it applies the insights of sociologists, historians, and political sci-entists to reframe the problem, Weiner's study demonstrates that the attempt to identify

individual student and teacher deficits has been unproductive and explains why the issue must be placed in a broader context that includes analysis of the systematic characteristics of urban schools.

Wilson, W. J. (1987). *The truly disadvantaged: The inner city, the underclass, and public policy.* Chicago: The University of Chicago Press.

The Truly Disadvantaged should spur critical rethinking in many quarters about the causes and potential remedies for inner-city poverty. As policy makers grapple with the problems of an enlarged underclass, they, and community leaders and concerned Americans of all races, would be well advised to examine Mr. Wilson's incisive analysis.

Winters, W. G. (1993). *African American mothers and urban schools: The power of participation.* New York: Lexington Books, an imprint of MacMillan, Inc.

African American Mothers and Urban Schools is a wonderful study that approaches the issue of alienation and participation in education conceptually and with strong databased answers. The basic thesis of her book is that participation and its educational benefits contribute to personal development.

4

Teacher Preparation for Family Involvement

Effective Strategies

Chapter Goals for the Reader

- To become familiar with the meaning of culturally relevant teaching
- To become familiar with strategies to help you become culturally aware of the similarities and differences that exist between you and individuals from a culture different from your own
- To learn how reading about different cultures can help you to become a culturally relevant teacher
- To understand how becoming a culturally relevant teacher can lead to developing a closer working relationship with families
- To become familiar with strategies to understand and appreciate cultures different from your own

Chapter Outline

Culturally Relevant Teachers Know How to Foster Better Home-School Partnerships

Culturally Relevant Teachers Learn about Themselves and Other Cultural Groups

    Personal Life Stories

    Cultural Self-Analysis

    Photos of Local Knowledge Sources

       Phase One: Making Culture a Personal Construct

       Phase Two: Teaching through New Cultural Lenses

       Phase Three: Mediating Cultural Constructs

Culturally Relevant Teachers Read about Different Cultures

    Autobiographies as Cultural Learning Tools

    Learning from Literature: Uses and Cautions

Culturally Relevant Teachers Can Learn About Families and Children From Early Field Experiences

    Field-Based Language Arts Methods Course

120

Chapter Overview

In the first section, I build the case and provide examples of why it is critical for culturally relevant teachers to know how to foster better home-school partnerships. I point out that several teacher educators are playing a significant role in enabling preservice teachers to have experiences that will better prepare them to work with children and their families from diverse cultural backgrounds. These programs are typically community-based projects through preservice methods courses and draw on parental knowledge to enhance student teaching experiences. Such programs and the strategies will help move preservice teachers toward gaining a deeper understanding of families, particularly from culturally diverse backgrounds.

In the second section, I discuss the need for culturally relevant teachers to learn about themselves and other cultures. Also, I suggest some strategies for how preservice teachers may learn to do this.

In the third section, I discuss using literature as a way for culturally enlightened teachers to learn about diverse cultures. Autobiographies of families are important sources of cultural information. Reading autobiographies will provide some background information to begin a meaningful conversation with families. When families are aware that you have taken the time, energy, and effort to learn more about their culture, it increases the likelihood that a fruitful relationship will develop. In the fourth section, I introduce several other programs and strategies that move beyond "reading about cultures" to actually "interacting with cultures." In particular, I provide two examples of how preservice teachers can do this—developing a family story and collecting parent stories of early literacy.

Introductory Scenario:
Dr. Edwards Speaks to Teacher Educators and Preservice Teachers

Many teacher educators have worked tirelessly to reform undergraduate programs so that preservice teachers can work effectively with students from diverse, racial, ethnic, and social-class groups in order to enable them to experience educational success. Creating educational equality for all students, especially for those of color and those who are located in high poverty areas, is at the heart of the multicultural reform agenda. James Banks (1995) explains that:

> There is general agreement among most scholars and researchers that, for multicultural education to be implemented successfully, institutional changes must be made, including changes in the curriculum; the teaching materials; teaching and learning styles; the attitudes, perceptions, and behaviors of teachers and administrators; and the goals, norms, and culture

of the school. However, many schools and university practitioners have a limited conception of multicultural education, viewing it primarily as curriculum reform that involves only changing or restructuring the curriculum to include content about ethnic groups, women, and other cultural groups. This conception of multicultural education is widespread because curriculum reform was the main focus when the movement first emerged in the 1960s and 1970s, and because the multicultural discourse in the popular media has focused on curriculum and largely ignored other dimensions and components of multicultural education...If multicultural education is to become better understood and implemented in ways more consistent with theory, its various dimensions must be more clearly described, conceptualized, and researched (pp. 3–4).

One way teacher educators can move closer to accomplishing what James Banks has suggested is to begin to prepare their students to become culturally relevant teachers. A strategy for doing this involves providing the opportunity to work with culturally different children and their families. Researchers like Florio-Ruane (1994) have captured the essence of why preservice teachers need to learn how to work with culturally different children and their families. In noting that preservice teachers themselves were generally "successful pupils" in school and entered the institution "familiar with its literacy practices," she suggested that such teachers may have difficulty finding "instructional ways to assist youngsters making the transition from home to school" (p. 53). As discussed in Chapter 3, this is especially true when preservice teachers have family histories that differ from their students. My plea to you is that you begin to assist youngsters in making the transition from home to school by becoming culturally relevant teachers. According to Ladson-Billings (1991):

> Culturally relevant teaching refers to the kind of teaching that allows minority [and poor] youngsters access to, and success in, school knowledge via their own culture; helps them to recognize and celebrate that culture; and empowers students so that they are able to critically examine educational content and process and ask what its role is in creating a democratic and multicultural society...Culturally relevant teachers are those who have specific conceptions about themselves and others, the kinds of classroom/community social relations they promote and the significance of knowledge in the classroom that they relate to these issues of student culture and educational critique (p. 236).

Ladson-Billings noted that "culturally relevant" teachers possess three important characteristics: (1) culturally relevant conceptions of self/others, (2) culturally relevant classroom social relations, and (3) culturally relevant conceptions of knowledge. A more detailed description of each of these characteristics is found in Table 4.1.

Many preservice teachers are surprised to find that their teacher education program has not prepared them to work with culturally diverse students and their families. It is likely, in fact, that an undergraduate education major will encounter little, if any, attention to the issue of parent involvement as part of their program. Williams, Jr., (1992) believes that the scant attention accorded to this issue communicates to these preservice teachers that "it is really not that important and all they need to know is their subject-matter" (p. 245). Williams, Jr., believes that teacher educators have sent this message because they have not fully accepted their responsibility for parent involvement. Safran (1979) agreed

TABLE 4.1 *Characteristics of Culturally Relevant Teachers*

Culturally Relevant Conceptions of Self/Others
Culturally relevant teachers see themselves as artists and teaching as a creative undertaking. They see themselves as a part of the community and their role as giving something back to that community…These teachers believe that success is possible for each student and a part of that success is helping students to make connections between themselves and their community, national, ethnic, and global identities (p. 236).

Culturally Relevant Classroom Social Relations
The classroom social relations of culturally relevant teachers are fluid and "humanely equitable" (as stated by Wilson, 1972) and extend beyond the boundaries of the classroom…The teachers demonstrate a connectedness with the students and encourage the same among students in their effort to build a "community of learners" instead of defining success as competitive individual achievement. This community of learners is urged to learn collaboratively and is expected to teach and assume responsibility for each other and the wider community (pp. 238–239).

Culturally Relevant Conceptions of Knowledge
Culturally relevant teachers believe that knowledge is continuously re-created, recycled, and shared…In assessing and evaluating students, culturally relevant teachers see excellence as a complex standard that may involve some postulates but take student diversity and individual differences into account. In other words, macro culture and standards are not ignored but neither are such postulates presented uncritically as superior to the students' ways of knowing and being (pp. 239–240).

with Williams, Jr., by stating that "While institutional practices must change if schools of education are to prepare teachers to work with parents so must the perspectives and practices of individual faculty members" (p. 110). I believe that the failure of teacher educators to prepare preservice teachers to work with parents has caused many preservice teachers to arrive in their classrooms on the first day of school not knowing exactly how to work with culturally diverse students and afraid to reach out to their families.

Even when teacher educators have decided to address parental involvement, they pursue it most often during the student teaching phase. The rationale for this is that their preservice teachers would gain the most insight on how to work with parents from field experiences. Kaplan (1992) informed us that in many cases "the assumption was that student teachers would experience these conferences firsthand and would be able to ask the supervising teacher specific questions" (p. 274). He revealed the inadequacy of this rationale when he observed that "Since the supervising teacher had little or no preparation in this area, it was apparent that firsthand experience was the sole criterion for how much or how little was discussed [about parent involvement issues]" (p. 274). McAfee (1987) admitted that even inservice programs for classroom teachers, which address parental involvement, have been limited by lack of time, money, and coordination.

Although firsthand experience is a good thing, it is much better when augmented by guidance and structured discussions about parent involvement in the teacher preparation program. In some teacher education courses, such discussion does occur and is aided by formal reading materials. Although such approaches can be useful, they, too, are often limited, as Foster & Loven (1992) noted, because "…teacher preparation programs often present an unsystematic approach to preparing preservice teachers to work with parents" (p. 14).

Several researchers have called for the need for preservice teachers to have actual hands-on experiences with cultural pluralism before their entry into real classrooms (Holm & Johnson, 1994; Hadaway, Florez, Larke, & Wiseman, 1993; Gollnick, 1992; Mills & Buckley, 1992). For example, Gollnick (1992) argued that "…a thorough understanding of the subject matter is just a beginning" (p. 68). Knowledge about how to apply that understanding in multicultural, experiential, and human interactions is key. However, Gollnick (1992) and other researchers have not taken the simplistic view, which "holds that if people from different cultural backgrounds interact, cultural understanding will automatically result" (Ozturk, 1992, p. 79). Instead, researchers like Gollnick & Chinn (1994) argued that "If individuals can learn to understand, empathize with, and participate in a second culture, they will have had a valuable experience. If they learn to live multiculturally, they are indeed fortunate" (p. 328). However, Gollnick & Chinn are painfully aware of the unfortunate fact that preservice teachers have had so few practical multicultural experiences. They revealed that:

> Educators are often at a disadvantage because they do not live, nor have ever lived, in the community in which their students live. Often the only parents with whom they interact are those few who attend parent-teacher meetings or who have scheduled conferences with them. In many cases, they have not been in their students' homes nor been active participants in community activities. To make our classrooms multicultural we need to learn the cultures of our students, especially when the students are members of oppressed groups (p. 296).

However, preservice teachers cannot afford to wait until their student teaching to interact with families. Certainly, no novice wants their first encounter with families to occur when they attend parent-teacher meetings or scheduled conferences. It is critical that beginning teachers have contact with families throughout their teacher education program. Garibaldi (1992) correctly noted that:

> "…[preservice] teachers must be afforded more opportunities to practice [their multicultural] skills, and in varied settings, through more clinical experiences throughout their undergraduate training. Furthermore, teacher education programs must take an active role in demanding that publishers develop textbooks that address issues relevant to and inclusive of multicultural populations. Finally, students who will teach must learn how to communicate more closely with the parents of their children and learn how to effectively use churches as well as civic and community-based organizations to motivate, encourage, and reward children's academic performance" (p. 36).

Unfortunately, most preservice teachers have not had these kinds of multicultural encounters with parents in their teacher preparation programs. However, there are several hands-on cross-cultural experiences that preservice teachers can participate in before entering the teaching profession. For example, Ogbu (1992) suggested that preservice teachers can learn about their students through (1) observing children's behavior in the classroom and on playgrounds, (2) asking children questions about their cultural practices and preferences, (3) talking with parents about their cultural practices and preferences, (4) doing research on various ethnic groups with children in school, and (5) studying published works on children's ethnic groups (p. 12). Gollnick & Chinn (1994) suggested that "…participation in community, religious, and ethnic activities can provide another perspective on the way students live" (p. 296).

Classrooms are becoming a rich tapestry, interwoven with people of diverse cultures and ethnic groups. The families of these children want their children not only to *survive* but also *thrive* in these multicultural classroom settings. Therefore, it is crucial that you get to know the families of the children you teach. Multicultural classrooms, philosophies, and curricula can benefit teachers and students. Multicultural classrooms that meet the instructional needs of *all* children will make parents feel comfortable with you as a teacher of their most priceless possession—*their child*. Developing approaches for involving diverse family populations in these multicultural schools and classroom settings is needed and holds a great deal of promise for improving the education of *all* children in schools today.

Reading required multicultural materials, listening to lectures, participating in class discussions, and completing class assignments designed to teach parent involvement allows you to process and think about information and expand your knowledge of multiple voices. In other words, when you have the opportunity to participate in these interactive experiences with diverse families it will allow you to reflect on and evaluate your role in bringing that information you learned in the university classroom to life. Although I believe you must come face-to-face with these multiple voices that you have read and heard so much about, these face-to-face interactions should be designed so that you can transfer your knowledge and interactions with diverse families to your own classroom when you begin to teach. Chapter 4 will move you closer to learning how to do this.

Culturally Relevant Teachers Know How to Foster Better Home-School Partnerships

As a preservice or experienced teacher, you can move closer to becoming a culturally relevant teacher by learning how to foster better home-school partnerships (Gardner, 1994) with parents and children different from yourself. As stated in Chapter 3, Joyce Epstein (1986) suggested that teachers must increase the amount of involvement of parents (including minority parents) who have little education. Epstein compared teachers who were active in seeking parental support with those who were not. Differences in these parents' reports of their involvement in learning activities at home from those of more educated parents were significant only in classrooms of teachers who failed to show leadership in parental involvement. Epstein concluded that teachers who got parents involved "mitigated the disadvantages typically associated with race, social class, and level of education" (p. 279). This is the power of what results when you learn to work with families.

In recent years, the perspectives and practices of individual members of teacher education faculties have accepted the task of preparing preservice teachers to work with families. Even though your institution might not be offering courses on parent involvement, despite this, you can learn from the examples that

I have included. Jones & Blendinger (1994) suggested that "Prospective teachers need to be knowledgeable about the importance of parent involvement because studies show that when parents are involved in their children's education, the children are more successful" (pp. 79–80). They further suggested that "The preparation of teachers for tomorrow's schools and classrooms should include providing future teachers with the knowledge and skills necessary for involving parents in their children's education" (p. 85). French (1996) contends that this recommendation raises an intriguing question: "How can teacher education programs prepare teacher candidates to be adept at establishing and maintaining effective relationships with parents and children?" (p. 335). She then suggested that teacher preparation programs might address this issue in several ways "...courses on parent counseling and parent training with lectures and reading about families, case studies, and other campus-classroom activities might impart knowledge and enhance the skills of teacher candidates" (p. 335).

One example of a course designed to increase teacher candidates' knowledge of how to work with parents was developed by Kaplan (1992). He developed a semester-long course entitled, *Parent Education in Home, School, and Society* for recent early childhood and elementary graduates. The general topics and instructional learning objectives addressed in the course included (1) "the nature of parental education instructional learning objective (ILO): (ILO: Students will demonstrate familiarity with effective home-school partnerships, past and present.), (2) theoretical frameworks (ILO: Students will demonstrate familiarity with themes of parental education that foster successful practice.), (3) subject matter—the knowledge base (ILO: Students will analyze the relationship of subject matter to process.), and (4) school (ILO: Students will develop an understanding of what schools can do to enhance parent/child interaction)" (pp. 275–276). Kaplan described the activities in the course as follows:

> Each week, material discussed is organized in such a manner as to elicit student involvement. One of the more popular activities is to have small-group presentations around one of the topics. Each group is held responsible for leading the discussion and supplying supplementary materials useful for the particular topic. Speakers have been utilized, as they are available. These [speakers] have come from the health profession, schools, social agencies, government agencies, parents and anywhere else expertise can be located (p. 276).

Also, some teacher education programs have prepared preservice teachers to become culturally relevant teachers by designing coursework that requires that preservice teachers participate in early field experiences, discussions, dialogue journals, and assisted reflections. Further, cousework has been designed that requires preservice teachers to develop personal life stories, construct cultural self-analysis, develop family stories, collect parent stories of early literacy, and participate in cross-cultural interactions. Still further, preservice teachers have taken courses that require them to view films and videotapes about diverse populations; listen to guest speakers; visit community agencies; and participate in community action projects as well as vicarious experiences and role playing (see Figure 4.1).

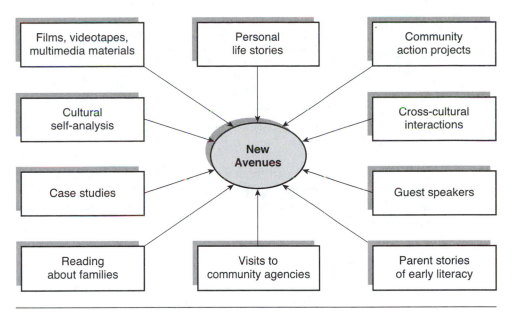

FIGURE 4.1   *Avenues for Understanding How to Work with Diverse Families and Children*

As these examples illustrate, parent and family involvement has been thought about for a long time but only recently have teacher educators begun to think of parent and family involvement as a topic that is important enough to include in teacher education programs. However, I applaud the efforts of teacher educators because I believe focusing on parent and family involvement is a step in the right direction.

Culturally Relevant Teachers Learn about Themselves and Other Cultural Groups

Culturally relevant teachers recognize and understand their own life history as situated within a particular cultural context. They are able to describe the ways in which their own family upbringing, social class, geographical location, and personal history have shaped their beliefs and values in specific ways. Patricia R. Schmidt (1996) captured why it is important for teachers to learn about themselves and other cultures. She stated that:

> Present and future teachers often have little knowledge of their own and other cultures because their life experiences have isolated them from minority cultures. Consequently, they may lack cultural understanding of minority students in their classroom. Additionally, knowledge of one's own cultural identity appears to be

a prerequisite for cross-cultural understanding. Since the research based on a sociocultural perspective emphasizes the importance of home/school connections for minority students' literacy learning, teachers must acquire the cultural and social awareness necessary to work effectively with diverse populations in their classrooms (p. 194).

I agree with Schmidt's observation and further contend that requiring preservice teachers to develop personal life stories, construct cultural self-analysis, and share photographs of their own cultures provides an excellent context for preservice teachers to learn about themselves and recognize the similarities and differences that exist between them and individuals from a culture different from their own. The benefit of employing these strategies enables the preservice teachers to become culturally aware, which will affect their teaching and interactions with diverse families and children.

Personal Life Stories

Analyzing one's background to understand the values and attitudes that are taken to the classroom and realizing that multiple perspectives exist are key components in successfully preparing culturally aware teachers (Adams, Pardo, & Schniedewind, 1993). Furthermore, becoming culturally aware is an important prerequisite to effectively leading others to respect diversity (LoBaugh, 1994). Life stories or cultural biographies of teachers and students are a means to promote self-understanding by examining one's life experiences. When shared with others, these life stories become a vehicle of communication about oneself. Fry & McKinney (1997) suggested that "In addition to reading literature and pursuing traditional means of understanding different cultures, developing life stories asks preservice teachers to examine culture or particular aspects of culture by creating a photographic essay" (p. 5). They concluded that "...personal reactions to essays through different expressive forms become powerful and effective. These forms may include journals, poetry, editorials, and drama" (p. 5). After asking the preservice teachers to develop a personal life story, Fry & McKinney interviewed preservice teachers. The interview emphasized (1) understanding culture from an individual or family viewpoint and (2) communicating with people from different cultures. Preservice teachers were asked to interview a person or family who was culturally different from them. Some chose to interview individuals who were ethnically different, whereas some chose other cultural aspects, for example, a wealthy, socialite mother was interviewed by a student who grew up in an impoverished family. The preservice teachers were asked to compare and contrast their culture with the interviewees. This experience proved to be enlightening and beneficial to preservice teachers. It helped them look inwardly and outwardly and compare their experiences to a differ culture. This might be an exercise that you might want to engage in. With all of what has happened in our country since September 11, 2001, it would be wise for all of us to get to know more about cultures that differ from our own.

Cultural Self-Analysis

While Fry & McKinney (1997) required preservice teachers to create personal life stories, Schmidt (1998) required her preservice teachers to construct a cultural self-analysis. Schmidt (1998) created a model to help present and future teachers become culturally sensitive so that they might begin to think about ways to communicate and connect with students and families from minority populations. The model is known as the *ABCs of Cultural Understanding and Communication*. Through literacy activities that included writing autobiographies, interviewing, and discovering the life stories of people from other cultures and performing cross-cultural analyses, present and future teachers studied differences and planned strategies for home/school communication. The following is a brief explanation of the ABCs model and its assignments: (1) Autobiography is written in detail, including key life events related to education, family, religious tradition, recreation, victories, and defeats. (2) Biography of a person culturally different is written from in-depth unstructured interviews that include key life events. (3) Cross-cultural analyses of similarities and differences related to the life stories are listed in chart format. (4) Cultural analyses of differences are examined with explanations of personal discomfort and admiration. (5) Communication plans for literacy development and home/school connections are designed with modifications for classroom adaptation (p. 28). Schmidt's course also included discussions of *Affirming Diversity: The Sociopolitical Context of Multicultural Education* (Nieto, 1996), *Multicultural Literacy: Mirroring the Reality of the Classroom* (Diamond & Moore, 1995), and *Hear My Voice: A Multicultural Anthology of Literature From the United States* (King, 1995). Every other week, guests from the Russian, Chinese, African-American, Latino, Native American, and Indian cultures were invited to tell their personal stories and respond to questions from the class. There were no examinations, but a three-ring binder was required for a record of class notes, thoughts, questions, and concerns to be shared with Schmidt at the end of the semester. Schmidt concluded by noting that:

> The ABCs model may serve as a means for teachers to develop comfort levels and communication when attempting to understand the children and families in their classrooms. Various modifications of autobiographies, interviews, and cultural analyses appear to be useful across the curriculum. Because the ABCs model deals with issues associated with family life, communication, education, religion, work, and socioeconomic status, present and future teachers see ways to connect topics with content areas. Knowing that life stories often focus on these topics may help teachers recognize subjects and literacy activities that could be integrated into the curriculum for culturally relevant pedagogy (p 37).

Cultural self-analysis is a powerful strategy because it first enables preservice teachers to think deeply about their own families, traditions, and so on. Developing an understanding of one's own cultural background is a necessary first step because only then are preservice teachers enabled to make cross-cultural analysis to compare and contrast similarities and differences.

Photos of Local Knowledge Sources

Allen & Labbo (2001) suggested that one way to create teacher education programs that build for culturally engaged teaching is through cultural memoir and photography. The undergraduate students that they teach at the University of Georgia are white, middle-class females; many of them attended schools without much economic or cultural diversity. Finding ways to help their students "see" their own cultures is part of the PhOLKS Project: Photographs of Local Knowledge Sources. Allen & Labbo met regularly with ten teachers to discuss insights about their students' out-of-school lives through the students' photographs and narratives and how they can use information to bridge cultural borderlands. As literacy teacher educators, Allen & Labbo investigated strategies for building a critical, culturally conscious professional community in which prospective educators could explore themselves as cultural beings who are teaching in a multicultural society.

Labbo taught reading methods one semester and then, in the second semester, taught the same group an advanced reading methods course; Allen taught language arts the second semester. Both courses incorporated a four-week, mid-semester practicum in culturally, linguistically, and economically diverse elementary schools. Allen & Labbo collected a variety of data in three phases across the two semesters.

Phase One: Making Culture a Personal Construct

In their writing workshop, the students researched and wrote Cultural Memoirs using existing photographs or taking new ones to document their own cultures and what was important to them at home and in their community. Labbo invited the students in her reading course to select something that they wanted to learn to do, and she asked them to keep reflective journals to find out more about themselves as learners. Students then wrote letters to their parents describing their insights on learning "something new" and on the implications for being able to understand the learning needs of their future students. Developing the cultural memoirs involved the following four steps:

1. Students in the language arts course engaged in a four-week genre study of memoirs during writing workshop, thirty to forty-five minutes of each ninety-minute class. They read and listened to excerpts from published memoirs that were deeply contextualized in time, place, and social issues. The professor read from her own in-process memoir (e.g., discovering at age nine that African-American children in her Texas town went to a separate school and reflecting on her beloved Oklahoma grandpa's patronizing view of Native Americans.

2. Students selected pictures representative of their lives, interviewed family members, and drafted narratives for each picture that were initially generally individualistic (e.g., "I am who I am because of my mother and father.").

The professor prompted them to reflect critically on how they became "cultural beings" by asking, "How did your parents shape you—by example, strict discipline, stories, teaching?" and asking them to situate themselves in particular times, places, and social issues. Students were asked to take additional pictures of taken-for-granted elements of their cultures: private and public schools, different parts of town, places of worship. They could access old newspapers or interview older family members to learn about events and issues such as education, jobs, immigration, civil rights, sexual orientation, and politics.

3. Students shared work in progress in individual conferences, small writing groups, and whole class sessions; dialogue and feedback shaped revision.
4. Students made choices about genre, writing style, and book layout. Some were frustrated by the lack of models and specific requirements; others felt this freed them. Students wrote children's pictures books, alphabet books, and texts that included family stories, letters to significant people in their lives, and poetry (p. 41).

Phase Two: Teaching through New Cultural Lenses

During the practicum, preservice teachers taught language arts through daily read-alouds and writing workshops; they also tutored one child in their class in reading. Children photographed what was important to them at home and in their community after brainstorming possibilities. Families were invited to narrate pictures in a school-home journal. Discussion of the photographs helping the preservice teachers in planning for instruction. The preservice teachers kept daily fieldwork journals with reports on writing and reading instruction, and they wrote case-study reports that included summaries of home-school connections and copies of children's photographic narratives.

Phase Three: Mediating Cultural Constructs

After their four-week field experience, the students discussed their case-study experiences and created a class matrix organized by grade level of their students' reading needs, the instruction they developed to meet those needs, the role the home and school photo process played, and insights about culturally engaged instruction.

The practices that Allen & Labbo explored with their students have the potential to build a self-reflective, culturally conscious community that maintains a balance between comfort in who they are and confrontation of themselves as cultural beings in a multicultural society. They cannot say which experiences affected their students in specific ways; there is no causal trail from activity to insight. It seems to them that, for their students, the elements of reading, discussion, and studying themselves as learners, cultural beings, and teachers all contributed.

PAUSE AND REFLECT

Construct a personal life story like the one Fry & McKinney described. Also, construct you own cultural self-analysis and assist an individual from another culture in understanding and appreciating who you are (see Schmidt, 1998). Further, allow your students to share with you pictures of their families and neighborhoods as a representation of their cultural background, and you, in turn, share with your students pictures of your family, neighborhoods, and so on.

Culturally Relevant Teachers Read about Different Cultures

Culturally relevant teachers read widely about the ethnic, political, and sociocultural backgrounds of the children they teach. However, they understand that personal narratives, fictional accounts, and sociological studies do not provide a complete or generalizable account of the way all people of a particular racial or social group think, behave, or believe. Rather, such teachers read to inform themselves of the multiple ways of seeing the world and the complex factors that influence personal histories. Culturally relevant teachers read to both expose themselves to other perspectives as well as to engage in reflexive examination of their own.

You might be asking yourself, "How does reading about different cultures relate to parent/family involvement?" Reading about different cultures will give you multiple lenses through which you can learn about a culture. Further, reading about different cultures will give you some personal insights and examples of what is important in these cultures, an understanding and appreciation of cultural interaction patterns, how parents interact with their children, how best to involve parents, and what training parents need to support their children's literacy development. More importantly, you will be able to formulate questions to ask members of these cultures when you have the opportunity to have face-to-face encounters with parents and children. Reading will provide you with background information to begin a meaningful conversation. When parents are aware that you have taken the time, energy, and effort to learn more about them, it increases your chances of having a fruitful relationship with these parents and their children. I am sure that most inservice teachers will agree with my last point. Also, I would like to add here that even if your teacher preparation program does not have a class on family involvement, the books suggested by Florio-Ruane and Runer & Roberts are ones that you can read on your own. Also, I encourage you to purchase Florio-Ruane's (2001) book, *Teacher Education and the Cultural Imagination: Autobiography, Conversation, and Narrative* to gain an in-depth understanding of how to participate in a book club. You might want to start a book club with a group of your colleagues.

Autobiographies as Cultural Learning Tools

The work by Florio-Ruane (1994, 2001) has resulted in one promising way teachers can learn how to teach outside their "villages." Florio-Ruane organized a Future Teachers' Autobiography Club, in which "members of the Club read and respond to ethnic autobiographies as a way to learn about literacy, culture, and identity in their own lives and the lives of persons whose backgrounds differ widely from their own" (p. 55). She revealed that the Autobiography Club members could have included men and women of varied races and social backgrounds, but she decided to include only white middle-class females because this group of teachers makes up the largest portion of American elementary teachers. All of the white female volunteers were seniors and did their student teaching in diverse classrooms.

Florio-Ruane chose six autobiographies to be read by the group: *The Road from Coorain, Lost in Translation: A Life in a New Language, I Know Why the Caged Bird Sings, Hunger of Memory, Lives on the Boundary*, and *White Teacher*. Florio-Ruane pointed out that although she convened the book talk meetings and selected the books, her comments in the group were modestly participatory rather than directive or evaluative. She also pointed out that her aim was not to lead a seminar but to encourage Club members to converse freely about the books. As a participant observer, Florio-Ruane wrote field notes after each meeting describing the conversational topics and dynamics of the group. She also audiotaped and transcribed the meeting conversations for closer analysis. Each participant recorded her reactions to the books and discussions in a personal sketchbook, which Florio-Ruane collected monthly and analyzed along with field notes and meeting transcripts. Florio-Ruane justified why she elected to use autobiographies by saying that:

> I chose the autobiographies to be read and discussed by the Future Teachers' Autobiography Club because they view life through the lens of literacy. The authors craft life stories as literature, dramatically recounting the multiple kinds and uses of language into which they were socialized both in and out of school. The narratives permit exploration of identity and power at the group and individual level and provide ways to gauge what is lost and what is gained when, upon entering school, their authors were enjoined not only to acquire new skills and linguistic operations but new perspectives on the world and new social identities (p. 56).

She found that "reading personal narratives of schooling and literacy may prompt preservice teachers to ask important educational questions" (p. 56) and paraphrased the following sample questions based on the work of Ferdman (1991):

(1) How is literacy defined in the individual's group and what is its significance?
(2) What significance do particular texts have for an individual's cultural identity?
(3) How do the particular pedagogical approaches or the texts used for the purposes of literacy in school relate to the learner's motives and sense of identity? (4) What messages does a reading and writing curriculum communicate about the

value of the learner's culture? and (5) What relationship does the learner perceive between the tasks assigned in school and his or her cultural identity? Must the learner change the nature of the self concept in order to do what is asked? (pp. 110–111).

Runer & Roberts (1994), both high school teachers, created an innovative way to not only develop sensitivity to multicultural issues but also a level of personal experience in relation to these issues. They worked to pass this sensitivity on to their students as well. They, like Florio-Ruane, recognized the importance of using multicultural literature and ethnic biographies as learning tools. Runer & Roberts were fortunate enough to be funded for two successful years by the Mellon Foundation to team-teach multicultural education with emphasis on literacy skills at an inner-city Career Academy on Chicago's southwest side. Demographically, their students were primarily Hispanic (seventy percent) and African American (thirty percent). Good portions of their students were on public aid and below grade level. Unfortunately, these situations were not the most damaging. Their students' energy was expended in a day-to-day struggle against gang-bangers and other social ills. In Chapter 3, you read about some of the issues children who live in poverty encounter. Sewell, Ducette, & Shapiro (1991) summarize those concerns about the environment for underclass and even lower-class children in the following commentary:

> The social reality into which children from culturally diverse backgrounds are born must be understood as a significant factor...it is a world in which their lives are battered by poverty, social isolation and often racial and ethnic inequities. It is an environment where crime, drug addiction, pollution and abuse are daily realities. There are urban and rural communities where children attend school physically and psychologically unprepared to learn. There are social conditions in which the nutritional status and health care needs of the children adversely affect academic achievement. It is a grim world far removed from the environment of America's privileged middle and upper class youth. It is a world in which taking and doing well on a standardized test is often irrelevant and sometimes impossible. It is a world in which children attend school environmental conditions, which make learning an insignificant objective, compared with the issues of personal survival (pp. 6–7).

Despite all of the personal challenges their students faced, Runer & Roberts did not ignore these issues and were keenly aware of the communities of poverty and fear in which their students lived. They also recognized that there is a need for the voices of the powerless and oppressed to be recognized and heard. Runer, a junior history teacher, and Roberts, a freshman English teacher, combined their classes for the purposes of studying different cultures. They chose autobiographies because they would provide their Hispanic and African-American students with role models for inspiration. Runer & Roberts felt that books based on exciting and true stories of men and women would be effective because "students, from early childhood, develop a natural interest in good stories and this continues through adulthood" (p. 25). The genre appealed to Runer & Roberts because "autobiographies promote the proper appreciation of diversity while guarding against the dangers of separation and fractionalism because they are written by people from every racial, ethnic, socio-economic, and religious group" (p. 26). Runer & Roberts assigned their students to read *Narrative on the Life of Frederick Douglass*. Runer & Roberts noted that their students "...appreciated the fact that literacy actually made the difference between slavery and liberation for Douglass as it gave him access to worlds never before dreamed of, worlds well beyond the world of his origins" (p. 26). They also assigned students to read *Farewell to Manzanar*, which deals with the shameful treatment of Japanese-Americans during World War II, and *Night*, which deals with the early life of Nobel Peace Prize winner and Holocaust survivor Elie Wiesel. Besides the autobiographies already mentioned, others used in whole, or partially, were *Autobiography of Malcolm X*, by Alex Haley; *Hiroshima*, by John Hersey; and *House on Mango Street*, by Sandra Cisneros. Runer & Roberts observed, "...during the semester we changed some attitudes for the better..." (p. 30). They confirmed "autobiographies, selected carefully and used appropriately, can help open a window to tolerance, cooperation, unity, and lack of fear for things and people that are different" (p. 30).

Learning from Literature: Uses and Cautions

As multicultural literature assisted Florio-Ruane and Runer & Roberts to teach cultural awareness, autobiographies can help preservice and inservice teachers gain insight into the lives and cultures of their future students and families. This point has received strong support in the research community. It has also been well documented that literature provides understanding of cultural narratives (Crawford, 1993; Van Dongen, 1987; Heath, 1982). Van Dongen (1987) stated that the uses and forms of narratives are significantly different from culture to culture. The stories of a culture may be integral to the culture or merely serve as entertainment. Crawford (1993) suggested, "examining the role of narrative in a culture it must be analyzed from its uses in daily routines, traditions, and rituals" (p. 78). She then posed three questions for readers to use as tools in the process of analysis: "What does a culture teach about the value of narrative? Does a culture use narrative for entertainment? What can be learned about the culture from narrative literature?" (p. 78). As an example of such analysis, Crawford recounts Van Dongen's account of Shirley Brice Heath's 1982 study of children from three different cultural groups in the United States:

> ...she depicted the groups as Trackton (working-class African Americans of recent rural origin), Roadville (working-class European Americans of Appalachian origin), and Maintown (middle-class, school-oriented). Narrative form and use differed across the cultural groups. Each used narrative differently. Although Trackton and Roadville people told stories, their structure differed. The Trackton stories were highly creative, fictionalized accounts, while Roadville's were factual with little exaggeration. Maintown's children, on the other hand, had a strong

literate tradition of story through oral reading experiences, story hours, and imag-
inative play (p. 78–79).

In this study, three distinct traditions emerged which help readers of narratives learn to place storytelling techniques into cultural frameworks. When thinking about these different narrative styles, it is important to heed the warnings of
Florio-Ruane about the process of contextualizing narratives. Readers must
remember that these narratives are individualized accounts within particular traditions. Perhaps, as Crawford suggested, such traditions can be regarded as "cultural influences" in a particular individual's development, influences that shape
that person's "narrative competencies." Relating this to children in the classroom
Crawford wrote that "...some children come to school who have been influenced
by stories heard from storybooks, whereas others have developed narrative forms
from stories that involve basic beliefs, traditions, and values of their culture. These
cultural influences need to be noted, valued, and appreciated by the school
because these influences can support literacy and literacy development" (p. 79). A
teacher's understanding of narrative modes and their uses in various communities can help children build bridges from home to classroom. It will also help if
teachers themselves act on Baker's (1983) suggestion that they "...develop a multicultural classroom when they acquire knowledge of culture—ethnic and racial,
religious, and gender differences—supportive of multiculturalism; develop a philosophy that values multicultural education in personal, professional, and community dimensions; and become involved in implementing multicultural
curriculum through the use of appropriate instructional techniques, strategies,
and materials" (p. 66). What Baker suggests is right on target, but some teachers
need on-the-job training to make this happen.

In one case, this on-the-job training has happened through university-school
partnerships, as illustrated by the work of Diamond & Moore (1995), who helped
inservice teachers organize their classroom instruction to mirror the new multicultural reality found in their classrooms. Specifically, they worked with teachers
and students for three years from three culturally diverse school districts—a predominately African-American, economically deprived district; a racially balanced,
economically varied population; and a predominately white, economically sufficient population. Through numerous, regularly scheduled visitations to classrooms, they discovered ways to help teachers acquire a sensitivity to multicultural
literature and ways to integrate multicultural perspectives across the curricula
(see Diamond & Moore, 1995).

The purpose of their program was to implement a multicultural literacy program that would (1) improve the educational achievement of students, particularly culturally diverse students and "at-risk" students, (2) heighten the cultural
awareness of all students, and (3) provide enrichment opportunities for all students. To achieve these goals, teachers and students engaged in practices and
strategies that are briefly highlighted in the following objectives: (1) To provide a
strong alignment between the written text and the cultural background, language,

and experiences of students of diverse cultures, racial groups, and linguistic backgrounds; (2) to heighten reading comprehension, writing quality, and vocabulary of elementary students; (3) to develop understanding and appreciation of one's own culture and the culture of others; and (4) to develop positive attitudes toward reading and writing (pp. 9–10). These objectives, which incorporated multiple ways of knowing and learning, were used to guide Diamond & Moore in developing their multicultural program.

Diamond & Moore's definition of multicultural literacy emerged from theoretical principles about culture, literacy, and learning. These principles, which laid the foundation for a multicultural literacy program, further evolved from their personal and cultural experiences, reading, and experiences while working with teachers and students from diverse settings. These principles are as follows: (1) Multicultural literacy is beneficial and fundamental for *all* students, not just students of diverse cultural and linguistic backgrounds. (2) Schools and teachers must embrace the cultural diversity of students and affirm the cultural beliefs, views, and personal experiences they bring to the classroom. (3) Teachers' positive attitudes and expectations of how students will perform in school have a marked effect on students' ability to achieve success. (4) Teachers must empower students as individuals and learners so that they receive validation for who they are. (5) Students' learning is enhanced when they can connect their personal cultural experiences with what they read and write. (6) Students learn best when they take an *active* role in the acquisition of knowledge and skills. (7) Students' learning is enhanced when they are encouraged to cooperate and collaborate, sharing and exchanging ideas, concepts, and understandings with others in the construction of knowledge (pp. 6–7).

These principles guided Diamond & Moore in the formation of their definition of multicultural literacy. Specifically:

> Multicultural literacy is the process of linking the cultural experiences, histories, and language that all children bring to school *with* language learning and academic learning that take place in the school. Multicultural literacy further activates silent voices, opens closed minds, promotes academic achievement, and enables students to think and act critically in a pluralistic, democratic society (p. 7).

PAUSE AND REFLECT

Obviously, reading about cultures different from your own can be very rewarding. If you are a preservice teacher, you should solicit the cooperation of a small group of your peers and organize a book club so that you can read about and share your thoughts regarding the diverse children in today's classrooms. If you are an inservice teacher, you should obtain on-the-job training by participating in university-school partnerships, like the one developed by Diamond & Moore (1995).

Culturally Relevant Teachers Can Learn about Families and Children from Early Field Experiences

The courses, which appear to have an impact on teacher thinking about cultural and ethnic differences, usually include field experiences related to minority cultures. Exposure to people and places seems to increase knowledge through first-hand experiences (Cochran-Smith & Lytle, 1992; Noordhoff & Kleinfeld, 1993). More specifically, recent research indicates that field experiences in culturally diverse settings may be a key component to effect preservice teachers' attitudinal and pedagogical change, necessary factors to achieve equity in school and society (Pine & Hilliard, 1990). Cooper, Beare, & Thorman (1990) concluded that as a result of cross-cultural teaching experiences combined with discussion, preservice teachers were more likely to develop culturally relevant teaching practices, an important prerequisite for minority children's success in schools (Ladson-Billings, 1993). Similarly, Pattnaik & Vold (1994) found that through assisted reflection, student teachers in an urban setting were more effective in recognizing consistencies and inconsistencies, in the cultural relevance of their teaching practices, when compared with their counterparts at other school settings. Once preservice teachers recognize the importance of culturally relevant teaching, they seek strategies to help them teach more effectively (LoBaugh, 1994).

Below are some examples of the types of field experiences teacher educators have developed for preservice teachers. They are ones that you can learn a great deal from. You might be saying to yourself, I wish we had "field experiences" like the ones described in these examples at my institution. Well, if these "field experiences" are not currently being offered by your institution, might be able to suggest that your institution consider including these "field experiences" as part of your undergraduate program. Oftentimes, institutions invite their currently enrolled and recently graduated students to make suggestions or give feedback on how to improve their teacher preparation program. Consequently, it gives you the opportunity to suggest that the field-based experiences proposed by Fry & McKinney (1997) and Jones & Blendinger (1994) be considered by your teacher preparation program. In the event that you are not able to do this, once you begin your teaching career, you might have the opportunity to become involved in a series of workshops on home-school relationships similar to the ones offered by Brand (1996).

Field-Based Language Arts Methods Course

One effort to make a field-based experience an integral part of preservice teachers' programs was created by Fry & McKinney (1997). They developed a field-based experience for elementary majors who were enrolled in a language arts methods course, taken one or two semesters before student teaching. Students in the language arts methods class met at the campus for the first eight class sessions, followed by a series of four meetings at a local elementary school. During the first eight weeks of the course, content focused on three interrelated components: *language arts, a multicultural context for teaching,* and *action research.* In addition to other topics in language arts, the instructor introduced each of the upcoming field experience assignments: (1) a classroom observation focusing on children's literacy development, (2) teaching a book discussion, (3) teaching a writing experience, (4) teaching a poetry experience. The students also maintained a dialogue journal with the instructor throughout the semester, and initial entries to this journal described their cultural backgrounds, attitudes toward diversity, and expectations for the teaching experience at the local elementary school. These entries were discussed and served as an introduction to issues in teaching language arts in a diverse society and, most importantly, served as a vehicle for students to confront preconceptions and cultural attitudes. Some students did share some aspects of their personal biography in journals, which they chose not to talk about with the class as a whole.

The third component of the course, action research, was presented as a form of reflective teaching. By asking the students to carefully study, plan, and reflect, they engaged in action research, an inquiry approach to understanding and improving teaching (Fueyo & Nueves, 1994). In this process, teachers became more responsive to students as a way to understand cultural diversity (Cochran-Smith & Lytle, 1992). The class members collaboratively outlined lessons for the upcoming field experiences. The plans were deliberately left open to adjustment so that the instructor could observe how the preservice teachers adapted, if at all, to the culture of the classroom. Students had the choice to work individually or with another person. The class visited the elementary school as a group, riding in a university van driven by the instructor. This allowed immediate, candid information related to the preservice teachers' perceptions of the field experiences and helped establish the sense of a cohort group regarding effective cross-cultural teacher preparation. The instructor observed each preservice teacher working with children. On several occasions, the instructor team-taught with students from a methods class. Each student submitted a description of their observation or teaching experience and a one-page reflection for each class assignment.

Taken together, the three components Fry & McKinney provided their preservice teachers with important ways to think about, discuss, and have experiences that will develop preservice teachers' ability to work with diverse people. Fry & McKinney's cohort of preservice teachers were fortunate to begin developing themselves as culturally relevant teachers while still in their preservice programs. Interacting with families could enhance programs such as theirs.

Incorporating Parent Involvement in Field-Based Assignments

Jones & Blendinger (1994) revealed that "strategies for reaching out to families are an integral part of the student teaching experience at Mississippi State University" (p. 81). They further revealed that: "Incorporating parent involvement instruction and field-based assignments as part of the student teaching experience helps student teachers gain practical experience in learning multiple ways to communicate and work with families" (p. 85).

The Mississippi State University students participated in intensive, guided experiences in parent involvement during their student teaching semester. According to Jones & Blendinger (1994), "specific objectives for the student teachers are to develop knowledge and skills that will enable them to (1) work with diverse families, (2) develop and implement activities for communicating with families, (3) create and carry out an at-home reading project, (4) conduct parent-teacher conferences, and (5) become aware of the wide range of activities used by teachers and schools to involve parents (p. 81). To achieve the first objective Jones & Blendinger described an activity designed to increase student teachers' awareness of family diversity. They stated "newly placed students are asked to draw a picture of the family they were raised in as a child using stick figures to represent family members. Next they are asked to draw what they believe to be an 'ideal' family. The students are divided into small groups and given the opportunity to discuss with others the similarities and differences of their two pictures" (p. 81). Jones & Blendinger reported that the students spent time exploring the ideal and the variations on the reality for many families today. This kind of interactive, practical, reality-based activity permeated the pedagogy and assignments in their parent involvement–learning project at Mississippi State University.

PAUSE AND REFLECT

Take a few moments and draw a picture of the family in which you were raised in as a child. Then draw a picture of what you believe to be an "ideal" family. With a peer, mentor teacher, or university professor, discuss your "ideal" and the variations on the reality for many families today.

Jones & Blendinger went on to describe the innovative ways in which these student teachers are charged to meet the program's learning objectives. They explained that:

After student teachers have developed an understanding of family diversity, they are expected to attend two additional sessions on parent involvement and complete two assignments during student teaching in order to gain practical experience in working with parents. The first session features a presentation by a principal from a local school district whose school has received widespread recognition for its parent involvement program (p. 82).

Other highlights of the program included a requirement that the student teachers develop an actual plan for parent involvement, that they implement a month-long project designed to motivate students to read outside of school and involve parents in their children's reading development, and that they participate in role-playing parent-teacher conferences. And, of course, students are encouraged to further their learning through participating in activities outside the class-room such as attending parent-teacher association (PTA) meetings, interviewing school staff, and going with teachers on home visits. These hands-on, experiential projects are proving to be effective. As Jones & Blendinger concluded:

> Feedback from the student teachers indicates they considered the parent involve-ment project a useful experience in learning how to reach out to all types of fami-lies. Student teachers felt better prepared to work with parents in their first teaching job. Almost all of the student teachers placed in culturally diverse class-rooms expressed a greater commitment to involving parents in their children's education (p. 85).

If you would like more detailed information on the particulars of the assign-ments the Mississippi State student teachers completed, do look into Jones & Blendinger's article.

Project Interconnecting Teachers, Children, and Homes (PITCH)

The PITCH program developed by Brand (1996) offered a set of inservice work-shops aimed at helping elementary and preschool teachers and administrators improve home-school relationships. The project emphasized developing and expanding classroom programs that promote literacy development. The Univer-sity of California Graduate School of Education, the Berkeley Unified School Dis-trict, and the Berkeley Public Education Foundation supported the workshops. Sixteen teachers from various schools were chosen to be a part of the project and received a small stipend for attending the workshops. They met monthly for five full-day Saturday sessions throughout one school semester.

During the sessions, teachers evaluated their individual school goals in rela-tion to home-school connections. Goals were set and teachers shared ideas about how to reach the goals, which included sending surveys home to parents. The idea was for teachers to compose their own strategies, instead of mandating methods in which to use them. This allowed the teachers to become the experts in their individual circumstances. The results of the survey helped the teachers begin the journey to improve home-school collaboration. They learned that parents often felt in the dark about the daily routine in school. Because of this, many teachers implemented a weekly newsletter to educate parents about the experiences that children have in school. Teachers also learned that parents who volunteer in the classroom wanted to have a better understanding of the connection between their activities and the curriculum. Parents wanted to be more authentically connected to the activities of the school day, which is parallel to the teachers' goals. The feed-back from parents facilitated the development of materials teachers could use to foster participation from parents. They also realized that having parents in the classroom was more valuable than they had expected, once a dialogue was started. Parents began to feel that they made valuable contributions to the educa-tion of their children.

PITCH was successful in making parental involvement meaningful for students, parents, and teachers by having teachers be the catalyst to developing and using strategies to create rewarding relationships. For this relationship to continue to grow, schools must maintain the momentum by providing research, time and encouragement to teachers.

PAUSE AND REFLECT

Jones & Blendinger provided their student teachers with numerous opportunities to interact with diverse families (i.e., at-home reading projects, parent-teacher conferences, etc.). If you are a preservice teacher, and if you don't have the opportunity to create and carry out an at-home reading project, at least go to a local elementary school and observe what occurs in parent-teacher conferences. If you are an inservice teacher and you have preservice teachers observing in your classroom, I encourage you to allow them to observe your interactions with parents during parent-teacher conferences. A few days after you have completed your conference have a debriefing session with the preservice teachers and answer questions they may have about what they observed.

Culturally Relevant Teachers Collect Data to Increase Their Knowledge about Families and Children

Collecting data provides the opportunity for preservice teachers to gain valuable insights into the values, beliefs, attitudes, and dispositions of families and children. As model programs for ways to improve preservice teachers' skills and expertise, the examples by French (1996) and Edwards et al. (1999) are excellent. The French examples allow preservice teachers to construct their own story about the family they visited. The Edwards (et al.) example provides the opportunity for families to tell their own self-reported stories about their home literacy environment. More importantly, these two examples provide preservice teachers with actual hands-on experiences with cultural pluralism.

Developing Family Stories

French (1996) described the Special Education Teacher Preparation Program at the University of Colorado at Denver and developed a course in which families in the community are the contexts for student research and study of family and parent issues. Students take the course in conjunction with another course on collaboration skills. The collaboration course emphasizes knowledge of problem solving and conflict management processes and communication skill development. The Collaboration with Families Lab emphasizes the dispositions, values, beliefs, and attitudes that permit application of skills to work with parents and families. Monies from a small teaching enhancement grant allowed French to employ the services of a parent coordinator who had worked as an involved parent of a child with disabilities in her local community and on the state level. Through her efforts, French was able to tap the resources of several existing parent support networks. The parent coordinator set up a focus group to obtain advice from ten parents regarding the kinds of knowledge, skills, and dispositions they believed vital to effective home-school relationships. The group resembled the larger community in racial, linguistic, socioeconomic, and cultural features. French asked the group of parents to think about the best teachers they had known and identify the knowledge, skills, and dispositions that those teachers possessed that enabled them to work well with parents and families. After they completed the lists, French drafted an initial syllabus for subsequent curriculum committee review and approval. She asked the focus group members to edit the draft and to add other thoughts. The advice of the focus group regarding the relationship of school professionals and families resulted in two overarching goals for the lab component of the course "…school professionals will have firsthand knowledge of families other than their own…School professionals will gain the knowledge, skills, and attitudes they need by participating actively in a family—the family serves as the laboratory for their study" (p. 336).

French taught the course for the first time during the fall 1994 semester. The content of the course initially consisted of forty-five hours of work with the parents, family, and student. In the syllabus, French directed students to select from the following list of possible activities and negotiate approval for others not on the list:

> …respite care, special family times (quinceaneras, bar or bat mitzvahs, birthdays), running errands with parents, child, and/or other family members, attend therapy, doctor appointments, hospital visits, meet/interview extended family, shadow students at school for a day, interview teachers, other service providers, take pictures, videos of the child and family, attend Individual Educational Planning (IEP), Individual Family Service Planning (IFSP), and/or Transition Planning meetings with parents/family, attend parent/family support meetings (e.g., advocacy group meetings, Metro Parents Encouraging Parents [PEP]), attend and/or participate in after-school or extracurricular activities with child/parent/family (e.g., Boy Scouts, athletic activities, swim lessons), attend state conferences with family/parents (e.g., PEP, Roundhouse, Inclusion, Crossroads), locate, visit, interview people in adult service agencies connected with the family, brainstorm together with family about upcoming transitions or personal futures planning (pp. 336–337).

The final product generated from the students' research was a Family Story. The focus group members saw little use for readings, library research, or background information. The parents believed that students could learn all they needed to know by participating in the family. On the other hand, French pointed out that the university has the tradition of using the scholarship of others to develop the knowledge of students. Consequently, when French developed the final course syllabus, she included a text, a set of required readings, and brief writing assignments. She selected Harry's *Cultural Diversity, Families, and the Special Education System* (1992) as a text because it described case-study research she had conducted with twelve families whose children were served by special education programs. French used a modified version of Harry's method of interaction with families as the model for students' own work in families.

The brief writing assignments consisted of a series of one-pagers that focused on a single incident, event, or circumstance and extracted from that situation a realization or significant learning that was reflected in their reading in some way. The one-pagers became data sources for the final project. The syllabus directed students to tell the story of a student and his/her parents and family in a Family Story, but suggested that there were many possible ways to do so. Among the suggestions were a slide-tape show, an edited video, an annotated photo album, and of course, a written paper. The criteria stated in the syllabus for the final project were:

> Clearly depict the family values and systems; engage in at least five different types of activities selected from the list or negotiated with the instructor and document the times and hours spent with the family; analyze how their own communication and interpersonal skills facilitated or hindered the relationship that actually developed with the family; analyze the relationship between the family and educational system—what it is like, why it is like it is, what contributing/inhibiting factors exist; identify the types of expertise and experience that the particular family and parents bring to the parent/professional relationship (p. 337).

The underlying assumption for the course was that spending time with parents and families outside of schools, having meaningful conversations, sharing the culture of the family, and reflecting on those experiences in light of the scholarly work of others would create in students the kinds of dispositions French intended. There were no examinations or other means of student evaluation included in the course. In the fall of 1995, French offered the course again. She made several changes in the course as a result of her initial findings. She increased the class contact time to 10 contact hours and decreased the family contact time to 30–35 hours. She emphasized debriefing and discussion of students' experiences in the context of the readings during class meetings, and French added a peer review feature for their Family Stories. French believed that the first group of students needed greater reassurance about their feelings of insecurity and their anxiety about venturing into the lives of families. The additional class time gave her the opportunity to facilitate the reflections of the second group and to guide their emerging senses of professional behavior with regard to their relationships with parents and family.

Collecting Parent Stories of Early Literacy

In our book, *A Path to Follow: Learning to Listen to Parents*, I, along with Pleasants and Franklin, suggest that collecting parent literacy stories is an excellent vehicle for helping teachers gain a better understanding of families and children and the literacy environments in which they live. This is a book that I would highly recommend you purchase. The book clearly outlines how to collect, analyze, and react to the parent stories that you collect. We defined parent stories as narratives gained from open-ended interviews. In these interviews, parents responded to questions designed to provide information about traditional and nontraditional early literacy activities and experiences that have happened in the home. We further defined parent stories through their ability to construct home literacy environments. Some examples of the questions used to collect parent stories are as follows:

- What do you and your child enjoy doing together?
- All children have potential. Did you notice that _____ had some particular talent or "gift" early on? If so, what was it? What did your child do to make you think that he/she had this potential? Were there specific things you did as a parent to strengthen this talent?
- Is there something about your child that might not be obvious to the teacher, but might positively or negatively affect his/her performance in school if the teacher knew? If so, what would that something be?
- What activities/ hobbies do you participate in as an individual? With your spouse or friends? As a family?
- Can you describe "something" about your home learning environment that you would like the school to build upon because you feel that this "something" would enhance your child's learning potential at school?

By using stories as a way to express the nature of the home environment, parents can select anecdotes and personal observations from their own individual consciousness to give teachers access to complicated social, emotional, and educational issues that can help unravel for teachers the mysteries around their students' early literacy beginnings. Still further, we pointed out that many parents have vivid memories about:

- The kinds of routines they did with their children
- Specific interactions they had with their children; observations of their children's beginning learning efforts
- Ways in which their children learned simply by watching them
- Perceptions as to whether their occupation determined how they raised their children
- Descriptions of "teachable moments" they had with their children
- Descriptions of things about their children that may not be obvious to the teacher but would help their children's performance if the teacher knew about them.

Additionally, many parents have scrapbooks, audiocassettes, videotapes, photographs, or other artifacts to share their children's literacy history.

Parent stories can provide teachers with the opportunity to gain a deeper understanding of the "human side" of families and children (i.e., why children behave as they do, children's ways of learning and communicating, problems parents have encountered and how these problems may have impacted their children's views about school and the schooling process). On a final note, we suggested that because teachers' evaluations of students are sometimes based on quick observations, they frequently fail to take into account the experiences that students have brought with them to school. Teachers are thus lacking vital information, which can help them better understand and teach their students. Parents can fill in some of the missing pieces by providing stories about their child's early learning experiences at home. Three examples of parent stories of early literacy can be found at the Web site that accompanies this book.

Summary

With the increasing diversity among children in public school classrooms, family involvement in teacher preparation is no longer optional. Preservice teachers must learn to familiarize themselves with cultures different from those of the children they will serve. I have discussed several programs and strategies that will assist preservice teachers to be effectively prepared for culturally relevant teaching. Such strategies include reading narratives about diverse cultures and developing family involvement components into teacher education methods courses. In addition, community-based programs will help preservice teachers to learn more about the families and communities of the children they serve. All of these strategies and programs will increase the likelihood of establishing a positive rapport and a close working relationship with families.

Chapter 4 Key Concepts _____

- The autobiographical work of Susan Florio-Ruane offers important insights for teacher candidates as well as inservice teachers. Her work highlights the importance of reading about different cultures in order to learn more about them.
- Multicultural literature and ethnic autobiographies can be learning tools for developing sensitivity to multicultural issues.
- Narratives in a culture must be analyzed from its uses in daily routines, traditions, and rituals.
- Preservice teachers need to be knowledgeable about the importance of parent involvement because studies show that when parents are involved in their children's education, the children are more successful.
- There are many avenues available to preservice teachers to understand how to work with diverse families and children (e.g., early field experiences, discussion, dialogues journals, assisted reflections, cross-cultural interactions, films and videotapes, guest speakers, visits to community agencies, and so on).

- Life stories or cultural biographies of teachers and students are a means to promote self-understanding by examining one's life experiences. When shared with others, these life stories become a vehicle of communicating about oneself.
- Cultural self-analysis provides preservice teachers with the opportunity to write their autobiography and compare and contrast it with the life story of an individual from another culture to assist them in understanding and appreciating cultural differences.
- Collecting parent literacy stories is an excellent vehicle for helping teachers gain a better understanding of families and children and the literacy environment in which they live.
- Preservice teachers need to have actual hands-on experiences with cultural pluralism before their entry into real classrooms.

Suggestions for Thought Questions and Activities

1. Organize a group of four or five students. Working in a group will allow you to survey more educators. Each group member should ask two or three professors, principals, or teachers to recommend a teacher whom they consider to practice "culturally relevant teaching." Ask the recommender to provide at least two examples concerning what they have witnessed the teacher doing.
2. Combine the list of teachers and examples. Do certain practices occur more often than others on the list? Categorize the examples to understand specific practices that are considered "culturally relevant."
3. Ask each group member to vote for the teacher whom they consider to have the "best practices" strictly based on the list of teachers and examples. Choose two teachers and call them. Explain the previous activities and explain that you want to schedule a time for the group to visit his/her class to witness "culturally relevant teaching in action."
4. During the visit look for specific examples of "culturally relevant teaching." If possible, take notes, briefly indicating what you see and hear. Also discuss your initial response to the teacher's actions. Type your notes, categorizing the actions and your responses.
5. Reconvene as a group to compare notes and discuss your visit. As a group, are certain practices more frequently noticed than others? Combine your information and make copies for all group members.

Internet Activities

- Search an online bookstore such as Amazon or Barnes & Noble for autobiographies. Look for an ethnic autobiography that interests you.

For Further Study

Diamond, B. J., & Moore, M. A. (1995). *Multicultural literacy: Mirroring the reality of the classroom.* White Plains, NY: Longman.

This pioneering text offers an invaluable discussion of the theoretical and practical issues surrounding the development of literacy in multicultural K–8 classrooms.

Edwards, P. A., with Pleasants, H. M. & Franklin, S. (1999). *A path to follow: Learning to listen to parents*. Portsmouth, NH: Heinemann.

The diverse and difficult needs of today's children far outstrip the ability of any one institution to meet them. Yet one of the richest resources for understanding a child's early learning experiences—parents—it quite often the most frequently overlooked. *A Path to Follow* suggests that parent "stories" can be a highly effective, collaborative tool for accessing knowledge that may not be obvious, but would obviously be of benefit.

Florio-Ruane, S. (2001). *Teacher education and the cultural imagination: Autobiography, conversation, and narrative*. Mahwah, NJ: Lawrence Erlbaum Associates, Publishers.

Making culture a more central concept in the texts and contexts of teacher education is the focus of this book. It is a rich account of the author's investigation of teacher book club discussions of ethnic literature, specifically ethnic autobiography—as a genre from which teachers might learn about culture, literacy, and education in their own and others' lives, and as a form of conversation and literature-based work that might be sustainable and foster teachers' comprehension and critical thinking.

Gay, G. (2000). *Culturally responsive teaching: Theory, research, & practice*. New York: Teachers College Press.

Geneva Gay makes a convincing case for using culturally responsive teaching to improve the school performance of underachieving students of color. She combines insights from multicultural education theory, research, and classroom practice to demonstrate that African, Asian, Latino, and Native American students will perform better, on multiple measures of achievement, when teaching is filtered through their own cultural experiences and frames of reference.

Kyle, D. W., McIntyre, E., Miller, K. B., & Moore, G. H. (2002). *Reaching out: a K–8 resource for connecting families with schools*. Thousand Oaks, CA: Corwin Press, Inc.

Reaching Out is an invaluable resource for compassionate educators interested in building strong relationships with their students' families. A dynamic team of teachers and teacher educators have combined their first-hand experience and in-depth research in this essential guidebook. By involving the entire family in the educational experience, teachers can bridge the gap separating home and school and help produce happier, healthier, and smarter kids.

Ladson-Billings, G. (1994). *The dreamkeepers: Successful teachers of African American children*. San Francisco: Jossey-Bass Publishers.

In *The Dreamkeepers*, Gloria Ladson-Billings explores the positive signs for the future. Who are the successful teachers of African-American students? What do they do? And how can we learn from them? Her portraits of eight exemplary teachers who differ in personal style and methods but share an approach to teaching that affirms and strengthens cultural identify are inspiring and full of hope.

5

Improving Two-Way Communication
Valuable Directions

Chapter Goals for the Reader

- To explore affordances and constraints of traditional "institutionalized" methods for interacting with parents (e.g., parent-teacher conferences, newsletters, parent-teacher organizations, and so on)
- To become familiar with "outside-the-box" techniques of recruiting and communicating with families (e.g., bar owners, ministerial alliance, people sitting on the street corner, and so on)
- To become familiar with the process of recruiting community leaders to support your school's program
- To identify ways to develop supportive networks in a large metropolitan area
- To explore some of the issues of working with bilingual families and families with special needs children

Chapter Outline

Overview Comments

Traditional Approaches

Nontraditional Approaches

Working with Special Needs Families
    Public Law 94-142

How to Recruit Parents and Solicit
Community Support

Networking in a Large Metropolitan Area

When to Recruit Community Leaders

Strategies for Identifying and Recruiting
Community Leaders

Chapter Overview _____

In the first section, I argue that schools must rethink what they want and expect from children, families, and communities. I then outline what schools should consider when planning the best environment for parents.

In the second section, I make the case that most parents are recruited by one-way and two-way forms of communication. In the third section, I discuss nontraditional approaches for recruiting and communicating with families, ways of working with special needs families, understanding of Public Law 94-142, ways to recruit parents and solicit community support, how to network in a large metropolitan area, when to recruit community leaders, and strategies for identifying and recruiting community leaders.

Introductory Scenario:
"Parents won't come to the school,
at least not the parents who need to come" _____

How many times have you heard teachers make the above statement? Well, I have heard teachers say this a thousand times. In the Introduction, I told you that I organized the *Parents as Partners in Reading Program* at Donaldsonville Elementary School (DES) located in Donaldsonville, Louisiana, a small, rural southern community. Hear I will share with you some background information on what occurred at Donaldsonville Elementary School especially as it relates to communicating and recruiting parents to participate in the book-reading program I developed. In addition to showing the parents how to participate in book-reading interactions with their children, one of the biggest challenges I faced was inviting to school these parents who in many ways felt uninvited.

When I asked the DES teachers the following questions, their answers provided me with more insight into why some of the parents might have felt uninvited: "What if the parents' literacy levels are too low to assist their children with homework assignments? What if families don't want to help their children or don't even want to walk into a school? What if they didn't like school when they were students? How do parents' literacies and families' own experiences as students in school contribute to or detract from their involvement in their children's learning?"

Clearly, school staffs must communicate to parents that they are welcome and wanted in the school. I think that the staff at DES really did want parents to come to school, but somehow the parents did not feel truly invited, so they didn't come. Consequently, the DES staff sought my assistance in helping them find ways to invite families to the school and provide them with skills to support their children's literacy learning.

During the spring of 1987, the Special Plan Upgrading Reading (SPUR) technical assistant for Ascension Parish Schools contacted me after reading a chapter that I was preparing for a book (see Edwards, 1989). This chapter highlighted the point that teachers should shift from *telling* to *showing* parents how to share books with their children. The technical assistant felt that the Donaldsonville parents needed assistance in how to share books with their children. She came to this conclusion because many of the DES children entered school with little or no knowledge of how to participate in book-reading interactions. This finding led the technical assistant to suggest that I develop a book-reading program at DES. She arranged a meeting with the principal and assistant principal of DES. The technical assistant's interest in my research stemmed from the fact that the principal, the assistant principal, and the teachers at DES had asked her to help them look for ways to increase the amount of parental involvement at DES.

The technical assistant described the racial tensions in the school, tensions between the predominately white faculty and the predominately black parent and student populations. The staff, sensing that the teaching professional was slowly turning white and the student population rapidly turning nonwhite, were extremely interested in opening lines of communication with the parents of the children they were serving. The technical assistant, a white female, felt that I, as an African-American educator, could bridge the gap among parents, teachers, and administrators.

What really convinced me to conduct the book-reading project at DES, however, was the commitment of the principal and assistant principal to the project. The principal expressed their support when I first met with her. In our conversation, she explained that she had been an educator for 37 years, including being a home economics teacher. This gave her, she said, a good understanding of child growth and development. She went on to say, "I am now encountering third-generation students—that is, I taught the grandparent, the parent, and now [the] grandchildren." She further explained that the area had changed greatly from the farming community of the 1950s to the chemical plants of today, resulting in job loss and unemployment. "Now, Donaldsonville," she said, "has two federally subsidized housing projects and several apartment complexes that are federally subsidized." Added to the economic problems was the fact that there was a high teen pregnancy rate, and many parents were illiterate or semi-literate. She said they had tried to make a difference, but a more structured approach was needed. She stated:

> I know the feeling of longing for the better things life has to offer. As a Depression baby of unemployed parents, I can relate to being hungry, being cold, and being rejected by peers from affluent circumstances. I have walked a mile to the grocery store because we did not have a car. I know that to rise from unfortunate circumstances, one must possess an education. No matter how hard one has to struggle and sacrifice, the price is small compared with the benefits of having that education.

She stated emphatically that she knew the parents wanted their children to succeed in school and they themselves were key to their children's success. She felt that her effort to unite home, school, and neighborhood would benefit considerably from my book-reading program. She concluded:

> Please agree to help us. The teachers feel that because many of our parents are illiterate they cannot help their children. The book-reading program you have described is exactly what we need (see Chapter 2 for fuller description of the book-reading program I developed).

I accepted the principal and assistant principal's offer to implement the book-reading program at DES. However, what I heard repeatedly from the staff was that the "parents won't come to the school, at least not the parents who need to come." You heard the principal admitting earlier that a large number of the parents at DES were illiterate or semi-literate. Yet, she and the staff at DES constantly sent out fliers to invite parents to come to school functions. France & Meeks (1987) have noted that unfortunately, "Function-ally illiterate and illiterate parents have been largely ignored by the schools, which go on sending home notices, report cards, homework assignments, information packets, survey forms, and permission slips as though they believe every parent can read and write" (p. 227). Their suggestion: "When there are indications that parents are failing to respond to parent involvement programs because of literacy problems, teachers should take time to call and arrange conferences during which they can describe some of the ways in which academic success can be fostered outside of direct instruction" (p. 226). Schools should therefore move from simply sending messages home to parents requesting their assistance to organizing programs to improve their skills so that they can provide the requested assis-tance. Henry Otto (1969) noted that:

> Communication is the key to building understanding, trust and mutual helpfulness between teachers and pupils, teachers and parents, teachers and principals, parents and pupils, and supervisors and their contacts with all who have an intimate relationship to a given school. Unless we can communicate with mutual understanding we remain strangers or nodding acquaintances at best. But to say that communication is the key doesn't tell much. We must know, understand, and practice the ins and outs of *effective* communication (p. 1).

Chapter 5 focuses on traditional "institutionalized" methods (e.g., parent-teacher con-ferences, newsletters, and parent-teacher organizations), as well as "outside-the-box" tech-niques of recruiting and communicating with families (e.g., bar owners, ministerial alliance, people sitting on the street corner, and so on). This chapter also addresses issues of commu-nicating and working with bilingual and families of special needs children and ways to make use of school resources that maximize the strengths and learning opportunities of both the home and community, as well as the classroom.

Overview Comments

Family-school involvement is a two-way street (Edwards & Young, 1992), and school professionals have to rethink what they want for children and what they expect from families and communities. Where should schools draw the line? Are schools the new and primary place where the interwoven needs of children are to be met (Edwards & Young, 1992)? Schools must do more than encourage parent and family involvement within a classroom that is often isolated from the broader context of the family itself. School must do more than become referral sources for other community agencies and service providers. Schools, in fact, are becoming the hub of a multiple-service brokerage for children and their families.

Several efforts currently under way are redefining the relationships of school, family, and community. School professionals are forging new alliances and partnerships with community organizations and agencies. Schools are expanding their definitions of "family" to include single parents, working parents, foster parents, grandparents, and others who have significant responsibilities for children. They are challenging the separateness of systems designed to support children and their families (Edwards & Young, 1992).

Once again, we call on the ecosystem model (Bronfenbrenner, 1979) to help in understanding the need for interrelationships for children and their families. School professionals are becoming more creative at developing styles and strategies that acknowledge this important interrelationship of the social context and the individual. Moving to broader notions of community alliances means moving beyond incremental thinking or assessing the needs of parents, teachers, and communities (Springate & Steglin, 1999). Edwards & Young (1992) make the following recommendations regarding the role of the school in establishing an environment conducive to child and family advocacy:

- Home/school strategies should be founded on the strengths of the families and their understanding of their own children.
- Efforts should be organized around preventive strategies. Therefore, school personnel must understand the children and families they serve, especially their social, personal, economic, and psychological stressors.
- Schools need to explore multiple models for reaching out to families and providing avenues to them for organizing and advocating for their needs.
- The school should view itself as an integral part of an ecosystem that supports the family, and the school should be able to refer families readily to needed resources within the community.
- Understanding the complexity of families and the new strategies needed for teachers and schools to reach out to them should become an integral part of teacher preparation programs (p. 100).

These recommendations require a drastic re-examination of the role of the teacher and the way in which she fulfills her academic responsibilities for children's learning. These suggestions require new roles for the teacher and new ways of thinking about achieving educational success for all students. In Chapter 4, you were introduced to some of the innovative strategies that teacher educators have employed to help preservice teachers learn how to work with families to begin to meet the goals discussed above. The progress some teacher educators have made is encouraging. However, by and large, teacher preparation programs do little to address the tendency for teachers to stay within the class, with doors closed, and wait passively for parents to seek to participate.

Just as young children thrive best under optimal conditions, parents are likely to do their best in an environment planned to meet their needs. Croft (1979) listed some considerations you should closely examine. They include:

- A *special place* where parents can meet or chat, such as a conference room, a coffee corner, a space set aside for the specific purpose of allowing parents to congregate. It should be easily accessible to the children's classroom.

- *Bulletin boards* where parents can readily see notices that are of interest. These might include up-to-date information about school regulations, announcements of parent meetings and workshops, daily center activities, reports on school meetings and policies, and information about educational opportunities.
- *Parent handbook* with information about the history of the school, how the organization is set up with job descriptions and responsibilities of each member of the administration, eligibility requirements, and funding information. Another section should include rules and regulations affecting the parents, such as holidays, the hours the school is open, routine information relating to illness, health requirements, permission slips, and phone numbers to call.
- *Free materials* such as newsletters, recipes, brochures, bulletins, information fact sheets, and educational materials. Parents are interested in information about such topics as tax laws, insurance, birth control, diet, and dealing with legal and emotional problems. If these materials are interestingly displayed and easily accessible, parents will make good use of them.
- *Lending library* of latest books and magazines with articles about child development, family concerns, and related topics. The library might also include toys, children's books, and records that families can check out to use at home.
- *Suggestion box* for those who are reluctant to voice their complaints or comments about various aspects of the program.
- *Clothing and food exchange* where outworn children's clothing or lost and found items can be made available to families in the school. Also, people who grow their own fruits and vegetables appreciate having the opportunity to trade surplus foods (pp. 26–27).

PAUSE AND REFLECT

How different is this image of a welcoming parent culture from that in which you have worked, observed, or learned? What barriers do you think exist to implementing some of these suggestions in a school with which you are familiar? What reasons for not implementing them do you think are typically given? How would you respond to criticisms of innovative ways for involving families? Imagine other possible "parent-family" school environments and practices.

Most of us will agree that at different times throughout the school year, parents are asked to become partners, collaborators, problems solvers, supporters, advisors, co-decision makers, and sometimes to be simply an interested audience (Henderson, Marburger, & Ooms, 1986). In whatever capacity parents choose to participate in school activities, one thing is evident. With few exceptions, each parent was recruited by means of traditional one-way and two-way forms of school communication: newsletters, telephone calls, and meetings. Atkin, Bastiani, & Goode (1988) pointed out that:

> Letters are probably the bread and butter of communication between home and school and the most frequent form of contact that a school has with its parents. Their very everyday nature perhaps makes them the most overlooked aspect of a home/school program; from the parents' perspective, however, the cumulative impact of regular letters conveys a great deal about a school's attitudes and intentions toward them (p. 146).

Also, they pointed out that: "...there are many occasions (bad weather, sanctions, closures) when letters have to be sent at short notice but better planning and some forethought could reduce the number of letters on individual matters" (p. 147). However, when Atkin, Bastiani, & Goode studied a large collection of letters sent out by schools, they found the range of topics the letters covered was vast, as Figure 5.1 shows.

Traditional Approaches

Most of us are familiar with the following forms of one-way communication Berger (1995) highlights in her book, *Parents as Partners in Education: Families and School Working Together*

August letters	district newsletters
handbooks	happy-grams
newspapers	parent questionnaire
spontaneous notes	suggestion boxes
yearbooks	

We might also recall the ever-popular two-way forms of communication she highlights:

back-to-school nights	breakfast meetings
carnivals	early-in-the-year contacts
exchanges	fairs
home visits	neighborhood visits
open-door policies	parent-teacher associations
picnics	Saturday morning sessions
school maintenance projects	school programs
suppers	telephone calls
workshops	

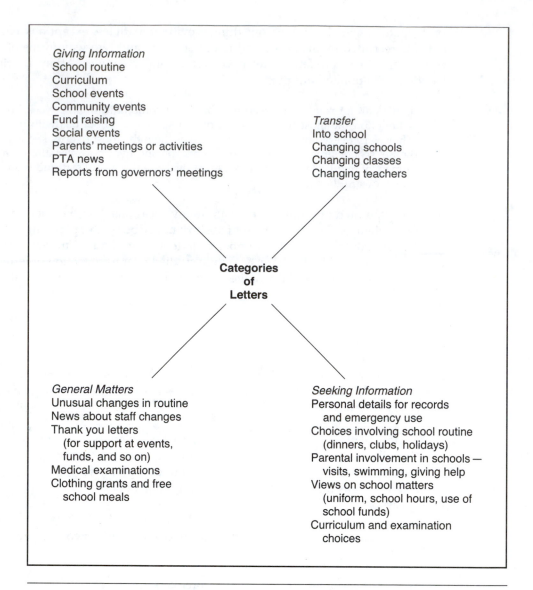

FIGURE 5.1 *Categories of Letters*

Source: J. Atkin, J. Bastiani (with J. Goode) (1988). *Listening to parents: An approach to the improvement of home/school relations.* New York: Croom Helm.

In addition to Berger's two-way forms of communication, Springate & Stegelin (1999) revealed that:

Parent-teacher conferences, home visits, parent meetings, classroom volunteer programs, and parents as members of boards and site-based decision-making councils all provide opportunities for ongoing two-way communication between and among school personnel and family members. Also, less traditional forms of two-way communication strategies are designed to meet the needs of working families and families involved in the care of younger children or other relatives. These strategies include family theme bags, classroom videos, and journal activities (p. 61).

Although schools have been using a variety of ways to communicate with parents over the years, for the most part, traditional approaches have been aimed at recruiting mainstream parents, especially those who are easy to reach. Usually, the more traditional approaches show little regard for the diversity of lifestyles or literacy levels among parents. As a result, few schools are communicating effectively with the very parents who would most benefit from a positive involvement in the school.

PAUSE AND REFLECT

What scheduling or resource problems do you envision might be made in a school if such suggestions were made? What are the benefits, described in previous chapters, that warrant the effort in re-imagining parent involvement practices?

As problems resulting from this imbalance grow, more researchers are beginning to encourage educators to examine the effectiveness of their current parent-involvement approaches. There are many parents who cannot read and write and who are unable to respond to the traditional forms of written communication sent by the school. Additionally, such parents often feel disenfranchised from their children's school through their history of failure. For these parents, new forms of communication must be devised. Karther & Lowden (1997) agree with this point noting that: "...schools may need to reconsider conventional assumptions and practices in order to build bridges to families who do not readily respond to traditional parent-school activities" (p. 41). School staffs should also seriously consider an issue raised by Nieto (1992). She noted that many of today's parents find that it is "...difficult to attend meetings or otherwise to be involved in the governance of the school" (p. 82). In Chapter 6, you come face-to-face with the reality that most of Morton's families, whether they held blue- or white-collar jobs, had little or no time to support the school in traditional ways.

Nontraditional Approaches

Sometimes asking community leaders to contact parents who have literacy problems will provide the incentive parents need to become willing participants in a literacy program. Another approach is to ask parents to contact other parents who would benefit from the program. Both of these grassroots methods can build strong ties between the home and school, which, if carefully nurtured, will improve with time.

Regardless of the approaches schools employ to involve both mainstream and nonmainstream parents in their programs, educators should be sensitive to the various literacy levels of parents. No longer can one type of communication be perceived effective with every group. Above all, educators should avoid making the mistake of using only one strategy for sharing information with parents. Unfortunately, many of the well-intentioned but uninformed educators do make this mistake, which communicates, to some parents, that they are insensitive to the diverse literacy levels of parents, or worse—the disparaging of them. Usually communication from such educators misses the mark altogether, either insulting the parents who read well or alienating those who cannot. Atkin, Bastiani, & Goode (1988) revealed that:

> Schools seeking to improve their relationship with parents and to create conditions where better communication can take place might well ask whether, as a result of our experience of listening to parents, we have come to any conclusions about which form of contact parents prefer? The answer, sadly for schools wanting a magic formula, is yes—different parents value differently different forms of contact! The hard fact is that parents are not a homogenous body any more than teachers are. They have their own individual ways of making judgments about schools, their preferred ways of seeking and receiving information, their own standpoints on the extent to which they wish to be involved with their child's education. The implications of this are that schools need to plan a range and variety of forms of contact in the knowledge that no one particular type will suit all parents...A school that offers both written reports and parent/teacher interviews may find attendance at the latter to be less than that at a school down the road [that] does not issue reports. Some schools have well-attended curriculum workshops while others will succeed with informal discussion with individual parents at coffee mornings. It is only by careful reflection and by seeking the views of parents that the appropriate range of contacts can be decided upon at a particular school (p. 128).

Atkin, Bastiani, & Goode contend that to assist schools with an analysis of the range and variety of a program, it is useful to focus on two dimensions of contact. These are (1) whether the form of contact is through the written or spoken word, and (2) whether the contact is with the individual parent, particular groups, or the parents as a whole (p. 128). They suggest that charting out aspects of the program in the form of a matrix along these two dimensions will illustrate range and balance, as well as the extent of the school's program. Figure 5.2 is a composite picture of what Atkin, Bastiani, & Goode found based on a number of schools to create a full range of practices.

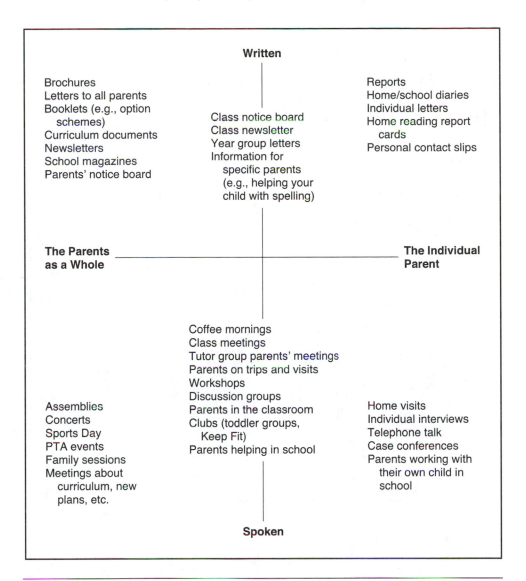

Written

Brochures
Letters to all parents
Booklets (e.g., option
    schemes)
Curriculum documents
Newsletters
School magazines
Parents' notice board

Class notice board
Class newsletter
Year group letters
Information for
    specific parents
    (e.g., helping your
    child with spelling)

Reports
Home/school diaries
Individual letters
Home reading report
    cards
Personal contact slips

**The Parents
as a Whole**

**The Individual
Parent**

Coffee mornings
Class meetings
Tutor group parents' meetings
Parents on trips and visits
Workshops
Discussion groups
Parents in the classroom
Clubs (toddler groups,
    Keep Fit)
Parents helping in school

Assemblies
Concerts
Sports Day
PTA events
Family sessions
Meetings about
    curriculum, new
    plans, etc.

Home visits
Individual interviews
Telephone talk
Case conferences
Parents working with
    their own child in
    school

Spoken

FIGURE 5.2   *Constructing a Profile of the Forms of Home/School Contacts: An Example*
Source: J. Atkin, J. Bastiani (with J. Goode) (1988). *Listening to parents: An approach to the improvement of home/school relations.* New York: Croom Helm.

School staffs can also use a communication checklist as a worksheet to help them evaluate the notification, preparation, content, and quality of face-to-face communication with parents (see Table 5.1). Table 5.2 can help school staffs evaluate the frequency, quality, content, and distribution of their school's written communication.

TABLE 5.1   *Communications Checklist*

Directions: This worksheet is designed to help you evaluate the notification, preparation, content, and quality of face-to-face communications with parents. In each square (if appropriate to that item) put a "+" for above average, a "0" for average, a "–" for below average. This quick check method will help you see strengths and areas in need of improvement. Add other communications not listed or criteria you feel are important.

Face-to-Face Oral Communication	Early Publicity	Multiple Methods of Notification	Adequate Preparation	Clear Purpose for Meetings or Contact	Agenda of Questions to Aid Preparation	Childcare	Translators Required	Helpful to Parents	Focus on Child	Attendance Goal
Classroom Orientations										
Back-to-School Nights										
Open Houses										
Parent Education Meetings										
Parent-Teacher Conferences										
Telephone Conferences										
Evenings with the Principal										
Coffee Klatches										
Home Visits										
Community Breakfasts										
Potluck Suppers										
Special Events										
Presentations to Community Groups										

TABLE 5.2 *Communications Checklist*

Directions: This worksheet is designed to help you evaluate the frequency, quality, content, and distribution of your school's written communication. In each square (if appropriate to that item) put a "+" for above average, a "0" for average, a "–" for below average. This quick check method will help you see strengths and areas in need of improvement. Add other communications not listed or criteria you feel are important.

Written Communications	Frequent	Easy to Read	Neat and Attractive	Encourages Responses	Important Information	Focus on Academics	Timely Distribution	Adequate Distribution	Translations Needed
Letters Home									
School Policies									
Discipline code									
Homework policy									
Health regulations									
Absences/tardies									
Course Requirements									
Meeting Notices									
Progress Notes									
Success Reports									
School Newsletters									
Class Newsletters									
Classwork									
Parent Surveys									
Learning Objectives									
Assignment or Activity Calendars									
Handbooks									
Classroom Policies									

Working with Special Needs Families

Many of you may not have specific training to work with single-parent families; minority children; or low-income, bilingual, handicapped, or migrant families. Some of you may have had more personal experiences in a variety of settings, but the sensitivity, understanding, flexibility, and insightfulness needed by a teacher under special circumstances are characteristics that are difficult, if not impossible, to teach in a college classroom. How then does a teacher prepare for work with families who have special needs? What do you do with the bilingual family, with children who are accustomed to a culture quite different from your own? What about the children who are poor? Or the child who has no mother or father? Are there "rules" a teacher can use as a guide? How can a teacher avoid making mistakes in unfamiliar situations? Hildebrand, Phenice, Gray, & Hines (1996) provided some good advice to teachers about the importance of communicating with diverse individuals and families. They revealed that:

> Communication with diverse individuals and families will become a necessity as you move into your volunteer and career roles in the helping professions. Communication is a two-way street between you and your clients, customers, patients, students or others. Communication probably requires some reorientation and new learning for you, as it does for most persons who branch out to serve others in the helping professions. Recall that, in a certain sense, we are all minorities to some of those we will serve, thus bridging the communication gap is essential.
>
> Intercultural communication has become an important science as business and political leaders have moved into the international arena. The skills they are learning have meaning for any of us working with people who are different from ourselves.
>
> Striving for *shared meaning* will be our goal. Shared meaning involves understanding each other in both written and spoken language, in body language, and in concepts. Achieving shared meaning will take time and effort on your part. Even if we speak the same basic language we may not fully understand another person. Humor is a case in point. With shared meaning we can laugh heartily; without shared meaning many things are simply not funny. However discouraged we become, we must still keep trying to communicate. "Meanings are in people" and striving for shared meaning is fundamental to building positive relationships (pp. 34–35).

Croft (1979) offers a word of caution. She revealed that:

> A family that is different or has special needs is not necessarily a "disadvantaged" family. Oftentimes, children who are handicapped in some way—whether physically or because of ethnic origin—are often brighter and more resourceful and bring a richer background of experiences to the school than their peers. It is easy for teachers with limited experiences to "feel sorry" for a child who is different in some way and to relate to that child and his or her family in a condescending manner. It is always more useful to focus and build on the strengths of the child and family (p. 37).

Croft also offers some words of advice for the teacher who is willing to expend extra effort to get more information, usually from the families themselves, and who is sincere in wanting to be more sensitive to the feelings and concerns of others. Such a teacher, Croft suggests, will find the task a rewarding one. Below are some principles Croft suggested that a teacher could do to work with families with special needs.

- Observe and listen. Watch for cues and relate to behavior that is familiar to you (separation anxiety, shyness, aggressiveness, and so on).
- Be patient. Parents and children from different sociocultural backgrounds may not want to deal with problems in the same way as others in the school.
- Be supportive. Encourage parents to express their feelings. Show them the ways you can reinforce their values.
- Build in successful experiences. Enable each child and parent to complete tasks responsibly and successfully.
- Use plenty of praise to reinforce their efforts.
- Be aware that it takes time to build confidence in you and the school.
- Do not push your knowledge and educational background on parents.
- Do not relate to poor and different families out of a sense of pity for them. They need compassion and guidance to develop their abilities, not have someone feel sorry for them.
- Makes rules and expectations clear. Keep them simple and few and follow up with supportive suggestions.
- Communicate your feelings honestly. "I feel helpless when Jose won't respond. Can we talk about it?"
- Admit your own lack of knowledge. "I don't know that much about Vietnam. Tell me about the school there."
- Accept the language of the child. Provide coordinated training to enable him or her to learn standard English while still retaining his or her native tongue.
- Adapt parent programs to involve special needs of all families.
- Parent involvement includes doing many things other than attending meetings. Let your parents help devise nontraditional parent involvement techniques.
- Incorporate the results of questionnaires and surveys into the curriculum where possible, but be careful not to build in failure or disappointment from false expectations.
- Identify mutual goals and start from where the family is at that moment.
- Programs and plans are more likely to succeed if they are developed around the immediate needs of the families (e.g., where to shop, how to save money, immigration procedures, birth control, medicine). In other words, academic tasks in the classroom should draw from and connect to the real life world within which children engage in literate ways of knowing and doing.
- Use complete sentences in talking with children, and encourage them and their parents to talk in complete sentences. Build discussion topics around their experiences.
- Do not be misled by standardized intelligence test scores. Use your own experience with the children to assess their educability.

- Instill a sense of cultural pride and self-worth through activities that encourage social interaction among all groups in the school. Parents and children learn from each other. Minority groups also have their prejudices and misconceptions about others (pp. 42–44).

Public Law 94-142

I know that I have been sharing with you how to work with special needs parents, but one group of special needs parents that you will hear a great deal about are the parents who have handicapped children or children with learning disabilities. In a sense, P.L. 94-142 is a law with which every teacher in a mainstreamed classroom should be familiar. The landmark legislation providing for the needs of the handicapped is P.L. 94-142. Section 3 of this law states:

> It is the purpose of this Act to assure that all handicapped children have available to them, within the time periods specified in section 612(2) (B), a free appropriate public education which emphasizes special education and related services designed to meet their unique needs, to assure that the rights of handicapped children and their parents or guardians are protected, to assist States and localities to provide for the education of all handicapped children, and to assess and assure the effectiveness of efforts to educate handicapped children.

Under the provision of P.L. 94-142, parents have these rights regarding their child's education:

- The parent must give consent for evaluation of the child.
- The parent has the right to "examine all relevant records with respect to the identification, evaluation, and educational placement of the child."
- The parent must be given written prior notice whenever a change in "the identification, evaluation, or educational placement of the child" occurs.
- This written notice must be in the parent's native tongue.
- The parent has an "opportunity to present complaints with respect to any matter relating to the identification, evaluation, or educational placement of the child."
- The parent has the right to a due process hearing in relation to any complaint.
- The parent has the right to participate in development of the individual educational program (IEP) for the child.
- Meetings to develop the IEP must be conducted in the parents' native tongue.
- Meetings to develop the IEP must be held at a time and place agreeable to the parent.

As you can see, special needs children and their parents are legally required to be given specialized attention. However, other parents you come in contact with may also need some special attention, regardless of whether the law or your institutional practices require or provide for it. One way to develop resources for the kinds of special assistance needed by some parents is to solicit community support. In the section below are my reflections on my experience soliciting community leaders to recruit parents for the book-reading program I developed at DES.

How to Recruit Parents and Solicit Community Support

Schools are burdened with immense problems that affect quality education and their relationship with families and the community. Unless educators begin to enlist the support and involvement of parents and community leaders to help resolve these problems, education and quality community resources remain in jeopardy. Haberman (1992) supports this point by arguing, "...teachers are needed in inner-city schools who are neither fearful of the inhabitants, nor ignorant of their lives, nor unwilling to interact with community organizations and institutions" (p. 38). I would argue that what Haberman purports holds true for all schools, not just inner-city schools. Literacy programs propose to answer some of these problems. But if programs, such as *Parents as Partners in Reading*, fail to involve the community, they too will be ineffectual. Forming a community network will make a difference. It will help people feel that they have a stake in the success of the program and in creating better human resources. The results will be a program that has long-lasting effects in the school community.

As I stated earlier, one of the criticisms of the programs designed for poor and minority parents is that they are based on the perception that such families "won't come to school because they are simply not interested in helping their children." To dispel this belief when implementing the *Parents as Partners in Reading* program, I asked for community support in recruiting parents for the book-reading program. A major component, I argued contributing to the success of the *Parents as Partners in Reading* program was the community. The principal and assistant helped in identifying key community leaders, such as the Ministerial Alliance, business leaders, school board members, and the local superintendent. They also suggested holding a series of meetings at the community center to solicit support from the "ordinary" townspeople (e.g., grandmothers and bus drivers), and contacting people just sitting on street corners about the role they could play in recruiting parents for the book-reading program. Each of these strategies proved to be successful.

The community support of the *Parents as Partners in Reading* program was overwhelming. Ministers, black and white, agreed to preach from their pulpits about the importance of helping children learn to read. They regularly urged parents to attend the weekly reading sessions to learn to help their children in school, noting the importance of literacy as a tool of faith.

A local bar owner emerged as a strong supporter of the reading program, informing mothers who patronized his establishment that they would no longer be welcome unless they put as much time into learning how to read to their children as they spent enjoying themselves at his bar. He provided transportation to school and back home for participating mothers and secured funds from the city social services department for child care for parents who otherwise could not attend. A grandmother organized a campaign to telephone program participants each week and reminded them of the scheduled meetings. I visited beauty salons, mom-and-pop restaurants, and local grocery stores to ask for their assistance in spreading the word about the book-reading program to the families in the Donaldsonville community. A bus driver offered to drive parents to the program each week, and the people sitting on the street corners began to talk about the program and encouraged all the parents they came in contact with to attend.

The outpouring of support from the community was duplicated at DES where school administrators, teachers, and the librarians staunchly supported the book-reading program. The teachers, as well as the school administrators and the librarian, enrolled in a family literacy course I taught to broaden their knowledge of literacy development in different family structures. Teachers also assisted in the development of training materials designed to show parents effective book-reading behaviors. The principal and assistant principal helped publicize the program in the community, driving parents to the program each week and creating a friendly and warm environment at the school for the parents. The librarian designed a computer program that listed the names of each child whose parent was participating in the book-reading program. For the first time in the school's history, parents were able to check out up to five books under their child's name. The librarian also kept a computerized list of books the parents were checking out. This information was shared with me, and the child's teacher. More importantly, the teachers, school administrators, and the librarian began to accept the parents as useful and reliable resources.

PAUSE AND REFLECT

What comes to mind when you read this? In what ways is this different from your experiences of parent involvement in school? How does this illustration force you to rethink your relation to the community in your role as teacher? What do you find interesting or scary to you in this example? What kinds of knowledge and expertise would you need as a teacher to organize an effort like this?

Networking in a Large Metropolitan Area

After reading what I did to recruit parents in the Donaldsonville community, you are probably saying to yourself, "I don't live in a small rural community, I live in a large metropolitan community. I have been extremely unsuccessful in recruiting parents to school events." How can I recruit parents to participate in programs like the *Parents as Partners in Reading* program in the school in which I teach? In the next section, I will share with you how to make contacts for recruiting parents in small rural communities, as well as in large metropolitan communities.

If you live in a large metropolitan area, many of the families you serve do not live in the community where the school is located. This creates its own kind of problems, namely, how you will get parents from across town to buy into the program and attend the sessions, and how you will become acquainted with the parents and communities in which they live.

I would recommend that you request the services of a demographer to determine the size, distribution, and vital statistics of the population in a given area. A demographer will provide valuable information about the families you serve and the significant contact you should make.

However, if your school or school district is unable to utilize the services of a demographer, you might contact some of the following organizations within the community where your parents live. They will provide information about families and the social pressures parents encounter. They might even offer suggestions as to how you can effectively recruit for the program.

- Social Services department
- Urban League
- Drug rehabilitation services
- Big Brothers/Big Sisters
- Shelters for abused women
- Law enforcement services
- Health department services
- Alcoholics Anonymous
- City council

In addition, you can obtain a map of the area(s) where your parents live and circle businesses, organizations, churches, and other community support groups that can help you identify and recruit community leaders. Have volunteers contact these sources by phone or letter, introduce the program to them, and invite them to a meeting. (See Figure 5.3 for a sample form for telephone canvassing.)

When to Recruit Community Leaders

Timing is very important when recruiting community leaders to participate in your program and to help you involve parents. Like a farmer who must plant seeds during a certain season to reap benefits of a good crop, you must recruit community leaders early enough to reap full participation and commitment from them. Leaders should not be contacted as an afterthought. Rather, they should be recruited long before the program sessions begin. You will find that most people in power positions prefer to be at the forefront of change, throwing their support

Child's name _____

Parent's name _____

Address _____

_____

_____

Phone _____

Best time to call or visit your home _____

Father's occupation _____

Mother's occupation _____

Best day and time for parents to attend sessions _____

_____

Comments:

FIGURE 5.3   *Sample Form for the Telephone Canvassing*

to winning teams that might bring them political gain. No one likes to be contacted late in the game when the very survival of a program might be in jeopardy.

Because community leaders often have linkages with families that teachers and administrators do not have, "parents and leaders," according to Swap (1987), "are more in need of each other's support than even before" (p. 1). Community leaders can help identify hard-to-reach parents and recruit them; devise alternative solutions to school problems and help implement them. Without a doubt, community leaders represent a powerful force that can support parents and teachers and help them achieve their goals.

Strategies for Identifying and Recruiting Community Leaders

- From the chamber of commerce, city hall, school board, or library, obtain lists of all of the organizations and local businesses in your community and the names of the people in charge.
- Contact key community leaders (ministers, bank presidents, the mayor, the director of adult education, retired teachers) and introduce your program to them.
- Telephone key people from each of the ethnic groups in the community and solicit names of other significant people and organizations. Select those who are well respected by their peers and who represent the ethnic groups you intend to serve.

As you examine your community to identify its leaders, look beyond the highly visible and articulate personalities of the dominant culture. Within every subculture, whether literate or nonliterate, there are powerful leaders (articulate in their own right) who directly influence his or her communities.

Brown (1987) says, "a nonliterate person may be very powerful within a nonliterate subculture" (p. 3). We should not, therefore fail to involve nonliterate as well as literate leaders of the community in the school's program. Often, the person considered most unlikely to get involved might be the very one who recruits the largest number of parents.

In Donaldsonville, Louisiana, for example, where I first piloted the *Parents as Partners in Reading* program, a bus driver surfaced as a key community leader. I also enlisted the owner of a tavern, who drove parents to the weekly sessions and also participated himself, and a Catholic priest who preached about the benefits of the program during his Sunday sermons. These people were not the mayor, the rotary club president, or school resource people. They were, however, the natural leaders of the community I was trying to tap.

The suggestions I have offered here for identifying and recruiting community leaders (natural or elected) are based on a model developed by Bronfenbrenner, Cochran, & Cross at Cornell University (see Figure 5.4).

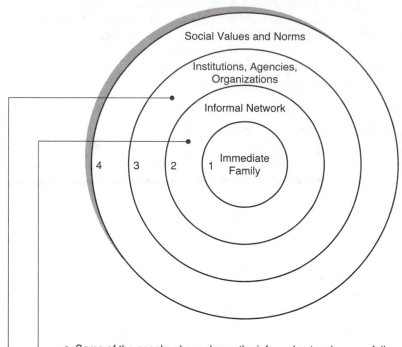

Some of the people who make up the informal network are as follows:

- Religious leaders/ministerial alliance/circle groups at church
- Grandparents/aunts/uncles
- Small neighborhood business owners
- Neighborhood groups/associations
- Teachers (retired and otherwise)
- Big Buddy, Big Brother, Big Sister organizations
- YWCA mothers, YMCA fathers

Some of the people who make up the circle of institutions, agencies, and organizations are as follows:

- Director of Adult Basic Education Programs (if available)
- Teen parent programs, such as Parents Too Soon
- Social Service department
- Housing authority
- Health department
- Fraternal organizations
- PTA or PTO groups
- Lions Clubs/Jaycees/Rotary/Kiwanis
- Chamber of Commerce

FIGURE 5.4 *The Social World of the Parent*

Source: Taken from Edwards, P. A. (1993). *Parents as partners in reading: A family literacy training program.* Second Edition. Chicago: Childrens Press.

This model identifies the people and environmental forces that affect a person. The inner circle represents a person's immediate family, usually people who live in the household. Each larger circle, radiating from the middle, represents a less immediate force. The next larger circle represents the individual's informal network; the people who influence him or her directly, either positively or negatively. Relatives and friends are part of this network, but it might also include teachers or religious leaders with whom the individual has a personal relationship. The third circle represents institutions, agencies, or organizations that affect the person, sometimes only indirectly. The largest circle includes the societal values and norms that affect individuals (pp. 1–2).

What each of the illustrations or strategies in this chapter has in common is a purposeful effort to use the parents, family culture, and experiences to support children's academic performance. These can be summarized as (1) urging teachers to create academic tasks that build on, extend, or develop areas of expertise, interests, or needs; (2) use of institutional and classroom interaction norms that explicitly acknowledge the cultural patterns from which children emerge and the resources they have available; (3) efforts to develop relationships where power and responsibility are shared between parents and teachers. These suggestions are all based on the assumption that both teachers and parents are of central importance to the academic success of students and equally critical in the development of school-based literacy expertise.

Summary

Like everyone else, parents thrive in a nurturing environment where they feel welcome and accepted. Schools must become more accommodating by providing comfortable areas for parents to congregate at school. Additionally, resources that increase parental awareness such as bulletin boards, newsletters, and magazines can encourage home-school communication. For many years schools have tried traditional methods of communication, however, these approaches may not be culturally sensitive and may not consider the various literacy levels of parents. Teachers need to learn important demographic information about the population that they serve to develop effective home-school connections. This information can be retrieved from demographers, Internet sources, or various agencies and organizations. Collecting parent stories, convincing parents to recruit other parents, and connecting with community leaders are additional ways that teachers can build stronger bonds between home and school.

Chapter 5 Key Concepts

- Schools need to provide an inviting environment for parents that may include but not be limited to a special gathering place such as a conference room or coffee corner, a bulletin board where parents can see notices of interest, parent handbooks with important information, a lending library offering recent articles concerning child development, family concerns, and a suggestion box.

- Yearbooks, spontaneous notes, and newsletters are examples of traditional one-way approaches to home/school communication.
- Traditional two-way approaches to home/school communication include back-to-school nights, home visits, and parent-teacher associations.
- Traditional approaches show little regard for the diversity of lifestyles or literacy levels among parents.
- Nontraditional approaches include asking community leaders and/or parents to contact other parents.
- Regardless of the types of approaches used, schools must be sensitive to the various literacy levels of parents, and should plan a range and variety of forms of contact.
- Striving for "shared meaning" should be every teacher's goal. Shared meaning involves understanding each other in both written and spoken language, in body language, and in concepts. It is fundamental to building positive relationships.
- Working with parents is an absolute must for every classroom teacher.
- Under the provision of P.L. 94-142, parents have specific rights regarding their child's education.
- Schools need to solicit community support to assist with addressing the immense problems that affect quality education.
- A demographer and/or various agencies and organizations can be utilized as resources to provide vital information about the student population in a given area.
- Community leaders who are well respected should be recruited to assist with building stronger bonds between home and school.

Suggestions for Thought Questions and Activities

1. During your next visit to your field experience, closely observe the students in the classroom. Based strictly on your instincts, write down information related to the students' socioeconomic status range, the types of parents that you think they may have, the type of neighborhood in which they live, family structure, home literacy practices, and any other vital information.
2. Interview the teacher to obtain information about the students in the class. Ask him or her if they have ever completed a demographic profile of their student population. If so, ask them to share how they completed the profile.
3. Compare your information with the teacher's information. What are the similarities? What are the differences? Many teachers use their "instincts" when determining the types of home-school connection methods would be most effective for their students. They make sweeping generalizations and base many of their decisions on stereotypes. Look at your observations and the teacher's information. Is it possible that either of you could fall into this "trap"?
4. Complete a demographic profile of the student population that you observed above. Use Internet resources, the school district's demographer, community agencies and organizations, and other sources discussed in this chapter. Compare your initial observations, the teacher's information, and the actual demographic information. Remember, your home-school connection practices must be based on the "truth," not your "instincts," and stereotypes that you hear from negative colleagues. Can you identify at least three community leaders who might be able to

assist you with parent recruitment if you were actually teaching? Share the names with your cooperating teacher as possible candidates to be invited as class speakers.

Internet Activities

- Using a search engine such as yahoo! or Proteacher, look for newsletters created by schools or individual classrooms. How are these newsletters organized? What information do they try to convey to parents? In what ways do they attempt to involve parents with the school?

- Using a search engine, look for parent-teacher organizations on the Web. Examine these sites carefully. What do they believe is the role of parents in the schools? Do they state any ideas about how teachers can get parents involved with their school?

- Using a search engine, look for a site that provides you with templates or a program for designing your own newsletter.

For Further Study

Atkin, M., Bastiani, J., with Goode, J. (1988). *Listening to parents: An approach to the improvement of home-school relations.* New York: Croom Helm.

> This book is of great practical value. It draws on the authors' work over the last decade to explore the links between listening to the parental perspective on a child's schooling and the development of more effective home/school practice. It describes the current scene, the philosophy and method for effectively listening, the development of familiarity and understanding with parents, strategies for encouraging a home/school program, and the development of effective practice. Included are accounts by parents with widely differing backgrounds and experiences on their role as educators and their dealings with their children's schools. The book concludes with a discussion of the important issues in home/school interaction and identification of the areas where further development is needed.

Harry, B. (1992). *Cultural diversity, families, and the special education system: Communication and empowerment.* New York: Teachers College Press.

> This book is primarily concerned with the way parents of minority students perceive the special education system, with specific attention to their views of the process by which their children are designated "handicapped."

McCaleb, S. P. (1994). *Building communities of learners: Collaboration among teachers, students, families, and community.* New York: St. Martin's Press.

> Sudia Palomo McCaleb presents a very powerful analysis of the dangers inherent to traditional schooling processes and examines some compelling alternative possibilities. Drawing not only from scholarly research and model experiences of progressive parent involvement programs throughout the country but also from her own ample experience as educator and activist, McCaleb describes the challenge and encourages her readers to engage in a critical personal reflection that will allow them to generate creative responses and liberatory practices.

Maiers, A. (2001). *The teacher-parent partnership in the primary grades: Pathways to communication and cooperation.* Chicago: Rigby Best Teachers Press.

> *The Teacher-Parent Partnership in the Primary Grades* is for all teachers who understand that working with families can and will make a difference in children's educational success. This powerful resource provides the tools for establishing open, dynamic school/home communication and cooperation.

6

Directions for Improving Family-School Partnership Preparation

Action Steps

Chapter Goals for the Reader

- To explore issues involved in creating a more systematic and structured parent involvement program through examination of the author's work with the staff at Morton Professional Development School

- To examine responses a group of preservice and experienced teachers gave to the question, "What does an elementary teacher need to know about parent involvement in order to structure it successfully?"

- To become familiar with a process for developing a scope and sequence of parent involvement activities grade-by-grade around curricular issues

- To critique scope and sequence examples developed by experienced teachers

- To analyze three sets of action steps that can be followed for developing and improving family-school partnerships

Chapter Outline

Chapter Overview

The first section draws on my experiences at Morton to describe the first set of action steps for creating a parent involvement program that involved: (1) developing definitions of family involvement, (2) deciding on types of family involvement, (3) examining perceptions of family involvement, and (4) implementing practices of family involvement. Also, I discuss the results of a survey of preservice and inservice around the question, *"What does an elementary teacher need to know about parent involvement in order to structure it successfully?"*

In the second section, I discuss in detail and provide examples of the second set of action steps preservice and experienced teachers should follow for developing and improving family-school partnerships. The second set of action steps are: (1) finding out about your school's history of involving families, (2) finding out about your school's parent involvement climate (i.e., present conditions, goals, bridges, barriers, first steps, and so on), (3) analyzing the profile of parent involvement at Morton, (4) constructing a demographic profile of Morton, and (5) conducting a community scan of your school's support network.

In the third section, I discuss the third set of action steps, which includes (1) examining *links* to government agencies, journals, organizations, and so on, (2) surveying families to determine if they feel capable, willing, and responsible to assist in their children's education, (3) getting in touch with your attitude toward parent involvement (parent profile), (4) assessing your readiness for increased parent involvement (plan of action), (5) documenting levels of family involvement at your school, (6) Developing a family-school planning calendar, (7) assessing your school's home-school partnership with families, (8) creating a school vision for a partnership, (9) creating a statement of your school's vision of family-school partnerships, and (10) developing an action plan for strengthening family-school partnerships.

Introductory Scenario:
"You're the expert, so tell us what to do"

Several years ago, Epstein (1988) reported that "Research on school programs for parent involvement has been limited up to now. That is why building programs and practices for productive family and school connections is just beginning" (p. 58). All too often, Sara Lightfoot (1978) has pointed out, the world of school and the world of home can be—and usually are—*worlds apart*. As a result, it is incumbent that school staffs *rethink, update,* and *redesign* their parent involvement initiatives to correlate with the families they now serve in the new millennium. In particular, school staffs should examine their views, concerns, wishes, and fears especially as they relate to involving parents in the educational support of their children. The Morton case example, as I will illustrate, represents an attempt to move beyond simply saying schools need to communicate with parents to describing how I facilitated one urban school's efforts to develop a structure for parent involvement.

Morton is a Professional Development School (PDS) that the authors of the Holmes Group Report, *Tomorrow's Schools,* have argued are places that are suitable for exploring issues like parent involvement. The authors of the report have carefully defined the mission, goals, and scope of a PDS as follows:

> By "Professional Development" we do not mean just a laboratory for university research, nor a demonstration school. Nor do we mean just a clinical setting for preparing student and intern teachers. Rather, we mean all of these together: a school for the development of novice professionals, for continuing development of experienced professionals, and *for the research and development of the profession* (p. 1).

The authors of the Holmes Group go on to detail what objectives are involved in creating a PDS. Specifically, they state that these schools are designed to help the teaching professional in the following six ways:

1. By promoting much more ambitious conceptions of teaching and learning on the part of prospective teachers in universities and students in schools
2. By adding to and reorganizing the collections of knowledge we have about teaching and learning
3. By ensuring that enterprising, relevant, responsible research and development is done in schools
4. By linking experienced teachers' efforts to renew their knowledge and advance their status with efforts to improve their schools and to prepare new teachers
5. By creating incentives for faculties in the public schools and faculties in education schools to work mutually
6. By strengthening the relationship between schools and the broader political, social, and economic communities in which they reside (pp. 1–2).

In the Morton case example, I address the final objective proposed by the authors of the Holmes Group Report. Current reform efforts address substance and fragmentation problems by connecting teacher education and educational research within PDSs (Dixon & Ishler, 1992; The Holmes Group, 1990; Rushcamp & Roehler, 1992; Winitzky, Stoddard & O'Keefe, 1992). In Lieberman's (1993) words: "Our challenge is to create a community that educates all of us, those in the university and those in the schools, a community that expands our relationships with one another and, in so doing, our knowledge and our effectiveness" (p. 9). At Morton, the staff and I struggled to bring our two communities together, especially in the process of supporting change in parent involvement initiatives. Lieberman (1993) discusses how "Miller & Silvernail (1991), working in a school-university partnership in Maine, describe the struggles for power and control between school-based [and] university-based faculty as they work together to create a professional development school" (p. 8). They found, as I did—that it is easy for the school staffs to want the "researcher" or "expert" to solve their problems. On the other hand, researchers often expect teachers will understand problems and solutions involved in school settings in the same ways that researchers construct them. As Lieberman noted, "Those involved in the inevitable conflicts that arise in the course of these collaborations might draw some comfort from the fact that the difficulty of building community and creating knowledge is in direct relation to the magnitude of the effects on organizations and individuals" (p. 9). Involving teachers in altering structures that have been in place for forty or more years is of great magnitude. And certainly the magnitude and seriousness of societal developments that necessitate this new structure are no less daunting. That these life conditions will call for a measured change in teachers' outlook on their own roles is understandably frightening.

Research that involves studying one's own efforts to transform an educational setting is often referred to as *action research* because it involves the systematic efforts to study the "actions" with which one is involved. Researchers who work within this tradition define a complex set of dynamics that undergird participation in the research process. Participation, a "powerful but slippery concept" (Elden & Levin, 1991), becomes empowering when defined as a "cogenerative dialogue." In a cogenerative dialogue, participants generate meaning by exchanging information from different frames of reference. For example, teachers, students, and parents have insider knowledge resulting from their experience within a particular locale (Fear & Edwards, 1995). In contrast, researchers have outsider knowledge, or what Goldenberg & Gallimore (1991) call "propositional knowledge"—that is, information from experiences, reading, dialogue with researchers, and observations that cuts across contexts. Although both insiders and outsiders bring different frames of reference to the dialogue, they communicate at a level where new frames can be generated.

Insiders and outsiders participate in a democratic dialogue and cogenerate meaning when the following assumptions are taken seriously:

1. The dialogue is a process of exchange: points and arguments move to and between participants.
2. All concerned have the possibility to participate.
3. Everyone is active in the discourse.
4. As a point of departure, all participants are equal.
5. Work experience is the foundation for participation.

6. Some of each participant's experience must be considered legitimate.
7. It must be possible for everyone to develop an understanding of the issue at stake.
8. All arguments that pertain to issues under discussion are, as a point of departure, legitimate.
9. The dialogue must continuously produce agreement that can provide a platform for investigation and practical action (Elden & Levin, 1991).

Empowering participation occurs when the cogenerative dialogue results in consequences that affect organization and utilization of valued resources. I thought that I had empowered participation and a cogenerative dialogue between the Morton staff and myself. However, as you'll learn later in the narrative description of my work with the staff, conflict emerged, specifically with the second-grade teachers, about the nature of the project and my role in the school. Obviously, I had not successfully constructed a cogenerative dialogue like this with one group of teachers.

Historically, researchers interested in educational issues have found it difficult to enact changes in schools and classrooms because of a variety of issues, including (1) teachers seeing researchers as experts who construct whole programs to be implemented, (2) teachers seeing themselves as a funnel through which programs are communicated to students and parents, (3) teachers seeing themselves as lacking agency, as not being an important part of constructing changes in their schools, (4) teachers seeing themselves as the recipients of directives issued from administrators, researchers, and parents, and (5) researchers misunderstanding the intricacies that are involved in implementation of broad programs and ideas. All of these issues are related to the problems inherent in the collaboration efforts I encountered at Morton with the second-grade teachers.

The Morton project illustrates up close the shift from "Who's to blame?" to "What dynamic is to blame?" In particular, you will see that what the second-grade teachers didn't understand was that the task was to have me present them with a structure, which all involved would use to discuss how to help organize the specifics of parent involvement. The staff and I, as the researcher, would then use that information to be co-creators of a program designed for parent involvement, specifically at Morton. My work with the Morton staff also provides insight into the need for a shift from "Who created the situation?" to "How was the situation constructed and what were the variables?" Notice again the shift from blame allocated to a person or set of people (e.g., parents) to understanding the systematic nature of educational problems. As you read this account, you will probably conclude that both the teachers and I were involved and interacting in ways that constructed a situation that was not the most beneficial for all involved. I believed that I had thought seriously about Hord, Rutherford, Huling-Austin, & Hall's (1987) assumptions about change based on their Concerns-Based Adoption Model (CBAM), which lead to the following conclusions: "(1) change is a process, not an event; (2) change is accomplished by individuals; (3) change is a highly personal experience; (4) change is best understood in operational terms; and (5) the focus of facilitation should be on individuals, innovations, and the context" (p. 6). I thought I had paid close attention to these assumptions, but something went wrong. In the next section, you will hear my account of what happened.

Description of the Events That Led to the Struggle

In working with the teachers at Morton, what evolved was a very complex set of issues centering on our beliefs about the goals and purposes of our collaboration efforts. In my attempts to help teachers rethink their parent involvement structures, practices, and purposes, I encountered some problems. My problems stemmed from the fact that the Morton staff thought they had already provided me with enough background information because they had participated in two structured individual interviews and two group meetings. A more detailed discussion of the two structured interviews will be highlighted later in this chapter. In the first group meeting, they described for me the parent involvement climate at Morton (i. e., present conditions, goals, bridges, barriers, first steps). In the second group meeting, I shared with them the demographic parent profile data that I had collected. As stated in Chapter 3, even though this data forced them to recognize that the parents and children at Morton in *1990* were very much unlike the parents and children some of them may have interacted with or remembered interacting with in *1952*, the Morton staff did not know how to respond to this new reality. They wanted me to solve the problem. What the Morton staff failed to understand, and perhaps I did not make clear to them, was that their participation in these activities was the *preliminary* basis for creating a structure for how to think about parent involvement at Morton.

The next phase, which precipitated the "major struggle," involved my attempts to try to move the staff to help me discuss the way the *structure* helps organize the *specifics* of the parent involvement initiative at Morton. In other words, I agreed with the teachers that they had provided me with rich information about past parent involvement initiatives at Morton, but much of that information was based on traditional modes. They needed to individually examine this information and try to come up with some new and revised ways of thinking about parent involvement. The way I thought that I could move teachers to think about the *specifics* of parent involvement was to have them do a *teacher profile*. In the following section, I provide a detailed account of the chain of events that I have outlined above.

Revisiting the Goals of the Home Literacy Project: A Background Description of the Struggle

Before the Home Literacy Project began, the existing parent involvement activities at Morton varied in substance and duration, much like the conventional activities described in the literature (Delgado-Gaitan, 1991; Epstein, 1987; Hess and Shipman, 1965; Lareau, 1989). At Morton, when teachers solicited parent participation in classrooms, they often wanted parents to perform mechanical tasks such as typing, editing, or binding children's stories. Such tasks offered little opportunity for significant involvement in curriculum, required the availability of parents during working hours, and involved no opportunity or expectation for reciprocity (i.e., seeking information or feedback from parents as "experts" of their children). Annual open houses and biannual parent-teacher conferences provided time for parents to see their child's classroom and get a brief overview of subject matter covered in a specific grade level. Teachers and administrators had set up parent-teacher association

(PTA) meetings, held parent-teacher conferences, made home visits, and encouraged parents to attend field trips and student performances. Although these events brought families and teachers together, they did not necessarily bring them together around specific literacy events or involve families in ways that would enable them to support children's literacy learning (Edwards, 1991).

Parent involvement is an integral part of the PDS philosophy and was part of the "package" for which teachers had signed on. They were well acquainted with what the PDS was trying to accomplish. Teachers did seem to make every attempt to contact all parents during regularly scheduled parent-teacher conferences. One approach employed by the principal was to ask the Morton teachers to make special efforts to hold parent conferences in the inner city for the parents of children who were bussed to school. This proved successful, and 98 percent of the parents usually attended conferences held in neighborhoods surrounding the school and in the inner-city site. In another attempt to contact parents, the principal rode the school bus on regular weekly intervals to share brief comments and see parents in the community. She also took student teachers on these visits to acquaint them with students' homes and living situations. Although these parent-teacher interactions were valuable, the teachers unanimously expressed a desire for more substantive and more frequent interaction. They joined the family involvement project specifically seeking alternative means to involve families in children's school lives, particularly in terms of understanding and supporting children's literacy growth.

I began discussions about parent involvement by defining specific principles that would drive our practices. I was determined that the needs and interests of Morton's parents and teachers would shape the structure and content of this family involvement project. Rather than simply imposing a preset or previously designed parent involvement program on the existing school structure, I wanted to create opportunities for the parents and teachers to talk together about their needs and goals. I held numerous meetings to discuss the goals and possibilities for a family involvement program. I developed and implemented the projects as I attempted to develop partnerships with teachers. Although it took almost an entire school year, I eventually developed a plan that involved families at three grade levels. More importantly, I was able to encourage both teachers and parents to help me in cogenerating these three projects (see Fear & Edwards, 1995). However, I must admit that the development of these three projects was not without a difficult and laborious struggle. Even though parent involvement at Morton was extremely traditional, the K-2 teachers said they wanted to move to a new way of involving parents. What people say sometimes is not initially congruent with what they do. The struggle began when the second-grade teachers felt that I alone should work out this new parent involvement "thing."

Struggling to Develop a New Model of Parent Involvement at Morton

When I entered the Morton Elementary School community there were expectations that I could move mountains because I was "the expert." As a new researcher entering this learning community, I was struggling to understand it. However, teachers were beyond the point of wanting to talk about the learning community because they had met with two other researchers over a two-year period and were weary of "just talking" about developing a learning community. They wanted action and they wanted it immediately. The message was clear: "Let's get this show on the road, if, in fact, there is a show." I was that "show" in their minds. I had authored a highly successful program for parents (see *Parent as Partners in Reading: A Family Literacy Training Program*, Edwards, 1993, 1990). This program had received national visibility. Although I had received recognition for a program for parents, that program had been developed in a completely different context from the one in which I was now working. Therefore, I too had to learn and explore the context of this school.

I reminded the principal and teachers that there are all kinds of schools around the country and different schools have different faculties, different faculties have different needs and aspirations, and different faculties communicate with different types of parent populations. I also reminded the principal and the teachers that there were two agendas—their agenda and my agenda. My agenda was to make sure that the projects were documented very carefully, and I strongly believed that their agenda should involve helping me define what parent involvement means in their learning community. It should be noted that even though in the two previous conversations the principal and the teachers shared with me their insights about the climate for parent involvement and they openly admitted to me that the parent involvement climate needed to be restructured, they were initially unwilling to help me restructure the parent involvement climate. In some cases, teachers felt that they had told me all of the information I needed to know to develop a new model of parent involvement at Morton. Being thrust into the position of leader precipitated a lot of jealously and hostility toward me. It was almost as if I was in a no-win situation. Teachers were unwilling at first to help me understand their learning community because I was "the expert," and experts are supposed to know everything. I am an expert on family/intergenerational literacy, but I was not an expert in this local context. I was struggling to understand the local context so that I could more effectively use my skills to bring parents, teachers, and children closer together in the Morton community. As a researcher, the teachers and principal viewed me as an outsider. They viewed me as being bossy when I asked questions. I viewed my role of asking questions as a way of entering the community.

In our weekly meetings, I tried to move them to expand their ideas from the interviews on why they thought parents needed to be involved, what they wanted them to do if they became involved, and what they wanted parents to do in connection with their classroom practices. These three questions were problematic for the second-grade teachers. The more I probed them as to what specific second-grade parent literacy project they felt "we" (meaning myself and the three second-grade teachers) should participate in, the more the second-grade teachers) thought that "I" (not "we") was simply floundering and had no ideas for helping them develop a project. In my opinion, the teachers were floundering because they seemed to not focus on what I asked them to do. I asked them to think about what they wanted second-grade parents to do, but the teachers had a very hard time coming up with specific ideas on what they expected of second-grade parents, even though they were second-grade teachers. My position was, "How can they expect me to know exactly what parents need to do, if they, who teach second-grade, do not know?" I continued to say to the teachers, "You have information about your parents that I do not have. I need to get an understanding of your local context so that I can begin to think with you about your local context. I realize that you have participated in group conversations and have shared your general feelings about Morton parents. What I would like for you to do now is to not generalize about the entire Morton parent population. Instead, I want you to talk specifically about the twenty or twenty-five parents of the children you teach daily." As a researcher, I felt the roles had been reversed. Teachers were now expecting me to play the same role researchers had asked teachers to play in the past. In the old model of collaboration, researchers gathered a great deal of data but the classroom remained the same. In my case, teachers were asking me to "fix the parent involvement situation" at their school and, more specifically, in their individual classrooms, without helping me to understand and/or change my views of parent involvement in this local context. I reminded the teachers that Carol Ascher (1988) says, "Parent involvement means different things to different people" (p. 1). I asked them to help me to begin to understand their views on what it means here at Morton especially in individual classrooms. To move K-2 teachers beyond simply discussing general goals for parent involvement, I developed the teacher profile as a vehicle for K-2 teachers to share with me their personal and specific reasons for wanting parent participation. The concept for the teacher profile was borrowed from the framework for teacher training in parent involvement developed by Chavkin & Williams (1988).

Unfortunately, having K-2 teachers complete the teacher profile caused a lot of grief for me. Teachers wanted me to listen to them, but they were unwilling to listen to me. However, I continued my struggle to be heard. I asked teachers to do profiles of themselves. I informed the teachers that I wanted them to include their perceptions of themselves as literacy providers. I wanted to know more about their teaching situations and what made them feel the strong need to have parents involved in the literacy support of their children. I explained to them that a *teacher profile* is a reflective description of who the teacher is as a literacy provider/facilitator (see Table 6.1 for a copy of the teacher profile chart). It also helps document the teachers' individual views on parent involvement. The profile depicts the teacher's philosophy of teaching and his or her views of how to teach content matter subjects (reading, writing, math, social studies, and so on). The profile describes strategies the teacher has employed and students' responses to these strategies. The profile further highlights techniques teachers have used to involve parents, their views on parent participation, and how to teach all of the students in their classes, especially at-risk students. The teacher profile asks teachers to reflect on the constraints, problems, and concerns they face daily in their classroom. Additionally, the profile asks teachers to describe how they presently cope with these issues and how they have coped in the past. The profile requests that teachers outline goals they have for children, parents, and themselves. They are also encouraged to shed light on how they expect to accomplish these goals. Lastly, the profile will include the teachers' descriptions of the new reading program and how they believe they can involve parents in the new reading efforts.

In addition to the information I requested in the teacher profile, the teachers felt that some other personal information should be included in the teacher profile. For example, they felt that background information on who the teacher is should be included (i.e., educational background, number of years in the teaching profession, grade levels taught, whether this is the school at which the teacher has taught or whether this is the first time the teacher has taught a particular grade level). They felt the profiles should also include information describing the teacher's understanding of individual children and information describing how the teacher provides reassurances to parents about their ability to teach all children and particularly their child. They wanted to include the number of years before the teacher plans to retire and what he or she plans to accomplish within that time frame, as well as the teacher's view of the school climate and the role of the teacher in conjunction with the principal.

Despite the fact that *all* of the K-2 teachers agreed to complete the teacher profile, two of the second-grade teachers passed in very sketchy profiles, and one of the second-grade teachers failed to complete it. As will be discussed in more depth later in this chapter, the second-grade teachers raised questions about the teacher profile and led an open attack on me about requiring them and other teachers to complete it. I must add that I did not require teachers to *write* a profile of themselves. I provided each teacher with a cassette tape for him or her to record their teacher profile, if they chose to do so. I had the teacher profiles transcribed and I shared the transcriptions with the teacher. I made comments on the transcription, and I asked the teacher to clarify, extend, or expand the section(s) of the transcription I had highlighted. In retrospect, I think this made teachers angry and defensive, because they

TABLE 6.1 *Teacher Profile Chart*

Part I (My Input as the Researcher)

What are your philosophy of teaching and your views of how to teach content matter subjects (reading, writing, math, social studies, and so on)?

What strategies have you employed and what were the student responses to these strategies?

What techniques have you used to involve parents?

What are your views on parental participation?

How have you attempted to teach all of the students in your classes (especially at-risk students)?

Describe and/or reflect on the constraints, problems, and concerns you face daily in your classroom. How are you presently coping with these issues and how have you coped in the past?

What goals have you outlined this year for children, parents, and yourself?

Provide a description of your reading program and how you plan to involve parents in the new reading efforts.

Part II (Morton Teachers' Input)

Provide some information on who you are as a teacher (i.e., educational background, number of years in the teaching profession, grade levels taught, whether or not this is the first time you have taught this grade level).

Provide some information which describes your understanding of individual children, and information describing how you provide reassurances to parents about your ability to teach all children and particularly their child.

Please indicate the number of years before you plan to retire and what you plan to accomplish within that time frame as well as the your view of the school climate and the role of the teacher in conjunction with the principal.

felt like I was critiquing them, which in reality, I was. I was not, however, critiquing their ideas but rather their effectiveness in communicating them. As has been discussed, a central idea in successful parent involvement programs is the ability to define specifically the ways in which parents can and should be meaningfully involved in the schools. This requires that teachers have a clear idea of their own beliefs and practices to be able to develop programs where parents are intrinsically involved in supported school goals. I felt that I was justified to ask for further explication on items in the teacher profile that I deemed were unclear to me as the reader of these profiles. Yet, some perceived this as an attack on their professional views. I knew that these teachers had their own specific and private thoughts and reasons for wanting parent involved in the education of their children, but many of these were tacit beliefs, unconsciously held and unavailable to me, as a researcher and facilitator. We needed to be able to make these beliefs transparent and part of the public discourse to move forward and create a plan that emerged from shared goals. This meant that I needed to clearly understand their own curricular practices and the goals, which shaped their views about parents and schooling.

The Group Meeting to Discuss the Teacher Profiles and "The Expert"

Kindergarten and first-grade teachers completed their teacher profiles; these profiles allowed me to gain a better understanding of how they thought about parents and children. As noted earlier, two of the second-grade teachers passed in very sketchy profiles, and one of the second-grade teachers failed to complete it. When I approached the second-grade teacher who failed to complete the profile, she responded by saying, "You do not have the right to approach me about this profile because you are not my principal." I felt that I did have the right to approach this teacher, because I was the principal investigator of the project in which she had willingly agreed to participate. Asking this second-grade teacher to complete the profile *appeared* extremely detrimental to me and a fatal blow to the project. The principal and the university coordinator called two meetings with all the teachers, to air their grievances and concerns about the project and the position of a researcher in their building. Unfortunately and, I believe, unfairly, I was not included in these meetings. From the notes taken at the meeting, one teacher stated, "Anyone who comes in this building should first come in as a guest. They shouldn't barge in and expect us to do things their way." Another teacher stated, "I don't have time to do things like a teacher profile." Yet, another stated, "The questions she asked us on the teacher profile are the ones teachers were asking her to explain all along." However, I did learn that one teacher came to the defense of my work with the teachers and the project itself. She stated that:

> I understood that the profile was part of the research process—she has asked us to talk about parent involvement in general at Morton, now she is asking us to discuss what we specifically want parents to do as it relates to literacy instruction in our own classrooms. In other words, she believes that grade level teachers *should* or *may* have similar parent involvement concerns around literacy. The concerns you have could lead to you developing a parent involvement program around *your* literacy concerns at *your* particular grade level. She has told us, and we agreed, that most of us have asked parents to help with parties and field trips...we know that helping with parties and field trips [and so on] has nothing to do with doing well in school. She is asking us to think about parent involvement in another

way. She wants "our new emphasis" on parent involvement to grow out of what we do in our classrooms. She is asking us to begin to think about creating a structure for parents around our curriculum, specifically our literacy curriculum. We can't ask her to do that for us. That is something we need to think about along with her. It's not her responsibility alone; we must play a part in this also. Just like we expect the parents of our children to join hands with us, she is asking us to join hands with her. I don't know what all the excitement and overreaction is about anyway. She did have the right to ask this teacher about her teacher profile. And the teacher should have complied with her request. If we want to be treated like a professional we should act like one. That's all I have to say.

The old saying that "good comes out of bad" proved true. This vigorous discussion proved to be cathartic for the teachers, and they realized that I was not the intruder they initially perceived. I was a person struggling to be heard. I was asking them to hear me, like they, for so many years, had been asking researchers to hear them. At this point, we began to move forward and talk. The teachers let me in, and we became co-learners. We found that the processes of exchange flourished when we began to learn how to criticize and trust the intentions driving our own criticism. Sharing the complexity of planning together and the mutual dependence between teachers and researchers were sources of empowerment for each of us. In particular, I was both empowered and pleased that the second-grade teachers had finally assumed leadership and accepted the assistance of myself and others in creating a structure for parents to be involved in the literacy development of their children rather than looking to us, who are outsiders, to be the change agents and leaders. Also, I was extremely pleased that the third-, fourth-, and fifth-grade teachers agreed to join the project because they believed in the premise on which the project was based—to invite parents to participate as curriculum literacy partners. What impressed me the most was that these third-, fourth-, and fifth-grade teachers had already examined their curriculum to determine how parents could support what they were doing in the classroom.

PAUSE AND REFLECT

Can you think of other ways that this situation could have been resolved? Discuss conflict resolution amongst educators in schools, including the notion of expectation on both sides. For example, when you invite people from the outside, are you trying to make parent involvement an event in your school or an ongoing program that structurally changes the way you interact with parents and children in your school? In your opinion, do you feel that I, as the researcher, was an intruder at Morton who made unfair demands on the teachers? Or do you feel that the teachers at Morton were making unfair demands on me by asking me to solve problems at their school and being unwilling to engage in the type of serious conversation I was pushing them to engage in through the teacher profile? Do you think parent involvement continues to remain an issue because all too often, teachers do not want to rethink their practices? Do you think the Morton teachers, like many teachers, felt more comfortable letting outsiders organize their parent involvement efforts so in the event the efforts fail, they can blame the outsider and not themselves?

Chapter 6, the heart of the book, describes for you the scope and sequence of parent involvement activities developed at Morton. It also outlines for you three sets of action steps for developing and improving family-school partnerships. After completing these action steps, you will have a good grasp of what you need to consider when thinking about family involvement. You will have the knowledge and background to help you develop and refine a definition of family involvement and examine your individual practices of working with diverse family populations. These action steps allow you to gain an understanding of the barriers that prevent families from becoming involved in the business of schools. Perhaps, more than anything else, these action steps serve as a guide for helping you (1) transform family involvement from mere rhetoric to actual practice and (2) develop yourself as a culturally relevant teacher who is able to bridge the gap between home and school.

In particular, you will enjoy reading the case study examples and vignettes, which highlight real teachers and parents, real struggles, and real efforts to involve parents in the educational lives of their children. You will also enjoy the opportunity to actively participate in the case study example. You will have the opportunity to evaluate the instruments I used with the teachers and parents at Morton, as well as the opportunity to react to the situations that arose in this setting. In other words, you can place yourself in the various scenarios by participating, on your own and with your peers, in the analysis and activities designed for the teachers and parents. You will have the opportunity to vicariously experience what it would feel like to develop a parent involvement program for diverse groups of families and children. Lastly, but more importantly, you can agree or disagree with the decisions I made and the strategies I designed at Morton. You can discuss whether you would have made the same or similar decisions or whether you would have designed the same, similar, or different strategies and activities if you taught at Morton. The chapter is designed with action steps to help you begin your journey of moving parent involvement from "high rhetoric to high practice."

New Parent Involvement Structures Emerge

Much has been written about the benefits of involving families in their children's literacy development (France & Hager, 1993; Handel, 1992; Edwards, 1991). A major focus of this work has centered around the question of how educators and families can better understand, cooperate, and communicate with each other to more effectively work together to support children's acquisition of literacy. One of the most important themes that have surfaced in the literature is the need for improving current structures for family involvement in schools (Edwards, 1996; Fear & Edwards, 1995). A second important theme is that families need to be heard; they need to be given time and opportunity to share their ideas, questions, and insights with teachers and administrators (Lynch, 1992). Simply put, teachers, administrators, and parents should become communicating allies in the education of all children.

In Chapter 2, you were introduced to terminology school staffs use to describe parent involvement initiatives (e.g., business partnerships, school-university partnerships, home-school-community partnerships, family literacy, and so on). At

Morton, the home literacy project can be defined as a curriculum-centered parent involvement project. Pizzo (1990) reports that parents should sustain strong attachments to their young children and advocate for them in the face of exceptionally adverse circumstances (p. 30). Supporting families provides a boost to the overall development of children. It seems reasonable to conclude then that a parent should be involved in their children's school curriculum. More than ten years ago, Seefeldt (1985) stated that schools should communicate with parents through the curriculum. She correctly noted that educators should do the following:

> Capitalize on the curriculum as a means of communicating with parents. It is an ongoing way to keep parents totally informed of their child's day, the school's goals and objectives, and the meaning of early childhood education. It's one way to begin to establish close, meaningful communication with busy parents...remember—informed, involved parents, those who are aware of what their children do in an early childhood program, are also supportive parents (p. 25).

Researchers like Keenan, Willett, & Solsken (1993) also believe that schools should communicate through the curriculum. The aims of their curriculum project were to strengthen the children's academic learning, foster school/home collaboration, and construct a multicultural community strong enough to nurture the diverse children of the urban elementary classrooms in which they worked. They believed that the project's focus on communication and meaning in the language arts provided a rich context for children's learning, but they also saw opportunities for further enriching their learning through new forms of parent participation in the curriculum.

Cummins (1986) argues that efforts to improve the education of children from dominated societal groups have been largely unsuccessful because the relationship between teachers and students and between schools and communities have remained unchanged. In his view, "The required changes involve personal redefinitions of the way classroom teachers interact with the children and communities they serve" (p. 18). He posits that school programs will be more successful at empowering minority children if (1) students' language and culture are incorporated into the school program, (2) community participation is encouraged as an integral component of children's education, (3) the pedagogy promotes intrinsic motivation on the part of students to use language actively to generate their own knowledge, and (4) professionals involved in assessment become advocates for students rather than legitimizing the location of the "problem" in the students. Although, like Cummins, I am particularly concerned with the success of children from dominated societal groups, I believe that his work speaks to school/home collaboration more generally and provides directions for raising all children in our increasingly diverse and complex villages. Unlike other approaches that focus on changes that families must make to support schools, I begin with ways that schools must change to support families.

Teachers and the whole school "family" have the responsibility for encouraging and facilitating parents' exposure to and integration into their children's classroom curriculum (Beane, 1990, p. 362). According to Knapp, Turnbull, & Shields (1990), all students must learn the culture of the school while they are attempting to master academic tasks. This is especially so for the disadvantaged learner. Lyn Corno (1989) summarizes well why the home and school should communicate around curricular issues. She noted that:

> ...With some shared understanding of their commonalities and differences, schools and homes should be able to work together to support each other in the development of a literate populace. There is, indeed, evidence that this is already occurring in certain enlightened contemporary homes and classrooms. It seems that the polarization of these subcultures may be transformed in important ways, and that families and classrooms wishing to move in this direction can benefit by a better understanding of the other's special traditions. Becoming literate about classrooms, then, is also in part becoming literate about the home; for this view suggests that effective classrooms are a blend of classroom and home—of family and knowledge workplace (p. 41).

First Set of Action of Steps

In this portion of the Morton Case Example, I describe the four-step process that the staff and I participated in to rethink parent involvement. As you saw in Chapter 2, there are many factors to consider in establishing a definition of parent involvement. First, who are the parents and what roles should they assume? Second, what kinds of involvement are advantageous for our school? Finally, what terms should be used to accurately portray the kind of parent involvement we want? From the many conversations I have had with school staffs in different parts of the United States, I have come to find that once entire school communities or individual classroom teachers begin to think seriously about parent involvement, they tend to think about it using the four-step process illustrated in Figure 6.1. In this chapter, you will hear how the Morton teachers used this four-step process.

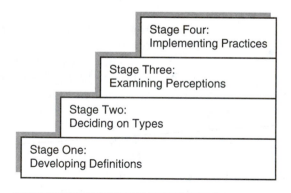

FIGURE 6.1   *Stages of Thinking about Parent Involvement*

These stages can be illustrated in terms of the questions asked to guide the process of improving parent involvement programs. These questions occur at both school and classroom levels.

School-Level Questions

Over the years, many schools, including Morton, have puzzled over questions such as the following:

- Should teachers and administrators formulate a singular/multiple definition(s) of parent involvement that represents the school's philosophy of parent involvement?
- Should schools develop specific policies about the roles parents may or should assume? (Edwards, 1999, pp. 83–84).

These kinds of questions are important for administrators to consider in that they set school policy. Principals and other school administrators might organize family nights or other types of events, but it is very important that these officials have thought about deeper and broader definitions of parent involvement (see Edwards, 1999). Further, schools have puzzled over the following question raised by Berger (1983):

Does the thought that parents could be involved as education policy makers in conjunction with the school interest or threaten you? (p. 1).

This question is very important because it acknowledges that school administrators can view more parent involvement as a blessing or a curse. Schools have also puzzled over questions like the following ones posed by Greenwood & Hickman (1991):

- What types of parent involvement have the strongest impact on different types of student achievement (e.g., higher order and lower order)?
- What types of parent involvement have the strongest effects on parent and student attitudes and behaviors?
- What parent and family characteristics influence student performance and parent involvement?
- What types of parent involvement work best with different socioeconomic status and ethnic families? (p. 287).

Classroom-Level Questions

In addition to these school-level questions, the Morton staff puzzled over the following questions that directly affect their individual practices of parent involvement:

- What should I do? How can I do more in my school/classroom to promote meaningful parent involvement?

- How should I reorganize my classroom instruction based on what I know about my students' home situations and their parents' ability to help them?
- What do I need to know so I won't offend parents, particularly parents of minority students?
- How should I interact with parents who have an ideology of parent involvement that conflicts with my own expectations?
- Should I only expect the parents of my students to be involved in their education? When the parents of my students choose not to be involved, should I seek out other family or community members to serve as advocates for these children?
- Should I begin to think about parent involvement initiatives in terms of my students' social, emotional, physical, and academic environment? Are my expectations for parent involvement unrealistic based on the families of the children I teach?
- How can I begin to rethink, in my school/classroom, the taken-for-granted, institutionally sanctioned means for teachers and parents to communicate (i.e., PTA meetings, open-house rituals at the beginning of the school year, writing and telephoning parents, and so on)? (See Edwards, 1999, p. 85.)

All of these questions reflect various stages in individual teachers' thinking at Morton about parent involvement, and these questions are an important part of the process of conceptualizing and understanding parent involvement. Furthermore, these questions help teachers to target the kinds of parent involvement they need for their classrooms. Teachers can ask these questions to begin generating specific ideas of parent involvement. More importantly, these questions can and should be included as part of staff development workshops to challenge teachers to reflect on a wide range of questions that need to be addressed when thinking about parent involvement initiatives.

Step 1: Developing an Informed Definition of Parent Involvement

Interviewing

In the fall of 1990, the Morton PDS staff invited me to their school to help them rethink and restructure parent involvement. I conducted two structured, individual interviews with each of the eight K-2 teachers and the reading specialist. The first interview was designed to assess their general thoughts about parent involvement (see Table 6.2). The second interview was designed to assess their thoughts regarding working with diverse parent populations, their beliefs about parent involvement/support of the school, and their reactions to parents' perceptions about schools (see Table 6.7). In my first group meeting with the principal, K-2 teachers, and reading specialist, I asked them to describe the parent involvement climate at Morton (e.g., present conditions, goals, bridges, barriers, first

TABLE 6.2 *First Structured Parent Involvement Interview*

Today I would like to chat with you to gather information and gain insights into some of the basic issues regarding parent involvement at Morton Professional Development School and in your classroom as we begin a concentrated collaborative effort to help parents become more involved in a "Literacy Community."

Inform teacher that the interview is being audiotaped. Encourage specific "teacher" stories to illustrate responses.

Think about Parental Involvement

1. Talk about how you feel about the role of parental responsibility as it refers to the school setting. Parent actions are different than ten to twenty years ago? Why?
2. Talk about your goals for parent involvement.
   - Attendance at meetings/conferences
   - Written correspondence
   - Classroom visits
   - At-home literacy events
   - Parental partnerships
3. Talk about how parent involvement affects your role as a teacher.
4. Talk about what you would like to know about a child's home situation to help you teach the child.
   - Schedule
   - Rules
   - Communication
   - Substance abuse
   - Family members
5. Talk about some of the types of parent involvement attempted during the past five years.
   District level
   School level
   Individual teacher level
   - Additional contacts
   - Innovative attempts
6. Talk about the response of these efforts.
   Why do you think this occurred?
   What was your follow-up?
   Your ideas?
   Your feelings?
7. When you received positive responses, talk about how you felt.
   Why?
   When you received negative responses, talk about how you felt.
   Why?

(continued)

TABLE 6.2 *Continued*

8. Talk about your own development of skills to relating to parents.
   District level
   College level
   "On the job"?
   Being a parent yourself?

9. Describe your present class:
   a. As learners
      • Physical characteristics
      • Academic level
      • Socioeconomic level
      • Behavior/management
      • Emotional/psychological
   b. Demographics of location of students' homes (neighborhoods, communities)
      • Areas of town
      • Amount of parental contact according to location, and so on
   c. parent characteristics
      • Age
      • Educational background
      • Level of school contact

10. Talk about the present types of parent involvement in your classroom.
    • In class
    • Treats
    • Fields trips
    • Other

11. Talk about the relationship you see between student achievement and parent involvement.

12. Talk about the parent involvement you would ultimately like to achieve with your students' parents (Utopian).

13. What type of "at-home" literacy program do you see as being carried out here at Morton?

14. As we work collaboratively as a Professional Development School, talk about MSU faculty's supportive role in this endeavor.
    • Research
    • Parent contacts
    • Community contact

steps). I also asked them to construct a parent involvement profile (see Henderson, Marburger, & Ooms, 1986). This profile requests school staffs to provide the percentage of time parents serve in specific roles within their school building (e.g., partners, collaborators, problem solvers, audience, supporters, advisors, and/or co-decision makers; see Figure 6.6).

Looking at the Responses from the First Structured Interview

This interview was designed to assess the Morton teachers' general thoughts about parents. We came together to begin working on their ideas of parent involvement at each grade level, so we could get a sense of how parents had been previously involved in the classrooms and how we could begin thinking of strategies to increase their parent involvement.

PAUSE AND REFLECT

Before reading further, take a few minutes and answer the first set of interview questions. You can answer them independently on paper, work with a partner in your class/group of colleagues, or work cooperatively with a cooperating/mentor teacher on these questions. After you answer these questions check your answers against the Morton teachers' responses and my analysis of these responses. Discuss which responses/analysis you agree or disagree with and why. Do you see a consistency in the teacher responses at Morton? Is there an integrated parent involvement approach at Morton?

Analysis of First Structured Interview

As you completed the first set of interview questions, you might have noticed that you had some definite ideas about parent involvement and what types of roles parents should play in their child's learning and academic achievement. Likewise, most of the Morton teachers were clear about how they felt about parent responsibility as it refers to the school setting, their goals for parent involvement, the techniques that they employed for involving parents, and the roles they wanted parents to play at home and at school to support their children's achievement. However, the voices spoke about parent involvement in very different ways, making a working consensus very difficult to achieve initially. Here is a sample of three teacher voices:

> *Mrs. Miller:* I feel that parent involvement is very, very important. More than that, I feel it is crucial if the child is going to achieve success in school. I do not believe for one moment that we can expect a teacher to do it all, whatever that means...it's just much easier if you've got some parent involvement. From a first grade teacher's point of view, it's wonderful, just ideal, if, when I get my children, they have been exposed to the "basics" or the readiness skills for learning to read...knowing their alphabet when they come to me, recognizing their letters...

> *Mrs. Novak:* My major issue is that I feel they, the parents, need to take more involvement before they even reach us...I hear more and more...Watching the news and reading articles...Instead of putting all of it

PAUSE AND REFLECT

At first glance, all of us would agree with Mrs. Miller that parent involvement is important, crucial to a child's success in school, and we can't expect teachers to do it all as she indicates. However, is it fair for Mrs. Miller to expect all of her children's parents to support their children's literacy development even if some of them are illiterate and do not have a sense of what she means when she says the "basics" or the "the readiness skills for learning to read"? Why or why not? Some parents do not feel confident or competent teaching reading and feel that they may hinder their children's success if they do the "wrong" things. What is your response to how some parents may feel about helping their children? What would you do about it? What other reactions do you have about Mrs. Miller's statement? Do you think that Mrs. Miller's belief about parent responsibility is fair? Do you think Mrs. Miller's assumptions about parent responsibility alienate some parents? Why or why not?

on a teacher in education what they are saying is that parents should get involved with their children's education. And I think we needed to get to that point. Teachers were being overwhelmed with, "It's our problem!" And I don't think parent involvement is totally our problem. In college, we should have learned how to work with parents, but we didn't. Sometimes I feel like parent involvement is not my job.

PAUSE AND REFLECT

As you can see, Mrs. Novak is overwhelmed and feels that parent involvement is not totally her problem or her job. Taking her cues from watching the news and reading articles, Mrs. Novak has made up her mind about what parents should do for their children even before their children enter school. What are your reactions to Mrs. Novak's statement? What would you do if you were Mrs. Novak? What do you think Mrs. Novak needs to do to change her thinking about parent involvement?

Mrs. Bowker: Okay, I think I see [parent involvement as] twofold. I think that there are some very specific objectives that they can help me to meet in the classroom, but I also see it as a supportive link to what we are doing in the classroom. So there are some specific things that I send home that I want parents' input and help with. [My goal is] [t]hat every parent is in my classroom at least twice a year to help. To actually, physically, know the routine, what we are doing, what we are going to do. So they volunteer to come and read stories, take a small group, count with students. I actually have a folder that's a parent helper folder where they just come in; they don't even have to see me. I explain it at the first open house where the folder is kept and what kind of things they can do. So I expect every parent to be in. And it has been met so far.

PAUSE AND REFLECT

Mrs. Bowker has identified very specific objectives for which she wants parent assistance. I wonder if Mrs. Bowker has stopped to think about whether her parents agree or disagree with the specific objectives she has outlined for them. Because Mrs. Bowker is so specific on how and what she wants parents to do, do you think that Mrs. Bowker would be unwilling to change the ways in which she wants parents involved? Do you think Mrs. Bowker's attempts to involve and invite parents to participate might in turn prompt some parents to select not to be involved and to feel uninvited?

You can see that each of the Morton teachers did think parent involvement was very important, yet each had a different perspective about how to define parent involvement and their responsibilities for fostering this involvement. Although each of the teachers had different definitions of parent involvement, they agreed to take particular "parts" of what each one of them thought "parent involvement" to mean to create a working definition. They also agreed to refine their definitions as they learned more about how to involve parents.

Preservice and Inservice Teachers' Views of
How to Successfully Structure Parent Involvement

In Chapter 2, you learned that parent involvement is embedded in multiple understandings, interpretations, and personal meanings. I argued that educators would continue to struggle to make the relationship between home and school one of depth until they define what they mean by and want from parent involvement initiatives. If preservice teachers did this then they would be more prepared and willing to work with parents, and inservice teachers would begin to rethink their parent involvement practices.

Since I speak frequently to preservice and inservice teacher groups around the country, I decided to survey some of these groups about what they meant by and wanted from parent involvement initiatives. I asked for volunteers to answer the question: "What does an elementary teacher need to know about parent involvement in order to structure it successfully?" A total of thirty-four inservice teachers and thirty-five preservice teachers responded in writing to this question. The inservice teachers were mainly from public schools in Michigan, Wyoming, Georgia, Illinois, and Texas, and the preservice teachers were from Michigan and Texas.

The years of teaching experience for the inservice teachers range from 5 to 25 years. The preservice teachers were doing their student teaching or were involved in a one-year internship program. Most of the inservice teachers were white women, with only a small percentage of them being African-American women and white men. Similarly, most of the preservice teachers were white women. However, the preservice teachers did include some Hispanic, African-American, and Asian-American women. Even though this sample is small, it is representative of the national teaching force. According to recent figures from the National Center for Education information, almost ninety percent of U.S. teachers are white, and about seven percent identify themselves as black, two percent as Hispanic, one percent as American Indian or Alaskan, and one percent as Asian Native.

In answering the question about what an elementary teacher needs to know about parent involvement, eight themes were identified across the responses: family background information, values and expectations, strategies for involving parents, how to communicate with parents, teaching parents, how to organize parent involvement, kinds of parent involvement, and home learning environment. Responses were coded and tallied to determine the number of inservice and preservice teachers who responded within each category. Because the question was open-ended, teachers could respond in multiple categories. The results are shown in Figure 6.2.

Family Background Information.   This category was the most common one mentioned by inservice and preservice teachers alike. It involved demographic information about the family, such as marital status, socioeconomic class, educational level, occupation, and parental school experiences. One preservice teacher commented:

> The first thing that a teacher needs to know about is the background of the child. What kind of home life is the child dealing with? What is the parental situation? Married, divorced, stepparents? If divorced, who does the child live with and are both parents involved in the child's life? (Preservice Teacher #1).

The inservice teachers surveyed echoed concerns with family background information. "A teacher needs to find out more about the parents of the children they are teaching. This would help the teacher figure out how the parent could be involved" (Inservice teacher #19). Some of the teachers seemed to believe that there was a relationship between the parent's own success as a student and their involvement. One teacher suggested:

> An elementary teacher needs to be aware of the different levels of parent (school) experience (their own) and be sensitive to their needs. [For] example, Some parents may have had bad school experiences earlier in their lives and [may] be afraid to participate in school activities. [For] example, other parents may be at school often (Inservice Teacher #15).

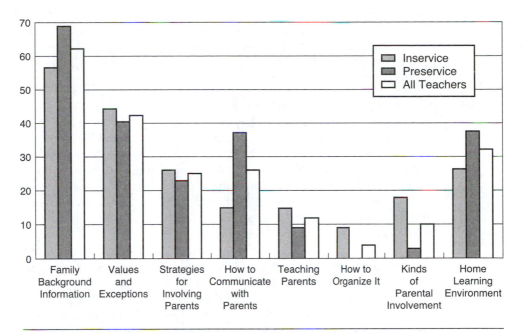

FIGURE 6.2   *What Do Teachers Need to Know to Structure Parent Involvement Successfully?*

Values and Expectations.   Values and expectations was the second most frequently mentioned category for teachers in both groups. Many of the teachers recognized that all parents do not have the same values and expectations related to education, as evidenced by comments such as, "What do parents expect from the classroom experience as a whole? How much of a part do they feel they play?" (Inservice Teacher #31); "What value of education do parents have?" (Preservice Teacher #25); and, "The teacher should be aware of families' cultures and values, how they relate with their children, and how they expect teachers to relate to their children" (Preservice Teacher #24).

Although many of the teachers acknowledged that parents may have differing values and expectations related to school, there seemed to be an underlying set of values and expectations that were "correct." One preservice teacher, for example, stated that teachers needed to know, "How to deal with parents who do not place value or importance in education" (Preservice Teacher #11).

Home Learning Environment.   Like the family background information, teachers felt that it was important to have knowledge about the child's home learning environment. This included the physical aspects of the home, such as, "Are there pencils, papers, and books in the home?" (Inservice Teacher #34); emotional

aspects, such as, "How does such an environment contribute to the type of emo-
tions a parent experiences? Is it a stressful environment or empowering environment?" (Inservice Teacher #1); and the nature of parent-child interaction, such as,
"Do they educate out of school, read at home, and do the homework with the
kids?" (Preservice Teacher #27).

How to Communicate with Parents.   Preservice teachers were more concerned
with communication skills (thirty-seven percent) than inservice teachers (fifteen
percent). Perhaps this related to the experience and skill that many inservice
teachers have acquired in talking with parents. Preservice teachers, on the other
hand, are less experienced talking to parents about problems that students are
having and may be apprehensive about doing so. Preservice teachers mentioned
challenging teacher-parent interactions, such as, "How to deal with conflicting
philosophies of education" (Preservice Teacher #11) and, "How do I handle an
angry parent?" (Preservice Teacher #35).

Some of the inservice teachers felt that communication skills were necessary
to promote parent involvement. One teacher wondered, "How can I talk with parents about them [struggling students] in a way that conveys a sense of urgency
but not a sense that there's nothing they can do anyway?" (Inservice Teacher #1).
Another recognized that teachers need to be careful not to "read too much" into
what a parent says: "We, as teachers need to know how to effectively communicative with parents who are reluctant, who have had "bad" school experiences,
young parents, and scrutinizing parents and how to understand what they say.
They may say things that we interpret negatively, but it's not meant to be negative" (Inservice Teacher #2).

Strategies for Involving Parents.   Twenty-five percent of the teachers surveyed
felt that teachers needed to know about effective strategies for involving parents
in their children's education. Some of the teachers seemed concerned about ways
of involving reluctant parents. For instance, one teacher asked, "How can I
encourage Title I parents to get involved? Many are afraid, intimidated, unmoti-
vated, uninterested, and unsure of how to be involved" (Inservice Teacher #1).
Similarly, a preservice teacher wondered, "How do I encourage a hesitant parent
to be involved?" (Preservice Teacher #35).

One of the preservice teachers was sensitive to the notion that teachers must
have a repertoire of strategies for involving parents. She explains, "Teachers need
to know how to engage a diverse group of parents in classroom activities/home
learning activities. They need a variety of strategies to meet a diverse group of
individuals" (Preservice Teacher #29).

Kinds of Parent Involvement.   The responses in this category acknowledged that
parent involvement could take a variety of forms. Teachers need to provide a
range of opportunities for parents to become involved in their children's education. According to one teacher:

An elementary teacher needs to be innovative about parent involvement. [For] example, some parents do well coming to conferences, open houses, and so on. Some parents may want to help in the classroom. Some parents may not want to come to school but do well by helping their child do their homework. Some parents may want to cut things out at home or drop off needed supplies and/or treats. Some parents may be doing their best at just getting their child to bed on time, fed, and dressed in the morning" (Inservice Teacher #15).

Although inservice teachers (eighteen percent) mentioned that teachers needed to be knowledgeable about the kinds of parent involvement more frequently that preservice teachers (three percent), one preservice teacher felt that teachers need to know, "How to work with different levels of parental support in school and home" (Preservice Teacher #11).

Teaching Parents.   This category of responses indicated that teachers needed to know how to teach parents how to be involved at school. An inservice teacher wondered, "How do we, without offending, help parents 'parent' (i.e., how children act toward adults comes directly from how they act toward their parents) (Inservice Teacher #1). Some of the teachers indicated that teachers should be knowledgeable about providing, "after school or parent classes/programs to help teach involvement skills and methods" (Inservice Teacher #6) and to know how to "develop parent workshops" (Preservice Teacher #14).

How to Organize Parent Involvement.   Comments in this category revolved around ways of structuring parent involvement. Issues such as, "How can you efficiently work with all the parents that want to be involved?" (Inservice Teacher #10) and, "How can you structure parent involvement to accommodate those with little education or literacy skills?" (Inservice Teacher #25) were included in this category.

This category was mentioned by nine percent of the inservice teachers but was not mentioned by preservice teachers. Perhaps this difference was related to the experience of inservice teachers in the difficulty of organizing parent involvement. Because most of the preservice teachers had not tried to organize parent involvement, they may not have been aware that this was a skill that teachers needed to have.

In short, the data from the teacher surveys suggested that teachers needed to have a great deal of knowledge and skill to successfully structure parent involvement. They need to know about family background, parental values, and expectations related to education and the home learning environment. They need to know strategies for promoting parent involvement, especially for parents who may be reluctant, and be aware of different kinds of parent involvement. Teachers need to know how to organize parent involvement and how to teach parents ways of being involved. Finally, teachers need to have communication skills that enable them to promote parent involvement.

Step 2: Deciding on Types of Family Involvement

When I asked the Morton teachers about the *type of parent involvement or roles they wanted parents to play in supporting their children's achievement*, the teachers' answers centered mostly on the roles parents could play at home, as well as the roles they could play at school. The answers to this question were so interesting that I decided to ask teachers in grades three through five what roles they wanted parents to play as well. Teachers' most common responses to this question across grade levels can be found in Tables 6.3 and 6.4.

Home-Centered Roles

The roles identified by the K-5 teachers at Morton resemble many of the *home-centered parent roles* Vukelich (1984) identified from her review of more than forty sources. For example, Vukelich reported that "read to your child," "be a good literate model," "provide books, magazines, and so on for your child to read," and "talk and listen to your child," were suggestions most frequently made for parent involvement. At the K-5 grade level, the Morton teachers overwhelmingly recommended to parents "have your child read to you." At the K-3 grade levels, teach-

---

TABLE 6.3   *Home-Centered Parent Roles Identified by Kindergarten through Fifth-Grade Teachers*

Common throughout all grades (K-5)
Have your child read to you

Common in grades K-1
Encourage practical reading (packages, signs, and so on)
Play with your child

Common in grades K-2
Take child on field trips/outings
Relate writing/words and experiences
Keep a journal

Common in grades K-3
Read to your child
Be a good literate model
Watch TV together
Encourage language use
Work on vocabulary

Common in grades 1 and 2
Provide challenges during reading time (interactive reading)

Common in grades 1-4
Review homework with child
Provide books in the home

Common in grades 4 and 5
Increase awareness of curriculum/teachers' goals

TABLE 6.4 *School-Centered Parent Roles Identified by Kindergarten through Fifth-Grade Teachers*

Common in grades K-5
Read to child's class
Attend open house, parent-teacher association meetings, conferences, workshops

Common in grades in K-3
Assist with projects/games
Flash cards
Chaperone (field trips)
Plan and direct parties
Work in school library
Help with school play
Listen to students retell stories
Drill child on vocabulary (teach root words and endings)

Common in grades 1 and 2
Work with slow learners
Teach songs to class

Common in grades 1-5
Check and file papers

Common in grades 4 and 5
Knowledge of the school's academic programs/reading program
Serve as resource person

ers recommended to parents "read to your child," "be a good literate model," "watch TV together," "work on vocabulary," and so on. At grades four and five, teachers only had one common recommendation for parents, which was "increase awareness of curriculum/teacher goals." Some of the *home-centered parent roles* at individual grade levels included the following: "Let your child help you sort clothing" (*kindergarten*), "give books and start a home library" (*first grade*), "reinforce correct English" (*second grade*), "draw up a contract with child" (*third grade*), "make every effort to become aware of child's strengths and weaknesses" (*fourth grade*), and "encourage your child to do outside reading" (*fifth grade*).

School-Centered Roles

I also solicited from the Morton teachers' *school-centered parents roles* what they would like for K-5 parents to assume. The roles that were common in grades K-5 were "read to child's class," and "attend open house, PTA meetings, conferences, workshops." In grades one through five, the only role commonly identified by the teachers was "check and file papers." In grades K-3, there were many common roles identified: "assist with projects/games," "flash cards," "chaperone (field trips)," "plan and direct parties," "work in school library," help with school play," "listen to students retell stories," and "drill child on vocabulary (teach root words and endings)." Teacher responses to this question by individual grade levels can be found in Tables 6.5 and 6.6.

TABLE 6.5 *Home-Centered Parent Roles at Individual Grade Levels*

Kindergarten
Let your child help you sort clothing
Label objects about the home
Show your child how to follow a recipe
Call attention to familiar sounds about the house

First Grade
Purchase books and start a home library
Give gifts of books on all occasions

Second Grade
Reinforce correct English
Provide a suitable place for child to study
Pay attention to the parent letter helpers that are sent home
Help child with crossword puzzles

Third Grade
Use dictionary and other references
Help child with creative thinking
Share favorite stories with child
Draw up a contract with child
Complete and read the Mini Page in newspaper
Set a limit on the number of books child checks out of the library each week

Fourth Grade
Show a continued interest in child's reading development
Make every effort to become aware of child's strengths and weaknesses

Fifth Grade
Work to reinforce what the teacher has taught
Encourage your child to do outside reading

Analysis of Teacher Responses

What might these teacher responses mean? First, teachers identified extremely traditional home- and school-centered roles. Soliciting parent assistance in "checking and filing papers," "assisting with project/games," and "flash cards" and so on are parent roles, which are expected to be fairly straightforward. For the most part, teachers feel they do not have to spend a significant amount of time explaining these roles to parents because many of these school-centered parent roles are considered to represent accepted and expected roles parents are willing to assume. Thus, most of these roles do not appear out of the ordinary for parents. Similarly, these roles do not communicate to parents that they are doing the teacher's job. Instead, most parents feel that in these roles they are supporting the teacher's efforts to do a *better job of teaching* their children. Lastly, but more importantly, these roles communicate to most parents that somehow they are fulfilling their civic responsibilities to schools.

I used this information with the entire staff to discuss some of the roles they had asked parents to assume in the past. Also, I used this information to discuss

TABLE 6.6 *School-Centered Parent Roles at Individual Grade Levels*

Kindergarten
Make picture books or a dictionary for the class
Use footprints to distinguish left from right

First Grade
Make bulletin board
Tape books
Review days, months, color words, and number words

Second Grade
Donate recreational reading materials to classroom
Help children to write a personal diary
Share interesting articles with class

Third Grade
Watch children read stories to lower-grade children
Watch children read silently and then check their comprehension
Illustrate stories that are read in class

Fourth Grade
Publicize the good points about the school's academic programs

Fifth Grade
Be the teacher's partner in your child's class
Observe children's interaction during reading

what plans they had for rethinking home and school roles parents might assume in the future.

Step 3: Examining Perceptions of Family Involvement

The second structured interview was conducted with Morton teachers in late September 1990, approximately five months after the first structured interview. Teachers were asked to carry their envisioned parent roles into particular scenarios. (See Table 6.7 for the questions in the second interviews.)

PAUSE AND REFLECT

Again, take a few minutes to answer this set of interview questions. You can answer them independently on paper, work with a partner in your class/group of colleagues, or work cooperatively with a cooperating/mentor teacher on these questions. After you answer these questions, check your answers against the Morton teachers' responses and my analysis of these responses. Discuss which responses/analysis you agree or disagree with and why. Do you see a consistency in the teacher responses at Morton? Is there an integrated parent involvement approach at Morton?

TABLE 6.7 *Second Structured Interview: Parent Involvement Scenarios*

SCENARIO 1

Getting parents "involved" in their children's education is widely accepted as critical to students' success in school. Many people agree that "Parent involvement is on everyone's list of practices to make schools more effective, to help families create a more positive learning environment, to reduce the risk of student failure, and to increase student success." Tell me what you think about parent involvement. I'd like to describe twelve parent/teacher interactions to you and ask you how you would handle the different kinds of parents in these situations.

Suppose you sent out three or four notices requesting a parent to attend a conference and received no response to your written communication. What would you do? Why is that what you would do?

Suppose you then telephone the parent and the parent promises you that he/she will meet with you after school. You wait for forty-five minutes, but the parent does not show up. What do you make of this?

Would you do anything about this?
If yes: What? Why would you do this?
If no: Why not?
What led you to this idea?

Suppose this was a white parent? How would you respond? Why is that the way you would respond?

Suppose this was a African American parent? How would you respond? Why is that the way you would respond?

Suppose this was a Latino parent? How would you respond? Why is that the way you would respond?

Suppose this was a Native American parent? How would you would respond? Why is that the way you would respond?

Suppose this parent was of the working class? How would you respond? Why is that the way you would respond?

SCENARIO 2

Teachers at Sear Roger School were talking about parent involvement and these are actual quotes. We'd like for you to comment on each of these quotes.

Parents won't come to the school, at least not the parents who need to come.
What do you think would lead a teacher to say something like this? Can you ever recall saying something like this yourself?

Parents don't want to become involved in their children's learning.
What do you think would lead a teacher to say something like this? Can you ever recall saying something like this yourself?

Parents don't seem interested in school.
What do you think would lead a teacher to say something like this? Can you ever recall saying something like this yourself?

TABLE 6.7   *Continued*

Parents don't show up.
What do you think would lead a teacher to say something like this? Can you ever recall saying something like this yourself?

Parents promise, but they don't follow through.
What do you think would lead a teacher to say something like this? Can you ever recall saying something like this yourself?

Parents only pretend to understand.
What do you think would lead a teacher to say something like this? Can you ever recall saying something like this yourself?

Parents do their children's work for them.
What do you think would lead a teacher to say something like this? Can you ever recall saying something like this yourself?

Parents worry too much about how the other kids are doing.
What do you think would lead a teacher to say something like this? Can you ever recall saying something like this yourself?

SCENARIO 3

At the same time the teachers were meeting to discuss parents, the Sear Roger parents were meeting in another room discussing teachers and these are some of their actual statements.

Teachers don't want parents poking about in school business.
What do you think might cause a parent to say something like this? What if a parent said this to you? How would you respond? Why? Do you think the parents of your students believe this about teachers in this school? Why?

Teachers only send home bad news.

Teachers don't do what they say they will.

Parent-teacher conferences are routine and unproductive.

Teachers teach too much by rote.

Teachers care more about discipline than teaching.

Teachers are obsessed with their occupational image.

Teachers are unsympathetic to parents whose background, social class, or language is different from their own.

Teachers feel that parent involvement is not their problem.

Teachers feel that parent involvement is too hard to administer.

Teachers don't make enough effort to understand children, they keep parents at bay with educational jargon, and they are more concerned with preserving their professional prerogatives than with helping kids.

Teachers worry about their professional independence and only want to get on with their jobs with as little interference from home as possible. (Henderson, Marburger & Ooms, 1986, p. 52).

Analysis of the Second Structured Individual Interviews

The second set of structured individual interviews with the eight K-2 teachers and the reading specialists was extremely interesting to watch. The teachers' and the reading specialist's responses to the three scenarios were what I would call *politically correct responses*. They failed to provide any differentiated responses in terms of how they would interact, for example, with a white, African American, welfare, or teen parent, or a parent who was reluctant to come to school. They also commented that they tended not to listen to gossip about parents, and they tried to talk directly to parents if they heard something positive. My personal response to these teacher statements was, "Hallelujah! Teachers have finally stopped listening to teacher lounge gossip!" However, I remained suspicious because I have firsthand experience of knowing that, in fact, teachers do in fact, gossip in the teacher's lounge. I was a teacher myself, and the lounge is the place where teachers let off steam. Because the teachers viewed me as an outsider, it is probable that they did not feel comfortable sharing with me what they really thought.

PAUSE AND REFLECT

Do you feel that the Morton teachers were being politically correct in their responses to the second set of interview questions? Why or why not? When you attempted to answer these questions, did you find yourself providing politically correct answers? Why or why not? Does your own attempt at political correctness prevent honest, open, and meaningful discussions/interactions with racially/culturally different parents? Do you think that in today's schools it is necessary to be politically correct? Why or why not?

Step 4: Implementing Practices of Parent Involvement

In Step 4, I describe the scope and sequence of parent involvement activities grade-by-grade around curricular issues. Very few schools schedule activities that they want parents to participate in throughout the school year in August. As a result, parent involvement does not become for families a set of structured activities that they can expect to participate in throughout the year. For information on the *Kindergarten Project*, please read Appendix A, which contains the September 1996 *Language Arts* article I wrote that provides a detailed description of how I assisted the Morton Kindergarten teachers in involving parents in the literacy support of their young children.

First-Grade Project

I asked first-grade teachers at Morton to describe their perceptions of parent involvement. The teachers responded by voicing frustration because they said that parents lacked respect for their children's gradual movement toward becoming readers and writers. One first-grade teacher expressed this frustration with parents by stating:

> We need parents to believe that when their kids work on something three days in class that they shouldn't take it off the refrigerator and throw it away. Some of the kids were coming back saying, "my mama threw that activity away," and then the kids were sort of disappointed that they were trying so hard in school and the parents were not supporting what they were doing at home.

The teacher continued by saying that:

> Parents don't understand what we're trying to say to them when we're talking to them about reading and writing. For example, several parents have said to me, "Yeah when they bring that home, there's not a word spelled right. There are no capitals. There are no periods. I can hardly read a thing. My kid reads it pretty good and tells me the story, and I think, gosh, this is what they're doing all day. And it went in the garbage."

After several discussions with the three first-grade teachers, I was able to help them understand the importance of closely examining their conversations with parents around reading and writing. I was also able to help teachers see that they needed to develop specific ways to help parents understand what was happening in first grade. I reminded the teachers that the children were trying to construct an understanding of reading and writing but that it was important to help their parents construct an understanding of how their children were developing as readers and writers (for more information see Fear, Edwards, & Harris, 1995).

My advice to first-grade teachers was consistent with the advice given by other researchers. For example, Edwards (1993) points out that "it is important to note that when children enter school not only are they affected by the new school environment, but their parents are as well" (p. 1). Fletcher (1966) reminded us that:

> Education is simply not something which is provided either by teachers in schools or by parents and family members in the home. It must be a *continuing* cultivation of the child's experiences in which *both* schools and families jointly take part. (p. 189)

Lightfoot (1978) makes clear that first-grade parents are greatly concerned about their children's academic development. She stated that:

> First grade is considered the critical period of family-school contact—when mothers [and fathers] are most distressed about releasing their child to the care of a distant person; when school is no longer a world of sandboxes and Play-Doh but a place for learning to read and write; where parents fear the external judgments made about the quality of their parenting during the first five years of the child's life; and when the child experiences the inevitable trauma of moving them from a relatively egocentric, nurturant home environment to the more evaluative, social experience of school (pp. 86–87).

I informed teachers that I believe that a good relationship between parents, child, and teacher should be a priority. Potter (1989) echoed my position by arguing that:

> Teachers have the important responsibility of working with and relating to families, not just children. Of course, the teacher's role with the child is different from that of the parent. The teacher has a more achievement-oriented approach where performance will be evaluated, but this cannot be done fairly if the teacher has no knowledge of the family relationships of the child. The teacher should strive to develop an environment where there is a *participatory role* for the family, which facilitates the parent-teacher-child relationship and so enables the teaching and evaluation of the child to be appropriate and just (p. 21).

Creating a First-Grade Parent Informant Group.   Based on our initial conversations about parents' struggles to support their children's learning, I helped the first-grade teachers organize a parent informant literacy group. The purpose of this group was to provide an opportunity for teachers, parents, and myself to participate in conversations that would facilitate parent understanding of how their children were developing as readers and writers. We used Marie M. Clay's books, *What Did I Write? Beginning Writing Behaviour* and *Reading: The Patterning of Complex Behaviour,* as guides for helping parents understand how their children were developing as readers and writers.

At the first meeting, I wanted to give the first-grade teachers the opportunity to lead the discussion with parents. I was disappointed, however, that the teachers were giving the parents global statements when they asked specific questions. Often, the answers teachers gave were only remotely related to what parents asked. For example, the teachers gave answers like, "Your child is doing fine," "They are just where I expected they would be," or "Trust me, everything will turn out just fine." My response to the answers that the teachers gave to parents was, "What do you really mean by what you said to parents?"

For the next meeting, parents requested that the meeting focus on child development. They wanted some specific examples of emergent literacy. Some of the discussion from this is highlighted as follows:

> A lot of us have grown up with this paradigm where everybody drew the same bunny [or] everybody wrote the same kind of Mother's Day card. We now accept all kinds of writing from the kids. If your child was born in January, and you have, I guess, another child that's born in September in the same classroom, would you expect the child born in September to be doing exactly the same thing that the child is doing that's born in January?

Parents all looked at each other and said, "NO." It made sense to them that children all enter the class at different levels with different amounts of experience. Therefore one cannot expect all of these children to be writing, reading, or moving at the same pace.

Some of the parents were starting to say, "Wow, no wonder his [or her] little face just drops when I throw his [her] papers away." They realized that children were getting conflicting messages: "My teacher thinks this is fantastic; my mother, grandmother, older brother, and sister—they don't think it's good." This began a lively conversation in which teachers, parents, and I all shared stories of children's development. One of the stories I shared seemed to strike parents as especially significant:

> You know, all of you had this baby who was eight, nine months old and when that child looked at a cup and said "cup" or said "cracker" or said "mama," you didn't say "No, excuse me, this is a cup that we drink out of, this is a cracker, [and] this is a cookie and if you want something to eat or drink, you have to pronounce everything perfectly. When your child was in kindergarten, first grade, [or] second grade, they may write a story [where] everything isn't spelled correctly. I hope you don't stop your child and say, "wait a minute; dog is d-o-g—it isn't d-o-s." You know what I mean?

By the end of that meeting, many made comments along the line of, "Yeah, maybe some of the things they've been bringing home I really need to praise."

At our third meeting, two important pieces of information that focused specifically on emergent literacy were shared with the parents. One was a brochure that I designed to help parents understand their children's reading and writing stages of development (see Figure 6.3). This brochure prompted a very productive and informative discussion among the parents, teachers, and myself.

The second important piece of information shared with the parents was an instrument that the first-grade teachers and I adapted from Mooney (1988), which allows teachers to talk more specifically about some of the attitudes, understandings, and behaviors of young children's reading development (see Appendix B). The feature of this instrument that the parents clearly identified with was that it provided the opportunity for their child's teacher to discuss with them the attitudes, understandings, and behaviors at three different developmental stages—emergent, early, and fluency. The parents were extremely pleased with the discussion around this instrument. They began to gain a better understanding of the point that children enter first grade at different levels of understanding. More importantly, they began to understand that they should be supportive of their child at whatever developmental level at which their child appears to be functioning. Parents were understanding better how learning to read is a process, not just an outcome of curricular activities.

Second-Grade Project

Like the first-grade teachers, second-grade teachers at Morton were also unsure of how they wanted to involve parents in the literacy support of their children. Teachers struggled to find ways to connect parent involvement activities to the curriculum in their classrooms. Consequently, two second-grade teachers, two researchers (Kathleen Fear and myself), a graduate student (Deborah L. Harris),

Children know that marks on paper have meaning. In the beginning, these marks do not look like letters. As children develop as writers, they use some or all of the following stages:

Pre-reading/Reading Stages

1. *Language Development*
   The child learns to mean, learns to talk, and talks to learn.

2. *Book Awareness/Book Talk*
   The child reads with the purposes of developing an awareness of what a book is (i.e., Once upon a time . . . .)

3. *Picture and Pretend Reading*
   The child tells the story from the pictures.

4. *Recite and Memory Read*
   The child reads/retells the story using the familiar story line.

5. *Conversation Reading*
   The child talks about the story that he/she has heard.

6. *Meaning from Print*
   The child understands that the story comes from print.

7. *Read Print*
   The child learns to read letters and words.

8. *Reading*
   The child learns and develops reading for communication and enjoyment.

Writing Stages

1. *Scribbling*
   Writing emerges by play/mimicking adults.

2. *Nonsense Letter*
   Written marks are used to express ideas and take form similar to letters and numbers.

3. *Mock Writing*
   Copies information using labels, signs, lists (i.e., K-Mart, McDonald's, and so on).

4. *Invented or Approximated Writing*
   Develops an awareness of written conventions (i.e., writing has meaning, letter/sound relations, space between words, and so on).

   My cat is nice.

5. *Early Writing*
   The child gains awareness of sentence structure, spelling, grammar, and punctuation. An awareness of writing organization appears.

6. *Developing Writing* The child is still learning the above skills. It takes time. Some correct spelling is seen in 1st grade.

   Kelsey is sick.

7. *Mature Writing*
   The child uses the writing process independently.

Reading/Writing at Home

As a parent, the most important thing you can do is let your child lead the way. Here are some suggestions for getting your child started at home:

1. Conversation: Talk to and with your child. Listen and ask questions.

2. Read to and with your child. Talk about it.

3. Visit places: library, store, etc.

4. Joke, sing, rhyme, read poems and fairy tales, retell stories together.

5. Provide opportunities for everyday reading: labels, signs, recipes, maps.

6. Provide writing area: crayons, markers, pencils, different paper, and so on, for exploration.

7. Designate area for displaying his/her writing.

8. Provide opportunities for everyday writing: notes, letters, grocery list, jobs.

9. Offer help when asked for and talk so he/she can understand.

10. Support your child's attempt in creating meaning. Don't be concerned with spelling.

FIGURE 6.3 *Children's Reading/Writing Stages*

and the reading specialist met during PDS release time to study and discuss parent involvement. In these study group discussions, the second-grade group decided to extend a program initiated by a student teacher. This student teacher had learned about an integrated reading and writing curriculum during a three-course literacy sequence that preceded her student teaching. At the beginning of the 1992–1993 school year, the student teacher assessed her students' development as readers and writers and began to implement the integrated curriculum approach she had studied. The second-grade teachers decided to work with her, because they saw writing as an important curriculum component and the school had participated in inservice activities related to writing three years before this experience.

The parent component of the new project grew out of changes in the literacy curriculum initiated by the student teacher and by two events that occurred simultaneously. The first event happened when, during regularly scheduled parent-teacher conferences, several of the parents talked with the teachers and the student teacher about the writing that children were working on at home. Although students were not assigned writing homework per se, some had independently begun preparing written pieces at home to share with their classmates the next day in school. Understandably, the parents of these students were curious about what was happening in the classroom. The student teacher explained the purpose of the writing that students were generating in school and shared student portfolios at these conferences. She also described students' responses to each other's written pieces. During the same week that parent conferences were held, the study group (i.e., researchers, graduate student, two second-grade teachers, student teacher, reading specialist) met to begin formulating a plan for involving parents in literacy instruction. The second catalyst for involving parents occurred when the reading specialist shared with the study group an article by Miller-Rodriguez (1991) that described a project that involved encouraging children to write by furnishing writing supplies that were sent home in "traveling writers' briefcases." The timing of these two events led to (1) the second-grade teachers deciding to follow up on the successes reported during parent conferences and (2) the need to reach out to more parents and students in a variety of ways.

Parent-Teacher-Student Teacher Informant Meetings. The second-grade team first extended conventional parent involvement practices by exchanging information at parent-teacher informant meetings. At these meetings the Morton second-grade PDS team shared portfolios of children's writing and videotapes of writing instruction with parents. The student teacher, teachers, and researchers focused on children's growth and their successes, whereas parents informed the group of their children's responses to school writing instruction. Parents also began to raise questions about the writing curriculum. The student teacher began to read examples aloud and discuss children's interests, successes, struggles, and uses of writing at school. Some parents joined in to affirm their children's growth and to describe their children's writing initiatives at home, whereas others raised concerns about their children's reticence and lack of initiative. Teachers shared their work, plans, questions, and uncertainties about differences in students' development as writers.

Rather than simply receiving information from teachers about their children's achievements, the parents contributed information on their own and raised specific questions in a public forum. In response to the group's remaining questions, the team planned a second meeting to discuss student progress. In addition, the teachers asked parents to share rides with additional interested parents, and they supplied six briefcases full of supplies for children to use at home. The success of these strategies led to the second activity that substantively changed the level of family involvement.

The parent informant meetings established a predictable structure for parents to communicate information about how their child was responding to instruction in school. Parents not only became more knowledgeable about the school curriculum, but they also contributed information about their children's struggles, concerns, and progress. They began to inform other parents and teachers about their children's desires and they made sense of the topics, audiences, and kernel issues in children's lives. Many parents gave each other ideas about how they wrote with their children and what ideas had stirred their children's curiosity.

Parents became more than recipients and overseers of assignments. Their creative responses also changed the dynamics of the informant group. There was a mutual sense of pride and enjoyment, shared by parents and professional educators alike, in reading the children's writing and explaining life situations and humorous events such as how a garage sale treasure (a plastic fruit-covered hat) became a critical component in a story. They also shared a mutual frustration over students who refused to write or share their work with their classmates. Rather than just expediting the meetings, teachers reaped rewards by openly sharing their struggles, as well as hearing from parents about the positive effects of their teaching. For example, one parent publicly praised the work of his child's teacher and described his responses to a relative who criticized the public schools within the district. Other parents described their child's excitement about writing with friends as a sleepover activity. Parents received support from the school and also from other parents.

Parents were truly involved in the group and the group process. The curriculum was not simply handed out, and parents were not just told about how their children were learning reading, writing, English grammar, and spelling. The informant meetings, in conjunction with the audiotapes, videotapes, invitations to the classroom, and journals, created an organizational structure for parent interpretation and expression. Parents could listen in on how their child's interests and problems were addressed during in-school writing conferences. More importantly, the videotaped instruction helped parents visualize and consequently discuss the community of readers and writers that teachers were attempting to build within the classroom. By changing the organizational structure of parent meetings and allocating resources to help parents gain access to information about the school, parents participated in more meaningful ways. They contributed and developed an interpretation of their child's reactions to school assignments, classmates, and their teacher as they developed strong parent-teacher and parent-parent relationships.

Parent Informant Journals. During the second informant meeting, parents began to raise questions about how they might respond to their children's writing, topic selections, and mechanical errors. These questions added a new level of complexity in the writing instruction taking place in the classroom. These children in the second-grade classroom had developed as very different writers and gained expertise in several different writing genres. For example, one student wrote a fantasy story that included a dialogue between a fork and a spoon, another student wrote about his goals as a Cub Scout, and another wrote about how he cared for his "pet slug." In response to parent questions, the team designed a method to show parents how teachers responded in school to children, depending on the child's development and writing purposes.

The teachers began to audiotape conferences with individual students during their regular classroom writing conferences. These tapes were sent home in the "traveler's briefcase" with a brief message to the parent at the end of the tape. Each child took a tape recorder and tape home for three days on a rotating basis. Parents could hear examples of how teachers were responding to their child, as well as the contents and mechanics in their child's writing. A parent journal was also sent home with the tape, and parents were encouraged to respond to the child's writing and also to the teacher's conference either orally or in writing or both, depending on their preferences.

The impact of these changes reached the parent community and the teachers and had an effect on the entire Morton staff. In response to the information and questions shared in the informant journals and meetings, additional times were scheduled, attendance increased, and parents began to ask more questions. Parents asked the team to continue the project with their children during the next year in third grade. The reading specialist and principal discussed the project with the third-grade teachers, and a student teacher was assigned to one of the third-grade classrooms to facilitate this project. Additionally, the first-grade teachers became involved when a first-grade tea was held so first graders could hear stories written by second-grade authors. During an end-of-year whole school PDS meeting, Morton teachers decided to request resources and organize meeting times to involve the entire school in the parent involvement project. In the end, changes in practices took place because implicit changes in thinking about parent involvement and literacy instruction took place simultaneously.

Third-Grade Project

The third-grade teachers approached me about working with them, fully aware of the fact that the goal of parent involvement at Morton was around curricular issues. They expressed their desire of wanting families to become involved in reading and writing with their children. In particular, they wanted to communicate to parents that there are close connections between reading and writing. I suggested and the teachers concurred that we should provide the parents with a specific focus and purpose for wanting to participate in the project. The teachers thought that the third-grade parent informant grade-level meetings could focus on *talking about writing*. At my suggestion, they purchased a book by Peter Stillman (1989) entitled *Families Writing*. I had told the teachers that, "I really like this book, because I thought that it would garner the interest and support of parents to participate." I then proceeded to give a description of the book:

> [*Families Writing* is a book that shows you how to record your] family's collective history, an accounting of what it is to be a member of that unique institution, *family*—a living record made of letters, poems, journals, anecdotes, family lore, tall tales, a variety of incidental jottings, authored by family members of all ages...This is writing for the very best of reasons—for the family's sake—and in this book, Peter Stillman helps you create a host of writing experiences that will draw yours closer together, not only for the moment, but across generations. In warm, engaging terms, Stillman explores the *whys* of family writing: its value in forging an unbreakable link between past and present, present and future; its incomparable role in keeping memories fresh; and its astonishing power for recall and discovery...[In this book] are also the *ways* of writing, some of them zany, all of them engrossing, that add up to [a] lifetime of family writing activities. These are keepsake items, rich with dreams, wishes, hopes, fears, the full gamut of human feelings. You'll feel fully comfortable expressing them in writing. And you'll feel fully capable of finding information on family customs and family members whose saint-like activities or roguish adventures are well worth pinning to the page...Stillman scoffs at the notion that you must be "creative" to do these things. He encourages you just to write, to say honestly whatever comes to mind, to write simply about simple matters: the homes you lived in, the trips you've taken, family cars, embarrassing moments, odd-ball relations, growing old. These are important. Your words will carry force...the book is a gold mine of anecdotes, almost a peek into the Stillman family's private album. Sprinkled liberally throughout are activities, events, and games that involve your whole family. They'll show you how enjoyable it is to write together...Most important, perhaps, Stillman instills a respect, even a love, for the writing process and its power to bring families together. That's only fitting. You and your family members are, after all, writing the book of your lives. (Taken from the back and front flap of *Families Writing*.)

After I read the description of the Stillman book, the teachers really got excited and responded by saying that they thought the parents would love this book. Agreeing that we would use the Stillman book to shape our conversations with parents, we set up four third-grade parent informant meetings to talk with the parents about the importance of writing and how they could help their children at home.

At our first meeting, we gave the parents a copy of Stillman's (1989) book *Families Writing,* and we showed a video by Lucy Calkins, *The Writing Workshop: A World of Difference*. The parents really loved the Calkins video and were extremely appreciative of receiving the Stillman book especially after I read the description of his book. What the teachers and I saw clearly was that the families viewed their participation in this project as personally beneficial to them, as well as a mechanism for supporting their children's development as both readers and writers. At the second meeting, the teachers and I provided the parents with some reading and writing strategies. We pointed out that "Reading and writing in grades 1–3 are essential processes through which children develop and refine their kindergarten emergent literacy behaviors. For primary-age children (approximately six to nine years old), reading and writing continues to serve their basic desire to express themselves and communicate print" (Keller, 1991, p. 63). The remainder of the meeting focused on sharing with the parents a list of strategies similar to ones compiled by Tompkins (1997). Tompkins argues that "there is no single definition of a *strategy* or a single list of strategies on which all researchers can agree" (p. 129). However, the teachers and I felt that the strategies compiled by Tompkins were ones that could be easily understood by parents. The twelve strategies that Tompkins believes that elementary students use when they read and write are as follows: (1) tapping prior knowledge, (2) predicting, (3) organizing ideas, (4) figuring out unknown words, (5) visualizing, (6) making connections, (7) applying fix-up strategies, (8) revising meaning, (9) monitoring, (10) playing with language, (11) generalizing, and (12) evaluating (pp. 129–133).

At the second meeting, the parents were extremely enthusiastic about the family writing they had done. One parent said:

> You were so right when you said that we would love the book on *Families Writing*. I shared the book with members of my extended family and they simply loved the idea of recording the family's history. We liked the book so much until we decided to take responsibility to record our family's history and assigned each family member a specific a story to write. We have a family reunion this summer and we think that the stories we share will be one of the most memorable events at the family reunion. This is a great book.

Another parent stated: "I got the same response from my family members." One parent said, "Even though you say that this project was developed to help us help our children with writing, I think the book has helped us record our family's history." A lively discussion continued for the entire hour-long meeting. However, one other parent's comment caught the our attention. He said:

> You know, over the years teachers have given us parents assignments that I have perceived as busywork, not well thought out. Rarely, did I see how these assignments would help my children. I am busy, and I don't have time for busywork. However, I must admit that this is the first assignment that I feel is helping my child, as well as [affecting] my entire family in a positive way. Thank you, thank you very much.

After this parent's comment, we could see in all of the parents' body language that they agreed with him. Our meeting ended. The teachers and I gave each other a high five. We were so pleased with the result of the second meeting.

In the third and fourth sessions, the parents continued to share with us their reactions to the Stillman book and the chapters that they found very interesting.

Hands down, they overwhelmingly loved the chapter on letters, words as gifts, and stories—of, by, and for the family. They shared pieces of their writing, and the teachers and I shared pieces of our writing. One parent shared a story that was not about her family's history, but her story caught our attention because it focused on how children are teased in classrooms and how teasing can have a lasting impact.

> I entered school when I was five years old. All of the desks in my classroom were right-handed desks and to make matters worse all of the scissors were right-handed scissors, but I am left-handed. My teacher looked at me strangely. My classmates laughed at me and said things like, "You write funny, and you cut funny too." I felt bad the whole time that I was in kindergarten. As I think back, the children tended to tease me on the playground and when the teacher was not watching. I am now so protective of my left-handed son. I don't want him to be teased. So far, I don't think that he has been teased. Teasing is very hurtful.

As the parent shared this story, the mood of the meeting changed and the parents agreed that teasing was hurtful. To change the mood of the meeting, a teacher shared a funny story about a Basset hound eating her lunch.

> When I was in the fourth grade, I went on a Girl Scout hiking trip. My mother packed a great lunch. It included ten bologna sandwiches, an apple, Babyruth candy bar, Cheetos, and a chocolate marshmallow pie. Of course, you know when I cut my ten bologna sandwiches in half, I had twenty sandwiches. However, while we were hiking around, a little Basset hound got into my lunch, and he ate the entire lunch. When I discovered this, all of the girls laughed and said, "You don't have anything to eat, and you are not going to have anything to eat because the dog ate your food, and we are not going to share with you." However, my Girl Scout leader made all of the girls share their lunch with me. The girls laughed, but I knew that they would share their lunch with me. As I think about it, it was funny. Years later, when I would see one of the girls in my Scout troop, the Basset hound story always entered the conversation.

All of us laughed and the parents and teachers asked me to share a story about myself. I said I did not want to make the mood sad again, but what occurred in my life as a teenager profoundly affected me, and the stories about my growing up tends to be discussed at our family gatherings. Of course, we also reminisce about other things too. One of my family stories can be found below:

> Growing up in the South during the mid-1950s and 1960s, I was thrust into the midst of the civil rights movement. I was escorted by federal marshals to a predominately white high school in Albany, Georgia, in the late 1960s. Some days, I came to school full of fear. However, I remembered the words of President John F. Kennedy; he said, "Let us never negotiate out of fear, but let us never fear to negotiate." I learned to negotiate in this setting. For example, I was the only African-American student in my Spanish class. Consequently, I had to do my Spanish conversations by myself. Two quotes by basketball coach legend John Wooden characterize how I felt at time. He said, "Do not let what you cannot do interfere

with what you can do." He also said, "Failure to prepare is preparing to fail." Determined not to fail my Spanish class, I would say, "Buenos dias, como esta usted." I would answer myself, saying, "Muy bien, gracias." My classmates laughed. My teacher appeared frustrated with my classmates, but did nothing to help me get a Spanish conversational partner. I understood why she did not assign me a conversational partner. During this period, had my teacher assigned me a partner, she would have had serious repercussions from parents. At the end of the first six weeks of school, I walked in front of my Spanish class and told my classmates that it had been extremely difficult to have conversations with myself and that I would greatly appreciate it if someone would volunteer to be my Spanish conversational partner.

General George Patton said, "Never tell people how to do things. Tell them what to do, and they will surprise you with their integrity." My classmates did surprise me with their integrity. To my surprise, six students volunteered. I accepted all six volunteers.

After I read my story, a lively conversation ensued. Many of the parents asked me if I felt angry, sad, and so on. I replied by saying, "I was frustrated and intimidated at first, but I realized that not all of the students liked what was happening to me. That's why so many students volunteered to be my Spanish conversational partner." After I shared my story and received responses to it, the meeting ended with us making plans for continuing this project the following year.

Fourth-Grade and Fifth-Grade Project

The fourth- and fifth-grade teachers unanimously agreed that they needed to focus their attention on content-area reading. We believed, like Harp & Brewer (1996), that "reading in the content areas has become a common topic in reading instruction" (p. 366). Also, we agreed with Hart & Brewer when they said that "reading and writing about content-area subjects present challenges to students far greater than those posed by the reading and writing of fiction texts" (p. 367). The fourth-grade teachers decided to focus on developing and understanding content-area reading, and the fifth-grade teachers wanted to continue refining the content-area reading needs of their students. Both groups of teachers felt that parent support around content-area reading would increase their students' reading proficiency. Therefore, the teachers decided to have combined parent informant meetings for the fourth- and fifth-grade parents.

As the teachers and I discussed the agenda for the parent informant meetings, I decided to share with them some of the information that I had read about content-area reading. The first piece of information that I shared with them came from Vacca, Vacca, & Gove (1995) who argued that:

Content-area textbooks are an integral part of schooling. In most classrooms, textbooks blend into the physical environment, much like desks, bulletin boards, and chalkboards. Even a casual observer expects to see textbooks in use in the elementary classroom. Yet, teachers often remark that children find textbooks difficult.

When students have trouble reading texts, we are acutely aware of the mismatch between the reading abilities students bring to text and materials and some of the difficulties of the text...to compensate for this, some teachers avoid textbook assignments. Instruction revolves around lecture and other activities instead of the textbook. Some teachers abandon difficult materials, sidestepping reading altogether as a vehicle for learning...In lieu of either abandoning difficult materials or avoiding reading altogether, we need to get answers to some very basic questions. How does the textbook meet the goals of the curriculum? Is the conceptual difficulty of the text beyond students' grasp? Does the author have a clear sense of purpose as conveyed to this audience? How well are the ideas in the text organized? With answers to these and other questions, teachers, [who] have some basis upon which to make decisions about text-related instruction, are exercising their professional judgment (pp. 412–413).

The teachers agreed with this perspective. In particular, they could identify with the questions that Vacca, Vacca, & Gove believed needed to be answered. Many of these same questions were ones the fourth- and fifth-teachers had pondered. I then read to them a quote by Burns, Roe, & Ross (1999), who stated that:

Reading in the content-area textbooks, such as those for social studies, science, mathematics, and other curricular areas, is often difficult for students. Content area textbooks contain *expository* (explanatory) material that can be harder for children to read than *narrative* (story) material. They also contain many new concepts...to read well in content area textbooks, children need good general reading strategies, including word recognition and comprehension, and reading/study strategies. If they cannot recognize the words they encounter, they will be unable to take in the information from the material. Without good literal, interpretive, critical, and creative reading comprehension strategies, they will not understand the textbook's message. And if they lack good reading/study strategies, they will be less likely to comprehend and retain the material (p. 407).

After reading this quote, I shared with the teachers that our parent informant meetings should focus on content-area reading, but we suggested that should address study skills as a part of these sessions. My rationale was based on research conducted by Ruddell (1999), who noted that:

Where once educators viewed reading and writing as important but essentially technical adjuncts to learning—that is, as learning tools or study skills, which learners use in the course of acquiring knowledge—they now understand that reading and writing are integral parts of the learning process itself. The study skills perspective was based on the belief that certain reading behaviors—for example, identifying main ideas, separating main ideas from significant details, and using graphs and charts—contribute to reading ability and thus to learning from subject area texts. The greater the reading/study skills, the more students could learn from text (p. 245).

He continues by saying that the study skills such as those listed below are critical for students to learn but should be taught in the context of literacy and content-area learning rather than in isolation. These embedded study skills are as follows:

1. Understanding and using book parts (tables of contents, indexes, marginalia, glossaries, and so on)
2. Alphabetizing, using headings and pronunciation guides, understanding abbreviations in reference sources (dictionaries, encyclopedias, atlases, and so on)
3. Using other references (telephone directories, newspapers, and so on)
4. Using the library (card files, databases, Dewey Decimal System, and so on)
5. Adjusting reading to purpose (skimming, scanning, intensive reading)
6. Reading graphs, charts, maps, globes, and other pictorial information
7. Notetaking
8. Finding main ideas, separating main ideas from important details
9. Outlining
10. Summarizing
11. Report writing

We decided to use two books to help us introduce the idea of study skills to the parents: *Reading Strategies and Practices: A Compendium* by Tierney & Readence (2000) and *Guiding Readers through Text: A Review of Study Guides* by Wood, Lapp, & Flood (1992). However, we made the decision to purchase the Wood, Lapp, & Flood book for the parents because *Guiding Readers through Text* combines a discussion of why and how study guides help students comprehend text with a focus on the most effective ways to use these guides in the classroom. The authors provide historical context by tracing the development of study guides as an instructional resource. For the bulk of the text, they present an array of study guides, explaining their purposes and illustrating their applications. They end with a set of guidelines that encapsulate the principles governing appropriate and effective use of study guides. Throughout the text, the authors present a balanced perspective on the value of these guides, making clear that they are a powerful resource but not a panacea. We also agreed with Wood, Lapp, & Flood when they stated that:

> Study guides are useful classroom tools because teachers cannot always provide one-on-one assistance to their students. Guides can act as personal tutors by focusing students' attention on important information and thus reducing the amount of print encountered at any one time. They can be valuable tools for enhancing instruction at any grade level and in any content field.

By providing the parents with a copy of the book by Wood, Lapp, & Flood and convening four parent informant meetings, we felt that the parents would better understand how to support their children's literacy development in the content areas. In our first meeting, one parent asked, "What is content-area reading?" I responded by saying, "Let me give you a definition of content literacy that I think will make it clearer what content-area reading is." A definition of content literacy has been offered by Vacca & Vacca (1996), who stated that:

> *Content literacy*—the ability to use reading and writing to learn subject matter in a given discipline—is a relatively new term that holds much potential for students'

acquisition of content. To better understand what it means to be content-literate in a discipline, examine the general construct of the term *literacy* and how it is used in today's society. Literacy is a strong cultural expectation in the United States and other technologically advanced countries. Society places a heavy premium on literate behavior and demands that its citizens acquire literacy for personal, social, academic, and economic success. But what does it mean to be literate? *Literacy* is a term whose meaning fluctuates from one context to another. *Literacy*, on one hand, may be used to describe how knowledgeable a person is in a particular subject. What do you know about computers and how to use them? Are you, for example, *computer-literate*? In the same vein, the term *cultural literacy* describes what an educated person should know about the arts, literature, and other determinants of culture (p. 8).

The rest of the meeting focused entirely on parents sharing with us that they did not know how to help their children with reading in the content-area subjects. One parent said:

I knew that my child was struggling, but I did not know how to help him. He would say, "Mom/Dad, can you help me?" We responded with, "Honey, just slowly read it again." I think the book on *Guiding Reading through Text: A Review of Study Skills* will enable my husband and me to help our son.

The other parents agreed with this parent and shared their own struggles with helping their children in the content-area subjects. Again, the teacher and I gave each other a high five because we sensed that we had once again appropriately addressed what parents felt they needed. In the second, third, and fourth meetings, we did activities with the parents from *Guiding Reading through Text: A Review of Study Skills* and other content-area reading texts like the one by Vacca & Vacca (1996). In the second meeting, we focused on the type of questions that should be asked based on the information readers need to answer the question. Vacca & Vacca (1996) pointed out that:

A reader draws on two broad information sources to answer questions: information in the text and information inside the reader's head. For example, some questions have answers that can be found directly in the text. These questions are *textually explicit* and lead to answers that are "right there" in the text. Other questions have answers that require students to think about the information they have read in the text. They must be able to search for ideas that are related to one another and then put these ideas together in order to answer the questions. These questions are *textually implicit* and lead to "think and search" answers. Still other questions require students to rely mainly on prior knowledge and experience. In other words, responses to these questions are more inside the reader's head than in the text itself. These questions are *schema-based* and lead to "author and you" and "on my own" answers (p. 48).

"Right There," "Think and Search," Author and You," and "On My Own" are mnemonics for question-answer relationships (QAR) (Raphael 1982, 1984,

In the Text:
Right There

The answer is in the text. The words used in the question and the words used for the answer can usually be found in the same sentences.

Think and Search

The answer is in the text, but the words used in the question and those used for the answer are not in the same sentence. You need to think about different parts of the text and how ideas can be put together before you can answer the question.

Or

In My Head:
On My Own

The text got you thinking, but the answer is inside your head. They can't help you much. So think about it, and use what you know already to answer the question.

Author and You

The answer is not in the text. You need to think about what you know, what the author says, and how they fit together.

FIGURE 6.4 *Where Are Answers to Questions Found?*

Source: Adapted from: Vacca, R. T., & Vacca, J. L. (1996). *Content area reading.* Fifth Edition. New York: HarperCollins College Publishers.

1986). QARs make explicit to students the relationships that exist among the types of question asked, the text, and the reader's prior knowledge. In the process of teaching QARs, both teachers and parents help students become aware of and skilled in using learning strategies to find the information they need to comprehend at different levels of response to the text. The procedures for learning QARs can be taught directly to students by teachers and can be reinforced by parents. See Figure 6.4 for the steps you should follow for teaching QARs.

The parents were excited and felt that they could implement these steps at home with their children. Overall, they felt that they finally had a strategy for helping their children in the content-area subjects. Our third and fourth meeting focused on some activities in *Guiding Reading through Text: A Review of Study Skills*. We answered the question, "What are study guides?" and we explained how study guides differ in two important respects from the typical practice of asking students to answer the textbook questions at the end of each chapter. Wood, Lapp, & Flood (1992) define study guides as follows: " Study guides—or reading guides, as they are sometimes called—are teacher-developed devices for helping students understand instructional reading material. Often study guides consist of a series of questions or activities related to the textbook or other material being used in class. Students respond to the questions or engage in the activities as they read portions of text" (p. 1). They further describe how study guides differ from other typical practices of asking questions by stating:

> "First, the teacher has control over the questions in study guides and can thus avoid the pitfalls of commercially developed textbook questions, which often are poorly constructed and require little higher-order thinking on the part of the students. Second, with study guides students don't have to wait until after they're done reading to find out what they are expected to know" (p. 1).

The parents really liked the study guide procedure and felt that they could use it effectively with their children at home. In our fourth meeting, we focused on the types of study guides (see Table 6.8).

The parents were surprised that there were so many variations of study guides. We shared with them that Wood, Lapp, & Flood (1992) believe that "...all study guides are essentially designed to develop two areas: (1) skills and strategies necessary for effective reading and (2) an understanding of a significant segment of a content area" (p. 5). The parents agreed and again communicated to us that they feel that the study guide idea would help them. The meeting ended.

What Can You Learn from the Scope and Sequence of Activities I Developed at Morton?

First of all, I hope that you were able to see how much the parents enjoyed participating in these projects. Rarely, do schools provide a forum for parents to speak freely about the school's literacy curriculum. As you can see, when schools do

TABLE 6.8   *Types of Study Guides*

Primary Objectives and Features	Guide
Broaden students' perspectives by making use of elaboration and prior knowledge	Point-of-View Guide
Help students monitor their comprehension through predicting, retelling, and outlining	Textbook Activity Guide
Promote peer interaction through discussion, retelling, brainstorming, and other activities	Interactive Reading Guide
Use peer interaction to solidify students' understanding and recall of information heard or viewed	Collaborative Listening Viewing Guide
Help students understand literal, inferential, and evaluative levels of information	Levels-of Comprehension Guide Learning-from-Text Guide
Enhance students' use of prior knowledge to infer, evaluate, and apply text information through open-ended questions	Guided Learning Plan
Activate students' prior knowledge and integrate it with text content; stimulate discussion	Extended Anticipation Guide
Teach various processes involved in reading (e.g., drawing conclusions, predicting outcomes, identifying the main idea, sequencing)	Processes-of-Reading Guide
Help students understand various organizational patterns of text (e.g., cause/effect, sequencing, comparison and contrast)	Pattern Guide
Help students understand the function of main ideas and supporting details through categorization	Concept Guide
Extend students' comprehension and recall of main concepts through the use of analogies	Analogical Study Guide
Help students develop purposes as they read segments of text; assist students with locating answers and differentiating assignments	Content Guide
Help students develop flexibility in reading rate	Guide-O-Rama Reading Road Map
Direct students' attention to text features (figures of speech, concepts, contrasts, main ideas) and help them develop strategies (using context, predicting, drawing conclusions) through the use of marginal notations	Glossing Process Guide

provide the opportunity for parents to participate, they feel, as did the Morton parents, comfortable sharing with teachers feedback that reflects their true feelings. A big plus at Morton was the ongoing feedback that teachers received from parents. Once families felt listened to, they were willing to put in more time. A critical point to remember is when families feel engaged, momentum for a project takes on a life of its own that benefits teachers, parents, and children.

Only a small amount of money was needed to purchase the briefcases, papers, audiotapes, and books in order to get the projects started. However, these projects were helpful in creating a substantial transformation of student literacy experiences. The collaborative nature of the process helped teachers develop more focused goals and objectives. There was a teacher and parent "buy-in and consensus" at each grade level. The project was building-wide, but the projects were individualized to each grade, which increased parent participation. Yet, another important feature of the scope and sequence of activities at Morton had to do with the ongoing nature of the program. In other words, we would meet periodically, and parents were encouraged to provide input into planning and organizing the workshop sessions designed for them. It is important to emphasize again that very few schools have developed a master schedule of parent involvement in August. However, many of us would agree that if parents enrolled their children in hockey, soccer, gymnastics, or piano lessons, at the beginning of the year parents would be provided with a master schedule of activities—the specific times and dates of activities at which their children would be expected to "show up." Unfortunately, many of these parents are not given at the beginning of the school year the specific activities (at different grade levels) that teachers expect them to participate in with their children.

One huge success at Morton was providing the parents in August with a scope and sequence of parent involvement activities. By doing this, it allowed par-

PAUSE AND REFLECT

Do you feel that pushing teachers as I did the Morton teachers in order to tailor their parent involvement initiatives to the needs of the parent population they now serve and around clearly defined curriculum issues is a step in the right direction? What did you like or dislike about these five projects? To continue what they have started, what do you do think Morton teachers should do next? How might these five projects be models for how educators across the country should begin to think about parent involvement? How do you think your own parent involvement initiatives could be molded around curriculum goals? Do you like the concept that parent involvement initiatives should be based on the curriculum? What similar projects could you implement based on your answers in the structured interview questions found earlier in this chapter? You can answer these questions independently on paper, work with a partner in your class/group of colleagues, or work cooperatively with a cooperating/mentor teacher.

ents to adjust their daily lives and schedules for the upcoming year and, thus, positively incorporate the suggested scope and sequence of activities into their daily lives and schedules. Moreover, both teachers and parents were able to contribute meaningful information to help each other. Lastly, but more importantly, parents were involved in ways that were central and significant, not peripheral to students' literacy instruction.

Developing a Scope and Sequence of Parent Involvement: Some Advice

Throughout the text, I continually alluded that you would learn how to develop a scope and sequence of parent involvement. Well, in the section below, I provide some background information to help you learn how to do this. In constructing a scope and sequence, one of the overarching goals is to help teachers and parents "get on the same page" by organizing and coordinating parent informant literacy groups, which will make school-based literacy practices and skills more accessible to parents (see Edwards, Danridge, & Pleasents, 1999). In essence, the goal is to make the school's "culture of power" (Delpit, 1995) explicit to parents so that they can familiarize themselves with school-based literacy knowledge (McGill-Franzen & Allington, 1991). You need to have a clear plan and set of goals that you would like to achieve at your grade level and decide how parents can assist with this plan or set of goals. In your discussions with your grade-level colleagues, you should address three significant points. The information below is based on a recent *Reading Teacher* article (see Edwards, McMillon, Turner, & Laier [2001]).

1. *Folk theories about students and families.* Taking a page from Bruner (1996), I make the assumption that teachers and administrators have "folk theories" about students and their families and that these folk theories influence the teaching and learning process. Folk theories are expectations, beliefs, and assumptions formed over time through personal and professional school experience; their gradual formation gives them a durable quality. Some teachers' folk theories tend to place responsibility for students' problems in school on the students and their families. Therefore, it is important to ask yourselves whether you make comments like "...my students come from violent neighborhoods and unstable homes and arrive at school lacking basic literacy skills. That's why it is useless to even try to work with their parents." Admitting that these folk theories exist is the first step in dealing with them.

2. *Cohesiveness of your instructional network.* Do you have any coordination within and between the different grade levels around literacy at your school? McGill-Franzen & Allington (1991) found that when children with reading difficulties receive a compartmentalized array of discrete literacy tasks that are unrelated (either across levels or between classroom and "specialist instructional contexts"), students make little progress in achievement. I would argue that this is good advice even if your school does not have many students with reading difficulties. The importance of developing a

cohesive instructional network is beneficial for all parties (i.e., teachers, parents, students, and so on). In particular, the cohesiveness of your instructional network will get parents to see up close what you expect of them and how they can support their children at each grade level.

3. *Developing a shared vision.* Studies of staff development tell us that teachers need to make curriculum and teaching strategies "their own" (Richardson & Placier, 2001). Studies of effective high-poverty school and teachers (see Taylor, Pressley, & Pearson, 2000) suggest that coordinated service delivery and articulated approaches to curriculum and instruction are important. This tension in the research suggests that although teachers should not be required to teach literacy from a "cookie-cutter mold," neither should curriculum and pedagogy be a matter of "anything goes" as long as a particular teacher is convinced it will work. It is important for teachers to have a shared vision to effectively guide instruction. Also, it will send a unified rather than fragmented message to parents. Parents can become confused and frustrated if different teachers are communicating conflicting messages to them.

Once you carefully think about the above three points, it will allow you to focus your thinking about developing a scope and sequence of parent involvement activities at your school. In Appendixes C and D, I have included several examples of what some teachers think should be a scope and sequence of parent involvement around literacy from kindergarten to fifth grade. (Two additional scope and sequence examples can be found on the Web site that accompanies this book at *www.ablongman.com/edwards1e.*) These teachers have outlined specific literacy activities that teachers should ask parents to participate in at home and/or school with their children. (In addition to the scope and sequence examples on the Web site, I provide the opportunity for you to answer the question, *"What does an elementary teacher need to know about parent involvement in order to structure it successfully?"* Additionally, you will have the opportunity to try your own hand at developing a scope and sequence of parent involvement on a grade-by-grade basis.)

Second Set of Action Steps

Step 1. Finding Out about Your School's History of Involving Families

In Chapter 3, you read a portion of Morton's history that focused on the issue of poverty. In this chapter, I share some additional information about Morton's history. This information sheds some light on why there might have been some apprehension on the part of teachers to reach out to parents. That's why I believe that one of the most important reasons for gathering information about your school is that it provides you the opportunity to examine whether your school has a past practice of extending a warm and friendly invitation to *all* parents. According to Purkey & Novak (1984), schools should be "the most inviting place in town" (p. 2). Four principles of invitational education were outlined by Purkey &

Novak: (1) people are able, valuable, and responsible and should be treated accordingly; (2) teaching should be a cooperative activity; (3) people possess relatively untapped potential in all areas of human development; and (4) this potential can best be realized by places, policies, [and] programs that are specifically designed to invite development and by people who are personally and professionally inviting to themselves and others (p. 2).

Today's school personnel must closely examine their school's history to determine if past policies and practices made parents feel invited or uninvited. Epstein (1988) noted that "schools of the same type serve different populations, have different histories of involving parents, have teachers and administrators with different philosophies, training, and skills in involving parents" (p. 58). Epstein's observation should encourage school personnel to ask themselves a number of questions:

1. What is our school's history of involving parents?
2. What is our school's philosophy regarding parents' involvement in school activities?
3. What training and skills do we need for involving parents in school affairs?

In addition, schools should examine Patrice Leblanc's (1992) steps for what works to increase parent and citizen participation (see Table 6.9).

The Morton Case Example: Morton Professional Development School and Its Community.   Morton serves elementary students who come from three distinct communities: a nearby trailer park, neighborhoods that surround the school, and the inner city. Children and families from these communities differ in many ways, including income, ethnic background, and educational experiences. The school is located in a primarily working class residential area on the edge of the inner city approximately six miles from a major research university. The school has an interesting parent involvement history, as reported by the first PTA president and a classroom teacher who taught at Morton for more than thirty-five years.

In 1952, when Morton Elementary School was built, it served primarily middle-class white families. These families were young first-time homeowners. The school for them served many purposes. Many of the community's social events were held at school. The school was also a place where the young families discussed national, state, and local politics; goals and aspirations for their children; and ways they could help the school better serve the needs of their children. An interview with the first Morton PTA president was quite revealing. She said that:

> In 1952, because there were few obvious differences between parents and children and teachers and administrators, Morton was a place where parents and teachers worked closely together. We were able to work closely together because we were friends, neighbors, [and] church members, and we even saw each other at the local grocery store. We shared so much in common. We had a shared sense of goals and aspirations for our children.

TABLE 6.9   *What Works to Increase Parent and Citizen Participation?*

The key to enhancing parent and citizen interactions with schools is knowledge of the factors that influence them. The following paragraphs suggest three steps to take in assessing these factors in your community and schools and how to move forward with that knowledge.

Step 1. Know the Culture.

1. What are the demographic and economic characteristics of the community and the school? (Look at race, ethnicity, socioeconomic status, and so on.)
2. Can the community by characterized as diverse or homogenous?

Step 2. Know the Politics.

1. What are the politics of the community?
2. How much dirty politics is there? (Individualism)
3. Are there open meetings with participation by everyone? (Moralism)
4. Do those in power see themselves as insiders and everyone else as outsiders? (Traditionalism)

Step 3. Apply What You Know.

1. If the community and school are white, middle-class, the two will have shared cultural values. If you share that culture, access is easy. You can then work toward the quantity and quality of participation that you desire by appealing to the established values and norms.

   If you do not share the culture of the community and school, your access may be more difficult. Here is where you need to use the politics of the community. If the community is individualistic, try approaching individual school personnel. Look for links related to economic development. Economic development ranges beyond money—starting a parent and citizen volunteer program is economic enhancement. It also gets your foot in the door. If the community politics are moralistic, chances are your participation is invited. If the community appears more traditionalistic, you need to use someone on the inside. Make connections and use them to get your point heard. Use whatever forms of parent and citizen participation that will work, given the local political culture.

2. If the community and school populations are diverse, look at the school personnel. Do they reflect the diversity? If not, one objective is to increase that diversity. Start with the school board. Again, use your political knowledge. Take an approach that fits with the political culture of the community and you'll have more success. For example, in an individualistic or moralistic community you might organize a group of interested parents and citizens to press for change. Start small but think big.

Source: LeBlanc, Patrice (1992). Parent-school interactions. In L. Kaplan (Ed.), *Education and the family* (pp. 132–140). Boston: Allyn and Bacon.

An interview with Mrs. Holmes, a teacher who had taught at Morton for more than thirty-five years, illustrates a crucial point in the ebb of parent relations at Morton and marks an important transition between the shared community of the early Morton Elementary School and the Morton of later development. Her comments raise an interesting set of issues that affect Morton even today. Mrs. Holmes reported that:

> In 1965 when schools were desegregated "the people in charge" never prepared us teachers to teach minority students nor did they have sensitivity sessions to discuss our fears, doubts, or opinions. If you tried to ask questions back then or appeared to be against desegregation, you were immediately labeled a racist. In other words, no one seemed to care about how we as teachers felt. The only apparent goal of those in charge was to physically bring together black and white bodies under one roof. At the beginning of desegregation, we teachers were so caught in our own perceptions of desegregation that we did not even stop to think about how the black parents felt. In retrospect, I would say, if those in charge informed black parents the same way they informed us; I can predict these parents probably had the same fears and doubts we as teachers had. When black children entered Morton, we (the teachers and administrator) saw a sharp decline in the number of events held at school. In the past, the school had been the center for community activities. Many teachers did not want to come back to school at night. It might sound stupid and crazy, but it was very real back then. Parent involvement as we had known it earlier, simply did not exist.

Ghosts in the School Building.   The accounts by the PTA president and the Morton teacher revealed two forms of parent involvement, one based on a shared sense of goals and aspirations and another based on discontinuity. The teachers who currently teach at Morton appeared unaware of the school's history and attempted to interface with parents as if no previous history existed. This failure to recognize the school's history proved problematic for both teachers and the school's administrator. It was problematic for them until I explained *how* ghosts exist in schools. These ghosts are invisible. No one can see them, but they do exist. Over the years, parent memories of these friendly and unfriendly ghosts signal to parents whether to feel invited or uninvited to come into school. My contention has been supported by Epstein (1988). She warned that schools should investigate their previous histories because "schools of the same type serve different populations, have different histories of involving parents, and have teachers and administrators with different philosophies, training, and skills for involving parents" (p. 58). Understanding the baggage that comes with the institutions will help teachers and administrators build and rebuild a foundation for effective communication.

The failure of schools to build or rebuild linkages between home and schools inadvertently encourages parents to maintain their frozen memories or their community's frozen perception of what that school was once like. This perpetuates the frustrations of teachers when parents say negatively, "Things will never change." Such a comment from a parent sounds simple and easily dismissible, but it may convey a very complex and intricate perception. The statement may sound like a personal complaint, but teachers must acknowledge the possible motivation behind it. To unpack such claims, we need to begin thinking more carefully about parent involvement and moving it beyond high rhetoric to high practice.

Step 2: Finding Out about Your
School's Parent Involvement Climate

In my first meeting with the Morton principal, K-2 teachers, and the reading specialist on September 15, 1990, I asked them to describe the parent involvement climate at Morton (e.g., present conditions, goals, bridges, barriers, and first steps; see Figure 6.5 for a pictorial description of these characteristics). In the section that follows you will read lengthy transcripts of what the Morton principal, K-2 teachers, and reading specialist had to say about the parent involvement climate. I share these lengthy transcripts with you because I want to provide the opportu-

FIGURE 6.5 *Pictorial Description of the Parent Involvement Climate*

nity for you to hear real voices of a real school staff struggling with a real issue—parent involvement. What you will learn from reading these lengthy transcripts is how intense the conversations around this topic can be. So when you become teachers or if you are already teaching you will at least have an example of what a conversation around parent involvement could look like. Please read this section critically because you will be asked to react to what you read.

My belief that the principal, teachers, and the reading specialist would feel more comfortable in a group setting proved to be correct. Their responses in this setting were, in my opinion, a truer representation of their private thoughts, feelings, and conceptions about parent involvement. Below are some of their responses concerning the parent involvement climate at Morton. In the first category of responses, the principal and reading specialist did not verbally participate in the conversation. Instead, the teachers took the leadership in describing the *present conditions* of the parent involvement climate at Morton. The teachers engaged in a lively conversation. They discussed conference rates and scheduling, conference convenience, parent appreciation activities, problems of working parents, problems of inaccessibility, transportation costs, positive phone calls to parents, tactics for recognizing "parent fatigue," sensitivity to parent differences, recognition of levels of parent participation, and admissions of little effort to involve parents. The teachers also discussed the principal's efforts to get parents to attend parent-teacher conferences. The following excerpts were taken from the first group meeting.

Mrs. Bell: ...Well, at Morton, we usually score very close to 100 percent of conferences held, so I'd like to work hard to maintain that, but it is not something that I see as a problem at Morton. I mean our administrator has set up conferences in the downtown area for those people who may not have transportation out here, and we usually always get 100 percent...I got 100 percent at my first conference last year and I expect 100 percent at the next one.

Mrs. Tate: [Our principal] really tries hard to get parents involved. For example, the conferences—I know on one occasion where she has made available the buses for parents to get in when they won't show up. Also going downtown holding conferences to try and get those people so all they have to do is walk out the door. Some do, some don't.... I have noticed the [principal] has the program at the end of the year if parents have helped and volunteered in the room. She gives them a luncheon, which is very nice. And then she involves them whenever we have the ice cream social at the end of the year they come in and work and help.

Mrs. Jones: I have parents come in if and when they can. What I've noticed though, over the past several years (and this seems to be getting to be the norm more than the exception to the rule) is that parents are having to work. They have to work to come out here and visit or to volunteer their services. They would like to do it. Many of them would like to do it but they need to work. I mean there is still rent to be paid, etc. And I really can identify with that. I do have some parents who will take an extended lunch hour and drive us on field trips and I am grateful to them for that, as far as working in the classroom, it is wonderful if they can come in and help you, but I find many times they simply cannot. Or they don't have transportation and you say that they can catch a [public transportation]. I don't say that, but I suppose we imply that they can catch [public transportation]. That's money.

Mrs. Terry: You name it, and we make phone calls about it. I'd like to think that I'm not a person who makes a phone call just because a child is naughty in the room. I try to put forth a conscious effort not to just make negative phone calls. So many times, I'll make a phone call because I want to know if a parent can drive for me. I'm still asking for their help. I have tried on many occasions to make a phone call to say your son or your daughter had a wonderful week in school.

Mrs. Benton: ...at our meet-the-teacher night, we have a sheet that asks if the parent would be willing to help...and we have it categorized by Valentine's Day party, Christmas party, drive on field trips, what have you...and we make sure they sign up. I mean we bring their attention to those sheets as they walk through.... And I take those sheets, and those are the ones that I call first for the things that I need for a particular thing. If I feel that I'm wearing one parent down or if I have a new parent, I'll call and say, "Mrs. Smith...I wonder if you can help out." And parents are very good about that. I have had a lot of parents who didn't sign up for anything, but they are especially good about sending things in.

Mrs. Jones: The last party we had was Valentine's Day, and one of the parents brought in a game. She got down on the floor with a group of kids and introduced the game, and the kids played. They really enjoyed it.

Mrs. Miller: ...field trips, classroom parties...That to me is very superficial. It is dated...Last week I had two or three parents...They were helpful and I appreciate that, but to me, that is an involvement on a much lower level. That's saying I will take a half day off of work, which is fine, but after they take off to drive for the field trip they feel like they put their service in for the year. I know we need that, and I am appreciative of that, but very few parents are willing at this point to...If you can't get them to make the commitment at school I would rather, much rather have them make a commitment at home to their child than to be in my class once a week correcting papers. I would rather have it at home.

Mrs. Andrews: I guess because I haven't really pushed parent involvement this year so that may account for one of the reasons why I wouldn't have a whole lot of parents working. However at the beginning of the year I did have one parent coming in and doing the computer with the class. She would take a group of kids and then the next week she would take another group. She stopped because she got a full time job, but she worked really well with the computer.

In the second category of responses, several teachers in the group made clear their *goals* for parent involvement. They revealed that they expected parents to read and react to the notes that they sent them. They further revealed the importance parents' awareness of classroom goals and parent involvement in children's educational development. Still further, the teachers discussed the importance of storytelling, books and crayons, and other creative children's materials.

PAUSE AND REFLECT

Do you think that the Morton teachers' discussion of the present condition is one of continuity or discontinuity? Why or why not? Are their comments realistic/unrealistic? Locate specific comments in the transcript to support your position. If you were a teacher at Morton, what would you do similarly or differently? You can respond to these independently on paper, work with a partner in your class/group of colleagues, or work cooperatively with a cooperating/mentor teacher on these questions.

Mrs. Green: I mean the goal would be for parents to read the notes, know exactly what the note said, and take the proper action.

Mrs. Green: It certainly makes it much easier if the school and parents are fully aware of what the goals are for any given classroom or any given child. For instance, it is so much easier for me as a teacher if I can say to a parent, "We are working on basic addition facts," and the parent helps his or her child at home.

Mrs. Jones: I just try to use parents in any way that I can.

Mrs. Andrews: Oh dear, my ultimate, ultimate, ultimate goal...Let me think for a minute. Well, I don't think I want that much. I would like to have parents who first of all made themselves available to learn what is going on in the classroom, whatever that means. It may mean taking off of work for a half day once a month and coming in to visit in the classroom, or drive on a field trip or something like that. So I'd like for them to really know what is going on in the classroom and be open or at least have some constructive criticism about what may or may not work for their particular child. I think that it's crucial. I think parents are going to need some involvement in their child's educational development.

Mrs. Turner: Be familiar with a book, whether it is a picture book or concept book. We have kindergartners that come and don't even know how to turn a page. So obviously there has not been reading in the home....There are places where you can get free books, you could come to school...There are schools in the neighborhood [the parent] could go to that school...They don't have to be new books; they could be old books, but that would be the responsibility of the parent. They should have some kind of books.

I also feel like it is not asking too much for a parent to have paper and crayons.

I would expect a parent to talk to a child through storytelling. You don't even need a book for that. I think if parents are shown how to share books with their children, they will enjoy it and their children will have a better chance of succeeding in school. That's why I think this program [meaning the *Parents as Partners in Reading Program*] is ideal. But I would expect that coming from any kind of home [or] socioeconomic level or whatever the program would be useful.

In the third category of responses, the principal and one teacher described in detail the *bridges* that they felt needed to be crossed before a "real" climate for parent involvement could be developed at Morton. For example, the principal and one teacher described directly meeting with parents, team partnership, parent commitment, and the necessity of developing a parent-child-teacher triangle.

Mrs. Tate, Principal: I think we're going to have to somehow have a face-to-face meeting with parents. And I guess I keep driving that home, and it sounds like we never do. We do. We really do. But, I think there's going to have to be more of it....maybe that means that we'll have to go to their homes...maybe we'll have to do that...for a time or two initially...And I certainly would be willing to do that.

I also think that we need to let the parents know and all staff know that I'm not in my little corner of the world and you are in your little corner...and they are in their little corner...That we are somehow a team. I don't know the answer as to how we can do that but I think maybe PDS is on the right track for that because I think parents have to look at it and feel that they are part of a team....And each of the PDS components has something to contribute to team building....Or it could be even called a partnership...That's right.

Mrs. Jones: Teaching would be a lot easier if [parents] would take their role seriously as the parent and as the pre-teacher of their child. When they are going through school, and I'm not saying every night a half hour, I'm saying when your child comes home with papers and you have seen that they've made mistakes and they have been corrected at school...To me I would think that would be a signal for you to say I need to work with my child on a few problems with my child or if it is a spelling lesson. I think that commitment needs to be present, and I know I can't guarantee every parent is going to do that, but if every parent would take some interest maybe twice a week for fifteen minutes or whatever my role would be much easier because also it adds to that triangle: the child, the teacher, and parent.

> **Mrs. Jones:** [*the reading specialist and several other teachers nodded their heads in agreement* that]...if you talk to the parent and you are working on the behavior or if you are working on academics...If you talk to the parent and you say, "Your child really needs oral reading at home. I am sending home a book." Obviously I let the child know what is going on, too. I think with that, like I said you are going right back to the triangle again. I think if the child knows...That 's why sometimes it is very good to have the child sitting right at the conferences with you when you are discussing the issue....I have actually had the child and the parent there and we set the behavior mode or something right in place with the parent and the child there. So the child knows exactly when the notes are going home weekly or whenever. I can't stress enough the triangle. If you are going to succeed you have to have all three, and so often we are lacking some of the parents so the child doesn't feel like there has been any follow through.

The goals the K-2 teachers had for parents were very explicit. For example, Mrs. Andrews stated that "...the goal would be for parents to read the notes, know exactly what the note said, and take the proper action." This teacher also revealed that she felt that parents should be aware of the teacher's goals. Mrs. Turner stated that she expected parents to "...be familiar with books...where to find books...talk to [their] child [and participate in] storytelling, [activities]."

The principal and the reading specialist were silent as the K-2 teachers described the present conditions for contacting parents and their goals for parent involvement. However, when the conversation shifted to describing the process for building bridges for parents to become partners in their children's learning, the principal, in particular, became extremely vocal.

Mrs. Jones agreed with the principal's comments, but she also shared with her peers that she felt that "teaching would be a lot easier if [parents] would take their role seriously as the parents and as the pre-teacher of their children." The reading specialist and several other teachers nodded their heads in agreement when Mrs. Jones stated that: "whether you [meaning the teacher] are working on academics, the parents need to support the efforts of the teacher." Mrs. Jones also received immediate approval from her peers when she suggested that children should be present when teachers discuss their expectations with the children's parents.

PAUSE AND REFLECT

Do you think that the Morton principal, K-2 teachers, and reading specialist's goals and bridges for parent involvement will succeed? Why or why not? Are the Morton staff's comments realistic or unrealistic? Locate specific comments in the transcript to support your position. What would you do differently or the same if you were a teacher at Morton? You can respond to these questions independently on paper, work with a partner in your class/group of colleagues, or work cooperatively with a cooperating/mentor teacher.

In the fourth category of responses, a number of teachers identified some of the *barriers* that prevented parents from becoming involved. The teachers discussed problems associated with parents' interpretations of notes and the confusion of parents receiving multiple notes. Further, the teachers discussed the tensions of training parents who rarely volunteer, difficulties with consistency in parent commitment, issues of confidentiality and privacy, and parents' personal ghosts.

Mrs. Terry: ...problems with notes being sent home. I don't know what the answer is but I guess I can't talk about my goals...until I talk about the problems. Realistically [parents reading notes] isn't what happens, and I don't think it's necessarily the fault of the parents. I mean sometimes as a teacher, I'll sit down and I'll write a note and to me it's clear as a bell...and the parent will get a completely different interpretation of it. So I don't know. I think that sometimes it's compounded when we send so many notes home at any one time and I'm talking about throughout the building...and this has been a concern of mine for a long time. On any given day the child may carry three, four, five notes home to be read. Maybe note is not the right word, but they have the flyer from YWCA or YMCA and they have something else from something else and something else from something else and then on top of that they may have a note from the teacher. Several of my parents have told me [this], and I had one just a few weeks ago. I said, "Did you get the note?" She replied "Well, maybe I did...but I want to tell you...I have four kids, and there's no way in the world I can read all the notes that are coming home."

Mrs. Bell: I have many notes from parents that say...They know what to do, if you just give them a little more time. So I'm wondering. Here we go back again I think with this communication thing...I mean we send the notes home and they just don't seem to do the job....Now I'm sounding like a failure here and I'm not...

Mrs. Benton: I find myself in limbo all the time because sometimes the parents, who would like to help [are] such a chore to have in the classroom. Not because they're there because I think it's wonderful that they can get there and just observe what a routine day in a classroom is like. You want to help.

Many of them don't have the basic skills to run the ditto machine, to run the copy machine, to check a paper. You say, "Just hand them the book." Well it's not always that easy. And I find that I have no time in my day to inservice them...and I find if you try to inservice them, you know they're here for a little while and then they're gone again. But there really isn't any time to inservice them. There must be an answer to this dilemma. I don't know what it is.

Mrs. Miller: Well, be on the lookout. If you say anything to a kid, make sure you can back it up...Sometimes they [children] will say you said this or that. I had that incident happen my first year where a parent came in about homework. This child would say one thing that really was not the right thing, and the information had been given out at open house about homework policy and the parents weren't there and I had sent it home by the child so if they had read it there would not have been that question. Back up what you say. Now with all the things that's going on now about "don't touch a child" you just have to stay on guard from anything risky.

Mrs. Novak: If a parent wants to come and volunteer in my room that's fine I just want to make sure that, in some rooms (not in mine, per se), the parents that come have been the ones who then complain in the neighborhood about this or that or about some child. I think you have to be very careful of that when you select the parent that the parent is there for very legitimate reasons. If they are...I don't think they should be correcting papers all the time. I think if they are working with children then when they come back into the classroom and discuss that child with you that it goes no further than that...I think you have to be careful with that as far as selection. A lot of times you get parents from the past who have another child coming to school soon and you know that parent well and you also work with that parent very well and that's fine, but taking on a new parent can be risky...And I think you have to say okay, this is not the type of parent I want in my classroom [and] then have the courage to say that...I personally want someone in my classroom who is there to help the child, not to criticize children.

Mrs. Miller: It is kind of a double-edged sword. If parents were going to choose to help me in the areas that I need, which would be tutoring, its very difficult to find parents who would make that commitment weekly and follow through. I've done that in years past, and they drop off. Even though you think you keep the interest high, it is very difficult to get an ongoing commitment from parents...With more than one or two...I mean if you're talking about a group of ten, I think you would have to sit down as a school maybe and say, "Okay, what could we really get the parents interested in enough that they would be willing to make this weekly commitment?" I have found that many parents as far as checking the tests have made a weekly commitment and I'm very appreciative of it, but it is something that can be done at home at night rather than coming to school.

  Part of the issue I think, too, with a lot of the parents in this school is that they don't see the school as a positive atmosphere because they themselves have not had real good experiences in school. They come here, and they feel intimidated, and you are starting from the beginning behind the eight ball. What you have to do at conference time is make them feel very comfortable with you and that is one step.

  When discussing the barriers that prevented parents from successfully participating in the affairs at Morton, Mrs. Terry and Mrs. Bell revealed that parents were receiving too many notes from teachers and did not have enough time to read these notes. For instance, Mrs. Terry reported,

"On any given day, the child may carry three, four, five notes homes to be read." Mrs. Bell admitted, "I have many notes from parents that say...They know what to do, if you [meaning the teacher] just give them a little more time." As the group continued to discuss the barriers they perceived as preventing parents from participating in the school affairs at Morton, the conversation shifted to teachers describing their own personal barriers, which can be categorized into fears, doubts, concerns, and reservations about parents participating in their classroom in particular. For example, Mrs. Benton stated that, "I find myself in limbo" and, "I find that I have no time in my day." Mrs. Miller warned of being accused of saying things that might be misinterpreted by parents. She said, "Well, be on the look-out. If you say anything to a kid make sure you can back it up...Now with all that's going on now about don't touch a child, you have to stay on guard from anything risky." Mrs. Jones further warned "If a parent wants to come and volunteer in my room that's fine I just want to make [sure] that...the parents [do not] then complain in the neighborhood about this or that about some child. I think you have to be very careful of that when you select the parent...I think if they are working with children then when they come back into the classroom and discuss that child with you that it goes no further...or don't get them to help you..."

PAUSE AND REFLECT

If you were a teacher at Morton, how would you remove the barriers to parent involvement that these teachers pinpointed (i.e., parent interpretations of notes, the confusion of parents receiving multiple notes, issues of confidentiality and privacy, parents' personal ghosts about school, and so on)? You can respond to this question independently on paper, work with a partner in your class/group of colleagues, or work cooperatively with a cooperating/mentor teacher.

In the last category of responses, a few teachers made suggestions that could be characterized as Morton's *first steps* toward improving the climate for parent involvement. They discussed effective communication, personal and positive interaction with parents, and communicating with parents as equals in the child's educational process.

Mrs. Bowker: I will always tell the child, "I talked to your mother" or "I talked to your father." To let them know that their parents have made an effort and that we are in constant communication...I do try to have a positive influence on the parents [and] the child. You know if a parent voiced a concern that I yelled at his or her child, then I'm probably more conscious of how I interact with that student.

Mrs. Dozier: My top thing would be to contact every parent initially before school starts, introduce myself, and have positive contact before I have to have a negative interaction with a parent. I would not let my first introduction with a parent be when there is a problem. I know that parents bring a lot of their own fears with them when they bring their children to school. So I would definitely contact them on a positive note and get to know them before I had to contact them on a negative note. I would help them feel comfortable with what's going to happen in my classroom. Let them know some of my background and what I'm looking forward to doing. Be clear about my expectations of what their child is going to learn in my classroom.

Mrs. Andrews: I just find that you treat [parents] as equals when they come to a conference...and you know that a lot of them will seem intimidated. Because they see me as a professional. If you step out of that role and say, "Look, this is what your child is doing, it is bothering me, and it must be driving you crazy at home too." You should be very honest and drop that role of "teacher" and just become a person who is sitting there and saying, "Look, we have a problem. Your child should be here, and I want us to work together to get him/her there. What do you see at home, what do you use at home? Does it work for you? Now we have to come up with a game plan. I know college didn't prepare me to address everything. My masters is in emotionally impaired in special education. So I had a lot of psychology, but I think basically, it is when you communicate to a parent you are the professional, but you become equals when you're talking and you admit that the parent knows much more about their child than you can ever know...so we should make parents our partners in learning.

Mrs. Jones: The first time you see an issue that needs to be dealt with, deal with it immediately instead of waiting until conference time and then all of a sudden the parent will say, "Why wasn't I contacted?" I think before it becomes a problem, when you see it as an issue, that's when you make the phone call and you make the written contact and you say, "This is an issue we need to deal with together." And again you create the triangle I mentioned earlier and I think that is important.

Despite all the barriers the teachers highlighted, they still described some of the *first steps* they had made to create an environment for parent involvement at Morton. For example, Mrs. Bowker stated that "I will always tell the child I talked to your mother or I talked to your father. To let [the child] know that their parents have made an effort and that we are in constant communication." Mrs. Dozier revealed that, "My top thing would be to contact every parent initially before school starts, introduce myself, and have positive contact before I have to have a negative interaction with a parent. I would not let my first introduction with a parent be when there is a problem." Lastly, and perhaps Mrs. Andrews reported one of the more impressive first steps. She reported that "...I think basically it is when you communicate to a parent you are the professional, but you become equals when you're talking and you admit that the parent knows much more about their child than you can ever know...so we should make parents our partners in learning."

PAUSE AND REFLECT

Do you think that the Morton staff's first steps toward improving the parent involvement climate will succeed? Why or why not? Are the Morton staff's comments realistic or unrealistic? Locate specific comments in the transcript to support your position. If you were a teacher at Morton, what would you do differently? You can respond to these questions independently on paper, work with a partner in your class/group of colleagues, or work cooperatively with a cooperating/mentor teacher.

Step 3: Analyzing the Profile of Parent Involvement at Morton

After the discussion with the principal, K-2 teachers, and the reading specialist about the present conditions, goals, bridges, barriers, and first steps toward developing a climate for parent involvement at Morton, I distributed a copy of *Construct a Profile of Parent Involvement in Your School,* which was developed by Henderson, Marburger, & Ooms (1986). I also provided for the principal, K-2 teachers, and the reading specialist the meanings as defined by Henderson, Marburger, & Ooms of the parent roles included in the parent profile (see Figure 6.6 for a pictorial description of the profile of parent involvement and Figure 6.7 for an estimate of the involvement of Morton parents). The parent roles are defined in the next section.

1. *Partners*: Parents performing basic obligations for their child's education and social development.
2. *Collaborators and problem solvers*: Parents reinforcing the school's efforts with their child and helping to solve problems.
3. *Audience*: Parents attending and appreciating the school's (and their child's) performance and productions.
4. *Supporters*: Parents providing volunteer assistance to teachers, the parent organization, and other parents.
5. *Advisors and/or co-decision makers*: Parents providing input on school policy and programs though membership in ad hoc or permanent governance bodies (p. 3).

After receiving and reviewing this information, the principal, K-2 teachers, and the reading specialist were asked to construct a profile of parent involvement at Morton. The results of their efforts can be found in Figure 6.7.

As shown in Figure 6.7, ninety percent of the Morton families were *partners* in their children's education, approximately seventy percent of the families served as *collaborators and problem solvers*, and slightly more than fifty percent of the families served only as an *audience*. Almost thirty percent of the families served as *supporters* and less than twenty percent of the families served as *advisors and/or co-decision makers*. It should be noted that these estimates are similar to those

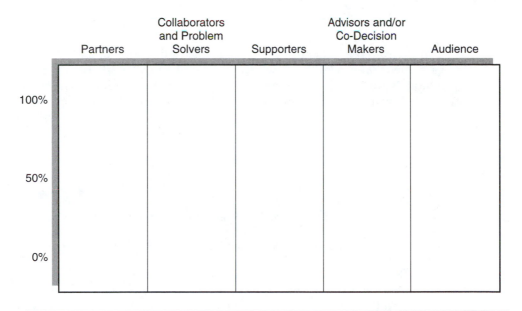

FIGURE 6.6 *Construct a Profile of Parent Involvement at Your School*

Source: Henderson, A., Marburger, C. L., & Ooms, T. (1986). Beyond the bake sale: An educator's guide to working with parents. Columbia, MD: National Committee for Citizens in Education.

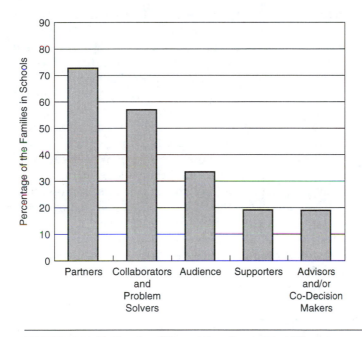

FIGURE 6.7 *Estimate of Parent Involvement at Morton*

reported by Henderson, Marburger, & Ooms (1986). Further, it should be noted that the estimates of parent involvement at Morton are consistent with Henderson, Marburger, & Ooms's contention that "Roles 1, 2, and 3 involve parents in activities that benefit their own child. Roles 4 and 5 largely benefit the school as a whole, with benefits accruing only *indirectly* to the parents' own child. This distinction is important because it may help to explain why so few parents are active in these last two roles, when it is less clear that their involvement will benefit their own child" (p. 13).

PAUSE AND REFLECT

Do you believe that the Morton's staff assessments were accurate in terms of describing the roles parents play at Morton based on the *Construct a Profile of Parent Involvement in Your School,* which was developed by Henderson, Marburger, & Ooms (1986)? Do you think that they had a difficult time placing parents, or was it an easy task? The results revealed that ninety percent of Morton parents served as partners in teaching their children. The percentage seems extremely high given the frustration with parents expressed by many of the Morton teachers in the two interviews. Did you come to the same conclusion? Do you think the Morton staff was trying to make their school look good? If so, why?

Step 4: Constructing a Demographic Profile of Morton

In addition to conducting two sets of structured individual interviews with the principal, K-2 teachers, and the reading specialist to get a sense of the parent involvement climate, I constructed a *demographic profile* of the entire parent population at Morton and a classroom by classroom profile (see the Web site for an example of a school and classroom demographic profile). The demographic profile data was collected from the information on the student data cards, which were located in the principal's office. A *demographic profile* is a composite description of the parent community that exists in a school building, as well as in individual classrooms. On the Web site that accompanies this book you can find a sample school district enrollment form and a sample of a student move-in/move-out information form. Even though I did not collect this information on the Morton families, this is information that can be collected to assist you in gathering additional information on the families and children you serve.

I informed the principal, K-2 teachers, and the reading specialist that once this demographic profile data was collected and analyzed, the principal, K-2 teachers, and the reading specialist could then decide how parents could best support parent involvement initiatives at Morton. Why did I decide to share with you the specific details and analysis of Morton? Well, for one thing, it will allow you to see what kind of analysis can be done with the data that you collect at your school. Also, you can learn something about the meaningfulness of this activity and how developing a demographic profile can affect your efforts both to increase parent involvement and improve literacy experiences for students. (See Figure 6.8 for demographic profile of Morton parents.)

Figure 6.8 describes the family structures of Morton's students. As noted in the pie chart, forty percent of the students live with both parents (mother and father), thirty percent of the students live with their mother only, and thirty percent live in alternative family arrangements (i.e., father only, aunt only, foster parents, father and father's girlfriend, mother and mother's boyfriend, grandmother and father, aunt and father, mother and uncle, dad and dad's girlfriend for six

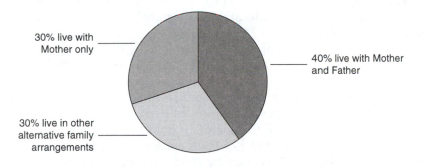

FIGURE 6.8   *The Family Structures of Morton Students*

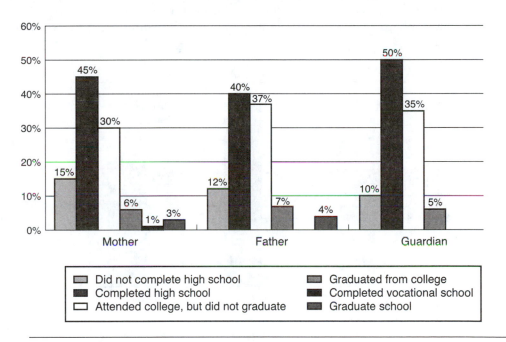

FIGURE 6.9   *The Educational Level of Morton's Families*

months and mother only for six months). Figure 6.9 describes the educational level of Morton's mothers, fathers, and guardians respectively. Only forty-five percent of the Morton mothers completed high school and one percent of them completed vocational school. Even though thirty percent of mothers attended college, only six percent of them graduated and less than three percent completed graduate school. The educational level of the Morton fathers was very similar to that of the Morton mothers. For example, forty percent of the fathers completed high school, and thirty-seven percent attended college but did not graduate. Only seven percent of the fathers completed college and four percent of them received graduate degrees. A slightly higher percentage of the Morton guardians received high school diplomas as opposed to the Morton mothers and fathers. However, the percentages in the other educational categories were very similar. For example, thirty-five percent of the Morton guardians attended college, but did not graduate. Only five percent of the guardians actually graduated from college.

Figure 6.10 highlights the percentages of Morton's mothers, fathers, and guardians in blue/white collar jobs. Most of the Morton mothers (seventy-five percent) and fathers (eighty percent) are blue-collar workers. Only twenty-five percent of the Morton mothers and twenty percent of the fathers are white-collar workers. Fifty-five percent of the guardians hold blue-collar jobs and almost an equal percent (forty-five percent) of them are employed in white-collar professions. Some of the *blue collar jobs* held by Morton mothers included waitress, lunch aide, nurses' aide, messenger, book marker, hairdresser, fast food service positions, service technician, house cleaning, cook, cashier, assembly worker. The *white-collar jobs* held by Morton mothers included personnel manager, benefit analyst, pharmacist, registrar, claims examination, insurance agent, registered nurse,

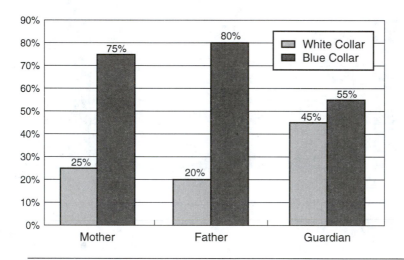

FIGURE 6.10   *Percentage of Morton's Mothers, Fathers, and Guardians in Blue/White Collar Jobs*

customer services representative, computer programmer, collections manager. The *blue collar jobs* held by Morton's fathers included plant guard, sweeper, furniture assembler, parking enforcement, deputy sheriff, truck driver, janitor, mechanic, mailman, athletic trainer, pest control, construction worker, welder, cabinet maker, barber, mowing & landscape. The *white collar jobs* held by Morton's fathers included psychologist, computer programmer, restaurant owner, professor, bank vice-president, engineer, controller, social worker, private investigator, minister. The *blue-collar jobs* held by Morton's guardians included cashier, sales, clerk, stock person, carpenter, paint repair, bus driver, dispatcher, car salesman. The guardians' *white collar jobs* included: engineer, professor, and owner of an accountant firm, lawyer, doctor, and realtor.

Figure 6.11 shows that ninety-six percent of the Morton families speak English in the home and only four percent of them do not. As noted in the pie chart, these other languages include Spanish, Greek, Arabic, Korean, Japanese, Farsi, and sign language. It should be noted that Spanish speakers comprised the largest number within the four percent of families who speak another language other than English.

Analysis of the Findings from the Demographic Profile of Morton. As you can see, many of the Morton families are employed on jobs that require them to work long hours. In fact, many of the Morton families work *shifts*, which means that their work hours are inflexible. It is extremely difficult for most of the families to leave their jobs to come visit their child's school during the *day* or *night* hours. In other words, it does not seem to matter whether the Morton families hold *blue or white-collar jobs*. What does seem to matter is that most of the *blue and white-collar workers* hold jobs, which prevent them from readily serving in some of the traditional parent roles teachers may wish for them to participate in. Yet, most of the Morton teachers I spoke with had not redefined their parent involvement initiatives to coincide with the work schedules of the *1990s* Morton families. It would be safe to conclude that there was a high probability that the Morton teachers did not have knowledge of the parents' work schedules even though that information was available on the data

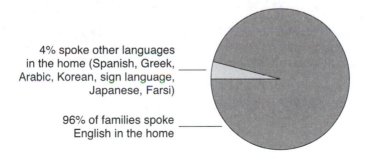

4% spoke other languages
in the home (Spanish, Greek,
Arabic, Korean, sign language,
Japanese, Farsi)

96% of families spoke
English in the home

FIGURE 6.11 *The Language Spoken at Morton in K-5*

cards located in the principal's office. It is my guess that most of the teachers had not bothered to check the data cards in the principal's office. This is just one way you might choose to analyze your data. You and your colleagues might want to consider other ways of examining the information you collect.

PAUSE AND REFLECT

Given the specifics of the demographic profile, what kinds of new, appropriate initiatives can you think of? Where could a Morton teacher begin to do things differently? Should Morton teachers do a demographic parent profile annually? Why or why not? Should Morton teachers have knowledge of parent work schedules? Why or why not?

Step 5: Conducting a Community Scan
of Your School's Support Network
One important beginning task is to get to know the community in which you will be teaching. You can go to the central office in your school district and obtain an attendance boundary map for the school of which you will be conducting a community scan. Spend an afternoon walking and/or driving around the area.

PAUSE AND REFLECT

Take a few minutes and make a rough sketch of the area where your school is located, noting streets and landmarks.

The sample list of questions that follows can provide you with some very insightful information about the families that your school serves:

- What is the predominant socioeconomic status of the neighborhood?
- What conditions are the homes in around the neighborhood? Are they mostly apartments, single-family homes, or a mix?
- What racial or ethnic groups are represented in the neighborhood? Which one is the majority group?
- What age groups are represented in the neighborhood? Which is the majority?
- Where are the public libraries located? Stop in the library and find out if there is a local newspaper, and if there is, skim it. Also find out if there is a local history you might read.

- Count the number of churches. What religions do they represent? Where are they concentrated?
- What is the economic base of the community? What industries are here? What commercial enterprises? What is the community's level of economic health?
- What services does the community provide for children?
- Where are the "hangouts"?
- How would you characterize the "tone" of the community? Optimistic? Busy? Depressed? Orderly? Unruly? Quiet?
- What other characteristics of this community stand out for you?

These questions are critical to understanding some of the community-level issues that might affect parent involvement at your school. Say, you find out where the "hangouts" are—so what? Well, these hangouts might be places where you can meet with parents to invite them to participate in your school's program. So often, teachers complain that they don't know where to contact parents. Hangouts can be a place to reach them. You might be asking yourself what kinds of services the community provides as useful in constructing parent involvement programs such as what I developed Morton. Again, when schools attempt to reach out to parents and parents are not just available to help their children, schools can have at their disposal *community organizations as family* (see Heath & McLaughlin, 1991), a concept a described in Chapter 2. The term *community organizations as family* broadens the definition of "parent" to include community leaders and youth workers (i.e., Boys and Girls Clubs of America, Future Farmers of America) who are invested in the lives, dreams, and development of the children in their care. More importantly, having at your disposal information on community services will not leave you saying, "This child needs help, I can't do it all at school, and I don't know who I can go to to ask for help." Community organizations might be the answer you have been looking for.

PAUSE AND REFLECT

Write a paragraph about how you might incorporate the knowledge you've obtained about the community into your teaching. How will it help you establish rapport with students? How will it help you develop good working relationships with parents? How can you use the information in your lessons?

Third Set of Action Steps

In the third set of action steps, I have included several activities that I did with the Morton staff, activities that I did with other schools, and activities that I think are great ones for schools to participate in. These activities will move you closer to understanding and the meeting the needs of the families you serve. For example, you will learn that your families feel capable, willing, and responsible to assist with tasks you might request of them. Also, you will learn how to document the levels of family involvement, how to develop a family-school planning calendar, and how to create a school vision of family-school partnerships.

- *Step 1: Examining links to government agencies, journals, and organizations.* Even though I did not use the Parent Involvement Questionnaire activity (found on the Web site that accompanies this book at *www.ablongman.com/edwards1e*) with the Morton staff, I think this is a great activity. In Appendix E, I have included a list of *links* to government agencies, journals, organizations, and so on. These *links* are invaluable in providing you with a wealth of information to broaden your knowledge of working with families and children.

- *Step 2: Surveying families to determine if they feel capable, willing, and responsible to assist in their children's education.* On the Web site, I have included an instrument called the Parent Involvement Questionnaire that you can use to survey families to determine if they feel capable, willing, and responsible to assist their children's education. I used this instrument to survey families in a large south Louisiana metropolitan school district. This information was extremely useful to the schools that participated in the survey study. In particular, the results prompted the schools to become more sensitive toward the families' feelings about participating in activities assigned by the schools. All too often schools readily make requests without considering the opinions/wishes of the families they serve.

- *Steps 3 and 4: Get in touch with your attitude toward parent involvement.* I also include another instrument called the Parent Profile that you can use to get in touch with your parents' attitudes toward parent involvement and a plan of action to assess parents' readiness for increased involvement in school (see the Web site for the Parent Profile).

- *Step 5: Documenting levels of family involvement at your school.* I have included an archival data form on the Web site for you to document levels of parent involvement in your school setting. So often teachers give homework assignments, with little or no awareness of how many school-age children are in a particular family or what their colleagues have requested of the same parent to help one or more children on a given night. Consequently, I invite you to organize a master schedule like the one found in Table 6.10 of the homework assignments so that you and other teachers will have an idea of how many and what types of homework assignments are being requested of children on given night.

- *Steps 6 and 7: Developing a family-school planning calendar and assessing your readiness for increased parent involvement.* On the Web site for this book you will find a home-school partnership-planning calendar for the months of September through August. On this partnership planning calendar, you can record the ways in which you partner with parents (i.e., communication, supporters, learners, teachers, advisory/decision-making).

Assignments

Name of Parent	Number Children Enrolled in School	Name of Child's Teacher (s)	Monday	Tuesday	Wednesday	Thursday	Friday

FIGURE 6.12 *Homework Master Plan*

Once you have completed the Archival Data Form and the Home-School Partnership Planning Calendar from the Web site, I invite you to use that information as a basis for answering the Home-School Partnership Assessment Questions found also on the Web site.

- *Steps 8 and 9: Creating a school vision for a partnership and creating a statement of your school's vision of family-school partnerships.*   After you have answered all of the questions found in the Home-School Partnership Assessment, you will be ready to complete the information requested in the Creating a School Vision for Partnership and Creating a Statement of Your School's Vision of Family-School Partnership—both found on the accompanying Web site. On both of these forms, I ask the question, *"What will your partnership program look like when your vision becomes a reality?"* and I invite you to write a statement of your school's vision based on parents' and the school staff's beliefs regarding the purposes of schooling and how parents and staff can work together to achieve those purposes.

- *Step 10: Developing an action plan for strengthening family-school partnerships.*   Lastly, on the Web site I provide you with an Action Plan for Strengthening Home-School Partnerships, which focuses on the following areas (i.e., home-school communications, home and school as supporters, home and school as learners, home and school as teachers, and home and school as advisory/decision-makers, advocates). In particular, I ask that you record the following information around the activities to plan to strengthen them as they relate to home-school partnerships: (1) what will be done, (2) purpose of the activity, (3) by whom, (4) when, (5) resources/training needs, and (6) evidence of success.

Summary

School-based collaborations between teachers and university researchers are often difficult to form. Chapter 6 provides an opportunity for readers to examine the development of an effective school-based parent involvement program beginning with initial communication problems that occurred between the teachers and researcher. These and other concerns were successfully addressed through open, honest discussions. The project moved forward as participants developed a mutual understanding and respect for the contributions and limitations of other participants. While working through the three phases of action steps, it becomes apparent that building home-school connections entails much more than asking parents to attend PTA meetings, parent-teacher conferences, and sponsor fundraising events. Developing home-school partnerships requires teachers to critique their own instruction, personal biases, and professional abilities. They must be able to clearly and precisely articulate specific ways that parents can reinforce the school's curriculum. Teachers must be committed to spend extra time to become extremely organized and plan ahead to provide parents with information needed to reinforce the curriculum.

One focus and message of this chapter reflects my belief that one of the primary roles of teacher educators is preparing preservice elementary teachers to involve parents in the literacy support of their children. Another message is to stress the importance of sensitivity to parents' personal literacy skills, needs, and concerns when soliciting the participation of diverse parent populations in literacy initiatives.

One way to use the information in this chapter might be to read it from front to back as an argument about the role of literacy in the research on home/school connections and the need to rethink or restructure parental involvement initiatives. When I wrote this chapter, I envisioned its use as a "how-to plan," in which the reader proceeds more or less from beginning to end and uses the evidence presented in the main body of the chapter to evaluate the author's analysis and thesis as it is presented and developed at the beginning and end of the book. This could stimulate readers to form their own explanations of what they observe and compare them to mine.

In closing, I believe that the ideas and strategies described in this book and in this chapter represent steps that will help preservice and inservice teachers accept responsibility for more effectively working with children and their parents. I hope preservice and inservice teachers will adopt and adapt the ideas described, making them their own, and molding them to their specific schools/classrooms and the needs of the communities they serve.

Chapter 6 Key Concepts

- Inevitable conflicts often arise when university researchers and schoolteachers attempt to form collaborations.
- Research that involves studying one's own efforts to transform an educational setting is often referred to as *action research* because it involves the systematic efforts to study the actions with which one is involved.
- Action research is especially empowering when participants generate meaning by exchanging information from different frames of reference (called *cogenerative dialogue*).
- *Propositional knowledge* is information from experiences, reading, dialogue with researchers, and observations that cut across contexts.
- Empowering participation occurs when the cogenerative dialogue results in consequences that affect organization and utilization of valued resources.
- Researchers interested in educational issues have found it difficult to enact changes in schools and classrooms for various reasons.
- To improve collaborations between researchers and teachers, a shift from blame allocated to a person or set of people (e.g., parents) to understanding the systematic nature of educational problems has to occur.
- Traditional forms of parent involvement offer little opportunity for significant involvement of curriculum, require the availability of parents during working hours, do not bring families together around specific literacy events, or do not involve parents in ways that would enable them to support children's literacy learning.

- Teacher profiles can be used as a vehicle for teachers to share their personal and specific reasons for wanting parent participation because parent involvement means different things to different people.
- Based on questions asked on the school and classroom level, the initial set of action steps include (1) developing definitions of family involvement, (2) deciding on types of family involvement, (3) examining perceptions of family involvement, and (4) implementing practices of family involvement.
- The second set of action steps focus on developing and improving family-school partnerships. Inservice and preservice teachers need to (1) find out about your school's history of involving families, (2) find out about your school's parent involvement climate (e.g., present conditions, goals, bridges, barriers, first steps, and so on), (3) construct a demographic profile of your classroom and school's parent population, (4) analyze the demographic profile findings of your classroom and school's parent population, and (5) conduct a community scan of your school's support network.
- The third set of action steps will complete the process of creating an effective home-school partnership. These steps include (1) examining *links to* government agencies, journals, and organizations, and so on; (2) surveying families to determine if they feel capable, willing, and responsible to assist in their children's education, (3) getting in touch with your attitude toward parent involvement (parent profile) (4) assessing your readiness for increased parent involvement (plan of action), (4) documenting levels of family involvement at your school, (5) developing a family-school planning calendar, (6) assessing your readiness for increased parent involvement, (7) creating a school vision for a partnership, (8) creating a statement of your school's vision of family-school partnerships, and (9) developing an action plan for strengthening family-school partnerships.

Suggestions for Thought Questions and Activities

You have read the entire book and completed the Suggestions for Thought Questions and Activities for each chapter. It's now time for you to practice interfacing with parents. After all, parent involvement is what this book is all about.

1. Form a study/support group of three or four people. Each member of the group should list the names of twenty parents. If possible, try to include parents from various cultures who may not be very involved in their children's education for whatever reason. Also, be sure to include parents from different socioeconomic backgrounds. Discuss the parent questionnaire with group members. In your opinion, are any important questions missing? Revise the questionnaire including questions from your group discussion.

2. Schedule a convenient time to complete your revised parent questionnaire with at least ten parents. It should take between thirty and forty-five minutes per interview.

3. Each group member should compile the information from the parents with whom they speak. Visually represent the answers on a chart or graph.

4. Reconvene the group and discuss the experiences of interfacing with parents and the information gathered.

5. Combine the parent responses. You should have approximately thirty to forty parent responses. If your group was the Parent Involvement Committee at Waterford Elementary School, discuss suggestions that you would make to the principal and teachers based on your collected data.

Internet Activities

- Using the same newsletters you found in Chapter 5, analyze them to see how they meet the needs of parents who speak languages other than English. Search the Internet to find an example of a school or classroom that attempts to bridge potential communication barriers.

- Using a search engine, look for parent support groups for children who have special needs. What do these groups advocate? In what ways do they encourage parents to be involved with the schools?

For Further Study[1]

Epstein, J. L., Sanders, M. G., Simon, B. S., Salinas, K. C., Jansorn, N. R., & Van Voorhis, F. L. (2002). *School, family, and community partnerships: Your handbook for action*, Second edition. Thousands Oaks, CA: Corwin Press, Inc.

The authors guide you through the process of planning, implementing, and maintaining a successful partnership between your school, students' families, and the community. The strategies they offer will help you (1) create "action teams" of principals, teachers, parents, and others to guide partnerships and keep them on track; (2) set up training workshops, discussions, and end-of-year celebrations to support your action teams; (3) link your partnership program to school improvement goals; (4) create specialized programs for use in middle and high schools; (5) network with other schools to share ideas and progress.

Hall, G. E., & Hord, S. M. (1987). *Change in schools: Facilitating the process.* Albany, NY: State University of New York Press.

This book summarizes nearly fifteen years of research in schools—research geared toward understanding and describing the change process as experienced by its participants. It addresses the question: "What can educators and educational administrators do on a day-to-day basis to become more effective in facilitating beneficial change?" This book provides research-based tools, techniques, and approaches that can help change facilitators to attain this goal.

The authors contend that, in order to be more effective, educators must be *concerns-based* in their approach to leadership. Early chapters deal with teachers' evolving attitudes, concerns, and perceptions of change, as well as their gradually developing skills in implementing promising educational innovations. Next, the authors turn to examine the role of the school principal and other leaders as change facilitators and present ways that they can become better informed about the developmental state of teachers and how to use these diagnostic survey and data as the basis for facilitating the change process. The emphasis is on practical day-to-day skills and techniques, showing administrators how to design and implement interventions that are supportive of teachers and others.

---

[1] You might have noticed that some of the references I included in Chapter 6 were published after I completed my work. I updated certain references to reflect the most current edition of these publications.

Each chapter presents not only the concepts and research of the authors but also translates the concepts in concrete applications, which illustrate the way; they can be applied to obtain genuine and lasting improvements. The book also contains an important discussion and description of the change process, focusing on teachers, innovations, and schools.

Fullan, M. (1993). *Change forces: Probing the depths of educational reform.* New York: The Falmer Press.

Change Forces debunks many of the current myths about the roles of vision and strategic planning, site-based management, strong leadership, consensus, and accountability. Drawing on research from successful organizations in business and educational systems, *Change Forces* identifies eight basic lessons about why change is seemingly chaotic and what to do about it. The book brings together the moral purpose of education to produce better citizens regardless of class, gender, and ethnicity, and the skills of change agentry necessary for individuals and systems to contend successfully with the forces of change.

Sarason, S. B. (1995). *School change: The personal development of a point of view.* New York: Teachers College Press.

In *School Change*, Professor Sarason has responded to the request to track the evolution of his ideas about school change by selecting papers and excerpts from his books that illustrate where his ideas came from. The result is both stimulating and surprising because on the surface the papers do not concern school change, but as he demonstrates, they contain concepts that were later to become essential parts of his point of view. This book is not a collection of papers or excerpts because for each of his selections he has written an extensive introduction that, collected together, could be a separate book. What comes through in this book is a picture of a major educator, theorist, and social observer who continues to develop and scan the current scene for confirmation or disconfirmation of his point of view, and he does this with wit and humor.

Sirotnik, K. A., & Goodlad, J. I. (1988). *School-university partnerships in action: Concepts, cases, and concerns.* New York: Teachers College Press.

Based on their own involvement in a number of promising partnership efforts, the editors and contributors have proposed a general paradigm for ideal collaboration between schools and universities: a mutually collaborative arrangement between equal partners working together to meet self-interest while solving common problems. Their contention throughout is that reasonable approximations to this ideal have great potential to effect significant educational improvement not ordinarily possible outside of such a collaborative relationship.

Vopat, J. (1994). *The parent project: A workshop approach to parent involvement.* York, Maine: Stenhouse Publishers. (Chapter 6)

This book provides a framework for implementing ways to get parents involved and informed. It is a complete sourcebook for teachers and principals that provides materials for conducting workshops with parents in areas of writing, reading, self-esteem, and community building.

Epilogue

Moving from High Rhetoric to High Practice

Let's face it. Parent involvement is a top priority in national debates and in debates at the local, state, and regional levels. The importance of parent involvement is acknowledged in the vision and mission statements of schools and school charters (McGilp & Michael, 1994). "Home and school should work together" is a refrain heard again and again, along with the mantra that parents must let their children know they care about education and support what the schools are doing (Edwards with Pleasants & Franklin, 1999, p. xv). In addition, many schools have communicated to parents that they are *wanted* and *needed* in the educational development of their children. Yet, as Joyce Epstein puts it, "Parent involvement remains high rhetoric and low practice." Despite recurring messages urging or demanding involvement, many parents remain completely isolated from the schools either because they have been alienated from schools in the past, or they perceive themselves as not having enough time and opportunity (Edwards with Pleasants & Franklin, 1999, p. xv). I am fully aware of this reality, and I wrote this book in an effort to help you as teachers or future teachers move parent involvement to "high practice and low rhetoric."

I have spent much of my career involved in efforts to help teachers develop meaningful collaborations with parents. What I have learned through this work is reflected in this present book, which I hope will help you in several ways. First and foremost, I hope this book has allowed you to develop a more in-depth understanding, as well as a practical and comprehensive view, of family involvement and its effects on children's literacy learning. I also hope that my book has helped you to feel more confident that you either have or can locate the tools and resources necessary to successfully involve parents in the educational support of their children. In writing this book, I have presented three sets of action steps that you can use in multiple ways. These action steps can serve as a starting point for gaining information; they can be adapted and modified to suit your specific needs and concerns, and they can be used at different points throughout the year to help you create parent involvement activities grade-by-grade around curricular issues.

In addition, I have also highlighted the benefits of traditional and nontraditional ways of recruiting and communicating with parents. In particular, I have encouraged you to ask the following questions: (1) How do these traditional and nontraditional approaches view or not view "parents as people?" (2) How can teachers analyze their own assumptions about parent involvement to alter what they do to promote or rethink it in their school setting?

Traditional and nontraditional approaches of parent involvement can be beneficial in creating family-school partnerships. Before you can begin to decide which approaches might be useful in working with the families you serve, you first must consider asking yourself the following questions: (1) What types of families does my school serve? (2) What techniques have I or my school used to involve families? (3) Which approaches I employed have been the *most* or *least* successful? Why? Once you have answered these three questions, you are ready to begin to think about the changes you would like to initiate. Keep in mind that the families you work with in a given year could be different from the families you work with the following year. Just as your students and their needs change from year to year so will their families. Consequently, it is important to remember that each year, you will need to assess the families you are working with and adjust the ways you work with them accordingly.

I recognize that teachers feel overburdened, but I suggest that by taking seriously the role of parents in the educational process and becoming specific about the actual help from families needed, burdens actually become lifted as responsibilities are shared. This requires that teachers and parents establish collaborative relationships around specific goals. With this in mind, I have attempted to suggest avenues that will lead you to a better understanding of both parents and children. Also, I have created a path for you to learn about yourself. I believe that this book provides a road map for expanding and broadening your knowledge of how to work with diverse families and children. My challenge to you is to begin to move parent involvement from "high rhetoric to high practice," and to join hands with colleagues in your school setting to make parent involvement a school-wide commitment.

"May the force be with you" and keep you excited about working with the families you serve and them excited about wanting to work with you.

Appendix A

Creating Sharing Time Conversations

Parents and Teachers Work Together

The following is the *Language Arts* article I wrote that illustrates how teachers can involve parents in improving the literacy of their young children.

CREATING SHARING TIME CONVERSATIONS: PARENTS AND TEACHERS WORK TOGETHER

PATRICIA A. EDWARDS

Sharing time, that venerable and sometimes questionable early childhood classroom practice, takes on new importance as teachers and families work together.

What Mary Jo Shared, written by Janice May Udry (1966), is a story of a little girl who never shared anything at school because she was too shy to stand before the other children and tell about anything. Udry writes,

> Almost every day her teacher, Miss Willet, would say "And Mary Jo, do you have something to share with us this morning?" Mary Jo always shook her head and looked at the floor.... "Why don't you ever share anything?" her friend Laurie asked. "I will some day," said Mary Jo. "I just don't want to yet." (p. 1)

Although this story was written 30 years ago, it mirrors the reality of many kindergarten classrooms today. Sharing time (also called "show and tell") is a recurring classroom language activity, where children are called upon to give a formal description of an object or a narrative account of some important past event (Michaels, 1981).

Unfortunately, too many children are often unsure and hesitant about what to share. As a result, when a teacher asks, as did Miss Willet when she asked "Do you have something to share with us this morning?" children often answer "no," as Mary Jo did. Similarly, when parents ask their children, as Mary Jo's father asked her, "Did you share something at school today?" many tend to say they did not. Though Mary Jo's teacher appeared to wait patiently for her to come up with ideas to share with her classmates, some teachers may unknowingly rush students to respond, and others may even try to force children to participate in sharing time. Over the years, many teachers have be-

come frustrated. Some have even contemplated abandoning sharing time as a part of their daily classroom routine. Many, however, would argue that sharing time can be an important event in the oral preparation for literacy (Michaels, 1981), and, in order to understand and alleviate the difficulties many teachers experience in helping children participate successfully in sharing time, different perspectives on this activity must be examined.

As a Michigan State University faculty member, I worked at Kendon Professional Development School in Lansing, Michigan, from the spring of 1990 to the spring of 1993. Kendon serves elementary students who come from 3 distinct communities: a nearby trailer park, neighborhoods that surround the school, and the inner city. Children and families from these communities differ in many ways, including family income, ethnic backgrounds, and educational experiences. The school is located in a primarily working class, residential area on the edge of the inner city.

While at Kendon, I asked the 2 kindergarten teachers, Mrs. Bowker and Mrs. Dozier, what parts of their programs they were least satisfied with. Both immediately said sharing time. Both teachers have taught kindergarten for over 25 years in a variety of urban school settings. About sharing time, Mrs. Bowker said:

> I'm not doing this again. This has no purpose. If I hear about tennis shoes, or that Barbie doll one more time.... You'd see kids looking around, thinking, "Oh, this is my sharing day," and they'd grab anything: "My dad bought this..." I was asking myself, "Why do we do this? What do we want them to learn from this, other than trying to make the others kids sit and listen."

Mrs. Dozier recalled the morning ritual of sharing time in the same way: "They'd bring in the same toy time after time and it was, after awhile, lacking in interest both for the other kids and for the teacher. And the ones who didn't have much wouldn't bring in anything!"

After thinking about the teachers' comments, I told Mrs. Bowker and Mrs. Dozier that, although the request for parents to support their children's educational achievement is not new, creating a structured opportunity for parents to support their children around a specific literacy event is new. Therefore, I recommended that we work together on involving parents in helping their children construct sharing time conversations. They agreed, and in this article I describe how they did this, including the parents' reactions to the new approach to sharing time, the problems created by the new structured approach, the impact of parental support of sharing time on student performance and self-esteem, and the new relationships that were developed between parents and teachers around this literacy event.

Making Changes

I asked the teachers, "What is it you want out of sharing time?" Mrs. Bowker replied, "Everybody knows what you want from sharing time." Mrs. Dozier responded, "Doesn't the term 'sharing time' imply what I mean and what I want from sharing time?" I said, "No, I don't know what you want from sharing time; please tell me." The teachers said that they "want(ed) children to stay on the topic, so that we can follow what the children are saying and so that we can ask them questions."

These kindergarten teachers highlighted an issue that Michaels (1981, 1986) has raised in her own research. She reported that when the children's discourse style matched the teacher's own literate style and expectations, collaboration was rhythmically synchronized and allowed for informal practice and instruction in the development of a literate discourse style. For these children, sharing time could be seen as a kind of oral preparation for literacy. In contrast, she noted that when the child's narrative style was in variance with the teacher's expectations, collaboration was often unsuccessful. For example, the teacher would frequently interrupt students while they were talking rather than guide or support them in making the most out of the event. She concluded that "sharing time could either provide or deny access to key literacy-related experiences, depending, ironically, on the degree to which teacher and child start out 'sharing' a set of discourse conventions and interpretive strategies" (1981, p. 423). Michaels (1981) also observed that.

> The discourse of the white children tended to be tightly organized, centering on a single, clearly identifiable

topic, a discourse style ... "topic-centered." This style closely matched the teacher's own discourse style as well as her notions about what constituted good sharing. In contrast to a topic-centered style, the black children and particularly the black girls, were far more likely to use a "topic-associating" style, that is discourse consisting of a series of implicitly associated personal anecdotes. (pp. 428–429)

In their experiences, Mrs. Bowker and Mrs. Dozier observed that white children as well as black children failed to employ a topic-centered style during sharing time. Based on this observation, Mrs. Bowker and Mrs. Dozier recognized the need to make changes in their sharing time program. During the summer of 1990,

> *I'm not doing this again. This has no purpose. If I hear about tennis shoes, or that Barbie doll one more time....*

Mrs. Bowker began looking for materials that might help change sharing time. Through her research, she found a commercially produced program entitled *Show and Tell: Structured Oral Language Activities* (Williams & Lewis, 1988). This program contains 19 different sharing time activities and a generic letter for the teacher to copy and send home weekly. The letter asks parents to talk with their children about a specific topic and to help them prepare to tell their classmates about this topic. Mrs. Bowker tried the letter and activities in a summer program, and the response of children and parents delighted her. She said, "This is it! If parents will do this in the summer when I don't even have a relationship with them, I know that this will work for me during the regular school year." After her successful experience with sharing time in the summer program, Mrs. Bowker shared the program with Mrs. Dozier. They adapted the published program to their own goals and introduced it in their classrooms in the fall of 1990. They believed their adaptation of the published program had several benefits: (1) It created a predictable structure for parents and children, (2) It allowed them to implement a structured oral language program in their classroom, and (3) It stimulated new ideas, motivating students to organize their thoughts and speak in complete sentences and encouraging parental involvement.

Although Mrs. Bowker and Mrs. Dozier generally liked the topics Williams and Lewis (1988) included,

Language Arts

they rearranged them into themed units and added a number of their own. Some of the topics Mrs. Dozier added included Family Celebrations, Teddy Bear Week, Valentine's Day Week, Making a List, My State Michigan, and Seasons. The family celebrations were intended to be a way for children to discuss things they did with their family. If children did not celebrate holidays, birthdays, or other special occasions, Mrs. Dozier tried to adjust the assignments for these students. For example, during Teddy Bear Week, students could bring their favorite teddy bears or books about a bear to school. This topic correlated with her special curriculum theme for that week. For Valentine's Day Week, students were asked to create a valentine for a friend or relative with materials sent home or materials they had available in their home. For My State Michigan week, she sent home a blank shape of the state of Michigan and asked parents to indicate areas that were important to their families. The children were then asked to explain these areas to the class and why they felt they were important. The topic Making a List invited students to make a list of anything they wanted. For instance, they could make a list of their friends and family members, as well as help their parents make a grocery list or a list of toys they wanted for Christmas. With the Seasons topic, Mrs. Dozier asked students to describe a favorite thing they liked to do during each of the seasons by drawing a picture and writing a sentence about the drawing.

Mrs. Bowker also added new sharing time topics but went a step further and organized the topics into thematic units. The thematic units and the topics within the units were as follows: Self-Awareness (This Is Me, My Neighborhood, My Favorite Color, All About Me, and My Year), Books and Writing (My Favorite Book, A Story By Me, The Public Library, Finger Puppets, and Making a List), Holidays (My Favorite Thanksgiving, My Favorite Holiday Season, Art Project, and A Valentine for Someone), Measuring (World's Greatest Cook), Senses (Mystery Tastes, Mystery Smells, Things to Feel and Guess, and What Is It?), Environment (Nature Hunt, The Weather, Plants, and I Found a Leaf), Families (This Is My Family and All About My Family), and Animals (Bears, Dogs, Cats, Snakes, etc.).

Parental Reactions

Although a few parents questioned the need for a new sharing time structure—saying things like, "Why couldn't a child just bring in a new toy to share, as older brothers and sisters had in the past?"—most responded enthusiastically to the new opportunities to help their children with a school assignment and to talk to them

regularly about age-appropriate subjects. In the spring of 1991, Mrs. Bowker and Mrs. Dozier asked parents to evaluate the program and list favorite and least favorite topics. "They said this made them make time for their children," Mrs. Bowker recalls.

> One parent wrote, "I wish I would have had something like this when I was growing up." She felt she and her mother would have been closer. "I wouldn't have started my family so soon." This was one who started having kids when she was 16 and she had 6 kids by the time she was 25.

A father wrote that he had missed several work-related promotions because he could not speak in front of an audience and, therefore, he appreciated the chance sharing time had given children to learn this important skill. Every week he and his 5-year-old daughter prepared for sharing time together, "and he did some really creative things. Like for the 'All about Me' he taped the 2 of them singing her favorite songs." His daughter played these to her classmates with great pride the next day.

Problems Created

Few important changes come without cost, and Mrs. Bowker and Mrs. Dozier noted several problems. First, because children and parents prepared eagerly for the morning ritual, sharing time now consumed far more of their already-full kindergarten day. As Mrs. Dozier pointed out:

> When you have kids taking 7 to 10 minutes, and you have 4 or 5 of them, you can't expect 5-year-olds to listen politely. When someone brings their whole baby album and their first pair of baby shoes, and the first dress they wore and the first food they ate—one went out and bought a jar of baby food to bring in—"And this is my baby spoon..."

She concluded that "lengthy performances of this sort can also create an act that is hard to follow." Mrs. Bowker recalled that one family prepared for the topic Where I Live Is Special by taking photos of every room in their house, labeling each one, and pasting the pictures to a poster board representation of their house. She continued:

> And the next day another child came in with pictures cut from a magazine of things that were exact replicas of things that he had in his house—"My mom has a Tiffany lamp and it's just like this one, and it comes from Sears..." And then the next child had only a picture that he drew of his house—which was the assignment. And that was the first time I had someone say,

Creating Sharing Time Conversations

"No, I will not share today." And I wouldn't have either.

Even though research supports the need to create a structure for parental involvement (Epstein, 1987), the structure for sharing time at Kendon Professional Development School was sometimes in conflict with the home structure because it demanded more of parents than had previously been demanded. Parents are busy people, and it is important for teachers to let them know ahead of time what is expected of them (Swap, 1987). Similarly, Epstein (1988) notes that "all families struggle with limited time, and they need understandable and useful information about how to help their children at home to become more successful in school" (p. 58). For example, some parents simply did not have the extra time needed to accommodate this new sharing time demand. One mother told Mrs. Dozier that she worked nights and weekends and could not fit preparation for sharing time into her family schedule. Both teachers helped parents in this position to think about alternatives, reporting that some of children prepared with grandmothers, aunts, or even elderly neighbors.

Finally, many parents responded to the teachers' letters by writing notes for a child's performance or trying to help the child to write. "They think of it as a project rather than a conversation," explained Mrs. Dozier. "School was a paper-and-pencil task for them, and they interpret school requests through the lens of their own experience."

Impact on Student Self-Esteem

Despite preliminary problems, Mrs. Bowker and Mrs. Dozier believed their kindergartners learned far more about listening in sharing time now that their classmates had something interesting to say. Both teachers scheduled several fluent students for sharing on Mondays, providing models for the less confident 5-year-olds. Each week they saw evidence that others had listened and taken note. They reported that students waited eagerly for their turns to share, for their moment in the sun. Mrs. Bowker and Mrs. Dozier recalled one child who was scheduled to have her tonsils taken out on her regular sharing day, but she insisted that her mother allow her to stop at school on the way to the hospital so she wouldn't miss her turn for sharing. Another student brought Mrs. Bowker a note asking to be sent home after sharing time: He had a fever and his mother wanted to put him to bed, but he would not hear of missing his turn to share what they had prepared.

Even though many of the students were extremely anxious to participate in sharing time, some were still shy. Clifford's progress over the course of the kindergarten year is described in the following excerpt synthesized from research field notes and interviews with Mrs. Bowker:

Clifford started the year having the sharing time project completed but not willing to get in front of the other children to show or tell. He just sat in the circle and held out his sharing time project for his classmates to see it. I noticed that he had drawn wonderful pictures and his mom had written several sentences they had practiced. He often mumbled isolated and disjointed words. He also maintained his seat in the circle. By the fifth week of sharing time, he moved to the Show and

> *...one child who was scheduled to have her tonsils taken out on her regular sharing day... insisted that her mother allow her to stop at school on the way to the hospital so she wouldn't miss her turn for sharing.*

Tell pillow in front of the group and showed his project and was using more sentences. Just 2 weeks later (the seventh week), Clifford was sitting very confidently in the chair designated as the sharing time chair. He had good eye contact, his hand gestures were synchronized with what he was saying, he walked around so each of his classmates could see whether the item he was carrying in his hand was large or small. He used very complex sentences and paused at appropriate times as if he was anticipating his classmates' questions and then answered the questions posed by them. Clifford's presentation was so organized, one could almost see his mother taking the nature walk with him and saying, "Cliff, these are acorns that have fallen off the tree. Squirrels eat these in the winter." With the support of Clifford's parents, his oral language development increased tremendously. By the end of the year, he would talk for 7 minutes. His posture, the smile on his face, the confident way he walked up to the sharing time chair would let anyone observing his sharing time performance know he enjoyed this activity. The only time Clifford didn't present he was very upset and sulked. He said Mrs. Bowker "should write his mother because she didn't do it!" He was absent and didn't get the assignment, then returned on his show and tell day.

Language Arts

Children enjoy sharing time when they are interested in their topic. Since all the children had the same topic, Mrs. Bowker and Mrs. Dozier reported that "the children were becoming 'topic-centered,' in terms of being able to think about 'What do I want to be able to talk about?' and to connect those thoughts together." "And they're doing that as listeners too," Mrs. Dozier pointed out. "They are listening for certain things. The reason they are listening for certain things is because every week all of the children have the same topic." Udry (1966), the author of *What Mary Jo Shared*, noted that when Mary Jo found a topic that all the children knew something about, they listened and offered their own thoughts on the topic. The "something" that all Mary Jo's classmates knew something about was their fathers. Consequently, when Mary Jo stood up and walked to the front of the room and announced to her classmates that she had brought her father so that she could share some of his experiences with them, it invoked a very lively, enriching, and interactive exchange.

A similar response one of Mrs. Bowker's students had from her classmates is described in the following episode developed from field notes and interviews:

On Tuesday morning, Darlene was the first on the schedule. She carried a green canvas sports bag to the front of the room, laid it on the table, and unzipped it. "What are you making?" asked Michael. "Bread," responded Darlene, smiling. On an easel where her classmates can see them easily, she arranged a drawing of a loaf of bread and 2 other sheets of paper. "I like bread," commented a little boy softly. Next, Darlene removed a tub of butter and a knife from the bag and laid them on the table. She saved the best for last. With a fine sense of drama she withdrew a large loaf of homemade bread wrapped in plastic wrap. Cradling it in her arms lovingly, she took her seat in the chair next to the table. "My mother and I put the bread on the table so we could draw it. Then my daddy cut it again. I have to keep it in here," she gestured toward the plastic wrap. "So it doesn't fall apart," a little girl explained. "Yeah," Darlene grinned. "Thank you, Jen." She paused thoughtfully. "It's called"—she paused again, then stood up to consult the paper on the easel. "It's a bread that . . ." she continued softly. "I can't hear what she is saying," piped a 5-year-old voice. "She does need to talk louder," Mrs. Bowker agreed, "but remember, you need to watch her very carefully. Darlene?" "It's a German bread," Darlene continued. "My Grandma's German." "We used powder to make the frosting. I don't know if there's a name of it." She glanced back at her recipe. "Maybe flour?" offered Mrs. Bowker. "We used flour and cream to make the frosting. And we used eggs and salt and braided it. And." Darlene's grin now encompassed her entire face. "I think it's the best bread in the

whole wide world. And the frosting is the best frosting in the whole wide world." She turned to Mrs. Bowker. "We made 2. One to stay home, one to bring here." "And will we have an opportunity to have some?" asked Mrs. Bowker. "Yes. And we can put some butter on it." "It smells very good," commented Mrs. Bowker. As Darlene tried to slide the bread back onto the bag, Tony commented that he had brought cookies and that the children will be allowed to eat them as well. Mrs. Bowker reminded him that at present they are hearing about Darlene's bread and suggested to Darlene that the bread could stay on the table and need not be fitted back into the bag. Darlene returned to her narrative. "We iced it, and then we put it in for . . . for this many minutes." She held the paper up for Mrs. Bowker's inspection. "For 40 minutes," Mrs. Bowker suggested. Darlene nodded, "When I was finished, then me and my sister punched it and my mom punched it, too. So we had the best punching in the whole wide world. Then we turned it over and let it rest until we were ready to make the frosting." After answering a classmate's question, she finished with a flourish. "Anytime you make it. I think it's the best bread in the whole wide world." Mrs. Bowker and Darlene agreed to serve up the bread and butter at the end of sharing time.

New Relationships Formed

Perhaps just as important as what the children learned is what parents and teachers learned. With my assistance, Mrs. Bowker and Mrs. Dozier organized parent forums to explain their ideas about sharing time and address the differences between sharing time and homework. These forums became a place for informal conversation and the exchange of ideas. At the second forum the teachers asked several parents to talk about how they made time each week for sharing time preparation. The conversation proved helpful for parents. Many commented that they learned strategies for assisting their young children with sharing time.

In the past, Mrs. Bowker and Mrs. Dozier assumed that low-income parents did not take the time to prepare their children for sharing time. They further noted:

The sharing time topics that we included in our new approach are topics that middle-class parents normally talk to children about. And these conversations help them to grow into good readers and good writers because they have this kind of information. We have many young and teenage parents that didn't have examples of good parenting, so we've tried to create a structure that makes conversation in the home a natural part of what we do.

What Mrs. Bowker and Mrs. Dozier did by creating a structure for sharing time is supported by Epstein

(1988) in her warning that "unless we examine both family and school structures and practices, we will continue to receive contradictory and often false messages about the capabilities of unconventional, minority, and hard to reach families" (p. 58). In the beginning, the teachers had made assumptions about low-income parents, but had not created a structure that would help these parents understand the school structures and practices.

Mrs. Bowker and Mrs. Dozier learned from the sharing time project that parents did care and that, regardless of economic background or race, they wanted to help their children learn. Both teachers noted that "they were 100% positive that if teachers provided parents with a structure, they would participate." Yet, Mrs. Bowker and Mrs. Dozier admitted that it is easy for teachers to draw the wrong conclusions. For example, Mrs. Bowker recalled a kindergartner who said she wasn't prepared to share because she hadn't brought anything in. That afternoon, when the mother picked the little girl up, she asked eagerly how the sharing time had gone. When Mrs. Bowker told her that the little girl had said she had nothing with her to share, the mother was astonished: "But it was right there in her backpack. We had a board game she wanted to talk about and a picture of her house . . ." Mrs. Bowker discovered that the kindergartner had not seen her mother pack these treasures in her backpack and had assumed that they were still at home.

Both teachers reported that the new approach to sharing time had made them more hopeful about the possibilities for involving parents productively in their children's literacy learning. They further concluded that they now saw the need to think carefully about what they wanted from families. They noted:

> Before we got involved in the sharing time project, we didn't know what we wanted parents to do. We had to

identify what we wanted them to do, and then, ask ourselves, "How do we communicate what that means?" Even though we had a few problems along the way, we think we were able to at least communicate to our parents the need to help their children create sharing time conversations. And I think we were successful. If we were not sure what our 5-year-olds were learning from sharing time 3 years ago, we, as well as our kindergartners' parents, now believe that this part of the curriculum contributes to the development of their literacy in important ways.

References

Epstein, J. L. (1987). Toward a theory of family-school connections: Teacher practices and parent involvement. In K. Hurrelman & F. X. Kaufmann (Eds.), *Social intervention: Potential and constraints* (pp. 121–136). New York: Walter de Gruyter.

Epstein, J. L. (1988). How do we improve programs for parent involvement? *Educational Horizons, 66,* 58–59.

Michaels, S. (1981). "Sharing time": Children's narrative styles and differential access to literacy. *Language in Society, 10,* 423–442.

Michaels, S. (1986). Narrative presentation: An oral preparation for literacy with first graders. In J. Cook-Gumperz (Ed.), *The social construction of literacy* (pp. 94–116). New York: Cambridge University Press.

Swap, S. M. (1987). *Enhancing parent involvement in schools: A manual for parents and teachers.* New York: Teachers College Press.

Udry, J. M. (1966). *What Mary Jo shared.* New York: Scholastic.

Williams, R., & Lewis, S. L. (1988). *Show and tell: Structured oral language activities.* Cypress, CA: Creative Teaching Press.

Patricia A. Edwards is Professor of Teacher Education at Michigan State University. She teaches, writes, and conducts research in the areas of family/intergenerational literacy and connections between home and school literacies.

Appendix B

Mooney's Instrument on Attitudes, Understandings, and Behaviors of Young Children's Reading Development

THE EMERGENT STAGE

Attitudes

Is keen to hear and use new language.
Shows pleasure in the rhyme and rhythm of language.
Enjoys "playing" with language.
Is keen to listen to stories, rhymes, and poems.
Expects books to amuse, delight, comfort, and excite.
Has an attitude of anticipation and expectancy about books and stories.
Expects to make sense of what is read to him/her and what he/she reads.
Is keen to return to some books.
Is keen to respond to some stories.
Wants to read and sees him/herself as a reader.
Is confident in making an attempt.
Responds to feedback.

Understandings

Knows language can be recorded and revisited.
Knows how stories and books work.
Thinks about what may happen and uses this to unfold the story.
Understands that the text, as well as the illustrations, carry the story.
Recognizes book language and sometimes uses this in speech, retellings, or play.
Understands the importance of background knowledge and uses this to get
    meaning.
Knows the rewards of reading and rereading.

Experiences success, which drives the child on to further reading.
Is aware of some print conventions, especially those relevant to directionality,
capital letters, and full stops.

Behaviors

"Plays" at reading.
Handles books confidently.
Interprets pictures.
Uses pictures to predict text.
Retells a known story in sequence.
Develops a memory for text.
Finger-points to locate specific words.
Focuses on word after word in sequence—finger, voice, and text match.
Focuses on some detail.
Identifies some words.
Uses some letter-sound links.
Reruns to regain meaning.
Explores new books.
Returns to favorite books.
Chooses to read independently at times.

THE EARLY STAGE

Attitudes

Is eager to listen to and to read longer stories.
Expects to be able to get meaning from text.
Is willing to work at getting meaning.
Sees reading as more than the words on the page.
Shows confidence in taking risks and making approximations, and sees these as
a way of learning.
Is confident in sharing feelings about and responses to books.
Is eager to confirm success by reading favorite and new books.
Is keen to read to others.
Seeks feedback.

Understandings

Shows increasing knowledge of print conversations.
Associates sounds with letter clusters, as well as individual letters.
Accepts miscues as a part of striving to get meaning.
Understands the importance of a self-improving system in developing oneself
as a reader.

Understands how real and imaginary experiences influence the meaning gained from books.

Increases sight vocabulary rapidly.

Understands how much attention needs to be given to text to confirm predictions.

Behaviors

Makes greater use of context for predictions.

Makes more accurate predictions.

Selects and integrates appropriate strategies more frequently.

Uses pictures for checking rather than prediction.

Reads on, as well as rereads to regain meaning.

Confirms by cross-checking to known items.

Chooses to read more frequently.

Copes with greater variety of genres and themes.

Copes with more characters, scene changes, and episodes.

Frequently explores books independently.

Builds up pace.

THE FLUENCY STAGE

Attitudes

Expects to take a more active part in interacting with the author's message.

Expects to meet challenges but is more confident of overcoming them.

Expects to discover new meanings on further readings.

Is eager to extend reading interests.

Is keen to take initiative in responding to books.

Expects others to consider his/her responses to books.

Does not expect to agree with everything that is read.

Sees books as providing answers to many questions.

Expects books to be a part of daily life and seeks time to read.

Understandings

Knows to focus on details of print only when meaning is lost.

Understands that taking risks and making approximations are an essential part of reading.

Is aware of a variety of genres and can identify elements.

Understands that authors and illustrators have individual voices and styles.

Understands how to adjust reading pace to accommodate purpose, style, and difficulty in material.

Knows how to use books to get information.

Knows how to use the library.

Behaviors

Samples text rather than focuses on every detail.
Uses increasing knowledge of letter clusters, affixes, roots, and compound words to confirm predictions.
Uses strategies of sampling, predicting, confirming, and self-correcting quickly, confidently, and independently.
Sets own purpose for reading.
Makes inferences from text and illustration.
Compares styles and forms.
Maintains meaning over longer and more complex structures.
Copes with longer time sequences.
Copes with more complex characters.
Copes with less predictable texts.
Chooses to read for pleasure, as well as for information.
Summarizes text for retelling.
Uses the table of contents.
Responds in various ways, including critically.

Appendix C

Sample of Teacher's Scope and Sequence of Parent Involvement Activities

Name <u>Lynette</u>   Grade Level <u>Third</u>

What does an elementary teacher need to know at each grade level (K-5) about how to involve parents in the literacy support of their children? What I am getting at here is—what should be the "scope and sequence of parent involvement" around literacy from kindergarten to fifth grade? In other words, what specific literacy activities should teachers ask parents to participate in at home and/or school with their children?

Kindergarten	First Grade

— Read books to their children
— Model reading books to establish the value of and pleasure in reading
— Go to the library and allow child to choose books
— Engage the child in authentic literacy events
  e.g.— Reading labels from cans and packages while shopping and unloading groceries
   — Discussing newspaper and magazine pictures
   — Noticing and attending to signs in and around the neighborhood
— Helping and encouraging and reinforcing any "home-work" assignments (e.g. letter of the week, and so on)
— Listening to their child tell or retell a story or event
— Create "family stories," traditions, and tell and retell them
— Be interested in their child's work, life, and thoughts
— Be positive in their responses, enhance good self-esteem
— Encourage verbal interactions, help child toward logical thought, sequencing, noticing and discussing details (precision in speech)
— Show you value your child's work
— Be as involved as time, and school and teacher, permit (within classroom, on trips, as volunteers, and so on)
— Monitor TV and video for content, appropriateness and time consumed
	Everything mentioned in kindergarten, plus: (these may apply to kindergarten also!)
	
	— Listen to your child read aloud
	— Know your child's curriculum
	— Be curious about your child's day, but ask specific questions
	
	(All of theses activities can be carried out at every grade level with adjustments made to accommodate reading and speaking proficiency.)

Second Grade	Third Grade
(Some of these are *appropriate at any age*.) Everything listed in K and 1 — Provide access to different kinds of books, including reference books (or computers, if available) — Encourage home journals or diaries — Play games that involve reading — Write thank-you notes, letters — Plan outings, parties — Make lists, etc. — Cook and read recipes	Everything listed in K-2 — Discuss neighborhood, community events (world events if appropriate... sports, and so on) — Allow your child to "teach you" how to do something

Fourth Grade	Fifth Grade
(Everything listed in K-3, adjusted for age and development)	
— Encourage independence in reading choices — Discuss TV shows, movies, videos — Ask more than superficial questions; ask thought-provoking questions — Encourage special interests, make information available — Encourage child to be challenged and provide the support needed (Vygostsky's zoped and scaffolding)	— Help your child be aware of the world around them (jobs, educational paths, and so on); help them become aware of their own responsibility for their own learning — Help them become aware they have choices (and that choices have consequences)

Appendix D

Sample of Teacher's Scope and Sequence of Parent Involvement Activities

Name <u>Sharon</u>   Grade Level <u>Fifth</u>

What does an elementary teacher need to know at each grade level (K-5) about how to involve parents in the literacy support of their children? What I am getting at here is—what should be the "scope and sequence of parent involvement" around literacy from kindergarten to fifth grade? In other words, what specific literacy activities should teachers ask parents to participate in at home and/or school with their children?

Kindergarten	First Grade
— Read to your child — Read favorite stories!! — "Play" with words 　— Poetry 　— Rhymes 　— Word games — Songs — Magnetic letters — Talk with your child — Have fun with literacy — Keep reading time relaxed — Model reading and show you enjoy it — Model writing—grocery lists, letters, thank-you notes — Encourage child to "write" thank-you notes	— Same as kindergarten — First grade is critical because it is when "reading" seems to click or not — Encourage child to read to you and keep it fun; don't pressure him/her — Give books and magazines subscriptions as gifts — Have your child help read recipes and cook — Provide lots of arts supplies, colored paper, line paper, textured paper for writing and drawing — Make books for your child to write their own stories

I started with fifth grade since that is the grade I teach. Many of the grades overlap since the modeling parents do and the activities are important at all ages. I see the depth of activities increasing, but most are the same.

Second Grade	Third Grade
Everything suggested in first grade, plus adding to the complexity of reading and writing tasks.	Same as fourth and fifth but not as complex. Keeping literacy "fun" is a must. Modeling continues to be an important factor along with supporting and showing an interest in child's reading, writing, and all literacy skills.

Fourth Grade	Fifth Grade
Same as fifth grade.	— Role model reading for information (newspapers) and for pleasure (books, magazines) — Read to and with their child if their child enjoys being read to — Encourage (insist on?) daily reading — Visit library, bookstore — Model writing letters, thank-you notes and encourage children to do the same — Review homework with child — Leave notes for your child — Encourage your child to keep a special diary and allow them to keep it private! Keep a journal yourself. — Encourage your child to be creative by writing and acting out plays, writing poems, and so on

Appendix E

Helpful Links

Government Agencies

Head Start
http://www2.acf.dhhs.gov/programs/hsb/

Office of Educational Research and Improvement
http://www.ed.gov/offices/OERI/

Parent Training and Information Systems Program
http://www.taalliance.org/PTIS.htm

Title I and Even Start
http://www.ed.gov/offices/OESE/CEP/cepprogresp.html
http://www.ed.gov/offices/OESE/CEP/evenstprogresp.html

Journals

Educational Leadership
http://www.ascd.org/readingroom/edlead/elintro.html

Language Arts
http://www.ncte.org/elem/la/

Phi Delta Kappan
http://www.pdkintl.org/kappan/kappan.htm

Primary Voices, K-6
http://www.ncte.org/elem/pv/

The Reading Teacher
http://www.reading.org/publications/rt/

Organizations

Alliance for Parental Involvement in Education
http://www.croton.com/allpie/index.html

American Library Association
http://www.ala.org

ASPIRA Association, Inc.
http://www.aspira.org

Black Hills Parent Resource Network
http://www.bhssc.org/sdprn/

Center for Social Organization of Schools
http://www.csos.jhu.edu/default1.htm

Center on Families, Communities, Schools, and Children's Learning
http://www.csos.jhu.edu/p2000/center.htm

Children's Home Society of Washington
http://www.chs-wa.org

Clearinghouse for Immigrant Education (CHIME)
http://www.igc.org/ncas/chime.htm

Colorado Parent Information and Resource Center
http://www.cpirc.org

Corporation for National Service
http://www.cns.gov

Dad to Dad
http://www.slowlane.com/d2d/

The Fatherhood Project
http://www.fatherhoodproject.org/

Fathers' Resource Center
http://www.fathers4kids.org

Florida Center for Parent Involvement
http://www.fmhi.usf.edu/cfs/dares/fcpi/

Families and Schools Together (FAST)
http://www.alliance1.org/fast.asp

Family Resource Project
http://www.alaskachd.org/family/

Greater Washington Urban League
http://www.gwul.org/

Institute for Responsive Education
http://www.resp-ed.org

International Reading Association
http://www.reading.org

Iowa Parent Resource Center
http://www.higherplain.org

Learning Disabilities Association of America
http://www.ldanatl.org

Mexican American Legal Defense and Education Fund
http://www.maldef.org

Missouri Partnership for Parenting Assistance
http://literacy.kent.edu/~missouri

National Association for Education of Young Children
http://www.naeyc.org

National Center for Fathering
http://www.fathers.com

National Center on Fathers & Families
http://www.ncoff.gse.upenn.edu/

National Center for Family Literacy
http://www.famlit.org

National Coalition for Parent Involvement in Education
http://www.ncpie.org

National Council for Family Relations
http://www.ncfr.com

National Institute for Literacy
http://www.nifl.gov

National Parenting Association
http://www.parentsunite.org

Northwest Regional Educational Laboratory
http://www.nwrel.org

Ohio Parent Information Resource Center
http://www.lys.org/OHPIRC2/index.html

Parent Partner
http://www.ecac-parentcenter.org/packets/parentpartners/index.shtml

National Black Child Development Institute
http://www.nbcdi.org

Parents Plus of Wisconsin
http://www.parentspluswi.org

Vermont Family Resource Partnership
http://www.vermontfamilyresource.org

Family Literacy

Family Literacy Foundation
http://www.read2kids.org/

National Center for Family Literacy
http://www.famlit.org

Parents and Children

Parents Place
http://www.parentsplace.com

Family Education Network
http://www.familyeducation.com

Family World
http://www.family.com

Parents as Teachers National Center
http://www.patnc.org

Parents Soup
http://www.parentsoup.com

Glossary

ABCs of Cultural Understanding and Communication Through this model, literacy activities that include writing autobiographies, interviewing and discovering the life stories of people from other cultures, and performing cross-cultural analyses, present and future teachers study differences and planned strategies for home/school communication.

Autobiography Club Members who are men and women of varied races and social backgrounds.

Collaboration To work with others toward a common goal.

Comprehensive Approach This method does not seek involvement from parent or family members for the sake of involvement or the benefit of a particular agency. Rather it works with, in, and through the family system to empower, assist, and strengthen the family.

Community Scan Community resources that the school can use as a support system.

Culture A system of values and beliefs about what is socially acceptable or unacceptable behavior.

Cultural Approach This approach focuses specifically on the needs of diverse families and emphasizes the fact that parents' cultural differences should not be viewed as deficits.

Culturally Relevant Teaching Refers to the kind of teaching that allows minority [poor] youngsters access to, and success in, school knowledge through their own culture, helps them recognize and celebrate that culture, and empowers students so they are able to critically examine educational content and process and ask what its role is in creating a democratic and multicultural society.

Demographic Profile A composite description of the parent community that exists in a school building, as well as in individual classrooms.

Developmental Approach This orientation seeks to help parents and families develop skills that benefit themselves, children, schools, professionals, and families and, at the same time, enhance family group and development.

Differentiated Parenting Recognizing that parents are different from one another in their perspectives, beliefs, and abilities to negotiate school.

Family All of the members of a household who reside under one roof; two or more people who reside together and who share similar goals and commitments; people who are related to each other.

Family Involvement Working with a child's parent or extended family.

Family Literacy Encompasses the ways parents, children, and extended family members use literacy at home and in their community. Sometimes, family literacy occurs naturally during the routines of daily living and helps adults and children "get things done." These events might include drawings or writings to share ideas; composing notes or letters to communicate messages; making lists; reading and following directions; or sharing stories and ideas through conversations, reading, and writing. Family literacy may be initiated purposefully by a parent or may occur spontaneously as parents and children go about the business of their daily lives. Family literacy activities may also reflect the ethnic, racial, or cultural heritage of the families involved (Morrow, Paratore, Tracey, 1994 as cited in Morrow, 1995, p. 8).

Family-School Partnerships The relationship that is created or that exists between families and schools.

Funds of Knowledge Those historically developed and accumulated strategies (skills, abilities, ideas, practices) or bodies of knowledge that are essential to a household's functioning and well being.

Generational Poverty Extends from one generation to the next.

Historical Approach Refers historically to the changes in the American family, the nature of family involvement in schools, and the effects of poverty on American families.

Home Literacy Ways in which families construct literacy in their home environment.

Humanistic Approach A point of view that sees "parents as people" and thus looks at them as individuals rather than a collective group.

Outside the Box Approach This approach involves using techniques like soliciting the assistance of bar owners, the ministerial alliance, hairdressers, or people sitting on the street corner to recruit and communicate with families.

Parent A person who raises a child.

Parent Education Program whose goal is to help develop parents in some way. For example, *Parents as Partners* attempts to teach parents how to work with their children.

Parent Involvement The multiple ways that parents work with their school or with their child in education.

Parent Informant Meeting A group meeting where teachers and parents collaborate on a grade-level literacy project.

Parent Stories Narratives gained from open-ended interviews. In these interviews, parents respond to questions designed to provide information about traditional and nontraditional early literacy activities and experiences that have happened in the home.

Parentally Appropriate Activities or interactions that are designed to meet the specific needs of an individual parent or a group of parents.

Personal Life Stories Analyzing one's background to understand the values and attitudes that are taken to the classroom and realizing that multiple perspectives exist and are key components in successfully preparing culturally aware teachers.

Photos of Local Knowledge Sources This approach involves finding ways to help preservice teachers "see" their own cultures (i. e., preservice teachers investigate their out-of-school lives through photographs and narratives) and how to use this information to bridge cultural borderlands.

PITCH (Project Interconnecting Teachers, Children, and Homes) The PITCH program, developed by Brand (1996), offered a set of inservice workshops aimed at helping elementary and preschool teachers and administrators improve home-school relationships.

Process Approach In this approach, families are encouraged to participate in certain activities that are important to the educational process, such as curriculum planning, textbook review and selection, membership on task forces and committees, teacher review and selection, and helping set behavior standards.

Situational Poverty A shorter period of poverty caused by circumstances (i.e., death, illness, divorce, etc.).

Social Capital The norms, social networks, and relationships between adults and children that are of value for children as they mature (i.e., it is the adults who *invest* in the children's development).

Scope and Sequence Grade-level family involvement activities that are developmentally based on the shared decision making and built around the elementary school literacy curriculum.

Task Approach This method seeks to involve parents in order to get assistance completing specific tasks that support the school or class program.

Teacher Profile A reflective description of who the teacher is as literacy providee/facilitator, the teacher's philosophy of teaching, and so on.

Textbook Children Those students that teachers, based on their background and training, perceive to be "normal."

Textbook Parents Those parents who participate in traditional activities such as baking cookies and who are available to come to school anytime teachers want them to.

Tourist curriculum Focuses on artifacts of other countries such as food, traditional clothing, folk tales, and household items.

Traditional "Institutional" Methods Parent-teacher conferences, newsletters, and parent-teacher organizations as a means for recruiting and communicating with families.

References

Adams, B. S., Pardo, W. E., & Schniedewind, N. (1993). Changing the way things are done here. *Educational Leadership*, 49, 37–43.

Adams, M. J. (1990). *Beginning to read: Thinking and learning about print*. Cambridge, MA: MIT Press.

Allen, J., & Labbo, L. (2001). Giving it a second thought: Making culturally engaged teaching culturally engaging. *Language Arts*, 79 (1), 40–52.

Ammon, M. S., Chrispeels, J., Safran, D., Sandy, M., Dear, J., & Reyes, M. (1998). *Preparing educators for partnerships with families* (pp. 1–40). *Report of the advisory task force on educator preparation for parent involvement.* (ERIC Document # 437369).

A nation at risk: The imperative for educational reform. (1983). Washington, DC: The National Commission on Excellence in Education.

Anderson, A. B., & Stokes, S. J. (1984). Social and institutional influences on the development and practice of literacy. In H. Goelman, A. Oberg, & F. Smith (Eds.), *Awakening to literacy* (pp. 24–37). Exeter, NH: Heinemann.

Anderson, R. C., Hiebert, E., Scott, J. A., & Wilkinson, I. A. G. (1985). *Becoming a nation of readers: The report of the commission on reading*. Washington, DC: The National Institute of Education.

Archambault, R. D. (1964). (Ed.) *John Dewey on education: Selected writings*. New York: Random House.

Arrastia, M. (1989). Mother's reading program. In *First teachers: A family literacy handbook for parents, policy-makers, and literacy providers* (pp. 31–34). Washington, DC: The Barbara Bush Foundation for Family Literacy.

Ascher, C. (1988). Improving the school-home connection for poor and minority urban students. *The Urban Review, 20* (2), 109–123.

Atkin, J., Bastiani, J., & Goode, J. (1988). *Listening to parents: An approach to the improvement of home-school relations*. Croom Helm, NY.

Au, K. H. (1993). *Literacy instruction in multicultural settings*. Forth Worth, TX: Harcourt Brace Jovanovich College Publishers.

Au, K. H., & Mason, J. M. (1983). Cultural congruence in classroom participation structures: Achieving a balance of rights. *Discourse Processes*, 6(2), 145–167.

Baker, A., & Soden, L. (1998). *The challenges of parent involvement research. ERIC Clearinghouse on Urban Education.* ERIC/CUE Digest Number 134.

Baker, G. C. (1983). *Planning and organizing for multicultural instruction*. Reading, MA: Addison-Wesley.

Barbour, A. C. (Winter, 1998–1999). Home literacy bags promote family involvement. *Childhood Education*, 75 (2), 71–75.

Baskwill, J. (1996). Conversing with parents through dialogue journals. *Teaching pre-K-8*, 26 (5), 49–61.

Beane, D. B. (1990). Say YES to a youngster's future: A model for home, school, and community partnership. *The Journal of Negro Education*, 59 (3), 360–374.

Becker, H. J., & Epstein, J. L. (1982). Parent involvement: A study of teacher practices. *Elementary School Journal*, 83, 85–102.

Bennett, C. I. (1999). *Comprehensive multicultural education: Theory and practice*. Fourth Edition. Boston: Allyn and Bacon.

Berger, E. H. (1991). *Parents as partners in education: The school and home working together*. Third Edition. Columbus, OH: Charles E. Merrill.

Berger, E. H. (1995). *Parents as partners in education: Families and schools working together*. Fourth Edition. Englewood Cliffs, NJ: Merrill.

Berlinder, D. (1986). "Does culture affect reading comprehension?" *Instructor*, 96 (3), 28–29.

Billingsley, A. (1968). *Black families in White America*. Englewood Cliffs, NJ: Prentice-Hall.

Blassingame, J. (1972). *The slave community*. New York: Oxford University Press.

Bourdieu, P. (1977). Cultural reproduction and social reproduction. In J. Karabel & A. H. Halsey (Eds.), *Power and Ideology in Education* (pp. 487–511). New York: Oxford.

Bourdieu, P. (1984). *Distinction: A social critique of the judgment of taste*, Nice, R. (trans.), (Ed.) Cambridge: Harvard University Press.

Bourdieu, P., & Passeron, J. C. (1977). *Reproduction in Education, society and culture*. Beverly Hills, CA: Sage.

Brand, S. (1996). Making parent involvement a reality: Helping teachers develop partnerships with parents. *Young Children*, 51, 76–81.

Bronfenbrenner, U. (1974). *A report on longitudinal evaluations of preschool programs*. (Report. No. [OHD] 76–30025). Washington, DC: Department of Health, Education, and Welfare.

Bronfenbrenner, U. (1986). Ecology of the family as a context for human development research perspective. *Developmental Psychology*, 22, 723–742.

Brown, C. (1987). Literacy in 30 hours: Paulo Friere's process in Northeast Brazil. In I. Shor (Ed.), *Freire for the classroom: A sourcebook for literatory teaching*. Portsmouth, NH: Boynton/Cook Publishers, Heinemann Educational Book.

Brown V. Topeka Board of Education, 347 U.S. 483, 1954.

Bruner, J. S. (1996). *The culture of education*. Cambridge, MA: Harvard University Press.

Burgess, J. (1982). The effects of a training program for parents of preschool on the children's school readiness. *Reading Improvement*, 19, 313–318.

Burns, P. C., Roe, B. D., & Ross, E. P. (1999). *Teaching reading in today's elementary schools*. Seventh Edition. Boston: Houghton Mifflin Company.

Carine, D. (1988). How to overcome barriers to student achievement. In S. Samuels & P. Pearson (Eds.), *Changing school reading-programs* (pp. 158–171). Newark, DE: International Reading Association.

Cassidy, J., & Vukelich, C. (1978). Survival reading for parents and kids: A parent education program. *The Reading Teacher*, 31, 638–641.

Cazden, C. B. (1999). Foreword. In C. Ballenger, *Teaching other people's children: Literacy and learning in a bilingual classroom* (pp. vii–viii). New York: Teachers College Press.

Cazden, C. B. (2001). *Classroom discourse: The language of teaching and learning.* Second Edition. Portsmouth, NH: Heinemann.

Cazden, C. B., & Mehan, H. (1989). Principles from sociology and anthropology: Context, code, classroom and culture. In M. Reynolds (Ed.), *Knowledge base for the beginning teacher* (pp. 47–57). Oxford and New York: Pergamon.

Chase, R. F. (Chair). (1987). *Report of the Asian and Pacific Islander Concerns Study Committee.* Washington, DC: National Education Association.

Chavkin, N. F., & Williams, D. L. Jr. (1988). Critical issues in teacher training for parent involvement. *Educational Horizons,* 66(2), 87–89.

Children's Defense Fund. (1996). Key facts about children. *Children's Defense Fund Reports,* 17(2), K1-K20.

Chomsky, C. (1972). Stages in language development and reading exposure. *Harvard Educational Review,* 42(1), 1–33.

Chrispeels, J. (1992). *Using an effective schools framework to build home-school partnerships for students success.* Paper prepared for the National Center for Effective Schools, Wisconsin Center for Education Research, School of Education, University of Wisconsin-Madison, Madison, WI.

Cisneros, S. (1992). *The house on mango street.* New York: Vintage Contempories Vintage Books.

Clark, R. (1983). *Family life and school achievement: Why poor black children succeed or fail.* Chicago: University of Chicago Press.

Clark, R. M. (1988). Parents as providers of linguistic and social capital. *Educational Horizons,* 66 (2), 93–95.

Clay, M. M. (1975). *What did I write?* Auckland: Heinemann.

Clay, M. M. (1979). *Reading: The patterning of complex behavior.* Portsmouth, NH: Heinemann.

Clegg, B. E. (March, 1973). *The effectiveness of learning games used by economically disadvantaged parents to increase the reading achievement of their children.* Paper presented at the annual meeting of the American Education Research Association, San Francisco.

Clifford R. M. (1997). Partnerships with families. *Young Children,* 52(3), 1–3.

Cochran-Smith, M., & Lytle, S. L. (1992). Interrogating cultural diversity: Inquiry and action. *Journal of Teaching Education,* 43(2), 104–115.

Coleman, J. S. (August-September, 1987). Families and schools. *Educational Researcher,* 16 (6), 32–38.

Coleman, J. S., Campbell, E. Q., Hobson, C. J., McParland, J., Mood, A. M., Weinfeld, F. D., & York, R. L. (1966). *Equality of educational opportunity.* Washington, DC: Government Printing Office.

Comer, J. P. (1980). *School and power.* New York: The Free Press.

Cooper, A., Beare, P., & Thorman, J. (1990). Preparing teachers for diversity: A comparison of student teaching experiences in Minnesota and South Texas. *Action in Teacher Education,* 12(3), 1–4.

Corno, L. (1989). What it means to be literate about classrooms. In D. Bloome (Ed.), *Classroom and literacy* (pp. 29–52). Norwood, NJ: Ablex Publishing Corporation.

Corbett, H. D., Wilson, B., & Webb, J. (1996). Visible differences and unseen commonalities: Viewing students as the connections between schools and communities. In

J. G. Cibulka & W. J. Kritek (Eds.), *Coordination among schools, families, and communities: Prospects for educational reform* (pp. 27–48). Albany, NY: State University of New York Press.

Crawford, L. W. (1993). *Language and literacy learning in multicultural classrooms.* Boston: Allyn and Bacon.

Criscuolo, N. (1974). Parents: Active partners in the reading program. *Elementary English,* 51, 883–884.

Croft, D. J. (1979). *Parents and teachers: A resource book for home, school, and community relations.* Belmont, CA: Wadsworth Publishing Company, Inc.

Crosset, R. J., Jr. (1972). *The extent and effect of parents' participating in their children's beginning reading programs: An inner-city project.* Doctoral dissertation, University of Cincinnati. (ERIC Document Reproduction Service No. ED 076946).

Cummins, J. (1986). Empowering minority students: A framework for intervention. *Harvard Educational Review,* 56, 18–36.

Darling, S. (1988). *Family literacy education: Replacing the cycle of failure with the legacy of success.* Washington, DC: Office of Educational Research and Improvement (ERIC Document Reproduction Service No. ED 332 749).

Delgado-Gaitan, C. (1987). Mexican adult literacy: New directions for immigrants. In S. R. Goldman & K. Trueba (Eds.), *Becoming literacy as a second language* (pp. 9–32). Norwood, NJ: Ablex.

Delgado-Gaitan, C. (1991). Involving parents in the schools: A process of empowerment. *American Journal of Education,* 100(1), 2–46.

Delgado-Gaitan, C. (1993). Research and policy in reconceptualizing family-school relationships. In P. Phelan & A. Locke-Davidson (Eds.), *Renegotiating cultural diversity in American schools* (pp. 139–158). New York: Teachers College Press.

Delpit, L. (1988). The silenced dialogue: Power and pedagogy in educating other people's children. *Harvard Educational Review,* 58, 280–298.

Delpit, L. (1995). *Other people's children: Cultural conflict in the classroom.* New York: The New York Press.

Derman-Sparks, L. (1989). *Anti-bias curriculum: Tools for empowering young children.* Washington, DC: National Association for the Education of Young Children.

Diamond, B., & Moore, M. (1995). *Mirroring the new reality of the classroom: A multicultural literacy approach.* White Plains, NY: Longman.

Diaz, S., Moll, L., & Mehan, K. (1986). Socio-cultural resources in instruction: A context-specific approach. In *Beyond language: Social and cultural factors in schooling language minority children,* (pp. 187–229). Los Angeles, CA: California State Department of Education and California State University.

Dixon, P., & Ishler, R. (1992). Professional development schools. *Journal of Teacher Education,* 43(1), 28–34.

Douglass, F. (1968). *Narratives of the life of Frederick Douglass.* New York: Signet Books.

Dye, T. R. (1992). *Understanding public policy.* Upper Saddle River, NJ: Prentice Hall.

Edwards, P. A. (1989). Supporting lower SES mothers' attempts to provide scaffolding for bookreading. In J. Allen & J. Mason (Eds.), *Risk makers, risk takers, risk breakers: Reducing the risks for young literacy learners* (pp. 222–250). Portsmouth, NH: Heinemann.

Edwards, P. A. (1990). *Talking Your Way to Literacy: A Program to Help Nonreading Parents Prepare Their Children for Reading.* Chicago: Childrens Press.

Edwards, P. A. (1990). *Parents as partners in reading: A family literacy training program.* Chicago: Childrens Press.

Edwards, P. A. (April, 1991). *Differentiated Parenting or Parentally Appropriate: The Missing Link in Efforts to Develop a Structure for Parent Involvement in Schools.* Paper presented at the Third Annual Roundtable on Home-Community School Partnerships, Chicago, IL.

Edwards, P. A. (1991). Fostering early literacy through parent coaching. In E. Hiebert (Ed.), *Literacy for a diverse society: Perspectives, programs, and policies* (pp. 199–213). New York: Teachers College Press.

Edwards, P. A. (1993). *Parents as Partners in Reading: A Family Literacy Training Program.* Second Edition. Chicago: Childrens Press.

Edwards, P. A. (1995). Combining parents' and teachers' thoughts about storybook reading at home and school. In L. M. Morrow (Ed.), *Family literacy: Multiple perspectives to enhance literacy development* (pp. 54–60). Newark, DE: International Reading Association.

Edwards, P. A. (1996). Creating sharing time conversations: Parents and teachers work together. *Language Arts, 73,* 344–349.

Edwards, P. A., & Danridge, J. C. (2001). Developing collaborative relationships with parents: Some examples. In V. Risko & K. Bromley (Eds.), *Collaboration for diverse learners: Viewpoints and practices* (pp. 251–272). Newark, DE: International Reading Association.

Edwards, P.A., Danridge, J.C., & Pleasants, H.M. (1999). Are we all on the same page? Exploring administrators' and teachers' conceptions of "at-riskness" in an urban elementary school. In T. Shanahan & F. R. Brown (Eds.), *48th yearbook of the National Reading Conference* (pp. 329–339). Chicago: National Reading Conference.

Edwards, P. A., Danridge, J.C., McMillon, G.T., & Pleasants, H.M. (2001). Taking ownership of literacy: Who has the power? In P.R. Schmidt & P.B. Mosenthal (Eds.), *Reconceptualizing literacy in the new age of pluralism and multiculturalism* (pp. 111–134). Greenwich, CT: Information Age Publishing Inc.

Edwards, P. A., & Garcia, G. E. (1991). Parental involvement in mainstream schools. In M. Foster (Ed.), *Readings on equal education: Qualitative investigations into schools and schooling* (pp. 167–187). New York: AMA Press, Inc.

Edwards, P. A., McMillon, G. T., Turner, J. D., & Laier, B. (2001). Who are you teaching? Coordinating instructional networks around the students and parents you serve. *The Reading Teacher,* 55, 145–150.

Edwards, P.A., & Garcia, G.E. (1995). The implications of Vygotskian theory for the development of home-school programs: A focus on storybook reading. In V. John-Steiner, C. Panofsky, & L. Smith (Eds.), *Interactionist Approaches to Language and Literacy* (pp. 243–264). New York: Cambridge University Press.

Edwards, P. A., with Pleasants, H. M. & Franklin, S. H. (1999). *A path to follow: Learning to listen to parents.* Portsmouth, NH: Heinemann.

Edwards, P. A., & Young, L. S. (1992). Beyond parents: Family, community, and school involvement. *Phi Delta Kappan,* 74 (1), 72–80.

Elden, M., & Levin, M. (1991). Congenerative learning: Bringing participation into action research. In W. Whyte (Ed.), *Participatory action research* (pp. 127–142). Newbury Park, CA: Sage.

Epstein, J. L. (1982). *Student reactions to teacher practices of parent involvement.* Paper presented at the annual meeting of the American Educational Research Association, New York City.

Epstein, J. L. (1985). Home and school connections in schools of the future: Implications of research on parent involvement. In *Peabody Journal of Education, Planning the School of the Future*, 62(2), 18–41.

Epstein, J. L. (January, 1986). Parents' reactions to teacher practices of parent involvement. *Elementary School Journal*, 86(3), 277–293.

Epstein, J. L. (1987). Parent involvement: State education agencies should lead the way. *Community Education Journal*, 14 (4), 4–10.

Epstein, J. L. (1988). How do we improve programs for parent involvement? *Educational Horizons*, 66 (2), 58–59.

Epstein, J. L., & Becker, H. J. (1982). Teachers' reported practices of parent involvement: Problems and possibilities. *Elementary School Journal*, 83, 103–113.

Evans, D. (1971). *An instructional program to enhance parent-pupil school interactions*. Arlington, VA: ERIC Document Reproduction Service No. ED 048342.

Evans, D., & Nelson, D. (1992). The curriculum of aspiring teachers: Not a question of either/or. In L. Kaplan (Ed.), *Education and the family* (pp. 230–242). Boston: Allyn and Bacon.

Fear, K. L., & Edwards, P. A. (1995). Building a democratic learning community within a PDS. *Teaching Education, 7*(2), 12–24.

Fitchen, J. J. (1981). *Poverty in rural America: A case study*. Boulder, CO: Westview Press.

Fletcher, R. (1966). *The family and marriage in Britain*. Harmondsworth: Penguin.

Florio-Ruane, S. (1994). The future teachers' autobiography club: Preparing educators to support literacy learning in culturally diverse classrooms. *English Education*, 26 (1), 52–66.

Florio-Ruane, S. (2001). *Teacher education and the cultural imagination: Autobiography, conversation, and narrative*. Mahwah, NJ: Lawrence Erlbaum Associates, Publishers.

Footlick, J. K. (Winter/Spring, 1990). What happened to the family? (Special Issue). *Newsweek*, 15–20.

Foster, J. E., & Loven, R. G. (1992). The need and directions for parent involvement in the '90s: Undergraduate perspectives and expections. *Action in Teacher Education: Linking teachers, schools, families, and communities. The Journal of the Association of Teacher Educators*, XIV (3), 13–18.

France, M. G., & Meeks, J. W. (1987). Parents who can't read: What the schools can do. *Journal of Reading*, 31, 222–227.

France, M. G., & Hager, J. M. (1993). Recruit, respect, respond: A model for working with low-income families and their preschoolers. *The Reading Teacher*, 46(2), 568–572.

Fraser, J. W. (1997). Preface. In J. J. Irvine (Ed.), *Critical knowledge for diverse teachers and learners* (pp. v–x). Washington, DC: American Association of Colleges for Teacher Education.

French, N. K. (1996). Connecting teachers and families: Using the family as the lab. *Journal of Teacher Education*, 47(5), 336–346.

Fry, P. G., & McKinney, L. J. (1997). A qualitative study of preservice teachers' early field experiences in an urban, culturally different school. *Urban Education*, 32(2), 184–201.

Fueyo, V., & Nueves, A. (1994). *Student teachers as researchers in multicultural classrooms: A continuing dialogue*. Paper presented at the annual meeting of the Association of Teacher Educators, Atlanta, Georgia.

Fuller, M. L. & Tutwiler, S. W. (1998). Poverty: The enemy of children and families. In M. L. Fuller & G. Olsen (Eds.), *Home-school relations: Working successfully with parents and families.* Boston: Allyn and Bacon.

Gadsden, V. L. (1994). Understanding family literacy: Conceptual issues facing the field. *Teachers College Record*, 96 (1), 58–86.

Gaj, N. (1989). Motheread, Inc. In *First teachers: A family literacy handbook for parents, policy-makers, and literacy providers* (pp. 27–30). Washington, DC: The Barbara Bush Foundation for Family Literacy.

Garcia, E. (1994). *Understanding and meeting the challenge of student cultural diversity.* Boston: Houghton Mifflin Company.

Gardner, S. (1994). Training for the future: Family support and school-linked services. *Equity and Choice*, 10(3), 16–18.

Gargiulo, R. M., & Graves, S. B. (Spring, 1991). Parental feelings. *Childhood Education*, 67, (3), 176–178.

Garibaldi, A. M. (1992). Preparing teachers for culturally diverse classrooms. In M. E. Dilworth (Ed.), *Diversity in teacher education: New directions* (pp. 23–39). San Francisco: Jossey-Bass Publishers.

Geiger, K. (1992). Heath, education, welfare: America's families and America's priorities. In L. Kaplan (Ed.), *Education and the family* (pp. 307–314). Boston: Allyn and Bacon.

Gilbert, S. E., & Gay, G. (1985). Improving the success in school of poor black children. *Phi Delta Kappan*, 67(2), 133–137.

Goals 2000: Educate America Act. H.R.1804. United States of America One Hundred Third Congress. (January 25, 1994). [On-line]. Available: http://www.ed.gov/legislation/GOALS2000/TheAct/index.html

Goldenberg, C. N. (1987). Low-income Hispanic parents' contribution to their first-grade children's word-recognition skills. *Anthropology and Education Quarterly*, 18 (3), 149–179.

Goldenberg, C., & Gallimore, R. (1991). Local knowledge, research and educational change. *Educational Researcher*, 20 (8), 7–17.

Gollnick, D. M. (1992). Understanding the dynamics of race, class, and gender. In M. E. Dilworth (Ed.), *Diversity in teacher education: New expectations* (pp. 63–78). San Francisco: Jossey-Bass Publishers.

Gollnick, D. M., & Chinn, P. C. (1994). *Multicultural education in a pluralistic society.* Fourth Edition. New York: MacMillan College Publishing Company.

Goodson, B. D., & Hess, R. D. (1975). *Parents as teachers of young children: An evaluative review of some contemporary concepts and programs.* Washington, DC: Bureau of Educational Personnel Development.

Gordon, I. J. (1969). *Reaching the child through parent education: The Florida approach.* Gainesville, FL: Institute for the development of human resources, College of Education, University of Florida.

Gordon, I. J. (1977). Parent education and parent involvement: Retrospect and prospect. *Childhood Education*, 54(1), 71–79.

Gordon, I. J. (1979a). The effects of parent involvement on schooling. In R. S. Brandt (Ed.), *Partners: Parents and schools* (pp. 4–25). Alexandria, VA: Association for Supervision and Curriculum and Development.

Gordon, I. J. (1979b). Parent education: A position paper. In W. G. Hill, P. Fox, & C. D. Jones (Eds.), *Families and schools: Implementing parent education* (Report No. 121) (pp. 1–5). Denver, CO: Education Commission of the States.

Gordon, I. J. & Breivogel, W. F. (1976). *Building effective home-school relationships*. Boston: Allyn and Bacon.

Greenwood, G., & Hankins, C. (1991). Research and practice in parent involvement: Implications for teacher education. *The Elementary School Journal*, 91, 279–288.

Grimmett, S. A., & McCoy, M. (1980). Effects of parental communication on reading performance of their grade-school children. *The Reading Teacher*, 34, 303–308.

Haberman, M. (1992). Creating community contexts that educate: An agenda for improving education in inner cities. In L. Kaplan (Ed.), *Education and the family* (pp. 27–40). Boston: Allyn and Bacon.

Haberman, M. (1993). Diverse contexts for teaching. In M .J. O'Hair & S. J. Odell (Eds.), *Diversity in teaching: Teacher education yearbook I*, (pp. 1–8). Forth Worth, TX: Harcourt Brace Jovanovich College Publishers.

Haberman, M. (1995). *Star teachers of children in poverty*. West Lafayette, IN: Kappa Delta Pi International Educational Honor Society.

Hadaway, N. L., Florez, V., Larke, P. J., & Wiseman, D. (1993). Teaching in the midst of diversity: How do we prepare? In M .J. O'Hair & S. J. Odell (Eds.), *Diversity in teaching: Teacher education yearbook I*, (pp. 60–83). Forth Worth, TX: Harcourt Brace Jovanovich College Publishers.

Haley, A., & Malcolm XI. (1965). *The autobiography of Malcolm X*. New York: Grove Press.

Hamby, J. V. (1992). The school-family link: A key to dropout prevention. In L. Kaplan (Ed.), *Education and the family* (pp. 54–68). Boston: Allyn and Bacon.

Handel, R. E. (1992). The partnership for family reading: Benefits for families and schools. *The Reading Teacher*, 46(2), 117–126.

Harrington, A. (1971). Teaching parents to help at home. In C. B. Smith (Ed.), *Parents and reading* (pp. 49–56). Newark, DE: International Reading Association.

Harris, T. L., & Hodges, R. E. (1995). *The literacy dictionary: A vocabulary of reading and writing*. Newark, DE: International Reading Association.

Harry, B. (1992). *Cultural diversity, families, and the special education system: Communication and empowerment*. New York: Teachers College Press.

Harp, B., & Brewer, J. (1996). *Reading and writing: Teaching for the connections*. Second Edition. Forth Worth, TX: Harcourt Brace College Publishers.

Hawkins, L. (1970). Urban schoolteaching: The personal touch. In N. Wright, Jr. (Ed.), *What Black educators are saying* (pp. 43–47). New York: Hawthorn Books, Inc.

Heath, S. B. (1982). What no bedtime story means: Narrative skills at home and school. *Language in Society*, 11(2), 49–76.

Heath, S. B. (1983). *Ways with words: Language, life, and work in communities and classrooms*. Cambridge, MA: Cambridge University Press.

Heath, S. B. (1989). Oral and literate traditions among Black Americans living in poverty. *American Psychologist*, 44(2), 367–373.

Heath, S. B., & McLaughlin, M. W. (1991). Community organizations as family. *Phi Delta Kappan*, 72 (8), 576–580.

Henderson, A. T. (1981). *Parent participation and student achievement: The evidence grows*. Columbia, MD: National Committee for Citizens in Education.

Henderson, A. T. (1987). *The evidence continues to grow*. Columbia, MD: National Committee for Citizens in Education.

Henderson, A. T. (1993). Foreword. In J. W. Rioux & N. Berla (Eds.), *Innovations in parent and family involvement* (pp. ix–xi). Princeton Junction, NJ: Eye on Education.

Henderson, A. T., & Berla, N. (1994). *A new generation of evidence: The family is critical to student achievement*. Columbia, MD: National Committee for Citizens in Education.

Henderson, A., Marburger, C. L., & Ooms, T. (1986). *Beyond the bake sale: An educator's guide to working with parents*. Columbia, MD: National Committee for Citizens in Education.

Hersey, J. (1979). *Hiroshima*. New York: Bantam Books.

Hildebrand, V., Phenice, L. A., Gray, M. M., & Hines, R. P. (1996). *Knowing and serving diverse families*. Englewood Cliffs, NJ: Merrill.

Hess, R.D., & Shipman, V. (1965). The socialization of cognitive modes in children. *Child Development, 36*, 461–479.

Hodgkinson, H. (1991). Reform versus reality. *Phi Delta Kappan, 73* (1), 8–16.

Hollins, E. R. (1996). *Culture in school learning: Revealing the deep meaning*. Mahwah, NJ: Lawrence Erlbaum Associates.

Holm, G., & Johnson, L. N. (1994). Shaping cultural partnerships: The readiness of preservice teachers to teach in culturally diverse classrooms. In M. J. O'Hair & S. J. Odell (Eds.), *Partnerships in education: Teacher education yearbook II*, (pp. 85–101). Forth Worth, TX: Harcourt Brace Jovanovich College Publishers.

Hord, S. M., Rutherford, W. L., Huling-Austin, L., & Hall, G. E. (1987). *Taking charge of change*. Alexandria, VA: Association for Supervision and Curriculum Development.

Houston, W. R., & Houston, E. (1992). Needed: A new knowledge in teacher education. In L. Kaplan (Ed.), *Education and the family* (pp. 272–277). Boston: Allyn and Bacon.

Huberman, M. (1987). How well does educational research really travel? *Educational Researcher, 16*(1), 5–13.

Huey, E. B. (1908). *The psychology and pedagogy of reading*. New York: MacMillan.

Hughes, J. M. (1979). A Commitment to parent education. In W. G. Hill, P. Fox, & C. D. Jones (Eds.), *Families and schools: Implementing parent education* (Report No. 121) (pp. 6–9). Denver, CO: Education Commission of the States.

Inocencio, E. B. (March 10, 1987). Testimony and comments of the Council of Asian and American Organizations, presented to the NEA Special Study Committee on Asian and Pacific Islander Concerns, Houston, TX. In R. F. Chase (Chair), *Report of the Asian and Pacific Islander Concerns Study Committee* (p.9). Washington, DC: National Education Association.

Irvine, J. J. (1992). Making teacher education culturally responsive. In M. E. Dilworth (Ed.), *Diversity in teacher education: New expectations*, (pp. 79–92). San Francisco: Jossey-Bass Publishers.

Jenkins, G. (1969). Understanding differences in parents. In N. Headley, H. Merhill, E. Mirbaha, & M. Rasmussen (Eds.), *Parents-children-teachers: Communication* (pp. 35–40). Washington, DC: Association for Childhood Education International.

Jenks, C., Smith, M., Acland, H., Bane, M. J., Cohen, D., Gintis, H., Heyns, B., & Michelson, S. (1972). *Inequality: A reassessment of the effect of family and schooling in America*. New York: Basic Books, Inc.

Joe, G. K. (March 10, 1987). Testimony and comments of the Council of Asian and American Organizations, presented to the NEA Special Study Committee on Asian and Pacific Islander Concerns, Houston, TX. In R. F. Chase (Chair), *Report of the Asian and Pacific Islander Concerns Study Committee* (p.9). Washington, DC: National Education Association.

Johnson, S. M. (1990). *Teachers at work: Achieving success in our schools*. New York: Basic Books.

Jones, L. T., & Blendinger, J. (1994). New beginnings: Preparing future teachers to work with diverse families. *Action in Teacher Education: Celebrating Diversity in Teacher Education. The Journal of the Association of Teacher Educators*, XVI (3), 79–86.

Jordan, C. (1985). Translating culture: From ethnographic information to education program. *Anthropology and Education Quarterly*, 16, 105–123.

Kagan, S. L. (1991). (Ed.). *The care and education of America's young children: Obstacles and opportunities*. Ninetieth Yearbook of the NSSE. Chicago: The National Society of the Study of Education.

Kaplan, L. (1992). (Ed.). *Education and the family*. Boston, MA: Allyn and Bacon.

Kaplan, L. (1992). Parent education in home, school, and society: A course description. In L. Kaplan (Ed.), *Education and the family* (pp. 273–277). Boston: Allyn and Bacon.

Karther, D. E., & Lowden, F. Y. (1997). Fostering effective parent involvement. *Contemporary Education*, 69 (1), 41–44.

Keenan, J. W., Willett, J., & Solsken, J. (1993). Focus on research: Constructing an urban village: School/home collaboration in a multicultural classroom. *Language Arts*, 70, 204–214.

Keller, M. F. (1991). *Reading-writing connections: From theory to practice*. New York: Longman.

King, L. (Ed.). (1995). *Hear my voice: A multicultural anthology of literature from the United States*. New York: Addison-Wesley.

Kochan, F., & Mullins, B. K. (1992). Teacher education: Linking universities, schools, and families for the twenty-first century. In L. Kaplan (Ed.), *Education and the family* (pp. 266–272). Boston: Allyn and Bacon.

Kozol, J. (1994). The new untouchables. In J. Krevotics & E. J. Nussel (Eds.), *Transforming urban education* (pp. 75–78). Boston: Allyn and Bacon.

Knapp, J. S., Turnbull, B. J., & Shields, P. M. (1990, September). New directions for educating the children of poverty. *Educational Leadership*, 48 (1), 4–8.

Krevotics, J., & Nussel, E. J. (Eds.). (1994). *Transforming urban education*. Boston: Allyn & Bacon.

Labov, W. A. (June, 1965). *Linguistic research on nonstandard English in Negro children*. Paper presented to the New York Society for the Experimental Study of Education, New York.

Ladson-Billings, G. (1993). Culturally relevant teaching: The key to making multicultural education work. In C. A. Grant (Ed.), *Research and multicultural education: From the margins to the mainstream* (pp. 203–217). Washington, DC: The Falmer Press.

Ladson-Billings, G. (1991). Returning to the source: Implications for educating teachers of black students. In M. Foster (Ed.), *Readings on equal education: Volume II qualitative investigations into schools and schooling* (pp. 227–244). New York: AMS Press, Inc.

Laosa, L. M. (1982). School, occupation, culture and family: The impact of parental schooling on the parent-child relationship. *Journal of Educational Psychology*, 74(6), 791–827.

Laosa, L. M. (1985). *Indices of the success of Head Start: A critique*. Paper presented at the conference "Research Directions for Minority Scholars Involved With Head

Start Programs," at Howard University, Washington, DC, sponsored by the U. S. Administration for Children, Youth and Families.

LeBlanc, P. (1992). Parent-school interactions. In L. Kaplan (Ed.), *Education and the family* (pp. 132–140). Boston: Allyn and Bacon.

Lareau, A. (1989). *Home advantage: Social class and parental intervention in elementary education*. New York: Falmer Press.

Lareau, A. (2000). *Home advantage: Social class and parental intervention in elementary education*. Second Edition. Lanham, MD: Rowman, & Littlefield Publishers, Inc.

Lazar, I. (1981). Early intervention is effective. *Educational Leadership*, 38 (4), 303–305.

LeGrand, K. R. (1981). Perspective on minority education: An interview with anthropologist John Ogbu. *Journal of Reading*, 24, 680–688.

Leibowitz, A. (1977). Parental inputs and children's achievement. *Journal of Human Resources*, 12, 242–251.

Leichter, H. J. (1984). Families as environments for literacy. In H. Goelman, A. A. Oberg, & F. Smith (Eds.), *Awakening to literacy* (pp. 38–50). Exeter, NH: Heinemann.

Leitch, M. L., & Tangri, S. S. (1988). Barriers to home-school collaboration. *Educational Horizons*, 66 (2), 70–74.

Lengyel, J., & Baghban, M. (1980). *The effects of a family reading program and SSR on reading achievement and attitudes*. (ERIC Document Reproduction Service No. ED 211925).

Lewis, A. E. (2001). There is no "race" in the schoolyard: Color-blind ideology in an (almost) all-White school. *American Educational Research Journal*, 38 (4), 781–811.

Lieberman, A. (1993). The meaning of scholarly activity and the building of community. *Equity and Choice*, 10(1), 4–10.

Lightfoot, S. L. (1978). *World apart: Relationships between families and schools*. New York: Basic Books.

LoBaugh, G. G. (1994). *Literature-based dialogue: Enhancing multiethnic curriculum for preservice teachers*. Unpublished doctoral dissertation, University of Oklahoma, Norman, Oklahoma.

Lynch, A. (1992). The importance of parent involvement. In L. Kaplan (Ed.), *Education and the family*. Boston: Allyn and Bacon.

Mahoney, E., & Wilcox, L. (1985). *Ready, set, read: Best books to prepare preschools*. Metuchen, NJ: Scarecrow Press.

McAfee, O. (1987). Improving home-school relations: Implications for staff development. *Education and Urban Society*, 19(2), 185–199.

McDiarmid, G. W., & Price, J. (1993). Preparing teachers for diversity: A study of student teachers in a multicultural program. In M. J. O'Hair & S. J. Odell (Eds.), *Diversity in teaching: Teacher education yearbook I*, (pp. 31–59). Forth Worth, TX: Harcourt Brace Jovanovich College Publishers.

McGill-Franzen, A., & Allington, R. L. (1991). Every child's right: Literacy. *The Reading Teacher*, 45, 86–90.

McGilp, J., & Michael, M. (1994). *The home-school connection: Guidelines for working with parents*. Portsmouth, NH: Heinemann.

McLaughlin, M. W., & Shields, P. M. (1987). Involving low-income parents in the schools: A role for policy? *Phi Delta Kappan*, 69, 156–160.

McWilliams, D. R., & Cunningham, P. M. (1976). Project PEP. *The Reading Teacher*, 29, 635–655.

Michaels, S. (1981). Sharing time: Children's narrative styles and differential access to literacy. *Language in Society*, 10(3), 423–442.

Michaels, S. (1986). Narrative presentation: An oral preparation for literacy with first-graders. In J. Cook-Gumperz (Ed.), *The social construction of literacy* (pp. 94–111). New York: Cambridge University Press.

Miller-Rodriguez, K. (1991). Home writing activities: The writing briefcase and the traveling suitcase. *The Reading Teacher, 45*(2), 25–26.

Mills, J. R., & Buckley, C. W. (1992). Accommodating the minority teacher candidate: Non-black students in predominately black colleges. In M. E. Dilworth (Ed.), *Diversity in teacher education: New expectations* (pp. 134–159). San Francisco: Jossey-Bass Publishers.

Mitchell, J. (1982). Reflections of a Black social scientist: Some struggles, some doubts, some hopes. *Harvard Educational Review, 52*, 27–44.

Moles, O. (1987). Who wants parent involvement? Interests, skills, and opportunities among parents and educators, *Education and Urban Society, 19*, 137–145.

Moles, O. C. (1993). Collaboration between schools and disadvantaged parents: Obstacles and openings. In N. F. Chavkin (Ed.), *Families and schools in a pluralistic society* (pp. 21–49). Albany, NY: State University of New York Press.

Moll, L. C., Amanti, C., Neff, D., & Gonazalez, N. (1992). Funds of knowledge for teaching: Using a qualitative approach to connect home and classrooms. *Theory Into Practice, 31* (2), 132–141.

Mooney, M. (1988). *Developing life-long readers*. Wellington, New Zealand: Department of Education.

Morrison, G. S. (1978). *Parent involvement in the home, school, and community*. Columbus, OH: Charles E. Merrill Publishing Company.

Morrison, G. S. (1988). *Early childhood education today*. Fourth Edition. Columbus, OH: Merrill Publishing Company.

Morrison, G. S. (1998). *Early childhood education today*. Seventh Edition. Upper Saddle River, NJ: Prentice-Hall.

Morrow, L. M. (1993). *Literacy development in the early years*. Second Edition. Boston: Allyn and Bacon.

Morrow, L. M., Tracey, D. H., & Maxwell, C. M. (Eds.), (1995). *A survey of family literacy*. Newark, DE: International Reading Association.

Moynihan, D. P. (1965). *The Negro family: The case for national action*. Washington, DC: United States Department of Labor, Office of Policy, Planning, and Research.

National PTA (2000). *Building successful partnerships: A guide for developing parent and family involvement programs.* Bloomington, IN: National Educational Service.

Neckerman, K. M., & Wilson, W. J. (1986). Schools and poor communities. In *School success for students at risk: Analysis and recommendations of the Council of Chief School Officers* (pp. 25–44). Orlando, FL: Harcourt Brace Jovanovich, Inc.

Neisser, U. (1986). New answers to an old question. In U. Neisser (Ed.), *The school achievement of minority children: New perspectives* (pp. 1–17). Hillsdale, NJ: Erlbaum.

Nieto, S. (1992). *Affirming diversity: The sociopolitical context of multicultural education*. New York: Longman.

Noordhoff, K., & Kleinfeld, J. (1993). Preparing teachers for multicultural classrooms. *Teaching and Teacher Education, 9*(1), 27–39.

Ogbu, J. U. (1974). *The next generation, an ethnography of education in an urban neighborhood*. New York: Academic Press.

Ogbu, J. U. (1992). Understanding cultural diversity and learning. *Educational Researcher*, 21(8), 5–14.

Ogbu, J. U. (1995). Understanding cultural diversity and learning. In J. A. Banks & C. A. Banks (Eds.), *Handbook on research in multicultural education* (pp. 582–593). New York: McMillan.

Olson, L. (April, 1990). Parents as partners: Redefining the social contract between parents and schools [Special Issue]. *Education Week*, 9 (28), 17–24.

One-third of a nation: A report of the commission on minority participation in education and American life (1988). Washington, DC: American Council on Education & Education Commission of the States.

Otto, H. J. (1969). Communication is the key. In *Parents-children-teachers: Communication* (pp. 1–4). Washington, DC: Association for Childhood Educational International.

Ozturk, M. C. (1992). Education for cross-cultural communication. *Educational Leadership*, 49, 79–81.

Paine, L. (1988). *Orientations toward diversity: What do prospective teachers bring?* Paper presented at the annual American Research Association, New Orleans, LA.

Paratore, J.R. (2001). *Opening doors, opening opportunities: Family literacy in an urban community*. Boston: Allyn and Bacon.

Pattnaik, J., & Vold, E. (February, 1994). *A study of student teachers' perceptions and practices of multicultural education in school/university partnerships*. Paper presented at the annual meeting of the Association of Teacher Educators, Atlanta, GA.

Payne, R. K. (1998). *A framework for understanding poverty*. Baytown, TX: RFT Publishing Co.

Pflaum, S. W. (1986). *The development of language and literacy in young children*. Third Edition. Columbus, OH: Charles E. Merrill.

Phelan, P. A., Davidson, A. L., & Cao, H. T. (1991). Students' multiple worlds: Negotiating the boundaries of family, peers, and school cultures. *Anthropology and Education Quarterly*, 22 (3), 224–250.

Pine, G., & Hilliard, A. (1990). Rx for racism: Imperatives for America's schools. *Phi Delta Kappan*, 71(8), 593–600.

Pizzo, P. D. (1990, September). Family-centered head start for infants and toddlers: A renewed direction for the project head start. *Young Children*, 45 (6), 30–39.

Potter, G. (1989). Parent participation in the language arts program. *Language Arts*, 66 (1), 21–28.

Powell, D. R. (1979). Organizational problems in institutionalizing parent education in the public schools. In W. G. Hill, P. Fox, & C. D. Jones (Eds.), *Families and schools: Implementing parent education* (Report No. 121) (pp. 14–18). Denver, CO: Education Commission of the States.

Powell, D. R. (1991). Parents and programs: Early childhood as a pioneer in parent involvement and support. In S. L. Kagan (Ed.), *The care and education of America's young children: Obstacles and opportunities*. Ninetieth Yearbook of the NSSE. Chicago: The National Society of the Study of Education.

Purcell-Gates, V. (1995). *Other people's words: The cycle of low literacy*. Cambridge, MA: Harvard University Press.

Purcell-Gates, V. (2000). Family literacy. In M. L. Kamil, P. B. Mosenthal, P. D. Pearson, & R. Barr (Eds.), *Handbook of reading research Volume III*, (pp. 853–870). Mahwah, NJ: Lawrence Erlbaum Associates, Publishers.

Purkey, W. W., & Novak, J. M. (1984). *Inviting school success: A self-concept approach to teaching and learning.* Belmont, CA: Wadsworth.

Raim, J. (1980). Who learns when parents teach their children? *The Reading Teacher, 34,* 152–155.

Raphael, T. E. (1982). Question-answering strategies for children. *The Reading Teacher, 36,* 186–191.

Raphael, T. E. (1984). Teaching learners about sources of information for answering comprehension questions. *Journal of Reading, 27,* 303–311.

Raphael, T. E. (1986). Teaching question/answer relationships. *The Reading Teacher, 39,* 516–520.

Rich, D. (1985). *The forgotten factor in school success—The family.* Washington, DC: Home School Institute.

Richardson, V., & Placier, P. (2001). Teacher change. In V. Richardson (Ed.), *Handbook of research on teaching* (4th ed.). Washington, DC: American Educational Research Association.

Richgels, D., & Wold, L. (1998). Literacy on the road: Guiding principles and practices for parent involvement. *The Reading Teacher, 42,* 508–512.

Rist, R. C. (1970). Student social class and teacher expectations: The self-fulfilling prophecy in ghetto education. *Harvard Educational Review, 40,* 441–451.

Roberts, F. (1979). Education for parenthood: Alternatives strategies for the public schools. In W. G. Hill, P. Fox, & C. D. Jones (Eds.), *Families and schools: Implementing parent education* (Report No. 121) (pp. 10–13). Denver, CO: Education Commission of the States.

Rodriguez, R. F. (1981). The involvement of minority group parents in school. *Teacher Education and Special Education, 4,* 40–44.

Rodriguez-Brown, F. V., Fen, R. L., & Albom, J. B. (1999). Hispanic parents' awareness and use of literacy-rich environments at home and in the community. *Education and Urban Society, 32* (1), 41–58.

Rosenthal, R., & Jackson, L. (1968). *Pygmalion in the classroom: Teacher expectations and pupils' intellectual development.* New York: Holt, Rinehart and Winston.

Roth, R. (1984). Schooling, literacy, acquisition and cultural transmission. *Journal of Education, 166* (3), 291–308.

Ruddell, R. B. (1999). *Teaching children to read and write: Becoming an influential teacher.* Second Edition. Boston: Allyn and Bacon.

Runer, C., & Roberts, L. (1994). Using autobiographies to teach multiculturalism and literacy. *Illinois Reading Council Journal, 22* (1), 25–31.

Rushcamp, S., & Roehler, L. (1992). Characteristics supporting change in a professional development school. *Journal of Teacher Education, 43*(1), 19–29.

Safran, D. (1974). *Preparing teachers for parent involvement.* Center for the Study of Parent Involvement, Orinda, CA.

Safran, D. (1979). Preparing teachers for parent involvement. In C. A. Grant (Ed.), *Community participation in education* (pp. 95–114). Boston: Allyn and Bacon, Inc.

Sarason, S. (1990). *The predictable failure of educational reform: Can we change course before it's too late?* San Francisco, CA: Jossey-Bass.

Schickedanz, J. (1986). *More than ABCs: The early stages of reading and writing.* Washington, DC: National Association for the Education of Young Children.

Schiefflin, B. B. & Cochran-Smith, M. (1984). Learning to read culturally: Literacy before schooling. In H. Goelman, A. Oberg, & F. Smith (Eds.), *Awakening to literacy* (pp. 3–23). Exeter, NH: Heinemann.

Schmidt, P. R. (1996). The ABC's model: Teachers connect home and school. *National Reading Conference Yearbook*, 47, pp. 194–208.

Schmidt, P. R. (1998). The ABC's of cultural understanding and communication. *Equity & Excellence in Education*, 31 (2), 28–38.

Scott-Jones, D. (1987). Mother-as-teacher in families of high- and low-achieving low-income black first graders. *Journal of Negro Education*, 56(1), 21–34.

Seefeldt, C. (1985). Communicate with curriculum. *Day Care and Early Education*, 13(2), 22–25.

Seeley, D. S. (1989). A new paradigm for parent involvement. *Educational Leadership*, 47 (2), 46–48.

Sewell, T. E., Ducette, J. P., & Shapiro, J. P. (1991). *Cultural diversity and educational assessment*. Paper presented at the American Psychological Association Annual Conference, San Francisco.

Shanahan, T., Mulhern, M., & Rodriguez-Brown, F. (1995). Project FLAME: Lessons learned from a family literacy program for minority families. *The Reading Teacher*, 48(7), 586–593.

Shartrand, A., Kreider, H., & Erickson-Warfield, M. (1994). *Preparing teachers to involve parents: A national survey of teacher education programs*. Working Paper. Cambridge, MA: Harvard Family Research Project.

Shelton, J. (1973). *An analysis of a family involvement communication system in a Title 1 elementary school: Final report*. Arlington, VA: ERIC Document Reproductrion Service No ED 082091.

Sherman, A. (1994). *Wasting America's future: The children's defense fund report on the cost of child poverty*. Boston, MA: Beacon Press.

Shockley, B., Michalove, B., & Allen, J. (1995). *Engaging families: Connecting home and school literacy communities*. Portsmouth, NH: Heinemann.

Shuck, A., Ulsh, F., & Platt, J. S. (1983). Parents encourage pupils (PEP): An inner-city parent involvement reading project. *The Reading Teacher*, 36, 524–528.

Sittig, L. H. (1982). Involving parents and children in reading for fun. *The Reading Teacher*, 36, 166–168.

Sleeter, C. E., & Grant, C. A. (1993). *Making Choices for Multicultural Education: Five Approaches to Race, Class, and Gender*, Second Edition. New York: Merrill.

Snow, C. E., Burns, M. S., & Griffin, P. (Eds.) (1998). *Preventing reading difficulties in young children*. Washington, DC: National Academy Press.

Spewock, T. S. (1988). Training parents to teach their preschools through literature. *The Reading Teacher*, 41, 648–652.

Springate, K. W., & Stegelin, D. A. (1999). *Building school and community partnerships through parent involvement*. Upper Saddle River, NJ: Prentice-Hall.

Stafford, F. P., & Hill, C. R. (1974). Allocation of time to preschool children and educational opportunity. *Journal of Human Resources*, 9, 323–341.

Stevenson, D. L., & Baker, D. P. (1987). The family-school relation and the child's school performance. *Child Development*, 58 (5), 1348–1357.

Stillman, P. R. (1989). *Families writing*. Cincinnati, OH: Writer's Digest Books.

Sutherland, I R. (1991). Parent-teacher involvement benefits everyone. *Early Child Development and Care*, 73, 121–131.

Swap, S. M. (1987). *Enhancing parent involvement in schools: A manual for parents and teachers*. New York: Teachers College Press.

Swap, S. M. (1993). *Developing home-school partnerships: From concepts to practice*. New York: Teachers College Press.

Swick, K. (1984). *Inviting parents into the young child's world: Practical guidelines for facilitating parent involvement*. Champaign, IL: Stipes.

Taylor, B. M., Pressley, M. P., & Pearson, P. D. (2000). *Research-supported characteristics of teachers and schools that promote reading achievement*. Washington, DC: National Education Association, Reading Matters Research Report.

Taylor, D., & Dorsey-Gaines, C. (1988). *Growing up literate: Learning from inner-city families*. Portsmouth, NH: Heinemann.

Taylor, D., & Strickland, D. (1986). *Family storybook reading*. Portsmouth, NH: Heinemann.

Teale, W. H., & Sulzby, E. (1986). *Emergent literacy: Writing and reading*. Norwood, NJ: Ablex.

Teale, W. H., & Sulzby, E. (1987). Access, mediation and literacy acquisition in early childhood. In D. Wagner (Ed.), *The future of literacy in a changing world* (pp. 173–206). New York: Pergamon Press.

Tharp, R. G. (1989). Psychocultural variables and constraints: Effects on teaching and learning in schools. *American Psychologist*, 44 (2), 349–359.

Tierney, R. J., & Readence, J. E. (2000). *Reading strategies and practices: A compendium*. Fifth Edition. Boston: Allyn and Bacon.

Tompkins, G. E. (1997). *Literacy for the 21st century: A balanced approach*. Upper Saddle River, NJ: Prentice Hall.

Tso, J. C. (March 9, 1987). Testimony and comments of the Council of Asian and American Organizations, presented to the NEA Special Study Committee on Asian and Pacific Islander Concerns, Houston, TX. In R. F. Chase (Chair), *Report of the Asian and Pacific Islander Concerns Study Committee* (p.9). Washington, DC: National Education Association.

Trueba, H. T. (1989). *Raising silent voices: Educating the linguistic minorities for the 21st century*. New York: Newbury House.

Tutwiler, S. W. (1998). Diversity among families. In M. L. Fuller & Olsen, G. (Eds.), *Home-school relations: Working successfully with parents and families* (pp. 40–66). Boston: Allyn and Bacon.

U. S. Department of Education (1986). *What works: Research about teaching and learning*. Washington, DC: Office of Educational Research and Improvement, U. S. Department of Education, *Statutes at Large*, vol. 89.

Vacca, J. L., Vacca, R. T., & Gove, M. K. (1995). *Reading and learning to read*. Third Edition. New York: HarperCollins College Publishers.

Vacca, R. T., & Vacca, J. L. (1996). *Content area reading*. Fifth Edition. New York: HarperCollins College Publishers.

Van Dongen, R. (1987). Children's narrative thought at home and at school. *Language Arts*, 64(1), 79–87.

Voss, M. M. (1996). *Hidden literacies: Children learning at home and school*. Portsmouth, NH: Heinemann.

Vukelich, C. (1978). Parents are teachers: A beginning reading program. *The Reading Teacher*, 31, 524–527.

Vukelich, C. (1984). Parents' role in the reading process: A review of practical suggestions and ways to communicate with parents. *The Reading Teacher*, 37 (6), 472–477.

Vygotsky, L. S. (1978). *Mind in society*. Cambridge, MA: Harvard University Press.

Weisel, E. (1989). *Night*. New York: Bantam Books.

Wertsch, J. V. (1991). *Voices of the mind: A sociocultural approach to mediated action*. Cambridge, MA: Harvard University Press.

Weston, W. J. (1989). *Education and the American family: A research synthesis*. New York: New York University Press.

White, B. L. (1975). *The first three years of life*. Englewood Cliffs, NJ: Prentice-Hall.

Wigfield, A., & Asher, S. R. (1984). Social and motivational influences on reading. In P. D. Pearson, R. Barr, M. L. Kamil, & P. Mosenthal (Eds.), *Handbook of reading research,* volume 1 (pp. 423–452). New York: Longman.

Willet, J., & Bloome, D. (1992). Literacy, language, school and community: A community-centered view. In A. Carrasquilo & C. Hedley (Eds.), *Whole language and the bilingual learner* (pp. 35–57). Norwood, NJ: Ablex.

Williams, Jr., D. L. (1992). Parental involvement in teacher preparation: Challenges to teacher education. In L. Kaplan (Ed.), *Education and the family* (pp. 243–254). Boston, MA: Allyn and Bacon.

Winitsky, N., Stoddart, T., & O'Keefe, P. (1992). Great expectations: Emergent professional development schools. *Journal of Teacher Education,* 43(1), 3–18.

Wissbrun, D., & Eckart, J. A. (1992). Hierarchy of parental involvement in schools. In L. Kaplan (Ed.), *Education and the family* (pp. 119–131). Boston: Allyn and Bacon.

Witherspoon, B. (n. d.). Parental involvement in Title 1: Policy, practice and promise. *www.Title1online.com* Education Funding Research Council.

Wood, K. D., Lapp, D., & Flood, J. (1992). *Guiding readers through text: A review of study guides*. Newark, DE: International Reading Association.

Young, L. S., Sykes, G., Featherstone, J., Elmore, R. F., & Devaney, K. (1990). *A report of the Holmes group tomorrow's schools: Principles for the design of professional development schools.* The Holmes Group, Inc.: Michigan State University, East Lansing, MI.

Ziegler, E. (1979). Introduction. In W. G. Hill, P. Fox, & C. D. Jones (Eds.), *Families and schools: Implementing parent education* (Report No. 121) (pp. ix–xiii). Denver, CO: Education Commission of the States.

Author Index

Subject Index